D1607802

The Rebirth of
the Habsburg Army

Recent Titles in
Contributions in Military Studies

The Rebirth of
the Habsburg Army

*Friedrich Beck and the Rise
of the General Staff*

SCOTT W. LACKEY

Contributions in Military Studies, Number 161

GREENWOOD PRESS
Westport, Connecticut • London

Library of Congress Cataloging-in-Publication Data

Lackey, Scott W.
  The rebirth of the Habsburg army : Friedrich Beck and the rise of
the general staff / Scott W. Lackey.
      p. cm.—(Contributions in military studies, ISSN 0883–6884
; no. 161)
  Includes bibliographical references and index.
  ISBN 0–313–29361–9 (alk. paper)
    1. Austria. Armee—History. 2. Austro-Hungarian Monarchy. Heer—
History. 3. Beck-Rzikowsky, Friedrich, Graf von, 1830–1906.
4. Generals—Austria—Biography. 5. Austria—History, Military.
I. Title. II. Series.
UA672.L33 1995
335′.009436—dc20   95–7897

British Library Cataloguing in Publication Data is available.

Library of Congress Catalog Card Number: 95–7897
ISBN: 0–313–29361–9
ISSN: 0883–6884

First published in 1995

Greenwood Press, 88 Post Road West, Westport, CT 06881
An imprint of Greenwood Publishing Group, Inc.

Printed in the United States of America

The paper used in this book complies with the
Permanent Paper Standard issued by the National
Information Standards Organization (Z39.48–1984).

10 9 8 7 6 5 4 3 2 1

To My Parents With Love

Contents

Acknowledgments

The vast enterprise of book writing necessarily reflects the efforts of more than just the author. This study of the late nineteenth century Habsburg army owes much to the work and dedication of many people. Without their unflagging confidence in my work and their assistance, I doubt if I would have had the strength and courage to endure the long process of research and writing, and--in the case of instructors, friends, and colleagues at the University of North Carolina at Chapel Hill,--of the many years of graduate study leading up to the finished monograph.

In six years of graduate study, two exemplary advisers have served as patient and understanding guides. As provost and dean of the college of arts and sciences when I arrived in Chapel Hill in 1984, Dr. Samuel R. Williamson could have easily begged off the responsibility for directing my degree program. From both a personal and professional standpoint, I am eternally grateful that he did not. Despite extremely heavy administrative responsibilities, Dr. Williamson devoted generous portions of his time to the careful examination of the current manuscript, always offering criticisms of a constructive nature with the intent only to improve the finished product and not discourage the author. Dr. Williamson's departure from Chapel Hill in 1988, and thus from the responsibilities of that campus, makes his devotion to this project all the more impressive, his caring assistance all the more cherished.

University regulations mandated the naming of a new academic adviser to oversee my graduate program following Dr. Williamson's assumption of his new duties as president and vice-chancellor of the University of the South. Professor Gerhard L. Weinberg was the natural choice, for he had served as my unofficial mentor within the department for years. Professor Weinberg's modern Europe seminars shaped my approach to the historian's craft, and I am deeply grateful for his lively interest in and constant commitment to a project far beyond the boundaries of his own research in Nazi Germany and the origins of World War II.

UNC history professors Konrad Jarausch, Josef Anderle, John Headley, and Roger Lotchin all took time from demanding schedules to serve as manuscript readers and to offer thoughtful comments and criticisms. They, too, have all demonstrated great devotion to my academic career, and I have profited more than they know from both their teaching and example. I should also like to thank Dr. Rodler Morris, command historian of the Combined Arms Center at

Fort Leavenworth, Kansas, for his kind consideration of the manuscript and his colleagueship throughout the 1990-91 academic year.

I should also like to extend special thanks to Professor Karl A. Roider of Louisiana State University, whom I encountered while researching the book in Austria. From our first encounter at an orientation meeting of the Austrian Fulbright Commission, Professor Roider took an immediate interest in my work and provided welcome colleagueship during the first two months of my stay in Austria. Professor Roider subsequently consented to read the manuscript in progress, and the finished product in no small measure owes its form to his helpful comments and criticisms.

This book owes much to the assistance of those Austrian academics, archivists, colleagues, and friends. Professor Dr. Gerald Stourzh helped in obtaining initial funding and served as my grant adviser during my year-long stay in Austria. Dr. Kurt Peball, then the director general of the Austrian State Archives, generously consented to see me and showed a keen interest in my research. Dr. Peter Broucek supervised my work at the *Kriegsarchiv* and proved ever willing to offer expert guidance through the mountains of relevant documentation. Dr. Rainer Egger of the same institution eagerly assisted my research in the military chancellery records. At the *Haus-, Hof- und Staatsarchiv*, Dr. Horst Brettner-Messler extended courteous support in my investigation of the foreign ministry archives and the private paper collections. As I told a gathering of the Austrian Military History Commission in April 1989, the Austrian State Archives and the graciousness of its custodians remain one of the best-kept secrets of the Alpine republic and one of its richest treasures.

I should also like to thank those Austrians whose interest and support sustained me during twelve long months of archival work. Dr. Lothar Höbelt, perhaps the brightest young Habsburg military historian in Austria today, absolutely showered me with attention during my stay in Vienna. He freely mobilized his vast array of contacts on my behalf and introduced me to a part of Viennese high society that I might not have otherwise encountered during the normal course of archival research. Dr. Höbelt proved of invaluable assistance in obtaining a renewal of my grant beyond its original six-month period. In this latter regard, I am also deeply grateful to Dr. Othmar Huber of the Austrian Ministry of Science and Research, who, despite responsibilities that went far beyond the administration of my Truman grant, took a deep personal interest in my work in Austria. I should also like to thank Dr. Huber and his wife for a most enjoyable evening of wine-tasting at their vacation home in Burgenland in July 1989.

Dr. Höbelt arranged for me to bring Friedrich Beck to the renewed attention of Austrian military historians in a talk before the Austrian Military History Commission in April 1989. I am, however, also indebted to Dr. Johann

Christoph Allmayer-Beck and Dr. Manfred Rauchensteiner, dual heads of the commission, for acting on Dr. Höbelt's recommendation and for their kind invitation to speak.

The last three months of my stay in Vienna were perhaps the most enjoyable, thanks to Friedrich and Gertrude Schauer and their neighbors, Rudolf Schöpf and family. The former graciously invited me into their home when my dormitory accommodations expired at the end of June 1989 and virtually made me a member of their family. When the Schauers left on a prearranged vacation, the Schöpfs both helped me with the management of the Schauer household and often provided me with entertainment after a hard day's work in the archives. I spent many an evening that summer over a bottle of Herr Schöpf's excellent wine. To both families, paragons of Austrian hospitality, I extend heartfelt thanks.

Professor Robert Kragalott of Ohio Wesleyan University kindled in me an interest in modern European history and has since my graduation in 1983 been a constant mentor and friend. I have attempted throughout my subsequent career to pattern myself after his example of excellence in scholarship and classroom teaching. Urged on by Professor Kurt Guddat, my other great undergraduate mentor, I continued my study of the language, culture, and literature of German-speaking Central Europe. Without his careful instruction in the German language, I would never have possessed the skills necessary to research this book. His tragic suicide in July 1989 deeply saddened all who knew him. These words and this book offer but an imperfect eulogy to one of the most devoted teachers and truly decent human beings I have ever known.

Finally, my parents, Don and Ethel Lackey, have offered their continued love and support during the curious enterprise of a professional historical career. They have been a constant source of encouragement and strength and have always been there to help in frequent times of need.

Abbreviations

Glstb.   Generalstab (General Staff)

HHStA   Haus-, Hof- und Staatsarchiv, Vienna

KA   Kriegsarchiv, Vienna

KZ   Kanzleizahl (Chancellery number)

KM Präs.   Kriegsministerium Präsidium (Presidium of the
                        Austro-Hungarian War Ministry)

MKSM   Militärkanzlei Seiner Majestät (Military
                        Chancellery of His Majesty)

OpB   Operationsbüro (Operations Section of the Austro-
                        Hungarian General Staff)

PA   Politisches Archiv (Political Archives, Austro-
                        Hungarian Foreign Ministry)

RMRZ   Reichsministerratszahl (Imperial Ministerial Council Number)

res.   reservat (classified document)

Introduction:
The Forgotten *Feldzeugmeister*

One bright September day in 1989, I stood on the Vienna Ringstraße at Schwarzenbergplatz waiting to board Tram No. 71 for the long ride to the *Zentralfriedhof.* My stay in the Austrian capital was drawing to a close and there remained one thing that I had to see before leaving for home. I had spent almost an entire calendar year researching a political-military biography of *Feldzeugmeister* (Lieutenant General) Friedrich von Beck in the Vienna archives. A visit to his final resting place at Central Cemetery seemed both a fitting conclusion and a requisite act of respect for a man whose life and career had served as my entry into the historical profession.

I had attempted the same trip the previous March on the assumption that the cemetery administration would be at work on a Sunday, generally the day of greatest visitation. Beck's name was not included among the list of the cemetery's "famous" occupants. The attendant at the main gate, a rather elderly gentlemen whose father perhaps served with Austro-Hungarian forces during the Great War, had heard nothing of a General Beck. Nor was a supposedly more knowledgeable colleague watching one of the other entrances to the labyrinthine maze of tombstones of much greater help. I was advised to return during the week or on Saturday when cemetery record-keepers could assist me in my search.

Devotion to archival work during the week and to the weekend pleasures of Vienna's "new wine" restaurants, cafés, opera, and theater postponed my return visit. With the research nearing completion, my thoughts again turned to the Central Cemetery, a journey which now seemed more obligatory than ever given the massive amount of material I had assembled on Beck's career.

My second journey, however, turned out to be almost as fruitless as the first. The administrative personnel initially appeared perplexed by an American's interest in a long-dead Habsburg general. Puzzlement soon gave way to consternation when they could not locate Beck in their registers for February 1920, the date of his interment at the Central Cemetery. Was I certain that he was indeed buried there? How did I know? And who was this General Beck anyway?

Reference to obituary notices found in the *Kriegsarchiv* somewhat allayed their suspicions that I might be making the whole thing up. In answering the last question, I quickly reverted to a hackneyed formula I had devised to explain my daily activities to Austrian students living on my floor of the residence hall: Friedrich Beck was the predecessor of the more (in)famous Franz Conrad von Hötzendorf, who led the monarchy's armed forces during World War I. This statement, accompanied by the supplemental information that Beck had headed Franz Joseph's military chancellery for fourteen years and his general staff for twenty-five, generally brought nods of understanding and appreciation from the sentimental Viennese.

In this case, it spurred the cemetery officials to greater efforts to find Beck's resting place. Frenzied searching still yielded nothing. No Friedrich Beck had been buried in the Central Cemetery in February 1920. At best, they could give me the location within the vast cemetery of a relative's grave -- someone who had first been buried elsewhere but was subsequently translated there.

With only this information to go on, I entered the cemetery grounds, determined to search for Beck on foot if the reference failed to yield positive results. The knowledge that Europeans often buried family members on top of one another offered little consolation as I made my way down the broad avenue toward the Karl-Lueger-Kirche where paths met to carry the visitor into all corners of this vast city of the dead.

As I strolled, I admired the elaborate tombstones which lined the main boulevard of the cemetery. Soon I began to recognize figures that had become familiar to me over the course of a year's research. There lay Heinrich von Heß, the chief of the general quartermaster corps and Beck's teacher and mentor. Over there was Franz Freiherr von John, architect of the Custoza victory and later war minister and chief of the general staff. Franz Uchatius, the inventor of the steel-bronze smelting process which allowed for the continued domestic production of Austro-Hungarian artillery in the late nineteenth century, rested in a place of honor. Beautiful flowers, no doubt planted at municipal expense, decorated the tombstones of these dead paladins of the defunct Habsburg monarchy. Beck, I thought, could not be too far distant from these other distinguished military men. I snapped a few photographs and moved on.

Upon reaching the church, I swung right toward a darker corner of the cemetery. Beck's relative was somewhere in the morass of lanes and byways. After fifteen minutes of searching, I found, to my amazement, Beck's grave. At first, I could not be sure. Great trees threw up leafy branches to obscure lettering worn by years of exposure to wind and water. But yes, the tall black pillar bore the name of *Generaloberst*[1] Friedrich Count Beck-Rzikowsky as well as those of his uncle, wife, and son.

I stood for a few minutes in silent reverence to this military man of peace. After a while, I stooped to clear away some of the undergrowth. Before leaving, I attempted to take a few pictures of the site, but even a flash could not sufficiently brighten the darkness. Without scrambling atop the stone, something that seemed almost sacrilegious, I knew that the names inscribed on the obelisk would never come out in my photographs.

I returned to the administration building with a sense of triumph. I had found someone resting within the cemetery who was not supposed to be there. The officials were dumbfounded. How could Beck be there without there being a record of it? After twenty minutes or so of much mumbling and pulling of hair, one of them found the answer. Back in 1920, those bodies interred in vaults (*Grufte*)--that is, in walled graves--were listed in a separate register. A check of these records soon revealed that a Friedrich Beck had indeed been laid to rest in the Vienna Central Cemetery on 10 February 1920.

This incident served to underscore an impression that had been building since I began work: Beck was the monarchy's forgotten general. As I stood silently in front of his grave, I reflected on Beck's obituary notice in the *Neue Wiener Tagblatt*. All of old imperial Vienna, in 1920 a tarnished memory in a city threatened with starvation in the aftermath of the World War, turned out to honor the close personal friend of Emperor Franz Joseph I. The latter's nephew, Emperor Karl I, wired his condolences to the Beck family from his exile in Switzerland and placed an imperial-sized order of flowers with city florists. In personal attendance were the Dutch and German ambassadors, the former Austrian Minister-President Max Vladimir von Beck (no relation), the former common minister of foreign affairs and finance Stephan Burian, the former *Obersthofmeister*[2] August Lobkowitz, the former director of Franz Joseph's civilian cabinet Alois Czedik, the former Austrian Defense Minister Friedrich Georgi, the Police President of Vienna Johann Schober, as well as numerous retired generals led by the last head of the imperial military chancellery Arthur Bolfras. Almost seventy years later, even those entrusted with the record-keeping of the cemetery had temporarily lost track of the man so honored by his contemporaries.

Beck's modern-day obscurity became almost a source of embarrassment to me as I pursued my research in the Vienna archives. My Conrad formula served me well in placing Beck in the minds of Austrian colleagues, most of whom were pursuing studies in fields other than history. It, however, quickly lent meaning and perspective to my work, for after a time I found much to admire in Friedrich Beck. A private mission began to take shape in my mind. I would fashion a political biography of a late nineteenth-century military leader of whom Austrians could justifiably be proud.

The archivists and historians with whom I met had of course heard of Friedrich Beck and fancied the idea of an American looking into the career of one of the old monarchy's military leaders. The shadow of the great Conrad, however, extended even into this more specialized realm. As the monarchy's last generalissimo, Conrad remains a defining figure in the political-military history of the monarchy. Already on my first day in the military archives,

Conrad stared at me disapprovingly from his high perch on an office wall. A few weeks later, a visit to Conrad's grave in Hietzing cemetery revealed a gigantic tombstone bearing a huge inscription arrogant in its simplicity: "FELDMARSCHALL CONRAD." The name of Gina von Reininghaus, the woman whose heart he planned to win by unleashing a world war, was relegated to an obscure corner of the massive stone financed by Austrian taxpayers. Two freshly laid wreaths from the Austrian *Bundesheer* offered evidence that public institutions continued to honor his memory.

By contrast, the old *Stiftskaserne*, to which the *Kriegsarchiv* had moved while still under Beck's administrative control, bore no portraits or other reminders of his long career in Habsburg military service. Beck had served as Franz Joseph's chief of the general staff for twenty-five years--over two and a half times longer than Conrad--and as head of his military chancellery for an additional fourteen years before that. Pictures of Franz Joseph and Archduke Albrecht guarded the reading room, but Beck, their longtime friend and colleague, was nowhere to be found. The 1867-1914 section of the Military History Museum in the Vienna Arsenal inexplicably failed to mention the man who exercised decisive influence over the monarchy's armed forces for all but the last eight years of this period.

Beck's obscurity is undoubtedly linked to a general neglect of Habsburg military history outside the Republic of Austria. In 1967 Paul Schroeder termed the field "an underdeveloped area which ought to qualify for Point 4 aid or the government's poverty program."[3] The situation has improved little since. This is especially true for the period between the 1867 Compromise and the appointment of Conrad as chief of the general staff in 1906. The lack of any real military "action" apart from the occupation of Bosnia-Herzegovina in 1878 and the relative decline over the subsequent decades of the monarchy's armed forces vis-à-vis those of the other Great European Powers made the last third of the nineteenth century uninviting to traditional military historians. Researchers, more interested in Austria-Hungary's increasing troubles in the Balkans during the decade leading up to World War I, have viewed military affairs of the preceding period as an uninteresting interlude between the monumental events of the 1850s and 1860s and those of 1914-18.

Fortunately, I was not without some historical assistance in my search for Beck. Since the appearance in 1930 of *Franz Josephs Weggefährte*, the name Edmund von Glaise-Horstenau has been inextricably linked with Beck and the history of the Austro-Hungarian army in the last half of the nineteenth century.[4] As an inter-war director of the Vienna *Kriegsarchiv*, Glaise-Horstenau had access to vast amounts of material unavailable to others, including the Beck diaries, lost for decades until very recently.[5] Indeed, his almost complete reliance on the latter gives his biography, at points, the character of a primary source.[6] However, it appears probable that he used little more than the diaries themselves and perhaps a few other bits of evidence from Beck's private papers in the writing of the biography.

More recently, Gunther Rothenberg has provided us with a survey of the Habsburg army during Franz Joseph's reign.[7] Excellent in his succinctness, Rothenberg broadly summarizes the developments in weaponry and military planning that occurred during Beck's tenure in high military office. The latter has also received detailed treatment in a Ph.D. dissertation by Dieter Degreif.[8] István Deák's new work offers, through a statistical study of two year-groups of Habsburg officers and a useful gleaning of some of the memoir literature, an interesting picture of life and career in Austro-Hungarian military service during the 1867-1914 period.[9]

The newest Austrian scholarship has centered on administrative history of the Austro-Hungarian military during Franz Joseph's reign. The Academy of Sciences volume on the armed forces offers a useful overview of administrative structures and army organization, influenced by the work of Walter Wagner, one of the principal authors of the volume, on the Austro-Hungarian war ministry to 1888.[10] The latter work is especially useful on the so-called "general staff question" of the late 1860s and early 1870s. The best work on the Austro-Hungarian general staff itself remains the massive unpublished manuscript by Colonel Oskar Wolf-Schneider von Arno.[11] Wolf-Schneider was preparing a multivolume work on the general staff for Styria Verlag when he died in the early 1950s. The manuscripts, contained in the collection of his private papers housed in the *Kriegsarchiv*, clearly demonstrate his command of the archival sources and provide an excellent institutional history of the general staff corps. The work is particularly strong in covering Beck's enhancement of the position of chief of the general staff after 1881 and improvements in war planning and mobilization capability.

This literature, however, did not completely answer all the questions about the development of the Austro-Hungarian armed forces in the late nineteenth century. How did the militarily inept monarchy of mid-century transform itself into the modern military state that existed by 1890? What was the nature of this transformation, and who were the major actors? What part did Beck play in this process?

A closer examination of these questions revealed that Friedrich Beck played the crucial role in the reform of the army after 1866. As head of the military chancellery between 1867 and 1881 and then chief of the general staff until 1906, Beck exercised often absolute control over the military destiny of the Habsburg empire. He took a leading role in the reorganization of the army after 1866 and emerged as the sole army representative capable of negotiating the military aspects of the 1867 Compromise with the Hungarians. By the mid-1870s, Beck made the emperor's military chancellery the focal point of power in the Austro-Hungarian army, overturning the system of ministerial dominance established after Königgrätz. The failure of the war ministry to organize an effective military intervention in the Franco-Prussian conflict of 1870 provided the main impetus for Beck's reforms.

Displacing ministerial absolutism, he erected a Prussian-style general staff with sole responsibility for military planning. The general staff functioned as the central nervous system for the monarchy's armed forces. Central general staff bureaus in Vienna formulated war plans to meet all political contingencies and devise mobilization, transportation, and logistical schedules. The central general staff bureaus formed the brain of the military organism. The periodic rotation of general staff officers to troop commands on the model of the Prussian *Truppengeneralstab* ensured the smooth execution of the brain's instructions during mobilization. Admission to and successful completion of the general staff course at the *Kriegsschule* determined membership in this elite officer corps. Staff rides and army maneuvers made sure that general staff officers remained well-honed in their craft of leading the army in wartime.

Beck shaped the role and missions of the general staff in 1874, a full eight years before he himself was appointed by Franz Joseph to lead it. Throughout the remainder of the 1870s, however, he exercised a dominant role from the military chancellery. In particular, he succeeded in forcing a reluctant Count Gyula Andrássy to place the acquisition of the Turkish provinces of Bosnia and Herzegovina on the foreign political agenda. In the spring of 1875, Beck convinced Franz Joseph to undertake a highly controversial tour of Dalmatia to demonstrate the sovereign's concern for the well-being of his subjects and those of the Turkish sultan in the neighboring territories.

The reemergence of the Eastern Question served to postpone any real reform in the Habsburg "way of war" until 1881, when Beck took over personal direction of the general staff. As chief, Beck oversaw the first systematic peacetime war planning in the monarchy's history. The deployment plans of the early 1880s, however, revealed that much work still had to be done in improving military readiness. In 1881 Austria-Hungary faced the possibility of a four-front war with Russia, Italy, Serbia, and Romania. The effective neutralization of most of these threats by the Habsburg foreign office by mid-decade did not deter Beck from pushing through a series of dramatic reforms aimed at increasing army readiness. Over the initial resistance of the war ministry and the inspector general of the army, he pushed through the reorganization of the army on a territorial basis to allow for a faster mobilization and deployment. Beck also obtained a significant expansion of the railroad network from the Austrian and Hungarian governments. In 1881 the Habsburg army could achieve war readiness in Galicia against Russia only after six weeks. By the end of the decade, this mobilization time had been cut in half.

Increases in the military strength of Great Power neighbors and the possibility of a multifront war forced Beck to call for the development of a people's army of unprecedented size. The militias established as a result of the 1867 Compromise would have to abandon their home defense role to join the common army in the field. At Beck's instigation, new levies (*Landsturm*) would take over home defense duties from the *Landwehr* and *Honvéd* militias of Austria and Hungary. The arming of untrained and unindoctrinated civilians in wartime, unthinkable in the 1860s, was approved under a mounting threat of war with Russia.

The 1880s, therefore, saw the radical transformation of Austria-Hungary into a modern military state under Beck's direction. The establishment of routine war planning against the state's probable enemies, the improvement of the rail network, and a slow strengthening of the fighting capabilities of the militias increased greatly the monarchy's capability of waging a successful war. The extension of the military service obligation to age forty-two in 1886 and the lifting of statutory limitations on the maximum size of the armed forces in the 1889 Military Law enabled the state to mobilize its manpower resources to an unprecedented degree in wartime. The development of both intelligence and counterespionage capabilities, coupled with the passage of emergency legislation restricting civilian rights in wartime, rounded out this picture of increasing effectiveness.

Beck's ability to carry out these reforms rested squarely upon his friendship with the emperor, a product of years of close contact at the military chancellery. Indeed, his virtual domination over military affairs can be viewed as a throwback to the early days of Franz Joseph's reign when another imperial favorite, Count Karl Grünne, ran the army. Unlike Grünne, Beck used his power to construct a sensible system of army administration with a purposeful distribution of power and functions among various military agencies. Beck recognized the war minister's highly important role in representing the army's interests before the Austrian and Hungarian Delegations and the need to maintain at least the appearance of ministerial control over the common forces. He therefore never attempted to free the general staff from its nominal subordination to the war ministry. But as chief of the general staff, Beck did insist upon complete autonomy in matters pertaining to the operational use of the armed forces and upon having the decisive voice in the determination of military requirements.

His sometimes turbulent relationship with the ministries of war and foreign affairs over the creation of the general staff corps and the imperialist agenda in the Balkans calmed considerably after Beck's transfer to the general staff in 1881. He made a concerted effort to coordinate political-military policy with both these agencies and never purposely undermined their authority or influence. He also cooperated closely with the Austrian and Hungarian governments to obtain passage of the much-needed *Landsturm* legislation in 1886 and improvements in the existing militia forces.

Without Beck's intervention, the reforms of the 1880s might never have taken place. The emperor, the war minister, the foreign minister, and the inspector general of the armed forces all at one time or another had opposed some or all of these measures. All had to be placed on the political agenda by Beck for consideration by the ministerial council and the Austrian and Hungarian ministries. But for Beck's intervention the territorialization of the army and the simplification of deployment and logistical planning that this reform entailed might never have occurred. Staff planning and the need to maximize troop strengths in Galicia for a likely war against Russia led directly to the creation of home defense levies in both halves of the monarchy. This reform, coupled with the lifting of the statutory ceilings on the army's wartime strength, allowed for an eventual total mobilization of Habsburg society for war.

Unlike his successor, Conrad von Hötzendorf, Beck never hoped to test the improved readiness of the Habsburg armed forces in war. In 1870 he opposed Austro-Hungarian intervention in the Franco-Prussian War as a senseless prolongation of the 1866 German civil war and pushed subsequently for the improvement of Austro-Prussian relations. While a keen advocate of Habsburg expansion in the Balkans, Beck worked assiduously throughout his career to avoid a confrontation with Russia and welcomed cooperation with St. Petersburg via the Three Emperors' League. When Russia threatened the monarchy with war in the aftermath of the Bulgarian crisis, Beck restrained the Austro-Hungarian military response in order to avoid war. Perhaps more than any other military leader of his age, Beck understood the moral and spiritual burdens involved in unleashing the military machines of Europe. Unlike his successor, he firmly believed that no conflict on the continent involving a Great Power could remain a local one. The growth of alliance systems would ensure that the next war would be a "great war."

These latter views alone make Beck a significant military figure of late nineteenth- and early twentieth-century Europe. No less than the elder Moltke, who, after all, had the experience of leading large forces in wartime, Beck realized the carnage of a modern European war. A political conservative, Beck saw in war the real danger of social and political upheaval, an overturning of the imperial regime to which he had devoted his life. From the quiet retirement of his Molkerbastei apartment in the center of Vienna, Beck sadly looked on while his predictions came true in the Great War.

As I stood before his grave in the shady corner of the *Zentralfriedhof*, I could not help but feel a bit sad myself over the historical fate of this military man of peace, this visionary of the Habsburg monarchy. Glaise-Horstenau's biography, still of tremendous use to specialists, has done little to enhance Beck's historical importance and reputation. The more recent administrative and political-social studies have largely failed to give him his due as the principal architect of the post-*Ausgleich* Habsburg armed forces. The present volume aims both to correct these deficiencies and to illustrate civil-military policymaking in the unique constitutional framework of the dual monarchy.

Chapter 1

Death and Rebirth

On 4 July 1866, remnants of the Habsburg North Army staggered away from the bloody battlefield of Königgrätz. The tired columns marched toward Olmütz, the army's base in Moravia where it had begun the campaign against Prussia. There Habsburg commanders hoped to regroup their shattered forces for a final stand in front of Vienna. On the fields of northern Bohemia, the retreating Austrians had left some 14,307 dead and wounded comrades. A further 29,906 had been captured or were reported missing. These losses, while not exorbitant by the standards of mid-nineteenth-century conflict, especially given the fact that nearly half a million men had been engaged, nonetheless stunned the Habsburg civil-military leadership. The army's inability to inflict comparable punishment on the Prussian enemy greatly magnified the impact of these high casualties.[1]

The loss of the Austro-Prussian War shook the very foundations of the Habsburg empire. Hungarian nationalists, led by Francis Deák and Gyula Andrássy, forced the creation of a dual monarchy, a constitutional arrangement that gave the Kingdom of Hungary its own government with autonomy in all areas except foreign and military policy.[2] The *Ausgleich* constitution of 1867 created a new "Austrian" state, an amalgam comprising all the non-Hungarian Habsburg territories, with functions and responsibilities identical to those given to the Hungarian government.[3] The armed forces also changed to reflect the new political realities. Most within the military recognized a need for reform, but there was little agreement on policies and goals needed to transform the defeated army into an effective fighting force that would simultaneously reflect the new dualist constitution of the Habsburg state.

Continuity and Reform, 1848-1866

Military reform preoccupied much of the early reign of Franz Joseph I, a fact often obscured by the catastrophic failure at Königgrätz. Details of military spectacle and regimen fascinated Franz Joseph, who rarely appeared in public out of uniform throughout his sixty-eight years as emperor.[4] This intense interest, however, did not translate into either professional military competence or an understanding of the organizational structures required to maintain the army's effectiveness during a period of rapid change in military science prompted by technological developments such as the railroad and telegraph. If anything, Franz Joseph's actions during his first twenty-five years demonstrate that he possessed no firm ideas on military science, administration, or organization. He distrusted army "intellectuals," those conscious of the innovations taking place around them and desirous of turning them to military advantage, and generally favored those who demonstrated courage and élan on the battlefield. His own squeamishness toward the carnage of war, amply demonstrated when the emperor quickly concluded the Villafranca peace soon after viewing the bloody battlefields of 1859, reinforced his admiration and trust of brave, but not necessarily competent, officers.

Franz Joseph also showed a strong early preference to rule, both in civil and military affairs, through familiar and trusted personages. This kind of favoritism, coupled with his military predilections, had disastrous consequences for the Austrian army and near fatal ones for the Habsburg state. Prior to the Italian War of 1859, it led to the rise of the *Generaladjutantur*, or adjutant general staff, a collection of officers distinguished more by noble birth than by military accomplishment headed by Franz Joseph's childhood tutor and friend, Karl Ludwig Count von Grünne. The count feared anyone of superior ability and encouraged the emperor's distrust of military intellectuals, just then beginning to organize around the *Generalquartiermeisterstab* (quartermaster general staff) and army legend Field Marshal Josef Radetzky's Italian Army headquarters. To counter their influence, Grünne courted aristocrats for his adjutant general staff, planting them throughout the army as a rival command and control system to the professional quartermaster general staff. In Italy, where the empire based its best-trained, combat-ready forces, Grünne retired the aging Count Radetzky, replacing him with the vain and incompetent General Franz Gyulai von Maros-Németh und Nádaska.[5] The Italian War of 1859, when units often received two sets of orders per day--one from the general quartermaster staff, the other from the adjutant general staff--demonstrated the large degree of Grünne's success.[6]

The unnecessary loss of the 1859 war to the Franco-Italian army forced a temporary abandonment of the favorite system. Post-war reforms, however, did little to improve the war-fighting capabilities of the Habsburg army. To restore the confidence of taxpayers in the armed forces, Franz Joseph consented to the re-establishment of a constitutional war ministry, eliminated in 1853 by Grünne, with responsibility for army administration. To prepare the army for its next war, the emperor placed his trust in General Ludwig von Benedek and the general quartermaster staff. Benedek met Franz Joseph's criterion for high military office. He had distinguished himself in 1848 as a regimental commander with Radetzky's army in Italy, winning the monarchy's highest decoration for bravery, the Maria Theresa Order. Until 1853, Benedek served as the chief of staff to the great Radetzky. Success at Solferino, where his corps covered the army's withdrawal, mandated a commanding role since the defeat in Italy discredited virtually the entire senior military leadership.[7]

In 1860, the general quartermaster staff appeared to be the coming institution within the Habsburg army like its counterpart in Prussia, the *Große Generalstab*. Founded in the late sixteenth century to administer logistics, the general quartermaster staff was actually one of the most venerable institutions in the army. Apart from a brief period in the early eighteenth century, when Prince Eugen of Savoy expanded the staff's competence to include tactical and operative questions, it remained small in size and mission.[8] Like their pre-Moltke counterparts in the Prussian general staff, members of the quartermaster general corps engaged mainly in triangulation (surveying), mapmaking, and the writing of detailed reports on the lands and peoples surveyed. Staff officers also served as clerical managers of divisional and corps offices when not assigned to staff headquarters in Vienna, where they assisted the chief of the general quartermaster corps in analyzing the military significance of technological breakthroughs and in determining fortification requirements for imperial defense.[9] After 1852 the newly established *Kriegsschule* (war college) educated staff officers in horseback-riding, military history, triangulation, and mapmaking, and foreign languages, a curriculum that bore a strong resemblance to that of the Prussian *Kriegsakademie*.[10]

Where the Austrian quartermaster general staff parted company with its Prussian counterpart was in the peacetime planning and preparation for war. Whereas the Prussians learned from past experiences such as the sluggish mobilization of 1850, the Austrians did not, despite opportunity to study the combat lessons of the 1848 Revolution and the Italian War of 1859. Responsibility for this crucial failure lies squarely with Benedek, whose personal distaste for the "green table" work of the military planner led him to ignore his duties as chief of the general quartermaster staff in favor of those he discharged as commander-in-chief of the Habsburg Italian Army and governor-general of Hungary. Stating "I conduct the business of war according to simple rules and I am not impressed by complicated calculations," Benedek preferred to remain with the troops in Italy rather than assume immediate direction of the staff in Vienna.[11] The general quartermaster staff did experience organizational growth during Benedek's tenure as chief, to include the establishment of bureaus for war planning, deployment, and military education. But Benedek's personal disinterest in staff work, coupled with burdensome responsibilities elsewhere, hampered the staff's ability to capitalize on administrative gains made over the rival adjutant corps after 1859. To his credit, Benedek recognized his neglect of the general quartermaster staff and asked to be relieved as its chief in March 1861. Franz Joseph's stubborn determination to entrust war heroes with the highest military responsibilities, regardless of their suitability for such positions, delayed action on this reasonable request for almost three years. As a consequence, the monarchy lacked detailed plans to prosecute the war with Prussia in 1866, a conflict long foreseen by many military and political observers.[12]

The Early Career of Friedrich Beck

On 1 July 1848, Friedrich Beck donned the white uniform of a second lieutenant in Habsburg service. His early career was at once typical of and extraordinary for general quartermaster staff officers of this time. Introduced to military service by a paternal uncle, whose connections as a senior civilian official within the *Hofkriegsrat* (Court War Council) bureaucracy gave the young man an advantage over others sharing his bourgeois background,[13] Friedrich Beck enrolled in the *Pionierschule* (Pioneer Academy) at Tulln near Vienna at age sixteen. The outbreak of revolutionary violence in his second year forced an early release of Beck's cadet class from the three-year course of instruction. Outstanding performance and family connections garnered for Beck a commission in the Grand Duke of Baden Infantry Regiment No. 59 during the 1848 Revolution. The young officer, therefore, experienced firsthand the manifold challenges confronted by the Habsburg army. Beck's staunch conservatism and loyalty to the Habsburg dynasty were quickly tested, but conservative upbringing and military indoctrination made him a reliable instrument of order in the hands of his superiors. While en route to join the army of Prince Alfred Windischgrätz, Beck informed on two fellow officers who had fraternized with student activists and dealt swiftly and successfully with several incidents of insubordination in the ranks.[14]

Beck, however, did not see action until the following year when he was ordered to Italy to join the line battalions of his regiment.[15] This transfer had a profound impact on Beck's future career, for it spared him the hardship of the bitter campaign against revolutionary Hungary. Unlike the vast majority of his colleagues in the Habsburg officer corps, Beck would later harbor none of their deep mistrust and resentment toward Magyar nationalists. Later in 1867, this made him the natural choice to spearhead the military negotiations with the Hungarians, which in turn laid the groundwork for his future dominance over the Austro-Hungarian military.

Reassignment to Italy brought Beck into contact with the best-trained, best-led forces in the monarchy: Field Marshal Josef Radetzky's Italian Army. Maintained in a constant state of preparedness by their commander, Habsburg forces in Italy practiced the only large-scale troop maneuvers in the monarchy prior to the *Armeemanöver* instituted by Beck in the 1880s. The Italian Army had also been called out at various times between 1815 and 1848 to suppress uprisings all along the Italian peninsula.[16] In 1848-49, it faced the dual threat of nationalist insurgency and foreign invasion, for the Kingdom of Sardinia-Piedmont threatened to capitalize on the monarchy's domestic difficulties. Radetzky, however, quickly quelled domestic unrest and turned back Piedmontese forces west of Verona.

In February 1849, Beck arrived at regimental headquarters in Verona during a lull in the fighting. Shortly after his coming, Sardinia broke the truce negotiated the previous spring and launched an invasion of Lombardy. Beck faced renewed disappointment when his unit, relegated to garrison duty, did not participate in Radetzky's final victorious campaign. However, two days after the cessation of hostilities, Regiment No. 59 stormed the town of Brescia, which had risen in forlorn desperation against Habsburg rule. Beck barely escaped death in the bitter fighting when he accidentally tripped over a fallen comrade, missing a bullet that cut down the man immediately behind him.[17]

Beck's combat performance won him the attention of his superiors, transfer to the general quartermaster staff, and promotion to first lieutenant in the summer of 1849. He served first with the Austrian forces besieging Venice. Following its surrender to Radetzky in August, Beck toured north Italian garrisons before becoming a brigade chief of staff in Vienna. In the latter post, he participated in the 1850 Austrian mobilization in Bohemia meant to bully Prussia into accepting a return of the pre-revolutionary Habsburg primacy in German politics. The unwillingness of Prussian conservatives to challenge Austria's leadership led to a rapid dissipation of the crisis and Beck's brief and final return to Italy, where he held a series of staff appointments.[18] The relatively little time spent with Habsburg forces in Italy would have a profound impact on Beck's attitudes and career. Unlike many of his contemporaries who would later attain high military rank, Beck never developed an attachment to the Italian provinces. Thus he never harbored personal revenge toward Sardinia-Piedmont, which would later eject the Habsburgs from Italy with French and Prussian assistance.

Following a year on the staff of the Vienna garrison, where he spent most of his time planning countermeasures against an expected resurgence of revolutionary violence, Beck gained admission to the first class of the newly established *Kriegsschule*. He graduated fourth in his class in the fall of 1854, was promoted to captain, second class and received permanent assignment to the general quartermaster staff. Beck's first appointment as a general staff captain was as a divisional chief of staff in Graz. He joined this command just when another great international crisis in the Balkans threatened the European peace. The Graz division participated in the mobilization ordered by Franz Joseph in the fall of 1854 to force Russia to evacuate the Danubian Principalities of Moldavia and Wallachia (i.e., the eastern portions of modern-day Romania). While the monarchy did not side against Russia in the ensuing Crimean War, its actions infuriated the Tsarist government, which naturally felt betrayed by the Habsburgs whose rule they had helped restore with blood and money only five years before. The Austro-Russian relationship would never fully recover from the enmity and suspicion generated by the Crimean crisis. Indeed, Beck would spend the vast majority of his time as chief of the general staff preparing Austria-Hungary for war against Russia.[19]

Beck received a major professional break when the chief of the general quartermaster corps, General Heinrich von Heß, made him his adjutant in the fall of 1855. Heß coupled an extraordinary grasp of future direction of military art and science with an almost total inability to build the general quartermaster staff into an institution that would execute his vision. Beck embraced many of the brilliant ideas his general failed to impart to others, including the vital importance of railroad and telegraph to success in late nineteenth-century warfare and the absolute need for detailed war plans for every possible political-military contingency. Indeed, Beck would assist Heß in the first real peacetime military planning in the monarchy's history and would later use many of Heß's strategic concepts in his own war plans of the 1880s.[20]   Under Heß, Beck developed early opinions as to the importance of the Balkans to the monarchy as an outlet for Austrian goods and an access route to rich Middle Eastern markets.[21]

On 1 September 1857, Beck was promoted to captain, first class and early the following year left his comfortable job as Heß's adjutant for a required two-year mapping assignment in southern Hungary.   This primitive region abounded with swamp fever and highwaymen and offered few comforts. The new captain, however, did what was expected of him. He hiked over the rugged countryside, drawing maps and composing descriptive pieces about area terrain and inhabitants.[22]   In 1859, as tensions rose between Austria and France over the issue of Italian nationalism, Beck petitioned General Heß for a combat assignment with the Habsburg army in Italy. The general agreed to cut short Beck's mapping tour and ordered him to Brescia to become chief of staff to General Sigismund Freiherr von Reischach.   His posting to Reischach's command proved key to Beck's future success. Reischach's brigadiers, Ludwig von Gablenz and Franz Freiherr von John, were extremely capable officers, both destined for high military office. Reischach gave Beck great latitude in the day-to-day operation of the division and its preparation for the coming war. More importantly, Reischach was highly regarded throughout the army with entrée to Emperor Franz Joseph.

The outbreak of hostilities in April 1859 found both the morale and readiness of individual units high, but the Austrian high command in traditional disarray. The field commander, General Franz Gyulai von Maros-Németh und Nádaska, began the campaign with no real operational plan of his own and rejected an aggressive one drawn up by his capable chief of staff, Colonel Franz Freiherr Kuhn von Kuhnenfeld. The army lacked maps of Sardinia-Piedmont, a fact which forced Beck to scour local stationary shops and bookstores to obtain them for his division.[23] Gyulai's early caution allowed the French army of five corps to link up with Piedmontese forces by 10 May 1859. Gyulai began a slow advance into the Piedmont, hoping that reinforcements from the interior of the monarchy would arrive before the French could appear in strength--a wish that went unrealized.[24]

On 4 June, the disorganized Austrian army collided with Franco-Italian forces near Magenta. Because of confusion in the Austrian rear area, the Reischach division could not enter the action until after 2 p.m. Beck and his commander led the division in a charge against the flank of the advancing French guard. At the height of the attack, Beck, dashing along the assaulting line to maintain order and discipline in the ranks, fell with a bullet in the left knee. Bleeding profusely from what appeared to be a serious and possibly incapacitating wound, the furious staff captain allowed himself to be taken from the field. The Reischach division wavered and then fell back, its attack bringing the day's fighting to an indecisive close. Austrian forces fought well and vacated the field only at the discretion of General Heß, who had arrived to assume direction of army operations.

After Magenta, the Austrian army conducted a series of fruitless marches and countermarches culminating in a bloody and inconclusive engagement at Solferino on 24 June. The battle found Beck on a hospital train bound for Vienna. Two days before, Beck received a surprise visit from Franz Joseph, who, on Baron Reischach's recommendation, conferred upon him the Order of the Iron Crown. This event, which marked the beginning of his long association with the emperor, proved key to Beck's later success for it bestowed upon him the "combat credentials" so esteemed by Franz Joseph. Fortunately for Beck, such distinction did not demand a high price. Within three months, physical therapy and sulfur treatments restored his leg. Within ten months, Beck was ready for a new assignment where he would confront Austria's next military challenge: the rising power of Prussia.[25]

Königgrätz: Death of an Army

In March 1860, Beck left Vienna for Frankfurt am Main to become the archivist and stenographer of the Federal Military Commission. The commission regulated the military affairs of the German Confederation, the

loose association of German states formed after 1815 on the model of the
Napoleonic Confederation of the Rhine. Most of the member states accepted
Habsburg leadership of the confederation. However, Prussia, enlarged by the
Congress of Vienna to act as a bulwark against further French aggression, also
aspired to a leadership role, particularly in the military sphere. During the
revolutions of 1848-49, German nationalist fervor had forced a brief Prussian
challenge to multinational Austria. In the early 1860s, Prussian nationalists led
by Otto von Bismarck renewed calls for an end to Austrian dominance of the
confederation.

When Bismarck became minister-president of Prussia in September
1862, he had the instrument he needed to realize his aim of unifying Germany:
the Prussian army. This army, soundly crushed by Napoleon in 1806, had
learned valuable lessons from the Napoleonic Wars and had spent much of the
intervening period recasting itself to master the new military realities of the
nineteenth century. The establishment of the Prussian general staff proved the
most important and enduring of the post-1815 reforms and the one that
permitted the exploitation of the emerging technologies of the railroad,
telegraph, and breechloading weaponry that would produce the lightning
victories of 1866 and 1870-71. An institutional "brain trust," the general staff
corps offered a hedge against the negative influence of militarily incompetent
sovereigns and courtier generals through continuous peacetime training in the
operational art.[26]

The appointment in 1857 of the quiet and unassuming Helmut von
Moltke as chief of the Prussian general staff gave an increasingly effective
organization a leader with the vision and focus to wield effectively the growing
military power of Prussia. Moltke shared Bismarck's view of the inevitability
of a showdown between Prussia and Austria for the leadership of Germany.
More importantly, he had a clear perception of Austrian military weaknesses
(particularly the lack of an effective general staff) demonstrated during the 1859
war.[27] Convergence of civil and military viewpoints on an eventual challenge
to Austrian leadership in Germany led to increasing Prussian aggressiveness in
the Confederation Diet and the military commission which served it.

As the secretary of the commission, Beck formally discharged merely
clerical functions in Frankfurt. In reality, he acted as the chief assistant to the
Austrian representative, Brigadier General Leopold Freiherr von Rzikowsky von
Dobrzicz, and as such, authored many of the formal rebuttals to Prussian
attempts to seize leadership of the confederation's military forces.[28] Beck
worked vigorously to divert attention from Prussian claims and to focus it on the
threat to the confederation posed by an expansionist France under Napoleon III.
He organized a subcommission to tour the existing German rail network and to
analyze its potential effectiveness in countering a possible French invasion.
Beck also drew up some rudimentary war plans calling for the concentration of

confederation forces along the central Rhine, with only weak flanking groups spread along the upper and lower reaches of the river--a deployment similar in concept to the one Moltke would employ in 1870. In an attempt to guarantee Austro-Prussian cooperation, Beck drafted a military convention providing for combined operations in the event of a French attack.[29]

Beck did not become deluded by his own schemes and kept his eyes open to the new developments in the Prussian army. In September 1861, he attended the corps maneuvers in Germany involving the Prussian contingent to the confederation army. Moltke's expert handling of the exercise, coupled with the primacy of the Prussian general staff over its conduct, greatly impressed Beck, who dutifully reported his favorable observations to Vienna. Thereafter, Beck became one of Moltke's greatest admirers and *the* greatest advocate for the establishment of a true Prussian-style general staff system in Austria.[30]

Beck soon got the chance to apply the lessons learned in Germany. In February 1862, he was ordered to Vienna to resume adjutant duties with his old mentor, Field Marshal Heß, then living in semi-retirement. A welcome promotion to major accompanied the appointment. This second tour completed Beck's education as a general staff officer, introducing him to the political realities of military preparedness with which he would contend for the remainder of his career. In 1860, Franz Joseph had elevated Heß to the House of Lords of the newly reconstituted parliament (*Reichsrat*). The general took his parliamentary responsibilities seriously and used his seat to lobby for military interests. Consequently, Beck's major task as adjutant was to gather information for the general's speeches in the house.

Topping the list of Heß's priorities was a drastic extension of the Austrian rail network. The general called for the construction of new lines linking Italy, the south German states, and Galicia with the interior of the monarchy to allow the army to counter threats to these areas. Heß's vision for railroad expansion became the basis for the concrete strategic planning and implementation by Beck himself in the 1870s and 1880s.[31] For his part, Beck convinced the general to argue in the diet and with the emperor for increased military commitments to the German Confederation, especially in northern Germany, in order to counter Prussian ambitions. Beck urged the buildup of Hannover into a major federal base and the stationing of Austrian troops in Hamburg in order to drive a wedge between the eastern and western halves of the Prussian kingdom. These projects were ignored by Foreign Minster Count Johann von Rechberg and Franz Joseph. Given the political-military realities of the early 1860s, an era of drastic military budget reductions, they probably had little choice. But in his diary, Beck joined the chorus of those lamenting Heß's lack of forcefulness and blamed the general's lack of courage to push important issues consistently with the emperor and the civilian leadership.[32]

In December 1863, Beck received orders transferring him to the adjutant general's office. While the adjutant general corps had lost much of its earlier power, in 1863 it still functioned as the emperor's personal office for military affairs. The appointment brought Beck into daily contact with the senior army leadership and, more importantly, with Franz Joseph himself. Despite an open policy of non-interference in military matters resulting from the unhappy experience of 1859, the emperor nonetheless remained keenly interested in army affairs and quite willing to influence events indirectly. The adjutant general's office, therefore, remained a powerful operational counterforce to the general quartermaster staff (renamed the general staff in 1865), especially since the latter suffered under an absentee chief and thus lacked leadership and direction for most of the 1859-66 period. In 1864, Beck, for example, assisted the Austrian field commander, General Ludwig von Gablenz, in preparations for the war against Denmark. The chief of the general quartermaster staff, General Ludwig von Benedek, preoccupied with an increasingly tense situation in Italy, took no part in the planning and preparation for the Danish campaign. [33]

At the adjutant general's office, Beck quickly gained a reputation as a capable and knowledgeable military planner, with a sharp grasp of the political-military realities facing the monarchy. His experiences at the Federal Military Commission and as Heß's adjutant made him a sought-after expert in German affairs and the Prussia-Germany theater of operations. As early as February 1865, Beck realized that an eventual Prussian attempt to seize control of Schleswig-Holstein--the spoils of the Danish War--would propel Austria into war.[34] In the fall of 1865, General Rudolf Rossbacher of the imperial war ministry entrusted Beck with the preparation of a war plan against Prussia. The war ministry did not make a similar request of the new chief of the general staff, General Alfred von Henickstein. The general staff, reorganized by Benedek to direct army operations, would only assume a war-planning role in the spring of 1866, after the naming of the field commanders.[35]

Beck's long association with Field Marshal Heß gave him a familiarity with existing Austrian war planning for a war against Prussia. On the basis of Heß's 1850 plan, Beck had written a series of papers calling for a swift advance through Saxony against Berlin. Like his mentor, Beck discounted the possibility of a Prussian invasion of the monarchy from Silesia without active Russian assistance. His plans recommended the concentration of the army at Gitschen, the precise location where in 1866 Moltke would propose to unite his widely scattered Prussian forces. [36] Indeed, in his *Operationsplan--Kriegsobjekt und Operationsobjekt*, Moltke later admitted that the geography of the Bohemian theater had given Benedek the opportunity for the piecemeal annihilation of the invading Prussian armies.[37] Unfortunately for Austria, neither the war ministry nor Benedek followed Beck's aggressive suggestions. They did, however, gain currency with the emperor, who favored a forward deployment in Bohemia to demonstrate to the anti-Prussian German states (Bavaria and Saxony) Austria's will to oppose Berlin's challenge to Habsburg leadership in Germany.

In the spring of 1866, the Austrian government possessed neither political nor military strategies to cope with the coming crisis with Prussia. Franz Joseph delayed choosing his field commanders until March and then made the wrong choices. The emperor's designate to lead the Habsburg North Army against Prussia, General Benedek, openly professed his unsuitability for command. Benedek would later claim that Archduke Albrecht, the leading dynastic figure in the army, forced him to accept the post and sacrifice his career to allow the Habsburgs to save face in the wake of an expected defeat.[38]

Insecure about his ability to direct operations in the northern theater after having spent the vast majority of his career in Italy, Benedek delayed his departure from Verona for over two months and did little to help plan the coming campaign. This he left to chief of the general staff General Alfred von Henickstein, who favored a conservative deployment around the Moravian fortress town of Olmütz. Henickstein argued that earlier war plans calling for a forward deployment in Bohemia had presupposed an Austrian numerical superiority that was no longer valid.[39] What the chief of staff failed to mention was that an Olmütz deployment presupposed a Prussian invasion from Silesia, an assumption unsupported by the widely scattered Prussian deployment that would become known to Vienna through excellent Saxon intelligence at the outbreak of hostilities. To make matters worse, Benedek appointed Brigadier General Gideon von Krismanich as his operations chief. Krismanich, described by historian Gunther Rothenberg as an eighteenth-century thinker preoccupied with logistics and lines of communication, reinforced Benedek's innate caution born of uncertainty in the North Army commander. Personality conflicts with Henickstein, named North Army chief of staff, would further impede staff work during the actual campaign.[40]

Although he had forsworn direct involvement in army operations after the battle of Solferino, Franz Joseph distrusted the conservative plans of Henickstein and Krismanich. In particular, he fretted over the foreign political impact, especially in Saxony, should the North Army remain stationary in Moravia. Knowing Beck to be an advocate of an aggressive advance, the emperor made him his special envoy to North Army headquarters. Franz Joseph hoped that Beck might convince Benedek to move the army into northern Bohemia.

Dispatched a total of four times to North Army headquarters during the campaign, Beck's achievements were enormous despite the ultimate outcome of the northern campaign. He convinced the king of Saxony to ally with Austria, a decision which meant the evacuation of his country. Beck also persuaded Benedek to overrule Henickstein and Krismanich and order the North Army to advance into Bohemia, an action which, had it been executed rapidly, might have changed the course of the campaign.[41] As it turned out, Benedek merely maneuvered between the three advancing arms of the Prussian armies and allowed them to concentrate beyond the Sudeten Mountains. This failure to annihilate the invaders piecemeal, coupled with a tactical doctrine emphasizing close assault in the face of the Prussian breechloading needle gun, produced the shattering losses of the campaign. On instructions from Archduke Albrecht, Beck convinced Benedek to evacuate the Austrian base at Olmütz after the Königgrätz defeat, saving the army from certain encirclement and total defeat. A Habsburg army, therefore, remained in being and ready to defend Vienna at the conclusion of the Nikolsburg armistice on 22 July 1866.

Political and Military Reform, 1866-1868

The loss of the 1866 war devastated confidence in Habsburg rule. Shouts and jeers accompanied the imperial carriage as it made its way along the Mariahilferstraße between Schönbrunn Palace and the Hofburg. The mayor of Vienna openly criticized the government for its inept prosecution of the war.[42] The conflict exacerbated political differences that had existed among the monarchy's nationalities before 1866. Constitutional change was inevitable if the empire was to remain intact. Hungarian nationalism posed the greatest challenge to the status quo, since it had rejected the reforms of the early 1860s that had marked the rebirth of parliamentary government. Before 1866, Magyar nationalists had demanded autonomy within the empire for the Hungarian kingdom. After the catastrophic defeat at Königgrätz, they could get it.

Fortunately for the Habsburgs, Hungary's political leadership in the summer of 1866 favored accommodation with the imperial government in Vienna. Franz Joseph responded to Hungarian willingness to negotiate by authorizing the creation of a Hungarian ministry headed by Count Gyula Andrássy, a man whom the emperor had condemned to the gallows for his participation in Kossuth's revolutionary government of 1848-49. On 29 May 1867, a reconstituted Hungarian parliament ratified a political compromise negotiated by Andrássy with Habsburg foreign minister Count Friedrich Ferdinand von Beust.

The political compromise, or *Ausgleich*, bestowed a strange mixture of permanent and impermanent, centralized and particular governmental institutions that would endure for the remainder of the monarchy's history. The official hyphenated name of the new state, Austria-Hungary, indicates some of its complex nature. The *Ausgleich* created three governments, each responsible in different measures to three different parliamentary bodies. National governments in Austria and Hungary, in theory responsible only to the emperor but reliant upon majorities in the Austrian *Reichsrat* and the Hungarian Diet to be truly effective, ran the affairs of two coequal and autonomous states. Representing the empire as a whole were the common ministries of foreign affairs, finance, and war. All three of these ministries, while each independently responsible solely to the emperor, had to obtain funding for their operations from a common legislature, known as the Delegations, consisting of sixty representatives each from the Austrian and Hungarian parliaments. The foreign minister functioned as a sort of unofficial prime minister, presiding over the common ministerial council in the emperor's absence. [43]

Because of its ubiquitousness in every province of the empire and the very nature of the enormous expenditures required for its support, the army formed the most important--and therefore contentious--bond between the newly autonomous halves of the Habsburg monarchy. Military outlays comprised the vast majority of the common budget and both "national" governments naturally took great interest in the form and future development of the army. For the Austro-German liberals, instilled with a hearty distrust of the military stemming from its brutal repression of liberalism in 1848-49, this interest took the form of tight parliamentary control over the military budget with the goal of keeping it as low as possible. Moderate Magyar nationalists, led by Andrássy, proved more accommodating toward the army's financial requirements, provided the army leadership agreed to certain changes in army organization.

Since the early eighteenth century, political Hungary had clamored for military institutions independent of all others within the multinational Habsburg empire. Hungarian nationalists had indeed made this a condition of their ratification of the Pragmatic Sanction in 1715. The shockwave of nationalism that swept over Europe in the wake of the French Revolution led to renewed calls for an independent Hungarian military. In 1839-40, the Hungarian diet demanded that all Hungarian troops wear national insignia, be led by Hungarian officers, and use Magyar as the language of service and command. [44] Except for the brief interlude of revolutionary upheaval in 1848-49, the imperial Habsburg government had effectively resisted these demands for a national army within a multinational empire. Control of the monarchy's military forces had remained with central imperial institutions of German character. Austria's defeat and expulsion from Germany by Prussia, however, challenged army unity grounded in a Germanic tradition.

The reopening of the military question, however, presented grave difficulties to ruling moderates in Hungary. They realized that Vienna would never accept popular radical interpretations of the Pragmatic Sanction that claimed it permitted the establishment of independent Hungarian forces. Moderates acknowledged that they would have to reach a military compromise that provided for the continued unity of the army while creating some sort of

Hungarian fighting force acceptable to Magyar nationalist aspirations.[45]   What they desperately required was someone within the military leadership with the vision and political adroitness to grant Hungary enough concessions to appease public opinion without alienating the emperor, the conservative Habsburg officer corps, and popular feeling in Cisleithania.   In short, Hungarian moderates needed a man to build them a golden bridge across the stormy waters of nationalism.   That man would be Friedrich Beck.

Beck played such a key role in the military *Ausgleich* only because the army leadership that emerged after Königgrätz proved utterly incapable of negotiating with the Hungarians.   The defeat produced a shake-up similar to the one that had followed the 1859 war.   The leaders of the Habsburg South Army, which had successfully blunted an Italian invasion of Venetia, bright figures on an otherwise bleak military landscape, rose to military power after 1866.   On 10 July 1866, Franz Joseph had appointed his cousin and commander of the South Army, Archduke Albrecht, commander-in-chief of all the monarchy's armed forces.   The same day, the emperor made Albrecht's chief of staff, General Franz Freiherr von John, chief of staff of the remnant forces gathering for a last-ditch defense of Vienna against the advancing Prussians.   Two months later, Franz Joseph named John both chief of the general staff and minister of war.[46]

In 1866, Albrecht was already well known for his opposition to Magyar nationalism because of his brutal tenure as imperial viceroy in Budapest in the immediate aftermath of the 1848 Revolution.   The archduke reacted with open hostility to suggestions of separate Hungarian military institutions and argued that they would cripple the monarchy's ability to wage war.   When in February 1867 the idea of a separate Hungarian war ministry began to circulate, Albrecht issued an order reaffirming army unity and loyalty to the emperor.   No Hungarian ministry, he declared, would ever have the right to issue commands to the army or influence its administration or organization.   German would remain the language of service and command for all who served in the Habsburg armed forces.[47]   This open hostility to Hungarian aspirations ensured that Albrecht would play absolutely no role in negotiations toward a military compromise.

War Minister John was simply overburdened with the matériel reforms brought on by defeat.   John insisted on the abandonment of the traditional white coats of the imperial infantry in favor of less conspicuous blue uniforms.   He also presided over the rapid, if often confused, transition from muzzleloading to breechloading small arms begun immediately after Königgrätz.[48]   These initiatives left John little time to ponder ways to appease Hungarian nationalism.

Where John collided with Hungarian interests was over the question of conscription.   The defeat of an empire of thirty million people by a kingdom of eighteen million had made a deep impression on the war minister.   The empire, he felt, urgently needed universal conscription laws that would tap the total strength of its war-fighting population. At the urging of John and a commission of senior generals, Franz Joseph signed universal conscription into law in December 1866. Unfortunately for the emperor, his war minister had neglected to coordinate this legislation with the Hungarians, who threatened to break off negotiations toward a political compromise. While the fire storm of Hungarian protest forced an embarrassed Franz Joseph to repeal universal conscription in February 1867, it neither caused John perceptible discomfort nor gave rise to introspection on methods that might reconcile Hungarian nationalism with military requirements.[49] With a complete absence of tact (a John trademark), John informed Andrássy in a 14 February 1867 crown council that the army expected Hungary to provide 40,000 recruits per year and coldly rebuffed the Magyar quid pro quo requiring Hungarian units to be stationed at home under officers approved by Budapest.[50] For the remainder of the year, John basically ignored the impasse over conscription and grew ever more irritable and hostile to the subject of Hungarians. On the last day of 1867, the war minister, frustrated with what he viewed as the inability of Hungarian nationalists to articulate their demands, sarcastically commented to Franz Joseph that maybe he should ask his Hungarian ministry exactly what it wanted in the way of military reform.[51]

The emperor, however, had no intention of letting the fractiousness of his commander-in-chief and war minister derail the compromise negotiations with Hungary. Already in February 1867, he had instructed his loyal envoy, Lieutenant Colonel Friedrich Beck, to sound out the Hungarian position on military reform in private meetings with minister-president Andrássy. Unlike Albrecht or John, who distrusted even moderate Hungarian nationalists, Beck grasped Andrássy's fundamental concern for the Great Power stature of the Habsburg empire and perceived therein a basis for a military compromise. Beck's appointment to head the emperor's military chancellery and the accompanying promotion to full colonel in July 1867 gave him the necessary credentials to negotiate the details of a military settlement.[52]

On 27 November 1867, the day before he was to meet Andrássy, Beck put on paper his ideas on the future of the Habsburg army under the dualist constitution.[53] Like John (and to a lesser extent, Archduke Albrecht), Beck believed that universal conscription had to form the centerpiece of any future military law. Beck also sided with army conservatives that a unified common army must be maintained, since it would have the imperial mission of protecting all the monarchy's territories from internal and external threats. He wrote that the army formed the glue which bound together the varied peoples of the empire and represented the ideal of national equality under Habsburg rule. The creation of a national Hungarian army would inevitably lead to demands by Czechs, Poles, and Croats for national forces of their own. Such a splintering of military power along national lines, Beck believed, would ultimately result in the political dissolution of the empire.

The political dualism already agreed upon, however, necessitated at least a partial abandonment of the unity principle. To counter radical nationalist proposals for an independent army, Beck argued for the establishment of a Hungarian national guard, or *Honvéd*, alongside a "common army" to which Hungary would still contribute men and matériel. A separate Hungarian defense ministry would maintain and administer the *Honvéd* in peacetime, although this ministry would have to submit periodic reports on the national guard's readiness to the imperial war ministry in Vienna. To maintain outward unity of the Habsburg armed forces, Beck proposed that *Honvéd* troops wear the same uniforms and receive the same basic equipment and training as those of the common army.

Beck's meeting with Andrássy revealed a surprising convergence of views on the major points of a military settlement. The minister-president announced that Hungary would accept both universal military service and a unified imperial army in exchange for a national guard under a Hungarian ministry. This *Honvéd* would assist the common army in wartime, but domestic peacekeeping would be its main mission. Indeed, the specter of the army as the instrument of imperial repression led Andrássy to insist that the common army be kept away from internal Hungarian affairs except in the utmost emergencies. Beck urged Franz Joseph most strongly to accept Andrássy's proposals as a basis for a military compromise with Hungary. In the light of more radical demands for a truly national army, Beck wrote, Andrássy's program appeared quite reasonable and moderate. A military compromise would moreover strengthen moderate elements in Hungary against dangerous left-wing opponents. An agreement with Budapest based on the Andrássy program, Beck concluded, was clearly in the best interest of the army.[54]

Over the strenuous objections of Albrecht and John, Franz Joseph ordered that the Beck-Andrássy exchanges form the basis of the deliberations of a general officer steering committee being formed by the war minister to redesign the army. On 31 December 1867, the emperor ordered John to convene the steering committee as soon as possible, since it would have to draft a new military bill for submission to the Delegations by mid-January.[55] When John tried to stonewall the compromise process by embroiling the war ministry in a budget dispute with the Austrian and Hungarian ministries, Franz Joseph removed him as war minister on 18 January 1868.[56]

The emperor's choice as John's successor, General Franz Freiherr Kuhn von Kuhnenfeld, proved a mixed blessing to the cause of military compromise. While recognizing the clear necessity for concession along the lines of the Beck-Andrássy talks, Kuhn distrusted the Hungarian political leadership and dismissed the Magyar people as racial inferiors to the monarchy's Austro-Germans.[57] Kuhn's aggressiveness, documented by his performance in the 1859 and 1866 wars,[58] ensured that the general officer steering committee would complete its formulation of a new military bill within two months. But his antipathy toward Hungarian aspirations also ensured that the product would fall short of actually cementing a military compromise. The steering committee report approved the creation of "militia" forces in both halves of the new dual monarchy with identical uniforms, equipment, and organization as the common army. After a little coaching by Kuhn, the committee also endorsed the concept of shared control of the militia in peacetime between the imperial war ministry and separate Austrian and Hungarian defense ministries.[59] But Kuhn insisted that the Hungarian militia retain both the German language of command (and German name, *Landwehr*, rather than the Hungarian *Honvéd*) and identical battle standards and uniform accouterments. Kuhn's bill stipulated that the militia would consist exclusively of older men, and would act as a sort of replacement pool for the common army during wartime. The general officer steering committee further limited the militia to infantry and cavalry, a restriction aimed at thwarting any future Magyar attempts to create a national army around a ready-made nucleus of the *Honvéd*. The war minister rejected outright demands for the stationing of units recruited in Hungary within the boundaries of the kingdom.[60]

Kuhn's draft legislation infuriated Andrássy. A portion of the annual Hungarian conscription, he argued, had to go to the *Honvéd*. A Hungarian national guard could only serve under the Magyar language of command. In an 18 June 1868 crown council, Andrássy tried to sidestep force design issues by suggesting that the ministers redraft the military bill to leave open the question of militia composition. To the exasperation of the war minister, Andrássy restated the nationalist demand for the home stationing of Hungarian common army units. The apparent recalcitrance of the Hungarian minister-president also angered the Cisleithanian ministers, who charged that Andrássy aimed to make the *Honvéd* a national Hungarian army.[61]

Angered by the rejection of his proposals, Andrássy opened direct communications with the emperor through his old negotiating partner, Colonel Beck. Indeed, even prior to the 18 June 1868 crown council, he had contacted Beck on a variety of topics related to the military bill. Specifically, Andrássy wanted Beck to get the emperor to concede the Hungarian language of command and national colors and battle standards to the *Honvéd*. While the summer of 1868 saw open acrimony between the war ministry and Budapest, Beck began the behind-the-scenes work that would secure the military compromise consistent with both defense and nationalist requirements.[62]

Beck first obtained Franz Joseph's assent to the Magyar language of command for Hungarian militia forces, the major stumbling block in the military negotiations. In exchange, Andrássy withdrew his demand for *Honvéd* artillery and agreed to postpone discussions on distinctive, nationalist uniforms, battle flags, and insignia until after the passage of a military bill.[63]   On 4 August 1868, Andrássy obtained from the Hungarian diet overwhelming approval (234-43) of the military law.[64]   Passage of the military bill in Cisleithania had to await the opening of the *Reichsrat* in October.   The majority Austro-German liberals offered significant opposition to the bill, hoping to obtain concrete limitations on the peacetime size of the armed forces.[65]   Their resistance forced Beck, Foreign Minister Beust, and Austrian minister-president Count Eduard Taaffe to launch a last-minute lobbying blitz to obtain passage of the military compromise by the end of November 1868.   On 5 December, Franz Joseph signed both the Austrian and Hungarian military bills into law.

But before he could make the military compromise final, the emperor had to call once again upon the head of his military chancellery to settle all the issues Andrássy had agreed to table the previous summer.   On 5 November 1868, Beck opened a final round of talks with *Honvéd* representatives.[66]   Initially, Beck's task appeared far from easy.   From their perspective, the Hungarians had already shown great understanding toward imperial desires for army unity.   Hungarian negotiators, led by Louis Kossuth's ex-minister of war, Anton Vetter Edler von Doggenfeld, did not appear favorably disposed toward further concessions in matters of uniform and insignia.   Given the distrust of Magyar motives in the military and the Cisleithanian government, Hungarian intransigence on these largely symbolic matters could still have derailed the military *Ausgleich*, even at this late stage.

Within the span of four days, however, Beck, with consummate diplomatic skill, had achieved total victory for the imperial position on all outstanding issues of the military compromise.   According to Glaise-Horstenau, Beck completely won over Vetter von Doggenfeld by conveying the emperor's fond memories of him as a childhood drill instructor.   Impressed by Beck's apparent liking and sympathy for Hungary, Vetter and his colleagues dropped initial demands for the red-white-green national colors for *Honvéd* battle flags and agreed to the adoption of the white battle standards of the common army. With the glib banter "same brothers, same caps," Beck obtained the committee's approval of common army headgear for the Hungarian militia.   Remembering the valiant resistance offered his old regiment by a group of Hungarian hussars during the 1848 Revolution, Beck got the Hungarians to concede the common army blouse for *Honvéd* cavalry.[67]

With the passage of the military law, the Habsburg monarchy completed its constitutional transformation from unitary to dualistic government.   Often ignored by subsequent historians anxious to stress the lack of progress in military affairs of later decades, the 1868 military law provided the legal basis for a great expansion of the Habsburg armed forces.   Whereas in 1866 the mobilized strength of the *k.k. Armee* stood at 600,000, the new law provided for the call-up of over one million men in wartime. An active service term of three years in the common army and two years in the *Landwehr* or *Honvéd* ensured the loyalty to the dynasty of these new forces. To help command this enlarged army, the law attempted to capture the imagination and support of the empire's middle classes by creating a new type of reserve officer, the one-year volunteer.[68] The new military legislation also preserved a common military structure, with an imperial war ministry in possession of administrative oversight of the common army, the *Kriegsmarine* and the militia forces. With the exception of the Hungarian *Honvéd*, German continued to provide the Habsburg armed forces with a common language of command and administration.[69]

In the two and a half years between Königgrätz and the successful conclusion of the military compromise with Hungary, the army had absorbed many of the hard lessons of the 1866 campaign. Under John's leadership, the army began rearmament with breechloading rifles and discarded impractical uniforms. The 1868 military law created an army which, at least on paper, equaled any of its European counterparts in size. It had also recast army organization and administration to coincide with the new dualist constitution.

While military reformers of the immediate post-war period emulated the Prussian model in many respects, they apparently had not yet grasped the central lesson of the Austro-Prussian War: to be truly effective, modern European armies required the centralized command and control mechanism of a general staff, manned by an elite corps of highly trained officers and entrusted with absolute responsibility for peacetime preparation for war and operative control in wartime. With the shock of the army's disastrous performance in 1866 fading quickly, the war ministry, entrusted by Franz Joseph with reviewing the army's command and control problems, would ignore the tremendous advantages of the Prussian system. Only Beck would consistently raise his voice in favor of a powerful general staff. Although Franz Joseph owed the success of the recent *Ausgleich* negotiations to Beck's efforts, he would continue for some years to ignore his calls for the reorganization of army command and control along Prussian lines. When the emperor finally heeded Beck's advice in 1874, he would bestow a permanence upon army administrative and command structures that they had not enjoyed since 1848.

Chapter 2

The General Staff Question

The Kuhn System

In the immediate aftermath of Königgrätz, the Habsburg high command addressed two of the most pressing issues: materiél shortcomings and the restructuring of the armed forces. The necessity to confront these delayed the correction of the still graver deficiencies exposed by the Austro-Prussian War: inadequate war planning and defective command and control structures. Still, the army high command, war ministry, general staff, and military chancellery all agreed on the need for reform. The question was what kind?

The poor performance of the North Army general staff during the 1866 campaign obscured the army's real need for a strong, independent, and well-trained Prussian-style general staff corps. Many senior officers blamed the general staff as directly responsible for the loss to Prussia. North Army field commanders flooded Archduke Albrecht's *Armeeoberkommando* with complaints about the incompetence of their general staff officers during the Königgrätz campaign.[1] Two former heads of the general staff, Ludwig von Benedek and Alfred von Henickstein, had left the service in disgrace, escaping court-martial only because of the emperor's mercy. Brigadier General Gideon von Krismanich, the former *Kriegsschule* instructor who had educated large numbers of general staff officers, suffered a similar fate.

In the immediate aftermath of defeat, the general staff had only one persistent proponent: Friedrich Beck. His enthusiasm for the institution stemmed from his personal observations of the Prussian system during his service in Frankfurt and his long association with Field Marshal Heß. As the latter's adjutant, Beck had advocated the reorganization of the general staff already in 1863.[2] In peacetime, he wrote, the general staff should gather military intelligence, conduct topographical surveys, and engage in strategic and tactical field exercises and problem-solving. In war, the general staff existed to assist field commanders in the deployment of their forces. Beck proposed the institution of regular large-scale maneuvers to hone staff skills.

In August 1867, one month after his appointment as head of the emperor's military chancellery, Beck wrote Franz Joseph an overview memorandum on the military affairs of the monarchy.[3]   In it, he strongly advocated a larger role for the general staff. Beck maintained that the general staff in wartime should have the primary responsibility for the strategic deployment of the army, while providing the necessary supplies and equipment to conduct the campaign. In times of peace, the general staff should concentrate on contingency planning and the related task of intelligence gathering on the capabilities of foreign armies. To increase the familiarity of general staff officers with the monarchy's myriad lands, Beck proposed the adoption of the Prussian system of general staff rides. These would provide general staff officers with a set of practical field problems for study, evaluation, and war planning. Beck wanted the chief of the general staff to take personal charge of general staff rides to ensure they fulfilled their intended purpose. In December 1867, Beck maneuvered to establish the position of the chief of the general staff in the post-Königgrätz reorganization of the army command and control structures.[4]   He wrote to the emperor that the chief of the general staff represented "the spiritual element" of the army. Both political necessity and practical considerations required that the chief of the general staff remain subordinate to both the minister of war and Archduke Albrecht's army high command headquarters. In wartime, the chief of the general staff would assist the commander-in-chief of the Habsburg armed forces in the direction of operations. In peacetime, he would help the war minister identify and determine military requirements. The chief of the general staff should attend all civilian ministerial councils that addressed military topics and be given an opportunity to express his opinions. He should participate in all military conferences, even those pertaining exclusively to army high command and war ministry matters. Above all, however, the chief's main task would remain the education of the general staff officer corps--over which he needed to exercise absolute control-- and the leadership of that corps in the planning and preparation for war.[5]

The current chief of the general staff, General Franz Freiherr von John, however, did not respond enthusiastically to Beck's proposals. Sensing that the monarchy had entered a liberal constitutional age, he concentrated most of his efforts on widening his authority as minister of war. As chief of the general staff, John remained subordinate to Archduke Albrecht, with whom he had a significant falling-out over credit for the Custoza victory.[6]   John wanted to use his newly emerging constitutional prerogatives as war minister to escape the domination of the archduke. What began immediately after the 1866 war as an amicable division of administrative and operational functions between the war ministry and army high command had degenerated by early 1868 into acrimonious debate over spheres of action and responsibility.[7]   Akin to Beck's concept, Archduke Albrecht wanted the chief of the general staff to function as his direct, personal subordinate on operational matters.[8]   John countered by pressing the emperor for the reduction of Albrecht's army high command staff to a couple of adjutants and a reduction in the archduke's functions to those of an inspector general: oversight of the education, training, morale, and war readiness of the force through direct observation.[9]   He promised Albrecht that the war ministry would consult him regarding the general staff issues of army organization, recruitment, armament, dislocation, order of battle, new regulations, and officer assignments within the war ministry and general staff. John viewed the latter, however, as unquestioningly subordinate to the war ministry, but did offer Albrecht the slight concession of periodic consultation with the chief of the general staff on all important operational questions.

By January 1868, however, John's position as minister of war had become extremely precarious. He had already angered the Hungarians by his refusal to work toward a military compromise and had alienated the Cisleithanian government with charges about its reneging on a military budget agreement. John's threat to undermine Albrecht's army high command now had the archduke wanting a new minister. John had rebuffed his only possible ally, Beck, by his failure to use the power of the war ministry to carve out an appropriate niche for the general staff within the military administration. The war minister had also angered Beck by pressing the emperor for strict limitations on the prerogatives of the military chancellery.[10]   Although John quite clearly wanted to remain as war minister, civil and military pressures combined on 18 January to force his resignation. On that date, Franz Joseph retracted his acceptance of John's earlier resignation as chief of the general staff--which Beck now officially noted for the record at the military chancellery as "never having occurred"--and removed him as minister of war.[11]   For the moment, John still remained chief of the general staff, a position he clearly did not want.

On the day of John's departure, Beck informed Franz Freiherr Kuhn von Kuhnenfeld of his appointment as war minister.[12]   Already one of the most distinguished men in the army, Kuhn had attracted Albrecht's attention for his defense of the Tyrol from Giuseppe Garibaldi's irregulars in 1866. In the late autumn of 1867, Albrecht had asked Kuhn to formulate his opinions on the proper position and role of the chief of the general staff within the military hierarchy. Kuhn's reply, which placed the chief of the general staff almost completely at Albrecht's disposal and removed him completely from the control of the war minister, mirrored the archduke's own ideas on the subject. This convergence of views led Albrecht to recommend Kuhn's name to the emperor as John's replacement.

Kuhn soon proved to be an extremely capable war minister, injecting new energy into the military administration. He provided the top-level resolve needed to settle the military *Ausgleich* with the Hungarians (admittedly with some timely assistance from Beck). Kuhn, however, also proved a man of considerable independence of mind with a corresponding strength of will to dominate military affairs from the war ministry. To accomplish this, Kuhn aimed at nothing less than the absolute alignment of military functions under total control of the war ministry.

Kuhn first targeted Albrecht's army high command for destruction. Although outwardly he initially enjoyed good relations with Albrecht, Kuhn harbored an intense dislike for the army commander that later bordered on physical aversion.[13] This hatred stemmed largely from the conflicting political perspectives of the two men. Kuhn, who considered himself a progressive, wanted to improve the army through the elimination of what he termed "reactionary feudal elements," including the primacy of a dynastic figure, apart from the emperor, over military affairs. To Kuhn, Albrecht was a throwback to the neo-absolutism of the 1850s--a man, the war minister wrote, who "dreamed of storming barricades."[14] On 2 September 1869, Kuhn described Albrecht in his diary as the incarnation of "Spanish absolutism, bigotry, ultramontanism, falseness and jesuitness." Kuhn took his position as a constitutional war minister seriously and sincerely believed in his responsibility to the people for the army. The continued existence of an army high command free from constitutional controls threatened this responsibility. Kuhn would not rest until he had achieved its eradication.

Success quickly crowned the war minister's efforts. Within a month of his appointment, Kuhn obtained the dissolution of the high command's administrative organs. The operations chancellery, the most important of the high command's bureaus, became the fifth department of the war ministry, losing its operational functions and becoming a statistical clearing house of data submitted to it by the other war ministry departments and subsidiary organs. The fifth department provided the minister with the vast amounts of information on the army's strength, organization, supply, weaponry, and fortifications needed to compile extensive war-readiness reports for the emperor.[15] A year later, Kuhn abolished Albrecht's title of army commander altogether, replacing it with a seemingly less important one of inspector general of the armed forces.[16] As his new title implied, Albrecht could continue to conduct inspections of military units and installations, but now had to submit all reports via the war ministry. Only on the "tactical issues" raised by his inspection tours could Albrecht report directly to the emperor. Kuhn promised to share with Albrecht all important information on the generalcy and had no objection to Franz Joseph showing his cousin certain documents involving changes in army organization.

On the other hand, Beck, because of his fundamental conservatism, enjoyed excellent personal relations with Albrecht. The head of the military chancellery, however, clashed with the archduke over the future development of the general staff. The size of the army high command bureaus mitigated against their effectiveness as a staff for the army commander in wartime. In peace, they assumed too many of the prerogatives Beck wanted to see reside within the general staff. Accordingly, Beck advised Franz Joseph to approve the substance of Kuhn's proposals, including Albrecht's transformation from army commander to inspector general. He, however, forcefully defended the emperor's right to consult with the archduke on the war readiness of the army. But with equal bureaucratic adroitness, Beck obtained the deletion of a provision for routine review of military chancellery records by the inspector general.[17]

Had Beck possessed any inkling of Kuhn's plans for the general staff, he would certainly have opposed his initial moves against Archduke Albrecht. In late 1868, Kuhn obtained Franz Joseph's permission to recast the general staff from a *Hilfsbehörde*, or supporting agency, to *Hilfsorgan*, or supporting organ. The war minister charged that the former term implied a degree of independence inconsistent with his position as the constitutional custodian of the armed forces. This realignment, which included the inspectors general of artillery, engineers, transportation, and uniforms, made the general staff directly subordinate to the imperial war ministry. The chief of the general staff corps reported to the war minister on the status and operations of the general staff corps, the pioneer regiment, the *Kriegsschule*, and the military-geographical institute. While the heads of the *Hilfsorgane* assumed complete responsibility for their branches and the accuracy of their reports to the war ministry, Kuhn reserved the right to preside over matters of promotion, the marriage of officers, service assignments, and transfers of all higher-ranking officers. The war minister also forbade the chief of the general staff and the inspectors general from issuing orders or memoranda directly to their service branches. All correspondence had to receive the war ministry's blessing first.[18]

Kuhn did not believe his task completed when the emperor approved his administrative proposals on 14 October 1868. The war minister aimed toward absolute control over general staff operations. To do this, he would have to obtain the ouster of the current chief, Major General Franz Freiherr von John. His diary entries make clear that Kuhn believed John did not possess the intelligence or professional knowledge to act effectively as chief of the general staff. He also just as clearly viewed the general staff as a "Jesuit caste" within the Habsburg military that would thwart the liberalization that Kuhn believed the tenor of the times demanded. The war minister aimed at nothing less than the complete elimination of the general staff corps and a scattering of its functions across the entire officer corps. Kuhn felt that this would engender a "meritocracy" within the Habsburg officer corps and end advancement on the basis of birth, family connections, and sycophancy.[19]

On 29 January 1869, Kuhn asked Franz Joseph to relieve John as chief of the general staff.[20]   That institution, the war minister complained, was "stagnating under his leadership." The general staff, Kuhn explained, needed a fresh personality, unburdened by past experiences, to lead it into the future. Kuhn added that John appeared to desire transfer to a post that offered him more independence of action (which he did not) and proposed that he be given command of the Graz military district.   John's propensity to irritate even his friends and allies hurt him now, as Albrecht and Beck, potential sympathizers with his position and vision of the general staff, did nothing to oppose the war ministry proposals. On 30 January, Franz Joseph relieved John as chief of the general staff "*mit Gnade*" (with grace), but without the customary decoration for meritorious service. With orders to assume command at Graz, John departed for Styria. Kuhn's true intentions for the general staff, apparently not transparent to Beck or Albrecht, became clear when on 18 April 1869, he nominated Brigadier General Josef Gallina, a war ministry section chief, to succeed John, not as the chief of the general staff, but merely its "director."   In so doing, Kuhn openly declared his intention of becoming his own chief of the general staff.[21]

Within a year, Kuhn moved to abolish the general staff as an independent officer corps. In 1869, he issued guidelines that designated field grade officer ranks (major, lieutenant colonel, and colonel) as "staff officer" grades. On 13 April 1870, the war minister proposed to open staff duties to all members of the Habsburg officer corps, provided they proved their suitability for such assignment through competitive examinations.[22]   This reform, Kuhn explained, would end the traditional favored promotion status of the general staff corps and introduce advancement based on talent.   The war minister informed Franz Joseph that the war ministry proposal would require a complete overhaul of existing promotion regulations and thus the emperor's approval as supreme warlord.

Influenced by Beck, Franz Joseph hesitated at the prospect of such a drastic reform. In a 10 May 1870 memorandum, Beck registered vehement opposition to Kuhn's abolition of the general staff corps.[23]   The head of the military chancellery argued that the general staff and its educational institution, the *Kriegsschule*, had produced some of the monarchy's finest officers. The 1859 campaign had revealed weaknesses, but the general staff had countered them by requiring staff captains to return to their original service branches for two years before rejoining the corps and thus strengthened officer contact with the troops. Beck also admitted that many troop commanders had complained about the shortcomings of general staff officers assigned to them. But he laid the blame for 1866 squarely on the shoulders of the general staff leadership, not the corps as a whole. And he noted that Franz Freiherr von John had since Königgrätz redoubled the earlier efforts to increase general staff contact with the troops by requiring all *Kriegsschule* graduates to return to combatant brigades as chiefs of staff before promotion to major.

Beck also disputed the war minister's claims that the proposed reforms would equalize promotion opportunities across army branches. Kuhn's promotion regulations, he argued, would do nothing to remedy current inequities in advancement between the various service branches. Moreover, those officers executing staff functions, arguably the most important to the army's ability to wage war, would lose their elite identity and clarity of purpose. To improve the quality of the general staff, the army should work to increase opportunities for general staff training, such as the conduct of large-scale maneuvers, rather than seek to broaden the talent base through the drastic measures advocated by the war minister.

Despite the vigorous support his arguments gained from Archduke Albrecht, Beck could not convince Franz Joseph to reject Kuhn's program.[24] In one of the rare instances in which he did not follow Beck's advice, the emperor ordered former war minister Count August von Degenfeld-Schonburg to chair a committee to consider Kuhn's reforms. Despite the strenuous efforts of Beck and Albrecht to load the committee with like-minded generals, Franz Joseph gave Kuhn and Degenfeld a free hand to determine the committee's composition, and thus almost guaranteed the war minister a favorable decision on his reforms.[25]

The Degenfeld committee, pressed onward by an anxious Kuhn, conducted eleven meetings between 28 July and 16 August 1870. On 17 August, Degenfeld presented Franz Joseph with the committee's findings, which amounted to a complete acceptance of the Kuhn reforms.[26] The general staff would vanish as an independent corps. Staff functions would henceforth be assigned to those who had demonstrated talent through competitive examinations. The committee abolished the special uniforms for all under the rank of full colonel. To avoid any impression of distinctness or elitism among those engaged in general staff functions, the committee ordered all lower-ranking staff officers to wear their branch uniform. The duties of the general staff "chief" remained the same as before, although the new regulations dictated that he needed only to be a general officer, not necessarily a senior one. The chief of the general staff remained completely subordinate to the war minister and would submit through him any recommendations for personnel assignments within the general staff bureaus, the *Kriegsschule*, and staff billets within combatant units.

Officially promulgated in 1871, the new promotion regulations marked a great victory for Franz Kuhn and the zenith of his power as imperial war minister. With the elimination of an independent general staff, Kuhn believed that he had created a rational, unified military system under the centralized direction of the war ministry. Within three years of taking office, Kuhn believed he had eliminated the division of military authority that had plagued the army throughout Franz Joseph's turbulent reign. Having successfully curbed the autonomy of such earlier power centers as the military chancellery, army high command, and general staff, Kuhn now perceived the war ministry as preeminent in military affairs and with no serious rivals for power.

But appearances were deceiving. There were still powerful informal forces that would ultimately overthrow Kuhn's ministerial system. No regulation could prevent Beck and Albrecht, bitter opponents of the war minister, from voicing their concerns directly to the emperor. As the head of the military chancellery, Beck reported daily to Franz Joseph on military matters. If the large number of memoranda found among Beck's private papers and the archives of the military chancellery are any indication, Beck did not hesitate to interject his own personal views. As a member of the imperial house and inspector general of the army, Archduke Albrecht naturally had access to the emperor at all times. Albrecht, too, was not hesitant to use his official position to combat the power and influence of the war minister with his cousin Franz Joseph. The emperor, of course, remained the one person with the authority to overturn Kuhn's system with the stroke of a pen.

The Franco-Prussian War and Its Consequences

Kuhn's opponents did not have to wait long for an opportunity to attack the inevitable weakness of ministerial centralization. Ironically, Kuhn began to sow the seeds of his own undoing when in January 1869 he trumpeted the achievements of his first year in office in his first annual war-readiness report to the emperor. In the event of war, he boasted, the army would consist of thirty infantry divisions, five cavalry divisions, and thirty-one reserve infantry divisions, excluding units assigned to garrison duties. By the end of 1869, Kuhn wrote, all of the mobilized army could be equipped with breechloading rifles and dressed in the new blue uniforms. The war minister admitted that he did not yet possess enough breechloaders to outfit both the Austrian and Hungarian militia, but added that this did not present a grave deficiency since these troops would serve only in a home-defense capacity in time of war. Matériel shortages remained, but these, Kuhn claimed, could be made up in the coming year. In any event, Kuhn pronounced the army ready for war.[27]

Kuhn weakened his position still further by boldly advocating an offensive war against both Prussia and Russia. On 14 July 1870--the day before France declared war on Prussia--he strongly urged Franz Joseph to intervene in the Franco-Prussian crisis. He feared that inaction would mean the final exclusion of the Habsburgs from German affairs and the secession of the Austro-German provinces from the empire.[28]   Kuhn warned that Austro-Hungarian intervention in a Franco-Prussian conflict would cause a dramatic widening of the crisis. Russia would come to the aid of Prussia, while the South Slav states would rise up against Ottoman rule in the Balkans. He added that Austria should not fear such events and that it had no better opportunity than the present to settle accounts with both Prussia and Russia. Russia's strength grew daily, and the military balance would only worsen if Austria waited. Even if Austria lost such a war, Kuhn concluded, its fate would differ little from what it could expect if Prussia won a lone contest with France. The dissolution of the monarchy, inevitable in either case, would only come sooner if Austria went down fighting.

The war minister's aggressive plans quickly unraveled. Kuhn's arrogance toward his ministerial colleagues made impossible a coordinated response to events in Germany. Moreover, the common ministry, joined by the minister-presidents of Austria and Hungary, angrily refused to endorse Kuhn's aggressive plans and favored at most a limited mobilization of the army to position the monarchy for the role of armed mediator.[29]   The emperor, worried that another war would utterly shatter Habsburg rule over the monarchy's culturally diverse peoples, authorized a partial mobilization that included a ban on the export of horses, the purchase of horses by the army, and the strengthening of certain fortifications.

Kuhn, however, refused to accept the government's negative verdict and continued to press for the expansion of the mobilization. In late July, he won the emperor's permission to call up all reserve personnel in the transportation, cavalry, and artillery branches and to begin the purchase of horses preliminary to full mobilization.[30]   On 3 August, he obtained Franz Joseph's approval to retain within the ranks those troops scheduled for discharge into the reserves and his agreement in principle to full mobilization at a later date.

But it quickly became clear that the war minister could not execute even the partial mobilization. On 30 August, Kuhn reported to his ministerial colleagues that he had been able to purchase only 53,000 horses to date and required another 33 million gulden to obtain the 30,000 additional animals needed by the army. At the same time, he advanced a demand for a further 40 million gulden for even more horses, artillery pieces, and uniforms.[31]   These new procurement demands--which nearly equaled the annual operations and maintenance budget for the entire common army--came as a complete shock to the emperor and his ministers. In May 1870, Kuhn had proclaimed that the monarchy possessed a trained, equipped, and ready force of 765,000 men and boasted proudly that no other Habsburg war minister had accomplished such a feat.[32]   The war minister brashly reaffirmed his claims about the army's war readiness in a letter to Franz Joseph the day after submitting his request for additional resources.[33]   Considering that a doubling of the military budget had not accompanied the twofold increase in army size accomplished in the 1868 military law, Kuhn exclaimed, the war ministry had done extremely well. Foolishly, the war minister again assured the emperor that the army had everything it needed in the way of munitions, armaments, and uniforms and offered to form a commission to validate his claims.

Unfortunately for Kuhn, Franz Joseph called his bluff and authorized the formation of a board of inquiry within the war ministry.   The board ultimately found the army woefully unprepared for mobilization and war in 1870.   The line infantry lacked 30,000 shirts and 28,000 uniform coats, and possessed 14,000 field caps of inferior quality.   The light infantry (*Jäger*) experienced a shortage of 5,000 coats, and the reserve cavalry lacked horses. According to the inquiry board, only the field artillery and the engineers were fully equipped and war ready in the summer of 1870.[34]

One serious shortage, glossed over by Kuhn's commission but of which Franz Joseph knew through Beck's military chancellery, concerned breechloading small arms.   Since Königgrätz, the war ministry had procured breechloaders in a most haphazard fashion.   In January 1867, the emperor had ordered the conversion to breechloading of the Lorenz muzzleloaders that Austria had taken to war the previous year.   The converted "Wänzl" pieces, however, soon revealed poor ballistic qualities because of their advanced age. The war ministry, therefore, contracted the Steyr arms manufacturer Josef Werndl to produce a metallic cartridge breechloader.   After extensive testing, the army adopted the resulting "Werndl" rifle as the standard infantry weapon on 28 July 1867 and simultaneously placed orders for 611,000 pieces.[35]

Werndl's establishment, however, proved woefully inadequate to the task of filling the massive orders placed by the Habsburg government.[36] Political opposition to extraordinary military expenditure, too, hampered the swift procurement of Werndl rifles.   Each piece cost Austro-Hungarian taxpayers about 50 gulden;   arming a fully mobilized common army required the expenditure of 40 million gulden, almost half of the annual army budget. This fiscal lump proved too large for the economy-minded politicians of the late 1860s to swallow, at least in one gulp.   In 1868, the Delegations approved over 14 million gulden for the new Werndl rifles and ammunition, but slashed outlays to under 1 million the following year.   In November 1870, Kuhn reported that the army possessed only 316,650 Werndl rifles and required an additional 302,810 pieces and 64 million rounds of ammunition just to meet common army needs, much less those of the Austrian *Landwehr* and Hungarian *Honvéd*.[37]   Large numbers of troops, he added, still by necessity used the larger caliber Wänzl.   Had Austria-Hungary gone to war in 1870, it would have done so with two main infantry weapons of different caliber. The logistical problems this would have created can only be imagined.

Throughout the autumn of 1870, Kuhn continued to push for an arms buildup for possible full-scale intervention in the Franco-Prussian War, despite the devastating defeat and surrender of French Emperor Napoleon III and his army at Sedan on 3 September. Kuhn, however, now fought a losing battle, as civilian support for even armed neutrality evaporated with what remained of the French professional army in September and October. On 5 November Franz Joseph dismantled Kuhn's partial mobilization. The emperor canceled the buildup of the artillery and transportation branches and discharged all the troops retained with the colors beyond their three years of active service. Under pressure from Hungarian interests, Franz Joseph also ended the ban on the sale of horses abroad.[38]

The End of the Kuhn Ministry and the Reemergence of the General Staff

More troubling for Kuhn, his enemies began to use the sad experience of the partial mobilization to undo the regime of ministerial dominance. Friedrich Beck remained the most persistent of Kuhn's critics. Alone among Franz Joseph's top advisers, Beck had rejected the idea of *revanche* against Prussia. Like the Prussian chief of the general staff, Helmut von Moltke, Beck had regarded the 1866 conflict as a German civil war, a painful and divisive experience not to be repeated unless the monarchy were absolutely assured of success. To the forty-year-old colonel, these conditions did not exist in 1870. As head of the military chancellery, almost every important document pertaining to the armed forces passed through his hands on its way to the emperor. Armed with the information gained through the normal discharge of his duties, Beck challenged Kuhn's optimistic war readiness reports. In 1870, he estimated that the army would be able to mobilize only about 500,000 men in Bohemia, a full 100,000 short of the number Prussia could deploy along the monarchy's borders. Moreover, it would take Austria-Hungary at least thirty days to assemble such an army, whereas Prussia could marshal its forces much faster.[39]

A week after the fall of Sedan, Beck stepped up his attack on the war ministry by submitting a memorandum to the emperor that sketched the essential military tasks left undone by the Kuhn administration.[40] Although Beck did not realize it at the time, this memorandum would become a blueprint for his future career as chief of the general staff. The Franco-Prussian War had shown that Prussia and its South German allies were capable of mobilizing an army of 600,000 men on their borders within three weeks. Had the Prussian military leadership not planned for all the details of mobilization in advance, such a swift concentration of force would have been unthinkable. Beck asserted that Prussia could mobilize equal numbers against the monarchy with equal swiftness, meaning that it could deploy over half a million men to Bohemia within three weeks. Under current conditions, it would take the monarchy at least thirty days to assemble its forces there. To compensate for its slower mobilization, Beck wrote, Austria-Hungary had little choice but to concentrate its forces at least ten marches from its northern border (i.e., between the Vienna Woods and Preßburg [Bratislava]), giving up vast portions of the monarchy to bloodless conquest.

Clearly, such a state of affairs could not continue. The invasion of an enemy army into the heart of the monarchy would disrupt the call-up of reservists in the border regions. Only a unified effort on the part of the war ministry, the civilian governments, and the general staff could improve the war readiness of the armed forces. The war ministry, which Beck freely admitted faced the most daunting challenges, had to draw up a wartime order of battle for the army before the onset of a war-threatening crisis.[41] In addition to stipulating the composition of common army divisions and corps, an order of battle must also take into account the mobilization of both the *Landwehr* and the *Honvéd*, the organization of their formations in divisions or corps, or their assignment to fortress duty.

To simplify mobilization procedures, the Habsburg monarchy would have to end its age-old tradition of stationing troops outside their home recruitment districts. Knowing that the emperor, and particularly Albrecht, who still vividly recalled the 1848 Revolution, would prove extremely hesitant to take such a dramatic step, Beck added that the shift to a territorial system should take place only as soon as political conditions permitted.

Beck also stressed that the war ministry needed to draw up and issue to the military commands exact instructions for the mobilization of forces under their control. Field commanders needed to have some idea what they had to do in the event of war. Beck added that the war ministry needed to establish severe penalties for those who failed to report for duty during a call-up, plan for the withdrawal of replacement units and their depots from threatened border districts, and make arrangements for its own evacuation should an enemy army approach the capital.

The war ministry also needed to supervise the stockpiling of the wartime requirements of a field army of between 400,000 and 600,000 men. The war ministry must ensure the continual storage of between two and three weeks' worth of supplies and enough munitions for two or three days of intense fighting at central depots for an army of this size. To hasten procurement of horses by the army in time of war--a major problem in 1870--the war ministry had to introduce a horse conscription law as an extension of the general service obligation.

Not unexpectedly given his earlier views, Beck reserved important functions for the general staff in increasing the monarchy's war readiness. The drafting of deployment plans to counter the moves of any enemy or group of enemies formed the central mission of the general staff. Deployment planning essentially took the war ministry's mobilization instructions a step further. Mobilization instructions placed the armed forces on a war footing within the recruitment areas; deployment plans directed their movements after mobilization to various locations depending on the nature of the threat. Calculating in advance where individual units would go would significantly accelerate the deployment of the army in the event of war. The general staff would also undertake studies of potential theaters of operation to assess area terrain, fortifications, and lines of communication. The general staff would use these studies to identify everything, including railroads, that the army needed to destroy in the event the enemy threatened to seize the area.

Unlike Kuhn, who largely disregarded the civilian political role in the defense of the monarchy, Beck realized the army's great need to obtain the agreement of the Austrian and Hungarian governments to provide for those security requirements that fell outside the normal military budget. In particular, the army required their decisive intervention for the construction of Carpathian railroads that would permit the reinforcement of Galicia by forces stationed in Hungary and eastern Austria. The Cisleithanian government had the additional task of identifying the exact position of all Bohemian, Moravian, Silesian, and Galician rolling stock to avoid its possible capture by the Prussians. Vienna also needed to accelerate the armament of the Austrian *Landwehr* and to mold it into a war-ready force of sixty-three battalions. The Cisleithanian government also needed to spearhead the organization of local levies (*Landsturm*) to defend those provinces bordering both Prussia and Russia.

In his conclusion, Beck wrote that Austria-Hungary could still achieve victory with an army of 600,000 men if it adequately prepared for war in peacetime. Before the outbreak of the next great international crisis, the army needed clear mobilization and deployment plans. This observation was a clear attack on Kuhn, whose general staff had done nothing to plan for the war minister's offensive war against both Prussia and Russia.[42] Without the existence of careful deployment planning, Beck concluded, Austrian success in any future war remained doubtful.

A week after Beck submitted his memorandum to Franz Joseph, the general staff submitted its own report to the military chancellery on measures it felt were needed to ensure the security of the monarchy. The memorandum, prepared by the general staff's railroad and telegraph bureau, largely reiterated Beck's theme that the current pace of mobilization would require the army to cede vast portions of territory to an invader. The general staff report, however, blamed the army's mobilization problems on the inadequacy of the monarchy's rail network rather than on organizational shortcomings. Particularly in the northern and eastern portions of the monarchy, railroads were relatively scattered and mostly single-tracked, limiting their effectiveness for the transport of forces. Expansion of the rail network, particularly the construction of lines connecting Transylvania and Galicia with the Austrian and Hungarian hinterland, remained an urgent requirement.

But the general staff did admit that the army had failed to exploit the capabilities of existing lines because of insufficient planning for the rail transport of troops. The general staff supported Beck's call for the drafting of a wartime order of battle, mobilization instructions, and deployment plans to meet all potential contingencies. Like Beck, the general staff favored the stationing of troops in their home recruitment districts and urged a solution to the problem of procuring horses during deployment, since presently this created the greatest delays in war readiness.

Kuhn took several months to respond to the Beck and general staff criticisms and proposals. Acutely aware of the impact of the recent miscarried mobilization on the prestige of his ministry, Kuhn summarized the lessons of the Franco-Prussian War in a report to the emperor on 3 December 1870. Recent political events, he wrote, had clearly demonstrated that peacetime preparations had the greatest impact on the speed and efficiency of army mobilization. The partial mobilization had uncovered matériel shortcomings which the war ministry would rectify as quickly as possible. To head off critics, Kuhn laid out specific initiatives being undertaken at the war ministry to meet the war-planning requirement. The war ministry, Kuhn exclaimed, had already prepared (albeit hastily) a wartime order of battle. The next logical step would be the formulation of detailed mobilization instructions to the various general and military commands which outlined procedures for their transformation to a war footing. Kuhn also proposed to augment the mobilization instructions with a series of "marching orders" to meet potential military contingencies. What the war minister exactly meant by "marching orders" is unclear, since he specifically excluded specific "deployment plans" (*Aufmarschpläne*) as envisioned by Beck and the general staff. Kuhn also remained equally silent on the matter of the latter's exact role in contributing to the war readiness of the army.

The war ministry, however, failed to pursue vigorously the preparation of either mobilization instructions or marching orders and thus eroded Kuhn's credibility still further. Preoccupied with procurement struggles with the Austrian and Hungarian governments and entangled in complex negotiations with Budapest over the abolition of the Military Border, which required, among other things, a complete revision of the 1870 wartime order of battle, Kuhn took over two years to submit even the simplest guidelines for a mobilization plan. In a report submitted to Franz Joseph on 23 March 1872, Kuhn stipulated only that the emperor could order either a full or partial mobilization and that war ministry plans would proceed from a date specified by him.[43] Kuhn admitted that the war ministry still had not drawn up a satisfactory wartime order of battle without which it could not begin preparation of concrete mobilization instructions. Two years later and only a few months before his dismissal as minister, Kuhn could offer only a framework for the necessary plans. Ultimately it was left to Alexander von Koller, Kuhn's successor as war minister, to complete the mobilization instructions in 1875.[44]

Kuhn's progress on obtaining passage of a horse conscription law was equally slow. The army had traditionally relied upon standing contracts with consortia of stud farmers to supply its needs. The mobilizations of 1866 and 1870, however, had proven this procurement method too protracted for modern requirements. After the Franco-Prussian War, Kuhn pushed both the Austrian and Hungarian governments to pass a law requiring breeders to place horses of military quality at the army's disposal in exchange for fair reimbursement. The Hungarians, whom such a law would primarily affect, proved surprisingly cooperative, reserving exemptions only for horses belonging to the imperial family and the civil government. It took Kuhn until April 1873 to iron out the details of the law, and only in 1876 did the horse conscription legislation finally become law.[45]

Kuhn fared little better after 1870 in the procurement struggles with the Austrian and Hungarian governments. While he secured overall increases in the army's operating budget during his last three years in office, even after the financial collapse of 1873, Kuhn made slow gains in the procurement of breechloading rifles and artillery.[46] While his civilian colleagues recognized the danger inherent in having two rifles of differing calibers in service simultaneously, Kuhn never got them to approve funds to make the necessary purchases. In February 1873, the war minister reported that the common army alone needed some 370,000 additional Werndl rifles.[47] Despite the personal intervention of the emperor, the civilians repeatedly slashed the army's procurement budget.[48] In February 1872, Kuhn lamented in his diary his inability to procure new steel-bronze 80mm and 90mm field pieces urgently needed by the army.[49] These guns would ultimately reach the troops only in 1876-77, over two years after Kuhn left office.

Delays in achieving war planning and procurement goals left Kuhn open to attack. From his position at the emperor's side, Beck continually criticized the overly centralized nature of the Kuhn regime. On 10 August 1873, he wrote Franz Joseph that "in no other European army is the war minister as powerful as ours" and charged that "one man could not fulfill all the necessary tasks."[50] The war minister needed a powerful chief of the general staff to assist him. Throughout the previous year, Beck had repeatedly urged Franz Joseph to overturn Kuhn's promotion regulations and restore the general staff as an independent corps.[51] The general staff had to perform the vital task of war planning, for, Beck wrote, "modern wars demand many and grandiose preparations, for which years of peace are required." Beck repeated his advice of September 1870: the general staff's chief function involved the preparation of war plans according to the political-military situation. The chief of the general staff needed complete independence from the war minister and should be allowed direct contact with the emperor on all questions concerning the direction of the general staff corps and army mobilization and deployment. The war minister already had enough to do in providing for the army's material wants, preparing the mobilization plan and presiding over the army administration.

In November 1872 Beck further elaborated his thoughts on the role of the chief of the general staff. Above all, Beck wrote, he had to be a high-ranking general officer and hinted that the current "director," Brigadier General Josef Gallina, did not possess sufficient seniority. A high-ranking chief of the general staff would more nearly equal the war minister. The chief of the general staff must personally direct the activities of the central general staff bureaus, collectively termed by Beck in imitation of the Prussian model "*der Große Generalstab*," in the execution of the "scientific," or war-planning, role. He should assume the sole responsibility for the selection of officers for the general staff, choosing only those who had both great mental and physical stamina. The chief of the general staff must also oversee their training at the *Kriegsschule*. He would post, with war ministry approval, other general staff officers to the various general, military, divisional, and brigade commands to serve as chiefs of staff (*Truppengeneralstab*). The chief of the general staff should function as the "coordinating agent" of the imperial war minister, and not strictly as the latter's subordinate. Beck urged cooperation rather than confrontation between the general staff and the war ministry.

Under Beck's concept, the *Große Generalstab* in Vienna would prepare the wartime order of battle for the field army, assist the war ministry in drawing up the mobilization instructions for the common army, *Kriegsmarine*, *Landwehr*, and *Honvéd*, and prepare deployment plans (*Aufmarschpläne*) for all possible theaters of war. The general staff bureaus would also follow the activities and development of foreign armies and investigate the wartime experience of other powers. The general staff bureaus would also engage in fortification planning for the monarchy as a whole.

The slowness of the Kuhn system in meeting the security needs of the empire emboldened Beck to strengthen his protests in 1873. On 14 December, he submitted yet another memorandum to the emperor arguing that the reorganization of the general staff ranked as *the* most important military question facing the monarchy, without which the vital business of war planning could not proceed.[52]   The reestablishment of the general staff corps was an absolute necessity. Beck forcefully argued for a substantial strengthening of the chief of the general staff's position within the military hierarchy. Administratively, the chief of the general staff should remain subordinate to the war minister, but in all matters concerning the well-being of his corps he should answer to the emperor alone. In time of war, the general staff and its agencies would assist line commanders in the direction of troops on the battlefield. In peacetime, they would assist troop commanders in their administrative duties or the chief of the general staff in war planning.

Beck also stepped up his attack on the war ministry. He complained of the war ministry's slowness in issuing mobilization instructions to unit commands. He noted the delay in updating the wartime order of battle, made obsolete by the dissolution of portions of the Military Border.[53] A new wartime order of battle must correspond as much as possible with the peacetime organization of the army in order to limit the amount of force restructuring needed during mobilization.

Beck cautioned that while the army needed the capability to mobilize to its full wartime strength in the shortest possible time, it also needed to direct its tremendous power toward a specific military purpose. Mobilization in place at recruitment centers would not measurably add to the monarchy's security. The army needed to possess deployment plans to give meaning and purpose to the marshaling of its military might. Here the general staff should play its greatest role, preparing mobilization plans in peacetime for every possible contingency facing the monarchy. The chief of the general staff would identify those international situations potentially requiring a military response. The deployment of the armed forces depended greatly on both international conditions, the military capabilities of potential opponents, and the potential theater of operations.

A second voice that Kuhn could not silence belonged to Archduke Albrecht. The inspector general of the army had waged a cold war against the war minister since 1869 when Kuhn had abolished the archduke's army high command apparatus. Unlike Beck, who used his position as Franz Joseph's personal military aide to press for fundamental changes in Kuhn's military system, Albrecht conducted a campaign of harassment against the war minister. The archduke used his social position to snub and isolate Kuhn within the officer corps. Kuhn complained several times in his diary that Albrecht would invite officers, even those of relative junior rank, to dine whom he knew had prior engagements with the war minister.[54] The officers in question could not, of course, turn down an invitation from a member of the royal family and the monarchy's only active field marshal and were forced to back out of their social commitments with Kuhn.

Albrecht also used his position as inspector general of the army to smother Kuhn with suggestions for reform. Although he undoubtedly believed in the absolute necessity of his proposals, Albrecht equally appreciated their harassment value against an already overburdened war minister. The inspector general argued with Kuhn over the reform of the technical branches of the army as well as the reorganization and expansion of the infantry and cavalry.[55] Albrecht also complained to Kuhn of the "slippage" of the Austro-Hungarian army vis-à-vis the German army and asserted that an increase in army size was absolutely necessary in order to restore the proper military balance based upon the respective populations of the two states.[56]   Kuhn also received unwelcome advice from Albrecht's younger brother and inspector general of artillery, Archduke Wilhelm, to increase the size of the artillery branch. The war minister pointed to the great expenses involved in artillery expansion and argued that more artillery would make the army unwieldy and immobile.[57]

Albrecht's greatest weapon against the war minister, however, were his inspection reports to the emperor on the war readiness of the army. These expressed, almost without exception, negative opinions on the quality of the troops, their equipment, weapons, and housing, and the conduct of maneuvers. Reporting on his inspection trips during 1872, Albrecht complained of the weak and sickly nature of the new recruits, particularly among the "lesser developed" Slavs and Romanians, and argued for both lower physical demands in the early weeks of training and an older induction age.[58]   The archduke lamented the poor quality of the food and housing of some of the units which he inspected, although he admitted that uniforms had improved dramatically.

Albrecht reserved plenty of negative comments for unit collective training. In 1872, the inspector general charged that while infantry training had improved, collective exercises of that year from the regimental upwards still were unsatisfactory.[59]   Albrecht wrote Franz Joseph that the new maneuver regulations of 1871 were not always followed, with the result that the earlier bayonet tactics, which had proven so fatal at Königgrätz, were still being taught. The cavalry, he added, needed much more practice in screening the army from enemy observation. Without going into specific details, Albrecht charged that the artillery arm was often not being properly employed.

Kuhn did not suffer Albrecht's criticisms gladly. In February 1872, the war minister had protested the inspector general's fitness reports to the emperor, which he maintained were overly critical.[60]   When he had accepted his current responsibilities in early 1868, Kuhn complained, the army had been in a state of complete disarray. Armament and equipment procurement had just started, and supply stocks were both qualitatively and quantitatively impoverished. The army had made great strides in both the procurement of new equipment and training under his leadership. The monarchy now possessed a wartime army of 800,000 fully armed and equipped men (again, an overstatement), an achievement which no other war minister could boast. In Kuhn's mind, Albrecht's petty criticisms[61] paled in comparison to these great accomplishments. Kuhn completely rejected the idea that some of the inspector general's observations might have some merit; he saw them only as personal attacks on his character and administration of the armed forces.

When the emperor appeared to accept Kuhn's explanations, Albrecht changed tactics. In April 1873, the inspector general praised Kuhn's annual war-readiness report for its clarity of expression and accepted its optimistic appraisal of the army's readiness for war.[62] The same year, however, Albrecht struck at the heart of the war minister's power. In a memorandum to the emperor, Albrecht pushed for the formation of a military cabinet consisting of the war minister, a *chief* (not director) of the general staff, the head of the military chancellery, and certain high-ranking generals and inspectors general, depending on the topic under consideration.[63] Albrecht described the purpose of the military cabinet as "the removal of the monarchy from the appearance that the one-sided views of the current war minister will or must necessarily be followed." The military cabinet would "relieve the war minister of a great responsibility, which he cannot, with all good conscience, bear alone."

To eliminate slowness and inefficiency within the military administration, Albrecht proposed a diminution of the war minister's powers. He proposed to remove the war minister completely from personnel decisions involving general officers and charged that Kuhn had abused his authority in this area by promoting friends and frustrating the careers of enemies. The emperor alone (whom Albrecht assumed he could influence) should make all senior military appointments via the military chancellery. War planning and collective training exercises should become the prerogative of the chief of the general staff. The general staff must remain a *Hilfsorgan* of the war ministry, but required a degree of independence in order to discharge its important strategic functions.

Albrecht's memorandum marked the beginning of the end for the Kuhn ministry. Franz Joseph's two most trusted military advisers, the inspector general of the army and the head of the emperor's military chancellery, had united in opposition to Kuhn's ministerial regime and had begun coordinating their proposals for a restructuring of the military administration. For the first time, Albrecht had endorsed Beck's idea of an independent and powerful chief of the general staff, entrusted completely with strategic planning and the general staff officer corps needed to execute that planning.

Kuhn might have overcome the opposition of Beck and Albrecht had he cultivated broad political support from the common, Austrian, and Hungarian governments. But relations between the war ministry and the civilians, never good, deteriorated further after the Franco-Prussian War. Foreign Minister Andrássy remembered Kuhn's loud objections to his proposal to procure

Gatling guns for the *Honvéd* at the height of the 1870 crisis, claiming them, as crewed weapons, to be artillery pieces and thus disallowed under the current militia statutes.[64] The war minister's undying hatred for Prussia-Germany also impeded the foreign ministry desire for a rapprochement with Berlin. Kuhn's relations with Budapest did not improve appreciably with Andrássy's departure for Vienna. In particular, Kuhn's dilatory response to Hungarian demands for the dissolution of the Military Border and the transfer of territorial sovereignty from the war ministry to the Hungarian government angered Magyar politicians.[65]

Kuhn's relations with the Austrian government, while less confrontational on individual issues, also remained poor. The Austrian government continually blocked war ministry efforts to increase the military budget. Ministerial councils often ended with heated arguments between Kuhn and Austrian Finance Minister Sisenio de Pretis. The Austro-German liberals in government and parliament, while they may have appreciated Kuhn's liberal constitutional convictions, did not want to pay for the renovation of the army or for infrastructure improvements desired by the war ministry.[66]

Even combined civil-military dissatisfaction could not have unseated Kuhn had he retained Franz Joseph's confidence, for only the emperor had the power to remove him as war minister. But relations between the two men had deteriorated following the Franco-Prussian War. Franz Joseph blamed Kuhn for the monarchy's inability to mount an effective intervention in the Franco-Prussian War after having pronounced the army completely war ready. The rumor that Kuhn harbored republican sympathies, given currency by Archduke Albrecht but vigorously denied by the war minister himself, also had likely reached the emperor's ear.[67]

For his part, Kuhn felt unloved by an emperor who had not fully rewarded him for his achievements.[68] The war minister complained of the emperor's lack of interest in his personal life, lamenting that the imperial court had taken no more notice of the birth of his two sons "than if a dog or a cat had come into this world." At the death of Franz Joseph's mother, the Archduchess Sophie, in May 1872, Kuhn was amazed at the emperor's apparent lack of sorrow or remorse and reacted with outrage when Franz Joseph questioned why he had not attended her requiem mass.[69] Kuhn felt the emperor cold, stolid, and simple-minded, attributes best exemplified by the court's mistreatment of its military servants whom, Kuhn observed, were discarded like "squeezed-out lemons" once they proved no longer useful.[70]

On 13 May 1872, Kuhn asked to be removed as war minister, asserting that he had lost the emperor's confidence.[71] Although Franz Joseph did not immediately agree, it had become increasingly apparent that Kuhn's days as war minister were numbered. Both Beck and Albrecht bombarded the emperor with complaints about the inefficiency of the "Kuhn System" and the chaos caused by the new promotion regulations. These had virtually eliminated extraordinary promotions in peacetime by requiring all candidates for the "staff ranks" of major, lieutenant colonel, and colonel to demonstrate competency through competitive examination.[72]   Beck charged that Kuhn's promotion system created disgruntlement throughout the officer corps.   Senior officers, for example, suddenly often found themselves subordinate to men many years their junior.[73]   Worse still, the abolition of a distinct general staff corps had accompanied the enactment of the new promotion regulations.   Kuhn's other great opponent, Archduke Albrecht, completely rejected the examination system, asserting that it would turn out merely "starry-eyed theoreticians" who had repeatedly failed the monarchy in war. Kuhn's exams, he charged, posed questions worthy of history's greatest military minds, and had to be graded with exceeding mildness if anyone were to pass them.

The organization of the general staff function within the army indeed remained the great outstanding question between the Kuhn and Beck-Albrecht camps. Ironically, the war minister himself unwittingly reopened the issue on 10 October 1872, when he asked Franz Joseph to approve certain minor reforms in the organization of the general staff. Specifically, Kuhn wanted to create the post of deputy director of the general staff at the rank of full colonel.[74] He also proposed to staff the military archives (*Kriegsarchiv*), then under general staff direction, with more war-experienced officers and to unify the foreign and domestic military surveying departments of the general staff.

The reaction of Kuhn's opponents was swift and decisive. Three days after Kuhn had submitted his program, Beck told Franz Joseph that, while the war minister's proposals might seem minor, in fact they actually would have far-reaching consequences for the future of the general staff.[75] Beck charged that Kuhn's reforms really amounted to a vote of no confidence in the general staff's current director, Major General Josef Gallina, since he had not been consulted about the anticipated changes. While Beck favored Kuhn's proposals uniting the military history department with the *Kriegsarchiv* and the joining together of the military surveying, Beck vigorously opposed the appointment of a colonel to act as the deputy director of the general staff. Such an officer would have important functions to discharge and would foreseeably remain at his post for quite a while. The general staff needed general officers leading it.

While it took him longer to formulate a response, Archduke Albrecht rejected Kuhn's proposals with equal vigor.[76]   From an administrative standpoint, Albrecht noted, Kuhn's restructuring of the general staff bureaus made perfect sense.   Still, like Beck, Albrecht decidedly opposed the war minister's domination of general staff operations. What the army really needed, wrote the archduke, was a *chief* of the general staff entrusted with the complete leadership of an independent general staff corps.

By early 1874, Franz Joseph began slowly to respond to the repeated calls from Beck and Albrecht for sweeping general staff reform and for a change in the working relationships between the war ministry and general staff. In January 1874, Franz Joseph authorized Albrecht to enter into secret negotiations with ex-war minister and chief of the general staff Lieutenant General Franz Freiherr von John, to discover under what circumstances he would accept reappointment as chief of the general staff. Albrecht had maintained close contact with John following the latter's dismissal as chief of the general staff in 1869. While commanding general at Graz, John had continued to serve as a sort of "shadow chief of staff" to the inspector general of the army, advising him periodically on matters of military importance.

At the same time he allowed discussions with John, Franz Joseph also instructed Albrecht to ask Alexander von Koller, then serving as commanding general of the Prague military district, if he would be willing to become war minister and to reestablish the general staff as an independent corps. Koller had long been a supporter of the Beck position on general staff reform. Both Beck and Albrecht had attempted, albeit unsuccessfully, to get him a seat on the Degenfeld commission in 1870. A respected senior general officer, Koller was their natural choice as Kuhn's successor.

Beck and Albrecht may have also had other motives for proposing Koller as war minister. Koller was an outsider to the military-bureaucratic scene in Vienna, and both Beck and Albrecht might therein have seen an opportunity to expand their own influence over military affairs. Koller also reportedly did not enjoy the best of health, a fact that conceivably might make him inclined toward a lightening of his burdens as war minister.[77] Albrecht and Beck obtained Franz Joseph's consent to Koller's appointment as minister if Koller could reach an agreement with John on the appropriate division of responsibilities between the war ministry and the general staff.

Koller did not disappoint his Vienna proponents. On 7 February 1874, Albrecht wrote John that Koller had agreed to take over the war ministry and to the reestablishment of the general staff as an independent corps.[78] Albrecht reported to John that Franz Joseph had been "impressed with Koller's clear perception of the problem" and apologized to John that the need to keep the Koller talks secret from Kuhn had made it impossible for him to meet personally with the war minister designate. Albrecht promised John that his appointment as chief of the general staff would occur simultaneously with the naming of Koller as war minister. He also relayed Franz Joseph's desire to obtain John's clear vision of his future position as chief of the general staff. Albrecht told John that the memorandum should leave out minor details and be ready by mid-March.

John's memorandum, submitted later the same month, revealed a thorough transformation of the general's thinking since his days as war minister.[79]   John demanded the complete independence of the general staff corps from war ministry direction, including the abolition of the latter's fifth department, which routinely reviewed and evaluated the work of the general staff. John insisted upon the power of choosing officers for the general staff corps. The chief of the general staff, he argued, needed authority over all questions involving the operative use of the army as well as its peacetime organization and deployment. He must also exercise influence over the conduct of collective training, military communications of all kind, fortification, and the assignment of general staff officers to troop commands. Matters internal to the general staff would include military surveying, the gathering of intelligence on foreign armies, the writing of military history, and the related administration of the *Kriegsarchiv*. The inspector general of the army would direct the various inspectorates general (cavalry, artillery, etc.) in matters of training, discipline, and personnel.

While John's ideas on general staff reorganization may have closely resembled those earlier expressed by Beck and, to a lesser extent, Albrecht, both now reacted sharply to John's memorandum. In particular, Beck felt that John's proposals were unrealistic and extreme, and, with Albrecht's assistance, he prepared a memorandum in response.[80] While Beck admitted the advantages of having both the chief of the general staff and the inspector general of the army exercise influence over army discipline and direct army training, he firmly believed that the monarchy could not afford to make any sudden changes that might shake soldier morale and confidence in the army leadership.   The complete division of operative command and administration advocated by John was impossible: nobody would take the job of constitutional war minister if this were attempted. Minor conflicts between and among the inspector general, chief of the general staff, and the war minister could all be overcome if the personalities involved were equal to the task. The new war minister and chief of the general staff had to work especially hard to look beyond petty jealousies toward the common goal of strengthening the empire's military power.

Beck continued: "the chief of the general staff is a *Hilfsorgan* and thus subordinate to the war ministry." His main task was to increase the war readiness and efficiency of the armed forces through careful planning for all possible military contingencies. To assist him, the chief of the general staff selected, with the advice and consent of the war ministry, a corps of officers schooled in the art and science of war. In addition to discharging duties with the central planning bureaus in Vienna, staff officers would also assist field commanders in their direction of forces according to centralized planning. The chief of the general staff would direct the theoretical and practical education of the general staff corps and alone would decide the best way to exploit the talents of its officers.

According to Beck, the future chief of the general staff would have to be consulted on all matters involving mobilization, order of battle, military education, and collective training. The emperor also must have the option to consult directly with him on political-military questions, the equipment and armament of the army, and the development of the infrastructure of the monarchy to satisfy military requirements, including the modernization and augmentation of existing fortifications and rail networks. Such consultations, however, had to proceed through the imperial war minister to ensure his constitutional position. The minister had to be given the opportunity to attach his own evaluations to general staff proposals before they were submitted to the emperor. In return, the war minister must include the chief of the general staff in all important war ministry conferences. In his conclusion, Beck reiterated an old theme: the chief of the general staff's primary mission remained the preparation of war plans to meet specific political-military situations. The chief of the general staff must exercise direct and absolute control over the general staff bureaus, including the Military Geographical Institute and the *Kriegsarchiv*, in order to carry out his vital security responsibilities.

John angrily lashed out at Beck's redefinition of the chief's role. On 11 April 1874, he complained to Albrecht that a chief of the general staff would have to be the greatest soothsayer of all time in order to function effectively under Beck's guidelines.[81] He would have to work simultaneously under (and thus satisfy) Franz Joseph, the war minister, and the inspector general of the army. John insisted that the chief of the general staff had to have a position of immediate responsibility to the emperor. "The army chief of staff must at the same time act as the chief of the general staff of His Majesty the Emperor." For all practical purposes, the general staff would remain a *Hilfsorgan* of the war ministry, regardless of the official expression of their relationship. The chief of the general staff needed direct contact with the emperor in order to discharge his important responsibilities involving the war readiness of the army. Those areas where Beck permitted the chief of the general staff to express his opinions, John felt, must belong within the regular sphere of his duties. John steadfastly rejected ministerial oversight of general staff functions through the Fifth Department, especially if no firm division existed between the war ministry and the general staff. He also defended an earlier position that the chief of the general staff exercise decisive influence over senior military appointments, arguing that the latter would be in a much better position to comment on a candidate's effectiveness and suitability for various posts than the war minister.

From Graz, John was powerless to force an acceptance of his views on his future position as chief of the general staff. When Franz Joseph composed his final decision on general staff reorganization, it was Beck and Albrecht, and not John, who guided the emperor's pen.[82] Franz Joseph's instructions to both Koller and John stressed that they must cooperate toward the common goal of improving the war readiness and efficiency of the army. The general staff would remain a *Hilfsorgan* of the war ministry and thus subordinate to it, but its chief would be allowed to submit reports to the emperor on his own initiative. These reports, however, would first go to the war minister, who could append any personal comments. The primary responsibilities of the chief of the general staff were the education of general staff officers and the preparation of war plans. The chief of the general staff could contribute to the war readiness of the army only through effective command of a well-trained and educated general staff officer corps. He must, therefore, oversee the theoretical and practical education of general staff officers and would exercise control over the composition of the general staff corps. All bureaus of the general staff as well as the Military Geographical Institute and the *Kriegsarchiv* were under his direct command. The chief of the general staff's autonomy within his own corps was limited only by budget considerations, which remained the responsibility of the constitutional war minister.

The war minister had to consult the chief of the general staff in all questions regarding the mobilization, order of battle, and collective training of the army. The chief of the general staff also had to exercise influence over the composition of military regulations and be allowed to make proposals on all questions of organization and political-military importance as well as on such purely military issues as fortifications, communications, equipment, and armament. The emperor himself pledged that he would make no major decisions in these areas without first obtaining the opinion of the chief of the general staff.

Franz Joseph concluded his instructions with Beck's old admonition that the most critical task facing the chief of the general staff was the preparation of war plans according to the political situation in Europe. These plans had to take into account all possible military contingencies, and the chief of the general staff needed to work with the war minister to draft sets of concrete instructions for each scenario. The chief of the general staff must also coordinate war planning with Archduke Albrecht, since the latter would assume overall leadership of the monarchy's armed forces in war.

In opting for Beck's moderate solution, Franz Joseph took the only practical avenue of general staff reform available to him in 1874. Kuhn had eliminated the general staff as an independent corps only three years before and had managed to convince his civilian colleagues to approve his new promotion regulations.[83] Beck himself still probably favored even greater independence for the chief of the general staff vis-à-vis the war minister and inspector general. He realized, however, that the power and influence of the imperial war ministry could not be reduced too swiftly without shaking civilian confidence in the military administration. To maintain this confidence, Beck believed that the general staff would always have to remain a *Hilfsorgan* of the war ministry and would agree to continue this subordinate relationship even after he himself became chief of the general staff in June 1881.

There now remained only the problem of easing the irascible Kuhn out of office, for as long as he remained, there could be no question of general staff reform. Koller, who had taken little part in the negotiations over the future war ministry-general staff relationship, indicated to Albrecht on 3 April 1874 that he was willing to take over as war minister under the Beck guidelines and consented to John's appointment as chief of the general staff.[84] John, while irritated that his objections to Beck's proposals had apparently been ignored, nonetheless agreed to become the chief of the general staff under a Koller ministry. Koller himself paid a secret visit the following month to Vienna to work out the final details of the transition.[85]

On 12 June 1874, Franz Joseph informed Kuhn that he would be relieved as war minister and would replace John as commanding general of the Graz military district. The emperor tried to soften the blow by awarding him the Order of St. Stephan.[86] In an audience on 14 June, Franz Joseph explained to Kuhn that he was being replaced as minister because "new organizations needed to be established." In his diary, Kuhn surmised that the reestablishment of the general staff as an independent officer corps lay at the root of his dismissal.[87]

With Kuhn's ouster and the reestablishment of the general staff corps, Beck achieved what had been his major military-organizational goal ever since he had become head of the emperor's military chancellery. Ever cognizant of political realities within the military hierarchy, Beck had accepted limitations on his earlier strident program of complete freedom of action for the general staff. Civilian sensibilities over ministerial responsibility had to be weighed in the balance of any military reform. Beck realized that any future chief of the general staff would have to consider the continued presence of Archduke Albrecht. Without his cooperation, a chief of the general staff would accomplish little.

John's actions during his final two years as chief of the general staff indicate that he, too, had learned that close cooperation between the top members of the military hierarchy remained a prerequisite for effective military policy. Unfortunately for the monarchy, John did not get much of a chance to put what he had learned into practice. Scarcely had John reestablished the general staff as an independent body when he died of a heart attack on the steps of the war ministry. His successor, Anton Freiherr von Schönfeld, did not have John's experience in dealing with the monarchy's major military figures. Schönfeld's failure to cooperate effectively with the war minister and especially the inspector general of the army, coupled with chronic illness, would greatly hinder his ability to devise meaningful military plans to meet the many dangers facing the monarchy in the late 1870s and early 1880s. Another five years would be needed before the general staff could begin to discharge this vital function. Only with his own appointment as chief of the general staff would Beck truly realize his vision for the general staff corps.

Chapter 3

The Eastern Crisis and
Beck's Rise to Power

Beck's Imperialist Ambitions

The early 1870s saw both the political and military leaderships of the monarchy increasingly concerned with that complex of issues known to diplomatic historians as the Eastern Question. The Franco-Prussian War, the pivotal event in the reorganization of the general staff into a potentially effective body, also changed both Habsburg foreign and military policy, for it completed Austria-Hungary's exclusion from German affairs. With its influence in Italy eliminated by the 1859 and 1866 wars, many thought the empire could regain lost prestige only through expansion in the western Balkans.

Even prior to the monarchy's fateful exclusion from Germany and Italy, Friedrich Beck had advocated Habsburg expansion in southeast Europe. He believed that the acquisition of Balkan territories would both secure Austria valuable trade routes to Asia and serve as a springboard for overseas expansion. Beck first developed these notions while Field Marshal Heß's adjutant in the mid-1850s. By the 1870s, his ideas had hardened into a deep conviction that the monarchy needed to expand to survive.[1] If the Balkans fell into the hands of a hostile power or a group of smaller states, Beck felt, Austrian industry and commerce would wither and die.[2]

After 1870, Beck's southward gaze focused on the two Turkish provinces of Bosnia and Herzegovina. These territories, Beck wrote in an August 1870 memorandum, formed the "hinterland" of the Habsburg Dalmatian coast.[3] Dalmatia, definitively ceded to Austria in 1815 by the Congress of Vienna, remained virtually cut off from the rest of the monarchy and was extremely vulnerable to landward attack. In particular, Beck feared that the autonomous Turkish principalities of Serbia and Montenegro might seize control of Bosnia and Herzegovina as a prelude to an attack on Dalmatia. Their conquest of the area would hold out the promise of a South Slavic kingdom to Serbs and Croats living within the monarchy's borders. This danger convinced

Beck that if Turkish rule over Bosnia and Herzegovina ever faltered, Austria-Hungary would have to move swiftly to occupy them. At most, the monarchy could accept Serbian occupation of northeastern Bosnia between the Bosna and Drina rivers in return for its acceptance of Habsburg expansion.

Beck, therefore, viewed the acquisition of Bosnia and Herzegovina as a life-or-death question (*Lebensfrage*) for the empire. Control of the region by any power other than Turkey would imperil the security of Dalmatia. Without Dalmatia, the monarchy would lose both its outlet to the sea and its Great Power status. Like the famous American theorist, Alfred Thayer Mahan, Beck conceived of international status in terms of naval power and access to maritime trade routes. If Austria-Hungary managed to gain an Aegean outlet, its Great Power stature would clearly benefit. Conquest of the Balkans, Beck believed, would also strengthen the army, since the region's "warlike" inhabitants would make excellent soldiers. The acquisition of Bosnia and Herzegovina formed the first necessary step on the road to Habsburg domination of the western Balkans. For Beck, open lines of communication to the Aegean had to be a major and consistent foreign policy goal. He hoped that Austria-Hungary would eventually expand to Salonika (Thessaloniki) and construct rail lines to Constantinople (modern-day Istanbul) with the aim of driving British and French products from oriental markets.

Balkan expansionism, however, did not find ready advocates among the political and military leadership of the early 1870s. Andrássy's foreign office focused on the rebuilding of the monarchy's international position and security through the improvement of relations with imperial Germany. War Minister Franz Kuhn rejected as ludicrous the idea that the acquisition of Bosnia and Herzegovina would contribute measurably to the defense of Dalmatia, stating that the fate of the province would be decided on battlefields elsewhere.[4] The war minister's attention remained riveted on Germany and a war of revenge against Prussia. Archduke Albrecht, too, had little use for wars of conquest in the Balkans and shared Kuhn's desire to settle scores with the new German empire. He did share Beck's view that Balkan imperialism would bring the monarchy economic gain and eventually garner public support, but was unwilling to sacrifice military preparedness on the northern frontiers to southward expansion.[5]

While Balkan imperialism might secure important markets and trade routes, their potential riches did not outweigh both the up-front costs and demographic implications of an expansionist policy in the eyes of the civilian politicians. The Austro-German liberals, who dominated the Cisleithanian *Reichsrat* during the 1870s, opposed the incorporation of additional Slavic territories within the empire. They also demonstrated a vocal unwillingness to shoulder the financial burdens of conquest and subsequent administration of territories acquired from Turkey. Rejecting physical domination of the region, the Austro-German liberals preferred to think more in terms of economic expansion and the establishment of a customs union with Serbia, Montenegro, and Bosnia.[6]

The Hungarians also disliked the idea of annexing neighboring Balkan territories for many of the same reasons. The Magyars, while dominating the political life of the Hungarian kingdom, made up less than 50% of the population. The addition of more Slavs into the monarchy would place them at an even greater demographic, and ultimately political, disadvantage. Pressure from the increasing number of Slavs might ultimately replace Hungary's hard-won dualism with a trialist form of government that gave Slavs equal representation in the affairs of the empire. Many Hungarian politicians also continued to harbor strong pro-Turkish sentiments stemming from the Ottoman government's willingness to harbor Hungarian refugees after the collapse of revolutionary Hungary in 1849. They took an equally dim view of an economic union with the region, since Balkan agricultural goods could then compete evenly with Hungarian products in Habsburg markets. Budapest accordingly opposed any policy that aimed at the dissolution of European Turkey.[7]

An imperial visit to Egypt for the opening of the Suez Canal in October 1869 and an uprising in Habsburg southern Dalmatia (Krivosije) upon the introduction of universal conscription did little to heighten permanent Austro-Hungarian interest in the Balkans at the start of the 1870s. Foreign policy focused on improving relations with imperial regimes in Prussia-Germany and Russia, an aim realized in the conclusion of the informal Three Emperors' League alliance in September 1873. Military efforts centered on increasing preparedness against Germany and Russia should diplomacy fail.[8] Kuhn and Albrecht pressed the civilians to fund both an extensive Carpathian rail system that would allow the rapid deployment to Galicia of forces stationed in the interior of the monarchy and an equally extensive system of fortresses that in war would defend the empire's northeastern frontier until reinforcements arrived.[9]

Beck vigorously supported Kuhn's agenda for railroad construction in Galicia. As head of the military chancellery, Beck wielded enormous influence, if little direct control, over railroad matters, since the Austrian trade and Hungarian communications ministries submitted construction and legislative/concessioning progress reports through him to the emperor. The military chancellery then used these reports to prepare quarterly or biquarterly summaries of railroad activities throughout the empire. While he welcomed the construction of the Carpathian lines, Beck did not lose sight of his plans for Balkan imperialism in his unofficial capacity as Franz Joseph's railroad adviser. In February 1872, he vigorously supported a proposal of the Budapest government for the construction of a line linking the Hungarian rail system with

Turkish and Serbian railroad projects. Beck tried to link this initiative with a similar Austrian proposal the following year.[10]

But Beck's dreams of trains running south brimming with Habsburg products and soldiers did not come to immediate fruition. Kuhn's war ministry refused to support the buildup of the monarchy's rail network in the south while Galician projects remained unfinished.[11] The financial crash of 1873 cooled civilian ardor for expensive railroad construction, particularly in the south, despite emerging Hungarian worries about the activities of Serbian agitators in Semlin (Zemun), just across the Save from Belgrade.[12] Foreign Minister Andrássy's difficulty in getting the Serbs and the Ottomans to agree to a link-up with Habsburg lines proved enough to kill prospects for a Balkan railroad for the time being.

Beck, however, began quietly to build up an imperialist faction within the army to lobby for Balkan expansionism as a foreign policy goal. Within the emperor's immediate entourage, he found an enthusiastic supporter in the person of Major General Friedrich Freiherr von Mondel, who owed his post as Franz Joseph's adjutant general largely to Beck's recommendation. More important to Beck was the support of the military commanders in Zara (Zadar) and Agram (Zagreb), Major General Gabriel Freiherr von Rodich and Lieutenant General Anton Freiherr von Mollinary von Monte Pastello. Rodich, whom War Minister Franz Kuhn labeled "a South Slav *par excellence*," shared the Pan Slav ambition of the unification of all South Slavs under one political unit. But unlike the Pan Slavs, who thought in terms of Serbia or Montenegro as the centripetal political force, Rodich hoped that the Habsburg empire would unify his people.[13] Rodich, who assumed the Zara command at the height of the Krivosije uprising, was not above using his position to stir up trouble in the neighboring Turkish provinces of Bosnia and Herzegovina and kept the military chancellery closely informed on conditions in the Balkans.[14] Mollinary, while he had sided with Franz Kuhn on the general staff issue and had sat on the Degenfeld commision which had drafted the war minister's promotion regulations, stood with Beck and Rodich on the question of Habsburg expansion in the Balkans.[15] Although differing views over army organization and his relative seniority vis-à-vis Beck kept him from becoming a close confidant of the imperialist camp, he nonetheless sympathized with its aims. As the senior military official on the monarchy's southern frontier and therefore the commander-in-chief presumptive of any Habsburg expeditionary force that might be sent into the Balkans, Mollinary remained a key and influential supporter.

The murder of a Turkish subject in Podgoriza (Titograd) by Montenegrins in the fall of 1874 gave Beck and his associates the opportunity to place the Balkans on the immediate foreign political and military agenda. In early January 1875, Rodich informed the military chancellery of an impending

Montenegrin declaration of war against the Ottoman empire and of the Dalmatian population's sympathy with the Slavic cause and hopes of armed Austrian intervention. While Andrássy ordered Rodich to keep a lid on domestic demonstrations in favor of Montenegro (using military force if necessary), Beck moved quickly to exploit the situation and set the stage for Habsburg military action.[16]   On 19 January 1875, he wrote War Minister Alexander von Koller asking him to determine, after consulting with Chief of the General Staff Franz Freiherr von John, which units could be transferred to Dalmatia without disrupting the wartime order of battle.[17]   Three days later, Beck wrote John asking him to name staff officers with suitable linguistic and cultural backgrounds for service in Dalmatia.[18]

Beck achieved a significant victory on 29 January 1875, when Franz Joseph summoned his civil-military leaders to deliberate on the growing unrest in the Balkans and to arrive at some sort of agreement on Austro-Hungarian policy to address the situation.[19]   The meeting marked the first in which Beck counted among the major policy participants. Supported by Albrecht, Beck obtained Andrássy's grudging acceptance of a clearly defined occupation zone in Bosnia and Herzegovina should conditions there deteriorate further. Beck interjected into the debate an 1869 general staff plan that anticipated Austro-Hungarian military action as far east as the Drina River frontier with Serbia, an area of operations that would permit the invasion forces full use of the Bosna River for communications.[20]   Since Habsburg forces would likely experience difficulty in distinguishing friend from foe in the early stages of the operation, they would have to seize key strategic points at Banja Luka, Sarajevo, Travnik, and Mostar quickly before resistance stiffened. Albrecht and Chief of the General Staff John therefore notified the conference that the occupation of Bosnia and Herzegovina would require the mobilization of 450,000 men, over half the wartime strength of the army.

Ultimately, the conference endorsed Andrássy's policy of assisting Ottoman efforts at pacification, permitting the Turkish army to use the Habsburg port of Klek to unload troops and supplies in the event of a Turkish-Montenegrin conflict. The conference, however, also directed the general staff to draw up a plan for the occupation of Bosnia and Herzegovina in the event Turkish rule over the provinces collapsed.   This foreign office-army understanding on contingency operations in the Balkans, however, lacked the support of the Austrian and Hungarian governments, which were not even invited to the conference or informed of its decisions.[21]

While he had achieved civil-military agreement as to the strategic importance of Bosnia and Herzegovina at the 29 January conference, Beck nonetheless remained dissatisfied with the results, since Austria-Hungary would not act under circumstances less than a total disintegration of Turkish rule in the provinces. Unwilling simply to await this happenstance, Beck resolved to set events in motion that would aggravate growing unrest among the Christian population of European Turkey. Within ten days of the conference, he wrote Rodich that he had recently broached the subject of an imperial tour of Dalmatia, an idea first proposed by the governor-general himself.[22]   Franz Joseph responded favorably to the idea and, through Beck, asked Rodich to prepare an itinerary for an exhaustive four-week tour of the province. The emperor showed a particular interest in Cattaro (Kotor), the southern Dalmatian port most threatened by Montenegro.

By April 1875, Beck and Rodich had made final the top-secret preparations for the trip.[23]   Lieutenant General Mollinary, the commander of Habsburg forces in Croatia, had noted a holiday mood among the expansionist conspirators during a routine visit to Vienna in March. Beck's handpicked successor as Franz Joseph's adjutant general, Major General Friedrich Freiherr von Mondel, told Mollinary of the preparations for the imperial tour. Mollinary expressed astonishment and exclaimed "then things will burn." In his memoirs, the military governor of Croatia called the trip "a shrewd move designed to set the provinces [of Bosnia and Herzegovina] ablaze and to give Austria a reason to intervene."[24]

Later the same month, Beck accompanied Franz Joseph to Dalmatia. The trip over the arduous road and trails of the primitive province, while wearisome, proved a great success. The native population greeted the Habsburg sovereign in great numbers;   citizens of the provincial capital Zara (Zadar) celebrated the arrival of the imperial party by illuminating both homes and harbor craft in an impressive display.[25]   On a few occasions, the emperor crossed the border into Bosnia, where he received a hearty welcome from the sultan's troops and Christian subjects alike. In Cattaro, Franz Joseph met with Prince Nikita of Montenegro, and Beck with the latter's father-in-law, the Voivode Vukotich, who promised "to protect the Austrian right flank" in an occupation of Herzegovina. Franz Joseph's presence in southern Dalmatia, Vukotich noted, showed that the Austrian emperor was much closer than the Russian tsar, and that Montenegro would follow Vienna's lead.[26]

The emperor returned to Vienna on 15 May. Within two weeks, the Christians of Herzegovina, emboldened by the interest in their welfare shown by the Austrian emperor, revolted against their Turkish overlords.[27]   The unrest quickly spread to neighboring Bosnia and increased in intensity.[28]   When local Turkish forces proved incapable of maintaining order, Habsburg Foreign Minister Gyula Andrássy attempted diplomatic intervention aimed at inducing the insurgents to lay down their arms, first via the consuls of the Great Powers in the area, then by a combined action of the European courts.[29]   The Christian rebels refused to abandon their struggle unless the European Concert guaranteed that the Porte would abolish the abusive tax farming system and declare religious equality.

The resumption of the fighting in the spring of 1876 led to renewed Austro-Hungarian diplomatic efforts to find a solution to the Balkan imbroglio short of European intervention. This time, however, Andrássy lost the consensus of the major European powers on his reform program. His proposals called for a two-month armistice to allow for the reconstruction of property destroyed in the bitter fighting and the injection of reflief aid to those left homeless. Great Britain's refusal to endorse them, however, killed Andrássy's last pacification initiative.[30]

Beck's expansionist party within the army actively opposed Andrássy's efforts to calm the situation in the Balkans. Both Rodich and Mollinary opened the borders of their provinces to Christian refugees from Bosnia and Herzegovina. By September 1875, Beck estimated that more than 22,000 had crossed into Austria-Hungary.[31] From his correspondence with Rodich, Beck clearly hoped that the financial burden of supporting these refugees would force the empire to intervene to restore order in Bosnia and Herzegovina. He turned a blind eye to the substantial assistance lent by friend Rodich to the insurgents, which, in addition to food and other supplies, also included some 8,000 aging but still effective Wänzl rifles and two million rounds of ammunition. The governor-general of Dalmatia also allowed Christian insurgents to establish supply depots within Austrian territory and permitted combatants to rest and recuperate there before returning to the fray.[32] Only when directly ordered by the foreign minister (supported by Franz Joseph) in January and again in February 1876, did Beck instruct Rodich to "urge" the Christian rebels to lay down their weapons and accept the promised reforms of the Porte.[33]

A dramatic widening of the crisis followed immediately upon the failure of the foreign minister's pacification efforts. In May 1876, Bulgaria revolted against Ottoman rule in support of their religious brethren in Bosnia and Herzegovina. At the same time, the sultan's Muslim subjects rose up against the Ottoman government because of its apparent willingness to cave into European demands for reform. By the end of the month, outraged mobs had murdered Sultan Abdul Aziz, and a new radically anti-Christian and anti-Western Murad V ascended the Turkish throne. Serbia and Montenegro declared war on the Porte at the end of June when the Turkish government refused to appoint Serbian Prince Milan Obrenovich viceroy of Bosnia and Herzegovina. Beck's maneuverings had achieved what Mollinary had predicted: the Balkans were burning.

The Serbo-Turkish War and the Russian Threat, 1876-1878

Beck and his imperialist co-conspirators had managed to transform a local insurrection into a full-scale Balkan war that threatened the peace of Europe. While he had achieved his aim of destabilizing European Turkey as a prelude to Austro-Hungarian military action, Beck, as head of the military chancellery, exercised little direct influence over preparations for the campaign that he hoped would come. Because of his access to the emperor, Beck had been able to set in motion events that might lead to an Austro-Hungarian invasion of Bosnia and Herzegovina. But he could not make certain through personal intervention that the army would be ready to move at the decisive moment.

That responsibility lay with the Imperial War Minister Lieutenant General Alexander von Koller and the Chief of the General Staff, Lieutenant General Franz Freiherr von John. Both men took this assignment seriously and had produced an operations plan within five weeks of the 29 January 1875 conference. The general staff maintained that at least five divisions would be needed to occupy Bosnia and Herzegovina. One division would invade Herzegovina from Dalmatia, two would march south from western Croatia toward Banja Luka and Travnik, and the remaining two divisions would advance down the Bosna River from Slavonia. The mobilization of this force would cost 3,785,000 gulden one-time and 2,817,000 gulden per month recurring. The war ministry added that it would be necessary to mobilize an additional seventy battalions within the monarchy to maintain public order during the operation.

But other than appoint Mollinary to lead the occupation when it occurred, little else had been done to prepare for military action, despite the increasing disintegration of law and order in Bosnia and Herzegovina. Both the war ministry and the general staff had other pressing matters to confront. Koller continued to wage the many procurement battles left over from his predecessor, including small arms purchases and the introduction of new 80mm and 90mm artillery pieces. The war ministry also labored hard to complete the mobilization instructions, without which definitive deployment planning was impossible.[34] John continued the task of reorganizing the general staff as an independent corps and had to work closely with Koller to obtain the necessary funds from the parsimonious Delegations. The Crash of 1873, which ended a period of budget surpluses, forced Koller and John to expend much effort in achieving their respective agendas. Approval of the Delegations for general staff reorganization, a prerequisite for detailed military planning of any sort, was not granted until December 1875.[35]

Just as the unrest in Bosnia and Herzegovina escalated and expanded to envelop European Turkey, unforeseen events removed both Koller and John from direction of Austro-Hungarian military affairs. Koller, increasingly unwell in the spring of 1876, requested his pension from the emperor in June of that year. John's departure came much more suddenly on 25 May when he died on the steps of the war ministry from an apparent heart attack. The exit of Koller and John created a sudden power vacuum within the army that would be only partially filled by their successors, Arthur Count Bylandt-Rheidt and Anton Freiherr von Schönfeld, who both required time to become acclimated to their new responsibilities. Bylandt, an artilleryman, had previously headed the war ministry's military-technical committee as a ballistics expert and had little experience in the larger administrative tasks that he would confront as minister. Schönfeld, selected by Albrecht and Beck mainly because the latter was still too junior in rank and seniority to assume the position of chief of the general staff himself, would prove a capable, if sickly, substitute for the robust John.

The transitions at the war ministry and general staff occurred at a potentially dangerous time. On 11 June 1876, with Serbia and Montenegro preparing to declare war on Turkey, a military conference ordered the 20th Infantry Division to Slavonia to thwart a Serbian-Montenegrin invasion of Bosnia and Herzegovina. Tensions in Vienna over the escalating Balkan situation, however, quickly eased when Andrássy obtained Russian recognition of Habsburg interests at the Reichstadt meeting in early July. On 10 July Beck penned a letter to Rodich informing him that Russia had agreed that Austria-Hungary would eventually be allowed to occupy Bosnia and Herzegovina.[36] Four days later, he added that earlier requests by Rodich to place forces in Dalmatia on a war footing were now considered premature, since the Balkan war had not yet produced definitive results.[37]

The diplomatic settlement with Russia gave the new military administration in Vienna time to prepare for possible contingency operations in the Balkans. Despite some early progress by John, preparations for the campaign were still inadequate. John's original concept called for the use of six infantry divisions to occupy Bosnia and Herzegovina. Then on 10 July 1876, the new war minister, Arthur Count Bylandt-Rheidt, informed Franz Joseph that current plans called for the mobilization of eight divisions, with five deploying to the Turkish provinces.[38] At the same time that it refined the invasion order of battle, the war ministry established a "mobilization department" to review all deployment plans submitted by Schönfeld's general staff. Over the objections of both Schönfeld and Deputy War Minister Franz Vlasits, Beck and Albrecht established another department to facilitate the war ministry's own mobilization instructions and preparations. Within a year, this led to the further development of a mobilization commission consisting of all war ministry department heads, the deputy chief of the general staff, and the heads of the general staff operations and railroad departments. The commission would gather following the emperor's issuance of a mobilization order to prepare the necessary telegraphic instructions to the combatant units, working from existing mobilization and deployment plans. This commission provided the basic framework for the mobilization of the Austro-Hungarian armed forces to 1914.[39]

Despite these organization reforms, Beck's military chancellery remained by far the most active agency in preparing for the occupation of Bosnia and Herzegovina. Beck took July 1876 to prepare a detailed set of instructions for Lieutenant General Mollinary, the presumptive commander of the Austro-Hungarian invasion forces.[40] For two years, these instructions would serve as the basis for all future military planning leading up to the occupation of Bosnia and Herzegovina in July 1878.

Beck began by stating that the occupation would not require as many forces as anticipated by the war ministry on 10 July. The deployment of four divisions--the 6th, 7th, and 36th Divisions of the Croatian-Slavonian XIII Corps and the Dalmatian 18th Division--should suffice to occupy the Turkish provinces. Ever aware of the civilian desire to cut costs, Beck reasoned that a less expensive, smaller force would have a better chance of obtaining the political approval of the Austrian and Hungarian parliaments. Despite the general anticipation of an easy Serbian/Montenegrin victory over Turkey in the current Balkan conflict, Beck did not expect the Slavic principalities to obstruct an Austro-Hungarian invasion of Bosnia or Herzegovina. Indeed, Beck struck out the portion of an earlier memorandum that pertained to possible operations against Serbia.[41] The military chancellery anticipated little or no resistance, particularly in Bosnia, given the absence of regular Turkish forces. In the face of only sporadic insurgent resistance, maintaining lines of communication with the monarchy would pose the greatest problem to Habsburg field commanders.

In his draft instructions, Beck also addressed issues that went beyond the scope of military operations. Beck wrote that the XIII Corps commander would be responsible for the establishment of a provincial administration that would cement Austro-Hungarian political authority in the region. He urged Mollinary to use existing institutions and the ruling Muslim elites as much as possible. Those public offices for which there were no appropriate native incumbents should be filled by Habsburg officers "familiar with the customs, usages, and languages of the people." Naturally, Croatian officers would be best suited for this kind of duty.

The greatest immediate problem facing the military commander would be the resettlement of the thousands of people who had taken refuge in Austria-Hungary and Montenegro during the crisis. While the army provided the native population with the means to rebuild communities shattered by civil war, it would also simultaneously have to disarm the various insurgent bands and break any armed resistance to Habsburg rule. Troops would also have to improve the roads and erect telegraph lines and later construct hospitals, depots, and fortifications.

His assignment of these far-reaching tasks to the commander of the occupation forces did not mean that Beck intended to give him *carte blanche* in dealing with situations as they developed in the provinces. Indeed, Beck stressed in his memorandum the direct subordination of the field commander to the war ministry. Only in matters of logistics did the invasion force commander have the right to direct communications to the army general command in Agram. He would receive orders directly from Vienna and was required to seek the approval of his actions from the war ministry, the general staff, or the emperor himself (through the military chancellery) on all important issues.

As the summer of 1876 progressed, the Serbo-Turkish War took a course unforeseen by most military experts of the day, including Friedrich Beck. Turkish forces, driven from Bulgaria by Christian rebels in May, rallied behind Osman Pasha and repulsed the joint Serbian-Montenegrin invasion of the Ottoman empire. In August, the Turks mounted a general offensive and defeated the Serbian army in a five-day battle at Alcksinach. As summer turned into fall, the Turkish government's desire to humilitate completely its rebellious Slavic vassal states threatened the general European peace. The Russians, who through various Pan-Slavic organizations, had sent massive amounts of aid to Serbia and Montenegro, expressed outrage at Turkish armistice terms that capped the future strength of the Serbian army and demanded an immediate cessation of hostilities. Through diplomatic channels, the Russian government informed Vienna that Russia would intervene to protect Serbia and Montenegro unless the Turks granted an immediate armistice. In a letter, Tsar Alexander II urged Franz Joseph to occupy Bosnia and Herzegovina in conjunction with a Russian invasion of Bulgaria.[42]

Possible unilateral Russian intervention in the Balkan conflict set off alarms within the Austro-Hungarian general staff. Given priority after the February 1872 military conference, general staff planning against Russia had become sidetracked by the Bosnia-Herzegovina contingency. In the fall of 1876, Schönfeld painted an overly gloomy picture of the geopolitical situation and of Austro-Hungarian military preparedness in a memorandum to Franz Joseph.[43] Inexplicably disregarding the poor showing of the Serbian and Montenegrin armies in the recent war, Schönfeld maintained that the monarchy would have to deploy forces in Galicia and along the Serbian frontier. He discounted the support Austria would get from victorious Turkish forces and completely wrote off the possibility that Germany and/or Britain would lend assistance, despite the interest of the two powers in sustaining the European balance and, particularly in the case of the latter, Turkish control of the

Dardanelles. Russia, on the other hand, could find ready allies in Italy and possibly even France.

Militarily, Russia would, therefore, completely outclass the monarchy. Anticipating that an Austro-Russian war would only break out after the commitment of forces to Bosnia and Herzegovina, Schönfeld informed Franz Joseph that Austria-Hungary would be able to field in Galicia only twenty-four infantry and four cavalry divisions for a total of 350,000 men to oppose Russia's twenty-nine infantry and twelve cavalry divisions, or some 416,000 men in Congress Poland and another twelve infantry and six cavalry divisions opposite Bukovina and eastern Galicia. The situation would be particularly grim in the early days of mobilization when Russian forces on the scene would far outnumber the peacetime Austro-Hungarian defenders stationed in Galicia. Worse still, the Russians could use their overwhelming superiority in cavalry to cut railroad and telegraph communications, wreaking havoc on the Austro-Hungarian mobilization and deployment. This would, among other things, mean that Habsburg defenders would, for the most part, lack artillery support, since all field artillery regiments save the one stationed in Galicia itself were scheduled for transport only on the thirteenth day of mobilization.

Schönfeld's memorandum became the subject of a top-level military conference convened by Franz Joseph on 13 November 1876 to debate the impact of the pending Russian intervention in the Balkan crisis.[44] The mobilization of the entire Russian army was expected within the next few days. The emperor warned that a war with Russia could easily arise out of a Russian intervention in the Balkan crisis, particularly if the Pan-Slavist movement forced the Russian government into making excessive territorial demands or to threaten legitimate Austro-Hungarian interests in the western half of the peninsula. Though still the junior member of the conference, Beck usurped for his military chancellery the general staff's military intelligence and planning functions by arguing that the monarchy needed to plan for troop deployments in Transylvania to guard against any forces Russia committed to fighting the Turks in the Balkans.

When Schönfeld rejected this notion, which would have meant the weakening of the main Habsburg effort in Galicia, Beck moved to undermine the chief of the general staff still further. Not wishing to repeat the sad experience of 1866 when the emperor and the military administration had made tardy and unfortunate selections for the top field commands, Schönfeld suggested the creation of an army high command, presumably led by Archduke Albrecht. Bylandt, not wishing to surrender the war ministry's hard-won prerogatives, had rejected the notion with the silent concurrence of both Archduke Albrecht and Beck.

Ultimately, the November 1876 conference adopted a defensive stance. The conference agreed to construct fortifications at Cracow, Olmütz, Przemysl,

Vienna, Budapest, and, in response to Beck's warning of a possible Russian threat from European Turkey, in the Carpathian passes leading into Romania. The conference also ordered the reduction of the Bosnia-Herzegovina invasion force to four divisions, an action that Beck had urged earlier to bolster domestic support for military action. At the suggestion of Schönfeld and Beck, the government quietly began to purchase horses and winter gear for the occupation forces to eliminate the possibility of being overcome by the events of the coming Russo-Turkish war.

The 13 November conference revealed that general staff autonomy in military planning still fell far short of the ideal expressed by Beck in the late 1860s and early 1870s. The conference proceedings indicate that the head of the military chancellery himself was not ready at that juncture to support a greater independent operational role for Schönfeld. Indeed, they signaled the emergence of Beck as a key player in any future combat deployment of the army. While he probably did not intend to infringe upon the chief of the general staff's role and missions, his active interest in operational questions would lead him to assume some of the chief's functions. When Schönfeld became incapacitated by illness immediately prior to the occupation of Bosnia and Herzegovina, Beck, by virtue of his abiding interest and role in shaping army operations, would be the natural person to oversee the invasion.

While ever anxious to realize his ambitions for the monarchy in the Balkans, Beck remained committed to a policy of peace and cooperation with Russia. With the motto "*clara pacta, boni amici*," he urged Franz Joseph to identify with Germany and Russia common aims and policies regarding the Eastern Question. In August 1875, Beck wrote that neither Russia nor Austria-Hungary could allow the unilateral intervention of the other in the Balkan imbroglio, particularly if such action appeared motivated by the prospect of territorial gain. The best solution for the monarchy would be to grant Russia limited territorial gains at Turkey's expense in exchange for its recognition of an Austro-Hungarian occupation of Bosnia and Herzegovina.[45]

Austro-Hungarian foreign policy during the winter of 1876-77 did not disappoint Beck. On 15 January 1877, Foreign Minister Andrássy initialed a convention under which Russia agreed to restrict its future military operations against Turkey to Romania and Bulgaria. Russia also promised not to seek Serbian and Montenegrin involvement and stated that Russian forces would only occupy Bulgaria for a short time following the expected victorious war with Turkey. The Russian government also agreed to include an Austro-Hungarian occupation of Bosnia and Herzegovina in a future peace settlement. For its efforts, Russia would receive Bessarabia and portions of Asian Turkey.[46]

The 24 April 1877 Russian declaration of war on the Ottoman empire and the initial rapid advance of the Russian army heightened military expectations in Austria-Hungary of an imminent occupation of Bosnia and

Herzegovina. On 21 June 1877, Beck wrote Rodich that the emperor might order the mobilization of the 18th Infantry Division in Dalmatia within a few days.[47] Two days later when Russian forces crossed the Danube into Bulgaria, Franz Joseph convened another military council on the status of army preparations in response to Balkan events.[48]

To date, general staff planning had taken into account both the anticipated occupation of Bosnia and Herzegovina and possible conflicts along the Italian, Galician, and Transylvanian frontiers. Upon mobilization, ten corps, the overwhelming majority of the army, would deploy in Galicia. Fears of Italian opposition to an Austro-Hungarian move in the Balkans, however, led Schönfeld to divert the first-line 36th Infantry Division from the occupation forces to strengthen Kuhn's III Corps and to replace it with the 41st *Honvéd* Division. This move unleashed a torrent of abuse on the chief of the general staff by the war ministry, which proclaimed Schönfeld's dispositions incompatible with the army's permanent wartime order of battle. The war ministry also attacked the general staff's logistics plan for the operation and its projections as to rail capabilities. Archduke Albrecht disliked the use of Hungarian troops in the occupation, citing current widespread pro-Turkish/anti-Slavic sympathies in Hungary and favored using the 42nd *Landwehr* Division, a Croatian unit. This time Beck tried to defend Schönfeld from his critics, but to no avail. The conference ordered the chief of the general staff to revise the order of battle for the invasion forces, including the reassignment of the 41st Division, and to revamp the supply plan. Franz Joseph also ordered the general staff to work closely with the war ministry in the formulation of additional contingency plans that would prepare the monarchy for any foreseeable outcome of the Russo-Turkish War.

The alarm during the early months of the Russo-Turkish War quickly subsided in July 1877 when Turkish resistance suddenly stiffened around the Plevna fortress in the Balkan Mountains of Bulgaria. By 21 July, the apparent stalemate had rendered the immediate mobilization of the Habsburg 18th Division unnecessary. Beck even permitted its commanding general, Major General Jovan Jovanovich, to go on leave.[49]

If anyone remained nervous at this point about events in the Balkans, it was Franz Joseph. Vacationing at Bad Ischl in early August, the emperor wrote Beck asking him to meet with Andrássy concerning the possibility of a preemptive mobilization against Serbia. [50] Despite statements to the contrary, Franz Joseph worried about Serbia's rearmament following its unsuccessful war with Turkey of the previous year and feared that the principality might use the Turkish preoccupation with the Russians to invade Bosnia and Herzegovina. Beck wired the emperor on 11 August that Andrássy had rejected the idea of mobilizing against Serbia, since the Budapest agreements had specifically designated the principality as a "neutral zone" between Austrian and Russian forces. As long as Serbia did not renew its war with the Ottoman empire or actually move troops into Bosnia, the foreign minister believed that Austria-Hungary should maintain correct relations with Belgrade.[51]

Beck appended no personal comments to his description of his interview with the foreign minister that indicated a differing assessment. Indeed, his instructions of the same period for the new presumptive commander of the occupation forces, Joseph Baron Philippovich von Philippsberg, demonstrate Beck's shared concern for correct appearances. These stressed that any Austro-Hungarian military action not "assume the character of a conquest by force, but that of a peaceful occupation." Beck was particularly anxious that the local population not regard Habsburg troops as enemies or conquerors, but as welcome protectors. Soldiers must avoid conduct that might arouse mistrust or embitterment that could lead to eventual resistance. Officers and men must convince the population that the Austro-Hungarian occupation served the best interests of the provinces. The monarchy would obtain this kind of atmosphere only if the operation were undertaken as a part of an international mandate. The healthy climate for an occupation of Bosnia and Herzegovina, so coveted by Beck, would almost certainly be lacking if the monarchy acted rashly in the midst of the Russo-Turkish War.

Franz Joseph followed the advice of Andrássy and Beck. Throughout the fall of 1877, he awaited a resolution of the Russo-Turkish War. On 10 December, the Turkish forces at Plevna surrendered. By year's end, the Russian army had taken Sofia and was slowly advancing on Constantinople. To the shock and alarm of the Habsburg foreign ministry, Tsar Alexander II transmitted peace proposals that directly contravened the Budapest agreements of January 1877. The tsar proposed to establish a large Bulgaria, dominated by a two-year Russian army of occupation. Bosnia and Herzegovina, earlier promised to Austria-Hungary, would become autonomous provinces within the Ottoman empire under the Russian plan.[52]

This sudden disavowal of his careful diplomacy with St. Petersburg deeply angered Andrássy. The foreign minister now pressed the emperor and his military leaders to order the mobilization of the entire armed forces of the empire in Transylvania, where they would be in a position to cut off the Russian field army in the Balkans from its sources of supply.[53] Beck, Albrecht, and Schönfeld united in opposition to military action, citing the cost in lives and matériel and irreparable damage to the monarchy's international standing that a war with Russia would bring.[54] Schönfeld reiterated his earlier objections to a deployment in Transylvania, a position which Beck did not support given the presence of a large Russian army in the Balkans.[55]

Franz Joseph convened a crown council on 7 February 1878 to discuss the full mobilization of the armed forces.[56] This crown council marked a watershed in Beck's career, for he was listed for the first time as an official participant, a clear indicator of his growing influence as a leader in military affairs. As head of the emperor's military chancellery, Beck technically had no place in a civilian crown council. It was the war minister who had the constitutional task of representing military interests in council, though he had the right to call upon the heads of his various *Hilfsorgane*, particularly the chief of the general staff or the head of the naval section, to report directly to the council on matters affecting their departments. By contrast, the fact that Schönfeld did not attend the 7 February crown council signaled his waning influence over the operational employment of the army. Indeed, his absence amounted to the suspension of the 1874 understandings that required the war minister to coordinate with the chief of the general staff on all matters involving the use of military force.

Andrássy took a stance similar to the one he advocated during the 1870 crisis: Austria-Hungary should declare total mobilization but call-up forces incrementally in order to spread the tremendous costs (310 million gulden according to a war ministry estimate) over a period of several months and thus increase the political acceptability of the action. Beck disagreed with this rather foolish notion and offered vigorous support to War Minister Bylandt's call for an all or nothing response to Russia's perfidity. Ever the compromiser, however, Beck offered that the army might get by on 60 million gulden during the first month of mobilization, a sum which could be raised from common resources and a 20 million gulden credit from the British government, which shared the monarchy's alarm at the prospect of a Russian-dominated Balkan peninsula. For Beck, British subsidies were key to the empire's ability to wage a successful war against Russia, since financial exhaustion would cripple the war effort long before a decision could be attained on the battlefield.

Franz Joseph, wiser and more cautious for his experiences in 1859 and 1866, ultimately sided with his military leaders. Russia was large and unconquerable. Even assuming victory in the initial battles, the monarchy's armies would soon find themselves overwhelmed in the large and hostile Russian landscape. Poor communications in the theater of operations would multiply the already staggering problem of supplying a million men for an extended campaign. In a 14 February 1878 audience, Beck drove home the military's perspective and put to rest the question of an immediate full-scale mobilization. He told the emperor plainly that the monarchy's military position was even worse than it had been in the disastrous years of 1859 and 1866. Italy would likely use the opportunity of an Austro-Russian War to invade the Tyrol, the Trentino, and Istria. This would require the army to position 70,000 troops in the Italian passes, still others to guard the southern frontier from Russia's Serbian and Montenegrin allies. Based on the public pronouncements of German Chancellor Prince Otto von Bismarck, Germany would not allow

Austria-Hungary to enjoy the fruits of victory even should fortune smile upon Habsburg arms.[57]

Beck estimated that an Austro-Russian war would cost 600 million gulden, an expenditure the civilian governments were not likely to approve. If Franz Joseph openly declared the conquest of the western Balkans to Salonika as a war aim, he might engender some enthusiasm from army and people for war. The mere eviction of the Russian army from European Turkey, however, offered insufficient compensation for the sacrifices required to defeat Russia. Given his great desire to see the empire expand in the Balkans, Beck sympathized with Andrássy's frustration at Russia's new unwillingness to honor earlier agreements. He nonetheless did not believe that military threats would provide the solution the monarchy required.

These warnings, coupled with pessimistic assessments by the general staff that the army would have to guard against an Italian invasion, staved off an immediate mobilization order and set political developments on a more peaceful course in line with Beck's more limited objective of territorial aggrandizement in the Balkans.[58] On 24 February 1878, a crown council approved a precautionary 60 million gulden credit to demonstrate to Russia and Europe Austro-Hungarian resolve in obtaining an agreeable peace settlement in the Balkans.[59] While it initially appeared to Beck that the Austrian and Hungarian governments might not validate the crown council decision, Russia's imposition of the punitive San Stefano peace on 1 March ensured swift approval of the credit by the respective parliaments before the end of the month.[60]

Approval of the financial means for military action in Bosnia and Herzegovina did not end Beck's difficulties in steering events toward his ultimate objective of an Austro-Hungarian occupation of the provinces. In April 1878, he deflected several attempts by Andrássy to cut the number of divisions slated for the occupation from seven to two. Beck's five-division compromise between extreme foreign office and general staff viewpoints ultimately formed the order of battle for the actual operation.[61]

The same month, the general staff joined with the foreign office to press the emperor to mobilize forces in Dalmatia and Slavonia to threaten both Serbia and Montenegro with invasion should they suddenly move to occupy Bosnia and Herzegovina.[62] Reversing its earlier stance, the general staff also called for the mobilization of the VII Corps in Transylvania to threaten the landward communications of the Russian army in the Balkans. Beck urged caution. Military demonstrations against the minor Balkan powers would back Vienna into a diplomatic corner without appreciably enhancing the monarchy's prestige. Russia would view a Habsburg mobilization in Transylvania as a provocation and would likely counter with a buildup in Poland.

Beck succeeded in holding military preemptive preparations in abeyance, permitting Andrássy's diplomacy to work toward a compromise. On

6 June 1878, the foreign minister signed an agreement with Great Britain pledging Austrian diplomatic support in cutting down the large Bulgarian state created by San Stefano and specifically to exclude a pro-Russian Bulgaria from the Aegean. Both powers agreed that a Russian occupation should last no longer than six months and be limited to a force of 60,000 men. In return, Britain gave tacit approval of an Austro-Hungarian occupation of Bosnia and Herzegovina.[63]

Despite the alignment of Britain with Habsburg interests, Andrássy continued to push for mobilization of forces in Transylvania to effect a Russian withdrawal from the Balkans in a political-military conference held on 6 June 1878.[64]   Beck, with the support of War Minister Bylandt, blocked this provocative step and limited preparations to the fortification of the mountain passes into Romania and the Dalmatian port of Cattaro (Kotor). On the issue of the mobilization of the forces slated for the now impending occupation of Bosnia and Herzegovina, civilian and military positions were reversed. The foreign ministry held to its earlier position that the army could execute the operation with only two divisions, while Beck and Bylandt called for the activation of all four divisions then slated for deployment. Franz Joseph ultimately agreed to a compromise that authorized the immediate mobilization of two divisions and that the execution of all preliminary measures, such as the purchase of horses and additional equipment, be made for the remaining two so they could later be brought swiftly to their full wartime strength.

The 6 June conference achieved less agreement as to how the monarchy proposed to administer the Turkish provinces once it occupied them, an issue raised by Beck and which showed him far ahead of his contemporaries in grappling with difficult problems. Beck explained to the conference that the political-military leadership would soon have to address matters of personnel and financial administration.   Andrássy demonstrated an aristocratic indifference to these thorny issues, dismissing Beck's observations with a glib remark that the Habsburg government did not need to work out a comprehensive administration plan for Bosnia and Herzegovina prior to the invasion. The military commander on the scene would merely govern through existing bureaucratic structures. Since large numbers of Austro-Hungarian troops were at his disposal, the military commander would not have to worry about the establishment of local police forces until after the demobilization following the completion of military operations. Andrássy's assessment showed an almost willful ignorance of the lawless conditions in Bosnia and Herzegovina (why else would Austro-Hungarian forces be needed to restore order and tranquility?), a miscalculation that would create substantial problems and opportunities for Beck during the occupation itself.

The Occupation of Bosnia-Herzegovina

On 28 June 1878, Andrássy obtained the approval of the Congress of Berlin for the Austro-Hungarian occupation, and subsequent administration, of Bosnia and Herzegovina. Three days later, the European powers awarded the monarchy the right to occupy the Sanjak of Novipazar, a strip of Turkish territory between the newly independent states of Serbia and Montenegro. Russia and Turkey, exhausted by their recent struggle, were powerless to resist the powerful Anglo-Austrian diplomatic combination backing these Habsburg gains. On 2 July, Franz Joseph ordered the mobilization of the two remaining divisions of the occupation force.[65]

While naturally pleased with the outcome of the Congress of Berlin, Beck nevertheless became increasingly nervous as the time for actual military operations grew near. On 23 May, he had written his friend Major General Rodich that the occupation forces would likely encounter resistance from the Turks and especially the Montenegrins, who coveted Herzegovina.[66] Five days after the mobilization of the last two occupation divisions, he wrote Rodich again complaining of Andrássy's remark that the occupation of the Turkish provinces would be more like a military parade than a combat operation. Beck wrote that the foreign minister was sadly mistaken and that Austro-Hungarian forces could expect determined resistance.[67]

Beck had good reason to be nervous, because the success of the upcoming occupation increasingly rested on his shoulders. Promoted in May 1878 to major general, Beck was now Schönfeld's equal in rank. This, coupled with Beck's position at the emperor's side in the military chancellery, lent great authority to his opinions and instructions, despite the lack of an official role in army operations. Schönfeld, whose chief responsibility was the operative employment of the army, had requested sick leave in June 1878, citing the reappearance of an old rheumatic affliction. Major General Maximilian Fischer, Schönfeld's deputy, chiefly handled the day-to-day bureaucratic operation of the general staff and was not trusted to assume a leadership role in army operations. Beck, now recognized throughout the army as an influential figure and the undoubted patron of the general staff, represented Schönfeld's logical surrogate as the operational head of the army during the occupation.[68]

On 25 July 1878, with Austro-Hungarian troops poised along the Save River and the Dalmatian border with Herzegovina, Beck read to a crown council the emperor's order to General Philippovich outlining the military and political goals of the occupation.[69] Beck had drawn up these instructions to the field commander entirely within the military chancellery with little or no formal coordination with either the general staff or Archduke Albrecht.

Beck defined the military task as the swift seizure of the most important political and military centers in the two provinces. In an attempt to circumvent the inaction of the crown council, he included Mitrovica, an important town within the Sanjak of Novipazar, on the list of points to be occupied. Beck stressed to Philippovich the absolute need for the local population to view Austro-Hungarian troops as peacekeepers and not conquerors. Habsburg commanders must avoid violent clashes with inhabitants and thereby undercut resistance forces. Beck did not anticipate much resistance from regular Turkish units but warned that the large number of irregular forces marshaled by Constantinople over the course of the previous three years might resist disarmament by Habsburg units. Apart from this general guideline, Beck gave Philippovich largely a free hand in accomplishing the military goals of the occupation with the proviso that he would have to submit regular progress reports to the emperor via the military chancellery.

Again circumventing the inaction he had encountered in the crown council concerning long-range policies and goals, Beck addressed in the imperial instructions the extensive political-administrative challenges that Philippovich would face upon completion of the military phase of the occupation. The most important questions would involve the protection of native lives and the safeguarding of property and property rights. Beck cautioned Philippovich, whose pro-Slavic sympathies were well known, that he would have to guarantee that the various nationalities, ethnic groups and religions received equal treatment by the Habsburg-supervised Turkish administration. The occupation government, however, should take special care to cultivate local Catholics, since they represented the most enthusiastic supporters of the monarchy. After the Catholics, the Muslim population should receive Philippovich's attention and protection, since it represented the more wealthy and educated element of provincial society. Beck hoped that the occupation government would eventually succeed in weaning away local Orthodox Christians and Muslims from their religious leaders outside the monarchy (i.e., the Greek Patriarch and the Sheik il Islam, respectively) and set up their own religious leaderships within the borders of the empire.

On 29 July 1878 Austro-Hungarian forces crossed into Bosnia and Herzegovina. The army mobilized an additional division in Croatia-Slavonia to assume the fortress and border patrol duties performed by troops involved in the operation. The 82,000 men of Philippovich's XIII Corps advanced along the Bosnia and Vrbas river valleys toward Sarajevo while Jovanovich's 9,000-man 18th Division marched up the Naretva into Herzegovina. The northern columns soon encountered fierce resistance from Muslim irregulars, forcing Philippovich to regroup his scattered forces in the Travnik-Zenica area on 4 August. Persistent insurgent attacks on his supply lines further hampered the XIII Corps drive on its objective: Sarajevo. While pleading with Vienna for reinforcements, Philippovich nonetheless took the Bosnian capital after extensive street fighting on 19 August. Jovanovich seized his objective, the Herzegovinian capital of Mostar, on 5 August, where he halted at the direction of the military chancellery.

Beck had negotiated with the war ministry and general staff for a reduction in the forces slated for deployment to Bosnia and Herzegovina to make the operation politically acceptable to the civilian governments in Vienna and Budapest. When operations stalled, however, he led the fight for substantial reinforcements for the campaign. Backed by War Minister Bylandt, Beck argued that when the army had drawn up the original order of battle, it had anticipated only having to "penetrate" the region. The army, Beck explained somewhat disingenuously, suffered what is now commonly known as "mission creep," since the invasion force was never meant to assume the expanded pacification mission mandated to Austria-Hungary by the Congress of Berlin. Franz Joseph, as he did in most military matters, heeded Beck's advice and ordered the mobilization of six additional divisions. These reinforcements would eventually bring the total number of troops deployed to Bosnia and Herzegovina to 153,000 men.[70]

These massive reinforcements, however, did not bring the campaign to a swift conclusion. While Austro-Hungarian troops had seized the political centers of Sarajevo and Mostar by mid-August, they still encountered locally stiff resistance in the countryside, particularly from Muslim irregular forces.[71] Philippovich aggravated the situation from a political perspective by not submitting regular situation reports to Vienna as required by the initial campaign orders issued to him by Beck. Philippovich's well-known hatred of both the Muslim population and the Hungarian soldiers under his command aroused concerns about his suitability to execute the political mission that would follow immediately upon the conclusion of military operations.[72]

The confused nature of guerilla warfare was undoubtedly responsible for Philippovich's silence in September and October. It, however, posed grave difficulties for the military leadership in Vienna eager to report victory and pending demobilization to the concerned civilians. On 29 September, Beck warned Philippovich that the emperor had to suppress an issue of the *Pester Lloyd* newspaper that had questioned Austro-Hungarian readiness for the occupation of Bosnia and Herzegovina. The army, Beck stressed, had to conclude operations quickly to forestall the reappearance of similar probing reports.[73]

Eventually, Philippovich wore out the patience of both the civil and military leaderships. On 1 October 1878, Chief of the General Staff Schönfeld proposed the commitment of an additional three divisions to bring the occupation to a swift termination. Franz Joseph, encouraged now by Beck and Bylandt, became irritated by his field commander's inability to conclude the military phase of the occupation. The emperor, therefore, greeted a proposal by Beck that a "high-ranking general" be dispatched to find out exactly what was happening in the provinces.[74]

Beck made the suggestion in the hope that he would be that high-ranking inspector general. He had good reason to believe that Franz Joseph would select him for the mission. Indeed, none among the emperor's inner military circle appeared suitable for the task. Archduke Albrecht and Bylandt-Rheidt were both far too senior for serious consideration, and Schönfeld's ailments precluded him from undertaking such a rigorous journey. Given the political-military mood within the crown council, any inspection tour was likely to result in Philippovich's removal from command. The emperor clearly needed someone with Beck's renowned diplomatic talents to accomplish this delicate task without offending a senior general officer who had, even if belatedly, accomplished the military goals of the occupation.

Unwilling to simply wait for answers from Sarajevo, Franz Joseph ordered Beck to undertake an inspection tour of Bosnia and Herzegovina as his personal representative. Beck was to report his findings directly to the emperor, bypassing both the war minister and the inspector general of the army.[75] On 31 October 1878, Beck had a five-hour interview with Philippovich, during which the latter announced his desire to return to his earlier command at Prague. Both generals agreed that a dissolution of the army command at Sarajevo should accompany Philippovich's departure and that his deputy, the Duke of Württemberg, or the commander of the 18th Infantry Division, Major General Jovan Jovanovich, should succeed him. The provinces would ultimately become a peacetime general command that in wartime would form the nucleus of an army corps.

Upon his return to Vienna, Beck made no effort to conceal the many problems facing the monarchy in Bosnia and Herzegovina. While he could report that the army had succeeded in breaking armed resistance to the occupation, practical problems of the political administration of the provinces, brushed aside earlier by Andrássy and the civilian governments, now demanded immediate attention.[76] Dashing both foreign office and civilian hopes, Beck reported that little remained of Ottoman government in the provinces and those Turkish officials still present were merely continuing their earlier mismanagement and would have to be replaced. He noted that the prospects for recruiting effective administrators from the native population, as envisioned by Andrássy and the civilians, were dim; lazy and ignorant, the population of Bosnia and Herzegovina could not hope to assume direction of their own affairs. Few among the local elites could read or write, either in Turkish or Serbo-Croatian. Schools were nonexistent, requiring Habsburg authorities to identify especially bright youths for education within the monarchy. Until the government could nurture such local talent, it would have to export to Bosnia and Herzegovina its own officials that had the requisite knowledge of Slavic languages.

Beck was equally grim in forecasting the ability of the provinces to bear the financial burden of their own administration, another of the basic assumptions of the Austrian and Hungarian civilian governments. The establishment of a court system and a local gendarmerie, both urgently required to uphold and administer a system of justice that formed the basis for the Berlin Congress mandate, would by themselves overburden already fragile provincial finances. The captured Turkish provincial treasury amounted to a mere 100,000 gulden. It would cost the monarchy 4.5 million gulden to create a police force alone, not to mention the sums that would be needed for the remaining civil administration and the maintenance of Austro-Hungarian forces in the area. Best estimates placed tax receipts at 7 million gulden per year. The Habsburg government, therefore, would have to commit substantial financial resources in order to establish the "western style" administrative system for Bosnia and Herzegovina assumed by the Congress of Berlin mandate.

Beck concluded with a number of recommendations that ultimately would form the basis of Austro-Hungarian rule in Bosnia and Herzegovina until 1918. Beck first recommended the fusion of the two provinces into the joint territory we know today, Bosnia-Herzegovina. In so doing, Beck rebuffed a suggestion by General Jovanovich that Herzegovina receive its own independent provincial government, citing the region's great poverty as the overwhelming consideration in favor of a fused provincial government at Sarajevo. Beck also blocked an early attempt by Jovanovich to address the so-called "agrarian issue," or the ownership of the vast majority of land by Muslims, which had originally ignited the civil war in July 1875. Impressed by the ferocity of Muslim resistance to the Austro-Hungarian occupation, Beck recommended that the Habsburg administration uphold all land tenure laws and property relationships that had existed under Turkish rule. This meant favoring Muslim landowners over Orthodox Christian peasants. The maintenance of the economic status quo would become one of the hallmarks of the Habsburg administration of Bosnia-Herzegovina and formed the basis for the Slavic discontent and separatism that would ultimately lead to the assassination of Archduke Franz Ferdinand, World War I, and the subsequent collapse of the monarchy.

Beck's concerns that the monarchy would be unable to achieve the social transformation of Bosnia-Herzegovina without serious unrest and/or renewed Ottoman intervention were valid in the fall of 1878. Muslim resistance to the occupation had forced the government to mobilize 278,000 men in support of the operation, almost one-third of the wartime strength of the common army. Habsburg forces had fought in eighty engagements and suffered nearly 5,400 casualties. Beck clearly feared that enactment of agrarian reform would rekindle Muslim resistance to Habsburg rule on a massive scale that would compel the army to mobilize most, if not all, its forces in order to quell it. This, in turn, might threaten the peace of Europe, especially if Russia saw an opportunity to settle old scores with those powers it held responsible for the unraveling of the San Stefano treaty.

Beck, too, may have been sensitive to army critics of his handling of the occupation, especially the massive buildup of forces after 1878.[77]   Beck, of course, did not alone make the decision to reinforce Philippovich. Both Bylandt and Schönfeld had agreed on the need for massive reinforcements in order to bring military operations to a swift conclusion. That Austro-Hungarian force did manage to pacify Bosnia-Herzegovina within a relatively short period of time was no minor achievement given both the rugged nature of the terrain and the poor road network in the provinces. Sixty-five years later, Marshal Tito would demonstrate the effectiveness of irregular forces in resisting even the best-equipped and highly trained occupiers over much the same ground. If anything, Beck should be criticized for his willingness to compromise with the foreign ministry that reduced the original troop commitment below levels needed to execute the occupation.

The ultimate success of the occupation of Bosnia-Herzegovina did serve to mark Beck as a leading military figure in the eyes of the civil-military leadership and of the public.[78]   While the general staff and the imperial war ministry had laid much of the groundwork for the campaign, it was Beck, and not Schönfeld or Bylandt, who represented the army at crucial conferences and who oversaw the conduct of the operation. Beck's trip report to the emperor formed the basis for the subsequent political-military administration of the new Habsburg provinces. Both admirers and critics alike saw Beck as the "coming man" in the army and Schönfeld's clear successor as chief of the general staff.[79] The age of Beck was dawning.

Chapter 4

The Beck System

Schönfeld Departs

On 7 January 1880 Franz Joseph convened a meeting to discuss the political-military situation of the monarchy.[1] The new foreign minister, Baron Heinrich von Haymerle, painted an uncertain picture. Pan Slavists might again lead Russia into conflict with Austria-Hungary in the Balkans. Italy, while it would never act alone, might attack the monarchy if the latter were engaged in hostilities elsewhere in order to obtain Istria and South Tyrol. Romania and Serbia were unknown factors, but Vienna needed to neutralize them either by diplomatic or military means. Haymerle wanted the drafting of annual deployment plans for the armed forces to meet all potential threats to the monarchy's security. Only then, he concluded, could the government view the future with confidence.

Haymerle's demands for increased military vigilance rankled Anton Freiherr von Schönfeld. The chief of the general staff angrily retorted that the hostile constellations described by the foreign minister had existed for years, and each had been the subject of intense scrutiny by the general staff. While the Balkan imbroglio had interrupted war planning against Russia, it also introduced new factors into the security equation. Serbia and Montenegro, for example, would undoubtedly assist Russia in any war in the hope of seizing Bosnia-Herzegovina from Habsburg control. Italy would also undoubtedly side against the monarchy. While the German alliance concluded the previous October would offer Austria-Hungary substantial military assistance, it added France to the list of possible adversaries.

Austro-Hungarian foreign and military policy should aim, therefore, to eliminate the possibility of a two-front war. Further, the isolation of Italy would eventually allow Austria-Hungary to launch a preemptive military strike against the weaker of its two major protagonists. Schönfeld wanted Haymerle to press the Delegations for money to construct a fortress system in Galicia to protect the army's rear during an Italian campaign. The general staff needed only to complete a new war plan against Italy that committed the majority of the armed forces to that theater. Current planning against Russia, he haughtily concluded, was entirely adequate for present needs.

Schönfeld's retort revealed just how much out of step he was with the prevailing attitudes of the civil-military leadership and, more importantly, how little he appreciated war planning as a dynamic process. While Franz Joseph, Albrecht, and even Beck sympathized with Schönfeld's desire to eliminate the Italian threat, they realized the political impossibility of such an offensive war. The monarchy would lose the German alliance, for it precluded aggressive policies by either party. Haymerle, backed by Albrecht, justifiably argued that Schönfeld's proposals ignored the real threat to Habsburg security, the Russian empire. Italy indeed would remain a factor in the security equation, but not a decisive one, for Italy alone could not defeat the monarchy. The inspector general wanted the general staff to examine further the deployment of the bulk of the army against Italy should diplomatic conditions change. But Albrecht pressed for an ongoing review of war planning versus Russia. Given the current situation, the general staff in particular needed to plan for both a two-front war against Russia and Italy and for a conflict with Russia alone that took into account the recent German alliance.

Chief of the General Staff of the Combined Armed Forces

Beck, who had already in effect replaced Schönfeld as the operative head of the army during the recent successful occupation of Bosnia-Herzegovina, maintained a prudent silence during the January 1880 conference. While personally on the best of terms with the chief of the general staff, Beck sat quietly as Schönfeld destroyed his credibility with the emperor, Foreign Minister Haymerle, War Minister Bylandt-Rheidt, and Archduke Albrecht. At the center of events within the military chancellery, he, of course, had closely observed Schönfeld's stormy tenure as chief of the general staff. Indeed, Beck had become Schönfeld's confidant. Already in November 1878, Schönfeld had complained to Beck of being ignored by both Albrecht and Bylandt and talked of resigning.[2]

The chief of the general staff seemed in continual conflict with the monarchy's other leading military figures. Immediately prior to the occupation of Bosnia-Herzegovina in July 1878, Schönfeld had fought off Bylandt's attempt to make the general staff's railroad section a war ministry department.[3] Schönfeld's cancellation of the annual general staff exercises of that year because of illness also irritated the war minister, who insisted that they be made up.[4] Albrecht and Schönfeld had clashed over their respective roles and competencies in war planning with Schönfeld complaining loudly of the inspector general's failure to represent general staff viewpoints with the emperor.[5]   The January 1880 conference initiated a feud specifically over the development of new plans against Russia. Franz Conrad von Hötzendorf, then a young staff officer, would later maintain that Albrecht disliked Schönfeld's disregard for social status in both admission to and advancement within the general staff. There is, however, no evidence to suggest that Albrecht pressured Schönfeld in this regard.[6]

Schönfeld's rheumatism during the initial phases of the occupation of Bosnia-Herzegovina ultimately proved decisive in cutting short his tenure as chief of the general staff. By leaving his post with military action imminent, Schönfeld had conceded his inability to direct field operations in a major war. While Schönfeld himself considered the success of the occupation a personal victory, virtually no one shared his opinion. Beck had clearly directed the operation from the military chancellery, something which even Schönfeld himself indirectly admitted in late September 1878 when he requested from Beck the relevant military chancellery files to allow for the preparation of the general staff study of the campaign.[7]   Beck, annoyed perhaps by the self-congratulatory tone of Schönfeld's letter and certainly by the bureaucratic untidiness of his request, coolly refused to hand over any records. He did offer to allow general staff officers to view anything they liked at the military chancellery.[8]

Schönfeld's relative isolation during the occupation was emphasized a month later when Franz Joseph awarded War Minister Bylandt the Great Cross of the Leopold Order for his work in the recent mobilization without bestowing a comparable decoration upon his chief of the general staff. Beck received full recognition for his services the following year, when the emperor pinned the Order of the Iron Crown, 1st Class upon his chest. Schönfeld again went away empty-handed. He complained to Beck, and the latter dutifully brought the chief of the general staff's grievance to Franz Joseph's attention.   While Beck sympathized with his friend's ambitions, he pointed to the impossibility of giving Schönfeld a medal for work in a campaign in which he had not immediately participated.[9]

In March 1881, Albrecht told Franz Joseph that Schönfeld no longer possessed his confidence and requested Beck's appointment as the new chief of the general staff. The emperor asked Beck for his opinion. While excited at the prospect of realizing his lifelong dream, Beck nevertheless did not want to appear over-eager for the job. He suggested Major General Wilhelm von Rheinländer, an old friend from his *Kriegsschule* days. Beck's intentions were honest;   he knew Rheinländer to possess both ability and the emperor's confidence, since he had earlier served as military tutor to young Crown Prince Rudolf.[10]   Rheinländer, however, declined the post, citing reasons of health, whereupon Franz Joseph again approached the head of his military chancellery.[11]

Beck demurred. While he had earlier supported the delineation of power and responsibility between war ministry, general staff, and the inspector general under which Schönfeld currently operated, Beck now demanded their revision. On 15 March 1881, he laid down in a memorandum to the emperor what amounted to his acceptance conditions for the post.[12] The chief of the general staff, Beck wrote, should be a congenial, well-educated and energetic man--qualities which, he professed, he never dreamed he possessed.

Beck defined the situation as follows: current regulations left uncertain both the role and position of the chief of the general staff. Preparing the monarchy for war constituted the main task of the general staff. The chief of the general staff needed to exercise control over the operative use of both *Honvéd* and *Landwehr* forces, since they would fight alongside the common army. The chief of the general staff would assist the supreme commander in the wartime direction of the armed forces and was, therefore, subordinate to him. Since the war minister remained responsible for maintenance, training, and supply, the general staff by definition retained its subordinate *Hilfsorgan* status. The chief of the general staff determined the military's imperative wartime needs and its desirable peacetime requirements; it remained the war minister's task to obtain everything possible within the current political context.[13]

The general staff and its bureaus should function as a giant operations center, charged with the task of preparing war plans to meet all possible military contingencies. As such, the chief of the general staff needed to have direct contact with both the emperor and Archduke Albrecht, the presumptive commander-in-chief of the Habsburg armed forces. Beck stressed that he had no intention of slighting the war minister by asserting access rights to the emperor and the archduke, and that no real changes need be made in the official working relationship between the war ministry and general staff.

Both Franz Joseph and Albrecht were pleased with Beck's memorandum, although the archduke made it perfectly clear to Beck that he expected the future chief of the general staff to obtain his opinions on and approval for all aspects of war planning.[14] Bylandt, however, expressed concern that Beck's proposals, especially those allowing the chief of the general staff direct access to the emperor, threatened the principle of ministerial responsibility for the armed forces. Beck quickly neutralized Bylandt's opposition by offering to nominate the war minister as Schönfeld's successor under his new guidelines. Bylandt, impressed by Beck's sincerity and by his repeated promises to work with, and not against, the war ministry, dropped his opposition to Beck's appointment as chief of the general staff.[15]

On 18 April 1881, Albrecht, acting on the emperor's instructions, ordered Schönfeld to request a long leave of absence and informed him that he would be replaced shortly as chief of the general staff. Schönfeld took the notification of his removal calmly and later did everything possible to assist Beck's transition, including evaluations of all the members of the general staff.[16]

On 11 June 1881, Franz Joseph officially named Beck chief of the general staff. Earlier in the week, the emperor had conferred the Great Cross of the Leopold Order upon him for his years of service as the head of the military chancellery. This decoration, awarded the war minister for the successful partial mobilization of 1878, was usually conferred upon senior commanding generals after years in office. Beck realized that the emperor's action might cause a great deal of hard feeling among the senior generalcy and had asked Franz Joseph to wait until he had earned this high distinction at his new post.[17]

On 14 June, Franz Joseph issued a circular decree defining the position of the chief of the general staff within the military hierarchy identical to Beck's earlier outline.[18] Beck's position differed from his predecessors in two significant ways: first, Beck was to be "the chief of the general staff of the combined armed forces," indicating that he would exercise influence over the operations of the *Landwehr*, *Honvéd*, and *Kriegsmarine*. Second, unlike Schönfeld or John, Beck would have direct access to the emperor on all matters related to the general staff, including army operations.[19] But he still would have to submit written reports and requests to the ruler via the war ministry. The general staff's *Hilfsorgan* status was thus reaffirmed. In a private letter to Bylandt, Franz Joseph granted Beck the right of direct correspondence in operational questions with both the various military commands and the military attachés.[20]

The subtleties of these changes were not lost upon the news media, which hotly debated the meaning of Beck's appointment. Excerpts from the Vienna press found among Beck's private papers indicate solid support of the emperor's decision.[21] One article noted that Franz Joseph's confidence in Beck amounted to an enhancement of the position and power of the chief of the general staff within army and state. Glaise-Horstenau writes that the Hungarian press made even more of an issue of Beck's close relationship with the emperor, charging that he was a court figure comparable to Grünne. Liberal papers in Austria correctly identified Beck's aim to run the general staff on the Prussian model but expressed unfounded fears that he thereby wished to erode the war minister's power and the principle of ministerial responsibility for military affairs.[22]

The Beck System

Glaise-Horstenau has written that wide segments of the army officer corps were both astonished by Beck's appointment and skeptical of his ability to become an effective chief of the general staff.[23]   Beck had not served with the troops since the campaigns of 1848-49 and had never held an independent field command. The general staff had even dropped his name from its rosters after his transfer to the military chancellery in 1863. While Beck had been an active proponent of the general staff and its mission, he had waged his struggle only among the limited circle of the emperor and his top military officials. His services to the general staff were, therefore, not immediately obvious to many in the corps, especially the younger officers.

Beck moved quickly to establish his authority over the general staff corps. On 2 July he set the tone in a speech to those staff officers currently assigned to Vienna.[24] Without bragging, Beck told them of his early service in the general staff and his constant concern for its well-being even during his long years of separation from the corps. He acknowledged that some of their faces were new to him but added that he was confident of their support. Beck tactfully included a few nice words for Schönfeld, whom he knew to have been a congenial and popular chief.

Preparing the army for war formed the first and foremost task confronting the general staff. Its officers, a product of rigorous selection, constituted an elite corps of the army best suited for the performance of this awesome task. Beck, however, stressed that the academic training at the *Kriegsschule*, shared by all assembled, provided only the basic tools for the completion of their common mission. Advanced academic training alone did not define the staff officer; he must show both concern for and commitment to the troops in order to avoid resentment and criticism of the corps within the army. Thus staff officers needed to possess physical stamina in addition to intellectual ability. In particular, Beck emphasized that good horsemanship was essential to the execution of the staff officer's duty. As an elite corps, the general staff had a number of privileges but with these came strenuous obligations and duties that needed to be pursued vigorously if its officers were to gain the trust and confidence of the army.[25]

Beck worked hard throughout the remainder of his career to develop these aspects of staff officer training. Despite the heavy emphasis in his speech on physical fitness and horsemanship, intellectual ability and exceptional educational performance remained the central qualification for admission to and advancement in the general staff. The *Kriegsschule* remained the forum for young officers to demonstrate such ability. Beck moved quickly to dispel any notions left over from the Kuhn era that the *Kriegsschule* should function as a sort of "military university" for the entire armed forces. While under the supervision of the chief of the general staff since 1867, army regulations had not clearly defined the *Kriegsschule* solely as a staff college. In 1882, Beck, with the approval of the war ministry, obtained its clear designation as the *Fachschule* of the general staff.[26] He simultaneously eliminated a series of courses in German literature and national economy, which Beck felt overburdened students and detracted from their more practical military course work.[27] This, however, should not be interpreted as narrow-mindedness, for Beck also broadened the teaching of history to include literature and culture.[28] He insisted upon extensive language training, including a thorough grounding in French and a knowledge of at least one of the monarchy's languages other than the officer's native tongue.[29]

Admission to the *Kriegsschule*, a prerequisite for any officer seeking a career in the general staff, remained extremely competitive. About one thousand first and second lieutenants gathered annually at their divisional and corps headquarters to take the preliminary entrance examination. All had to have served with the troops for at least three years and needed the permission of their regimental commanders to take the exam. Only about 20% made it through a first cut.[30] Those who passed went to Vienna for a second battery of tests lasting several days. Only approximately a quarter of these finalists ever saw the inside of the *Kriegsschule*. Considerations of birth, family, wealth, or nationality exercised no influence over the acceptance or rejection of aspirants.[31]

The forty or so officers entering the *Kriegsschule's* two-year program shouldered crushing academic loads centering on military science and foreign languages.[32] They also received instruction in such non-military subjects as natural sciences, international law, and cultural history. In addition, the young officers were subjected to an intensive regimen of horseback-riding, an aspect of their training particularly dear to Beck. The chief of the general staff took a great interest in the education of the future officers of his corps and presided each year over both the written and oral final examinations.

The top twenty-five or so graduates received trial assignments with the general staff, where they continued their practical education in general staff work. Beck monitored their progress closely, even to the point of grading some of their written assignments himself.[33] Those who performed satisfactorily received after a few years both permanent assignment with the general staff and promotion to the rank of captain. Those not accepted were returned to the line, where they found themselves junior to their less gifted colleagues who had not undergone their rigorous training, for time spent both at the *Kriegsschule* and in attached service with the general staff did not count toward regimental seniority. The relatively few officers that the general staff could accommodate each year led to increasing resentment toward the general staff among *Kriegsschule* graduates in the regular officer corps.[34]

Even those line officers who had not undergone the ordeal of the *Kriegsschule* resented their colleagues in the general staff. Most of this animosity stemmed from the rapid promotion opportunities open to general staff officers. As Gunther Rothenberg has pointed out, general staff officers were on average six to eight years younger than their counterparts of equal rank in the line.[35] In 1875, corps officers attained the rank of colonel, generally the highest regular service grade within the general staff (with the exception of the chief and his deputy), at around age forty-five. Line officer advancement varied by service branch. Cavalry officers generally reached the rank of colonel at an average age of forty-six, infantry officers at almost fifty-two, their colleagues in the artillery at fifty-five, if at all. As a consequence, most of the monarchy's generals by the turn of the century had been general staff officers. Uniform regulations allowing staff officers to wear distinctive "bottle-green" tunics and feathered hats made them even resemble generals and accentuated the corps' connections with the upper echelons of the army.[36]

Ill feeling toward the general staff increased throughout Beck's tenure in office. Pressures soon arose to expand the *Kriegsschule* to permit engineers and artillerymen to attend its technical and strategic courses and to enlarge the school in general.[37] Artillery and engineering officers complained that their early training had slighted tactics and strategy, thus making it virtually impossible for officers from these branches to pass the entrance examinations. The unrealistic anticipation was, of course, that if more officers were admitted to the *Kriegsschule*, more would enjoy the rapid promotion benefits of its graduates.

Beck realized the folly of such expectations and initially resisted attempts to redefine the *Kriegsschule's* role as a general staff school and only grudgingly permitted a widening of its functions.[38] In 1886, Beck headed a commission with the aim of recasting the *Kriegsschule* as the "highest military educational institution of the common army."[39] Beck delayed the commission's work for as long as possible. He realized that expanding the size of the *Kriegsschule* would only serve to heighten tensions within the officer corps, for the general staff would never be in a position to incorporate more than a fraction of the graduates and would have to turn away many excellent candidates. In 1894, however, he allowed the doubling of the annual classes, which thereafter numbered from between eighty and one hundred officers. In 1900, the artillery advanced course, with Beck's blessing, was entirely incorporated within the *Kriegsschule*. The impetus for these reforms came from Heinrich von Pitreich, then commandant of the college and later minister of war, who argued that the merger better served the educational requirements of artillery officers and greatly simplified their training.[40] At the turn of the century, less than half of war college graduates could ever hope for a posting to the general staff corps. As a result, many fine officers returned to the line angry and disillusioned with nothing to show for years of effort.[41] They often brought with them tremendous debts, for as students they received only a small stipend, far less than even their meager lieutenant's pay.[42]

Beck, however, made sure that those accepted into the general staff earned the privilege of rapid promotion. Any who thought their training ended with graduation from the *Kriegsschule* were quickly disappointed. Duty with the general staff itself formed one continuous educational experience. Beck purposely assigned new staff officers to duty with the central bureaus in Vienna so that he could get to know them personally and eye their progress. To bridge the gap between line and staff and to ensure that staff officers did not begin to view their work in war preparation too abstractly, Beck adopted the Prussian example of rotating general staff officers to troops assignments.[43] In peacetime, they would assist divisional and corps commanders in routine administration, and in the event of war, with the direction of their units according to war plans drawn up by the general staff in Vienna.[44] Staff officers then faced yet another round of tests, based on these practical experiences, for promotion to major.[45]

Beck demanded that the training and education of the general staff corps form an ongoing process under his personal supervision. He intensified the practice begun by his predecessors of holding annual general staff rides (*Generalstabsreisen*) on the Prussian model.[46] Unlike Schönfeld, Beck insisted upon directing them in person.[47] These three-week field exercises played an important role in the practical training of general staff officers. Carried out in areas of potential future conflict, predominantly in Galicia and northern Hungary but also along the western and southern borders of the monarchy, staff rides familiarized young officers with situations they might face in a real war and gave them experience in issuing orders. Beck also used the opportunity afforded by staff rides to observe his subordinates under pressure. He purposely made these graded exercises extremely rigorous, insisting that the participants, generally captains and first lieutenants, work around the clock, riding and reconnoitering in all weather by day, writing reports and orders at night by candlelight. The chief led by example, often remaining in the saddle from dawn to dusk, and pushed himself as hard as his men. The exercises were designed to simulate the actual duties of general staff officers in wartime, and Beck strove to make them as realistic as possible.[48] Like admission to the *Kriegsschule*, participation in the *Generalstabsreisen* was gradually widened to include engineering, pioneer, supply, and medical officers from the common army as well as those designated for staff duties in wartime in the *Landwehr* and *Honvéd*.[49]

After Albrecht's death in 1895, Beck also led the so-called *Generalsreisen*, or field exercises for general officers. Lieutenant General

Philippovich, the commander-in-chief of the occupation of Bosnia-Herzegovina, had already in 1875 pushed for the establishment of exercises similar to those of the general staff for brigade, divisional, and corps commanders, some of whom had never belonged to the general staff. The Balkan uproar and the feverish military planning that accompanied it had prevented serious consideration of the proposal until the early 1880s. Beck resisted Albrecht's attempts to allow general officers to attend the general staff exercises and also initially refused to lead the *Generalsreisen*, citing his relatively junior standing within the generalcy.[50] Albrecht, therefore, took over the direction of the first ten annual exercises, although in his last years relied heavily upon Beck's assistance. After 1895 Beck, now without any intermediate military figure between himself and the emperor, was the logical choice to lead the *Generalsreisen*. Like the general staff exercises, Albrecht, then Beck, eventually broadened the scope of the *Generalsreisen* to include a substantial general staff component, since staff officers would function as the executors of orders given by the field commanders.[51]

In addition to these major exercises, Beck organized each year eight smaller, but otherwise identical outings (*kleine Generalstabsreisen*) for staff officers currently serving with the troops. In the 1890s, he instituted staff rides for military supply and transportation officials (*Intendanzreisen*) under the direction of general staff officers in order to give them valuable experience in providing for the material needs of the army in a war situation. After 1900, the telegraph bureau of the general staff held special telegraph exercises for new staff officers to test field applications of communications equipment.[52]

During winter months, war games took the place of field exercises. Beck had been an early and ardent promoter of war games in the Habsburg army as a practical supplement to field exercises.[53] In 1870, he had helped organize the first informal war games in the Austrian capital which formed the model for those instituted by General Gallina a year later.[54]

Like the *Generalstabsreisen*, staff war games had their origins in early nineteenth-century Prussia, where they developed from chesslike beginnings to realistic campaigns played out on gridded mapboards according to increasingly complex rules incorporating the variables of war.[55] Gallina's early program called for two war games per month between December and March, but participation was limited to staff officers serving in Vienna.[56] During the Schönfeld and Beck eras, the deputy chief of the general staff led these exercises in the capital. The IV Corps chief of staff in Budapest also held an annual series of war games, as did many of his counterparts at the various other corps headquarters.[57]

Beck, of course, realized that field rides and war games could never replace the command experience of full-fledged maneuvers. Again, Prussia formed the model upon which the new chief of staff based his ideas about how maneuvers should be conducted. Present at the Prussian exercises in 1861, Beck had admired Moltke's great control over their conduct.[58] He had also marveled at the great number of troops involved and became a firm proponent of exercises pitting two corps against each other. Until the mid-1880s, the largest maneuvers held within the Habsburg monarchy were limited to division-sized units, and emphasis had been placed upon exercises at the brigade and regimental levels.[59] Prior to 1881 Albrecht had directed the larger maneuvers, although the chief of the general staff sometimes acted as his deputy.[60] And often it was the war minister, and not the chief of the general staff, who assessed the effectiveness of the exercise upon its conclusion.[61]

The early 1880s, however, proved a poor time for the immediate realization of Beck's goals regarding army maneuvers. The monarchy had just undertaken an expensive occupation of Bosnia-Herzegovina, and civilian governments pressed the war ministry to cut costs. Maneuvers, a non-maintenance item in the military budget, were among the first to fall victim to financial stringency.[62] An unimpressive divisional maneuver in 1880 under Schönfeld's direction also did little to help Beck's efforts to enlarge the scope of realistic peacetime exercises. Beck moved swiftly to suppress the publication of a general staff report on the unfortunate episode and prepared feverishly during his first months as chief for the fall maneuvers in Upper Hungary.[63] Beck's great success in directing the latter allowed him to keep the idea of corps maneuvers alive for the next several years, when both the uprising in Bosnia-Herzegovina against the introduction of conscription there and the territorial reorganization of the army served to prolong the suspension of most larger exercises.[64] Meanwhile, the new chief of the general staff bided his time, conducting cost studies of the Prussian corps maneuvers in order to provide the war ministry with accurate projections for similar exercises.[65]

Some divisional maneuvers resumed in 1883. The following year saw the first regular corps-level exercises in the monarchy's history. The Brünn and Preßburg corps fought each other in an exercise lasting several days. The experiment proved such a great success that one corps-level exercise took place each year thereafter. Since Franz Joseph took an active part in these corps maneuvers, regardless of weather conditions, they became known as the "*Kaisermanöver*," or imperial maneuvers.[66] In 1893 the first exercises involving more than one corps on each side, something without precedent among the armies of Europe, were held at Güns (Köseg) in Hungary. Because of their fantastic expense, the monarchy could afford to conduct these so-called "*Armeemanöver*" only twice more, once in 1900 around the Carpathian town of Jaslo and again in southwest Bohemia in 1905. Franz Joseph usually thanked Beck at the conclusion of the corps maneuvers and always expressed satisfaction with the general staff's direction of the five-day exercise.[67]

Beck also led the way in expanding Austro-Hungarian maneuvers to include the *Kriegsmarine*, *Landwehr*, and *Honvéd*. As chief of the general staff, Beck placed great emphasis upon cooperation with the naval arm and in the training of staff officers in strategic and tactical use of naval forces. He instituted both joint exercises between the general staff and the naval officer corps and landing maneuvers using both land and sea forces.[68] A firm believer in the need to develop *Landwehr* and *Honvéd* units to the same level of effectiveness as those of the common army, Beck wholeheartedly agreed to Hungarian suggestions in 1886 that militia forces take part in the yearly large-scale exercises.[69]

Although Albrecht technically still directed the larger exercises until his death in 1895, it was Beck who undertook the actual preparations, involving both paperwork and personal inspections of proposed sites a year in advance.[70] After 1895 Beck bore the sole responsibility for the corps exercises. The chief of the general staff did not view this as a burden; indeed, after 1896 he added a second annual corps-level maneuver to an already full schedule.[71] Beck strove to, and largely succeeded in, making the corps maneuvers as realistic as possible. He often used them to conduct operational tests of the latest technical innovations such as aerial balloons and armored cars.[72] Austro-Hungarian maneuvers became known throughout Europe for their high quality, surpassing even those of Beck's original model, Prussia-Germany.[73]

The corps maneuvers also aroused great interest among the peoples of the monarchy. In 1902, Beck would write Franz Joseph that no sooner had one maneuver ended than the press began to debate the location of next year's exercises. He complained that media interest even extended to predicting which corps would participate in the coming maneuvers, which would obviously have some impact upon where they would be held.[74] Beck actually gloried under all the attention and was gratified that the corps maneuvers had aroused such comment. Indeed, apart from their obvious military benefits, Beck believed that showing off the common army's capabilities strengthened its role as the major centripetal force of the empire.[75]

Beck attended and even led some of the lesser exercises. For example, he took charge of the special cavalry maneuvers each year.[76] After Albrecht's death, Beck often observed the target practice of various units, in effect usurping the normal duties of the inspectors general appointed to assume the tasks of the late field marshal.[77] He would even at times leave the capital for several days to observe the training of individual units and garrisons.[78] Beck also regularly examined the maneuvers of the railroad and telegraph regiment, created at his urging in 1883 and placed under his direct command.[79] As chief of the general staff, Beck presided over the pioneer regiment, oversaw the education of pioneer officers and attended unit maneuvers as well until 1893, when he relinquished control to an inspector general of pioneers, a position created following Beck's unification of the pioneer and engineer branches of the technical service.[80]

Beck, however, spent most of his time in Vienna, as did much of the general staff corps. Those officers not serving with the troops were assigned to duty in one of the staff's central bureaus. These included directorate, operations, intelligence, mapping, railroad, and telegraph departments. The directorate handled all personnel matters of the general staff as well as its correspondence with outside agencies. The operations department had the central task of war planning, including the formation of deployment plans to meet probable war scenarios, the wartime order of battle, and evaluations of army readiness, organization, and armament on the basis of data provided by the mapping, railroad, telegraph, and intelligence departments. The so-called *Evidenzbüro*, or intelligence office, analyzed the strengths and weaknesses of foreign military forces as well as their weapons, equipment, and fortifications. The *Eisenbahnbüro* determined the military's rail requirements in wartime and worked with the operations department in the formulation of timetables for the various deployment plans. After the formation of special railroad troops in 1883, it oversaw their organization and training. Officers of the telegraph department prepared for telegraph use in wartime, including cooperation with civilian authorities in curtailing non-military traffic and the erection of new field telegraph lines to connect the army in the field with the communications network of the monarchy. Consequently, it also oversaw the training and organization of the railroad and telegraph regiment. Still other staff officers were assigned to the *Kriegsarchiv* and the Military Geographical Institute.[81]

Beck made few changes in the organization and duties of the central bureaus of the general staff. In 1889 he allowed the railroad department to become a joint agency of the general staff and the war ministry. The telegraph department followed suit in 1900. Also in that year Beck established an "*Instruktionsbüro*" to handle both admissions examinations and the test for promotion to major as well as the general staff war games. The wearisome task of mapping, once such an important aspect of a staff officer's training, gradually fell from the list of his requisite duties during Beck's tenure as chief of the general staff.[82] This might have owed to Beck's own dislike of sketching and drawing, one of the few areas of general staff work in which he had not excelled as a young officer.[83]

Some corps officers found employment outside the normal rotation between the troop and staff assignments.[84] Several staff officers, for example, were always attached to the emperor's military chancellery, and after 1898, to that of Archduke Franz Ferdinand as well. Others had duties as "wing adjutants" to the inspector general of the army, Archduke Albrecht, the war minister, and Beck himself. Still others with special abilities or backgrounds served as military attachés in countries whose military capabilities were of

importance to the security of the monarchy.[85]   Beck dispatched general staff
officers to observe the 1885 Serbo-Bulgarian War and the turn-of-the-century
conflicts in the Ottoman empire, East Asia, and South Africa.[86]   Indicative of
his commitment to military education, Beck also used large numbers of general
staff officers as teachers in the various military academies and cadet schools,
many more than had been give this duty under the regime of his predecessors.[87]

To assist him in daily operations of the general staff bureaus, Beck, like
his two immediate predecessors, had a deputy chief.[88]   That these all were
highly capable officers proved an immense help to Beck, particularly in the
1880s, when he needed to devote his full energies to the formation of strategic
policies and increasing the war readiness of the armed forces. While August
von Pitreich would complain of the thankless nature of the deputy's function,
for his uncle held the post in the 1890s, Beck made it a point of acknowledging
the services of his deputies before social gatherings of the general staff.[89]   Beck,
however, reserved the right to decide all important matters, even when his
absence from the capital left the deputy chief nominally in charge.

Beck demanded a lot from his officers but strove to lead by example,
taking on even the most rigorous and unpleasant duties. Through a variety of
devices, from private office meetings with the most junior officers to personal
direction of the *Generalstabsreisen*, he attempted to lead by personal example.
"Beck was a slave driver," remarked one staff officer, "but one rarely felt the
whip."[90]   He mixed freely with his subordinates and organized dinners at
fashionable Vienna hotels for corps officers serving in the capital. Yet Beck
never let familiarity detract from the task at hand.[91]

In 1890, Archduke Albrecht praised Beck's direction of the general
staff, noting a vast improvement in the quality of corps officers during the
latter's first ten years as chief.[92]   Admirers began to speak of a "Beck System."
Not all of its products, however, liked what Beck had created. Major General
Maximilien Ritter von Hoen, who capped his general staff career as director of
the *Kriegsarchiv* during the First World War, charged that Beck's centralization
of authority within the general staff did not encourage independent thought
among staff officers.[93]   The general staff, Hoen remarked, educated helpers, not
leaders suitable for army command. Those who today might be praised for their
"interpersonal" skills were distrusted by Beck, despite his own obvious abilities
in this area. Long drill, both in the classroom and on the field, molded the
general staff corps into a separate and special caste within the armed forces,
trained to think and respond alike to any military situation. Uniformity of
thought fostered an inclination toward forcing even the unpredictable human
factors of war into tidy models and tables. Moreover, general staff involvement
in the smallest details of anything pertaining to the war readiness of the armed
forces inexorably led to its domination of all aspects of the military
administration.

However, only by careful examination of the details of war--logistics, lines of communication, railroad timetables, the determination of staging areas-- could the general staff provide for the monarchy's security. The system of general staff education, formed by Beck and his predecessors, while perhaps not well-rounded, prepared general staff officers for the complex and detailed task of war planning. General staff officers *did need* to think and act with what would appear to most as rigid uniformity, if one million soldiers were to function efficiently in war. Those general staff officers attached to the divisional, corps, and army headquarters had to understand the rationale behind the deployment plans they executed. Such an understanding could be achieved onlt if the members of the general staff were trained to examine military situations in the same way.

Hoen's criticisms, while they illuminate the flaws inherent in all general staff systems, fail to evaluate their utility, indeed their necessity, for Austria-Hungary at the time of their formation and solidification during the late 1870s and early 1880s. In 1881, Austria-Hungary faced a staggering strategic situation. With the exception of the common border with Germany, behind every one of the monarchy's frontiers stood a potential enemy. Schönfeld's stop-gap administration of the general staff had addressed the most immediate war planning needs of the late 1870s. The government's preoccupation with the Eastern Crisis, however, had prevented the general staff from tackling the roots of the monarchy's security problems--a confused army organization, an inadequate communications network, and an incomplete utilization of the national militias. By 1880 Schönfeld had demonstrated an intellectual rigidity in regard to the ongoing nature of military preparation and had to be replaced. While Beck threw a lot of personal vigor into his new post, he nonetheless needed the assistance of a dedicated corps of officers, rigorously and perhaps rigidly trained, in order to begin the hard work of correcting these grave problems. The industriousness of the general staff, coupled with the great prestige and influence of its chief with the emperor, would go far in the 1880s toward minimizing the military threats to the monarchy.

Chapter 5

Defending the Dual Monarchy

In the winter of 1882 Russian cavalry general Dimitrievich Skobelev delivered an inflammatory speech in St. Petersburg denouncing the Habsburg monarchy as Russia's main enemy. The civil-military leadership in Vienna reacted with alarm when Tsar Alexander III, who had succeeded to the Russian throne after his father's assassination the previous year, did not immediately denounce the speech.[1] By 1882 Austro-Russian relations had outwardly recovered from the shocks of the Great Eastern Crisis of 1875-78. The two powers had already in 1881 negotiated a renewal of the Three Emperors' League, and Alexander III hastened to reestablish monarchical solidarity among Europe's three great empires. Clearly he feared the revolutionary violence that had claimed his father's life. The renewal, unlike the original accord, even took written form and bound the signatories to cooperate in Balkan affairs.[2] But the Austro-Hungarian government had little real confidence that the improved relationship with St. Petersburg would provide the monarchy with lasting security.

Indeed, the foreign ministry had at the political-military conference of 7 January 1880 conceded the inability of diplomacy alone to shield Austria-Hungary from the aggression of its neighbors.[3] Baron Heinrich von Haymerle, Andrássy's successor at the *Ballhausplatz*, wanted increased vigilance from the general staff and institutionalized war planning that recognized both foreign political and military developments. For Haymerle, Russia remained the greatest enemy, since it alone could defeat the monarchy. By virtue of the Dual Alliance of 1879, Austria-Hungary might expect the support of the German empire in countering Russian aggression. But Haymerle cautioned the civil-military leaders to remember that Germany would have to deploy substantial forces to guard against a French attack in the West. Italy, Serbia, Montenegro, and perhaps Romania, while they might join Russia in an attack on the monarchy, could not alone threaten its existence. The general staff must, therefore, direct its main energies toward improving Austria-Hungary's war readiness against Russia, with subsidiary planning to meet threats posed by these other states.

Schönfeld, however, declined to revise existing war plans dating from the late 1870s, even though these took into account factors, such as the occupation of Bosnia and Herzegovina, which were no longer relevant. Indeed, the chief of the general staff believed that a preemptive attack on Italy, the weaker of the monarchy's two Great Power adversaries, posed the only solution to the current strategic dilemma of a multi-front war. Schönfeld ignored the diplomatic complications of his aggressive scheme and seemingly believed that a ring of fortifications in Galicia would serve either to deter or, in the worst case, to blunt Russian intervention in an Austro-Italian war.

Unlike both his predecessor Schönfeld and his successor Conrad, Beck did not seek a solution to the monarchy's military problems in an offensive war and agreed to a large extent with the foreign office assessments of the international situation. In a March 1880 memorandum to the emperor, Beck warned that an offensive war against Italy might cause a general European "explosion" with unforeseen outcomes.[4] While he calculated that Austria-Hungary would possess considerable advantages in a conflict with Italy, Beck doubted if the other Great Powers, particularly Russia, would permit Rome's humiliation.[5] And like Haymerle, Beck expected that the Austro-Hungarian Balkan frontier would also not remain quiet, particularly in the event of military complications with Russia. Serbia and Montenegro resented the monarchy's occupation of Bosnia-Herzegovina and could only be regarded as enemies. The Bulgarian army, commanded by Russian officers, also constituted a potential foe.[6] An alliance with Romania might possibly counteract these Balkan adversaries, while the German alliance would help Austria-Hungary meet any Russian onslaught. However, Beck warned the emperor against an over-reliance on Germany to solve the monarchy's security problems.

Beck and the German Alliance

Despite the latter view, the new chief of the general staff perceived the German connection as vital to waging a successful war against the Russian empire. Beck had realized the need for Prussian assistance as far back as 1854. If both powers coordinated their military efforts, they could encircle and annihilate Russian forces in the exposed Polish salient between East Prussia and Austrian Galicia.[7] In 1860, Beck had urged the conclusion of a defensive alliance with Prussia against France, hinting that the existence of such an agreement might have prevented the Italian disaster of the previous year.[8] During the Franco-Prussian War, he successfully fought the revanchism of Albrecht and Kuhn and worked to keep Austria-Hungary neutral. A fervent proponent throughout the 1870s of friendly ties between his natural and adoptive homelands, Beck naturally welcomed the signing of the Dual Alliance in October 1879.[9]

Beck, however, soon realized that this agreement did not go far enough in defining the obligations of the signatories in the event of war. He wanted an intensification of relations to include concrete plans for military cooperation. In Beck's view, the alliance would remain ineffective without some sort of agreement over war strategy and goals. Already in December 1879, Beck corresponded directly with Bismarck, urging a further military definition of the Austro-German alliance.[10] The German chancellor, however, preferred the ambiguity of the original treaty, fearing that a closer understanding might encourage Austro-Hungarian aggressiveness in the Balkans and unleash a dreadful war with Russia. The Prussian general staff, faced after 1879 with the grim potential of a two-front war against Russia and France, however, began to favor closer ties with its Austro-Hungarian counterpart.[11]

In Austria-Hungary, Beck stood alone in his desire for close military cooperation with Germany. The upper echelons of the Habsburg officer corps still smarted under the monarchy's humiliating defeat by Prussia in 1866 and resented the latter's subsequent military successes. Although as commander of the *Süd Armee* he had not faced Prussian forces directly, Albrecht nonetheless distrusted Bismarck's German empire and entertained hopes for a reversal of the 1866 verdict. Although by 1880 virtually no one entertained further thoughts of *revanche*, the inspector general nevertheless continued to dislike the arrogance of the Prussian general staff. In a letter to Beck, Albrecht complained of public statements by Moltke blaming the monarchy for centuries of German weakness and criticizing the current condition of its armed forces.[12] War Minister Bylandt, though he did not share his predecessor Kuhn's hatred for Prussia-Germany, nonetheless did not push for the exploration of the military implications of the 1879 alliance. Schönfeld likewise regarded the German alliance at best as a means of covering Austria-Hungary's rear in an Italian war.

In 1880 few of the monarchy's top military leaders wanted to expand relations with Germany. Under Baron Heinrich von Haymerle, the *Ballhausplatz* encouraged inaction in this aspect of Austro-Hungarian foreign relations. In the January 1880 political-military conference, Haymerle quickly rebuffed a suggestion by Albrecht that the Austro-Hungarian general staff enter into negotiations with its Prussian counterpart concerning joint troop deployments in a war against Russia.[13] The foreign minister feared the existence of a "war party" in Germany bent upon a disastrous war with Russia. Franz Joseph, who shared Haymerle's unfounded fears that the Germans would consider war if guaranteed substantial Austro-Hungarian support in a Russian campaign, ordered that the general staff conduct no closer discussions concerning the distribution of forces upon the activation of the Dual Alliance.[14]

Haymerle's unexpected death from a heart attack in October 1881 brought a sudden shift in foreign office attitudes. Beck, now chief of the general staff, obtained the consent of Haymerle's successor, Count Gustav Kálnoky, to discuss matters of mutual strategic importance with the German ally. Supported now by Albrecht, who favored a closer understanding as a means of holding Germany to its obligations, Beck and Kálnoky managed to convince the emperor to reverse his 1880 decision forbidding military conversations with the Germans.[15]   Since both the German and Austro-Hungarian governments had recently renegotiated the Three Emperors' League with Russia, any meeting between the respective general staffs had to take place under the utmost secrecy. After some back-channel negotiations, both agreed that the newly appointed Prussian *Generalquartiermeister*, Alfred von Waldersee, would visit the vacationing Friedrich Beck at the alpine resort of Strobl in early August 1882.[16]

The Strobl discussions would form the basis for Austro-German military cooperation throughout the remainder of the 1880s and provide the essentials for Austro-Hungarian strategic doctrine against Russia until 1914. While not an advocate of a preventive war against Russia, as his actions during the Eastern Crisis illustrated, Beck nonetheless favored an offensive strategy should war with Russia become necessary. The Austro-Hungarian chief of the general staff envisioned a two-pronged advance of allied forces aimed at cutting off and annihilating the Russian army inside Congress Poland. Habsburg forces, deploying on both banks of the Vistula, would strike first toward Lublin before turning northward to link up with the Germans advancing from East Prussia. Waldersee, who, as later events would prove, favored an aggressive political as well as military posture against the nominal Russian ally, promised a forcing of the Russian flank along the Niemen River at Grodno within a week of the mobilization order. On mobilization plus ten, a force of 70,000 men would breach any Russian defense of the Vistula and create an opening for a general advance of the German army along the right bank after the twentieth day of the war. The Prussian quartermaster general also offered Beck the use of the German Silesian railroads to assist in the deployment of Austro-Hungarian forces in central Galicia.

Beck then asked the most pressing question from the Austro-Hungarian standpoint: how many divisions would the Germans commit to the east, given their ever-present concerns for the security of the western border? Waldersee conceded that the Prussian general staff had to take into account the possibility of a two-front war but promised that in any event Germany would deploy some twenty line and six reserve divisions--a force of over 400,000 men--to the eastern theater of operations. This answer greatly pleased Beck. He was now confident that Germany would honor both the spirit and the letter of its alliance commitments.

Having considered the central issues, Beck and Waldersee turned to peripheral matters. Since the alliance forces would begin the campaign separated by hundreds of miles of enemy territory, Beck, fearing the domination of the more efficient Prussian military machine, argued against the formation of a combined allied command before the link-up of Austro-Hungarian and

German forces in central Poland. Waldersee did not raise any objections to this proposal but instead tried to lead the discussion away from purely military considerations and into areas of political sensitivity for Austria-Hungary as well as his own country. Specifically, Waldersee wanted the allies to frame any war against Russia as one for the liberation of Poland and accept the enlistment of Polish volunteer forces to fight in the later battles of the war. Beck, who clearly dominated the talks, rejected Waldersee's idea out of hand since it involved political, and not military, considerations: such matters, he stated, would have to be handled through diplomatic channels.

Waldersee's questions concerning potential allies in a conflict versus Russia met with a more direct response from the Austro-Hungarian chief of the general staff. Beck quickly dispelled Waldersee's doubts about the desirability of Turkey as an Austro-German ally, noting that, despite their defeat in the recent war, Turkish forces might prove effective in countering any military action on Russia's behalf by Serbia, Montenegro, Bulgaria, and Romania and could possibly tie down large numbers of Russian troops in the Caucasus. Both expressed uncertainty about Italy's attitude, despite the conclusion of the Triple Alliance the previous May, which bound the Italian government to benevolent neutrality in the event of a war with Russia alone and active assistance should more than one power attack one or more of the signatory powers.[17]

Beck followed up the Strobl discussions, for which he had garnered high praise from both Franz Joseph and Archduke Albrecht,[18] with another more impromptu meeting the following month with Helmut von Moltke. Waldersee had pressed for the establishment of permanent communications between the general staffs via the military attachés rather than the foreign ministries, citing overriding concern for military secrecy since presumably contacts might eventually include the exchange of deployment plans. While Beck had reserved judgment on this issue, Albrecht wholeheartedly embraced this *modus operandi* as a safeguard, as he wrote Franz Joseph, against Bismarck's "Falstaff-like" gregariousness. Albrecht also feared that Bismarck's great antagonism toward von Moltke, which had built up over the course of Prussia's last two wars, would interfere in the effective military cooperation between the two powers.

Beck apparently went to Breslau with no intention of pursuing further talks with either Waldersee or Moltke. He had clearly obtained from the former the necessary commitments and at the moment saw little need for further discussions. Moltke, who because of his high public profile had been forced to send his deputy Waldersee to make the initial contact with Beck, was very anxious to meet his Austro-Hungarian counterpart. On the third day of the maneuvers, Moltke made a private and unexpected call on Beck at the latter's hotel and talked with him for one hour.[19]

Moltke agreed with the basic assumptions of the Strobl meeting. In a war against Russia, Germany and Austria-Hungary would immediately have to go on the offensive.[20] Otherwise, if allowed to mobilize undisturbed, the 1.5 million man Russian army would overwhelm the allies. Moltke urged Beck to take steps to hasten the slow Austro-Hungarian mobilization in Galicia, which in the fall of 1882 would take almost six weeks. He also pushed for the transfer to Galicia of the corps currently slated to guard the Siebenbürgen passes into Romania. The latter, with a Hohenzollern king, would surely remain neutral.

Despite Moltke's great prestige, Beck managed to press for his own agenda in the interview. In particular, he wished to confirm Waldersee's commitment of twenty line infantry divisions to the eastern front. Moltke pledged that Germany would remain on the defensive in the west, declaring that 100,000 men dug in around the fortified works of Metz and Strassbourg would suffice to repel any French invasion. The Rhine River would also prove a formidable obstacle to an advancing French army. Beck obtained Moltke's agreement that no supreme allied headquarters would be needed in the east, a matter of great concern to the Austro-Hungarian general staff given the greater prestige of the Prussian army and its leadership. As long as the general staffs were in agreement as to the prosecution of the war, Moltke declared, there would be no need for a joint command structure. Beck also convinced Moltke to jettison Waldersee's plans concerning Poland, and both affirmed that their respective countries possessed no territorial ambitions in the region.

Beck's discussions with Waldersee and Moltke cemented the friendship and cooperation between the Prussian and Austro-Hungarian general staffs and laid the groundwork for the strategic planning of both powers throughout the 1880s. Both sides followed up these initial contacts with ongoing communications. On 29 October 1882, Beck congratulated Moltke on his twenty-fifth anniversary as chief of the Prussian general staff and praised his creation of a model institution.[21] The same day, Molkte wrote the Austro-Hungarian military chancellery, indicating his satisfaction with his exchange of views with Beck at the Breslau maneuvers.[22] In February 1883, Moltke agreed to an exchange of all military intelligence concerning Russia which Beck had requested via the Austro-Hungarian military attaché in Berlin, Baron Steininger.[23] The latter remained in particularly close contact with Waldersee, whose warlike proclivities became increasingly apparent to Beck by the end of the year.[24]

The allied military discussions, however, did not succeed in changing Bismarck's attitudes toward the alliance. In a conversation with Crown Prince Rudolf in March 1883, Bismarck denied the anti-Russian character of the Dual Alliance, despite the circumstances surrounding its formation.[25] The German chancellor favored the maintenance of the general military obligations of the original alliance. A two-front war presented grave dangers for the new German empire, Bismarck told his guest, and he would not consent to any measures that might bring one about.

Bismarck's fears, however, were unfounded. Politically, the monarchy had just as little to gain from an offensive war against Russia as the German empire--and just as much to lose. In the early 1880s, the political and military leaderships expected that a war of aggression in the east would give rise to a general European conflict, forcing a multifront war upon the monarchy. Moreover, the military discussions with the Germans highlighted the inability of the Austro-Hungarian armed forces to execute even their assigned mission in the Russian campaign, much less simultaneously defend the country's eastern, southern, and southwestern borders.

Moltke had pointed out the most glaring deficiency in the Austro-Hungarian defense posture: slow mobilization. While the German army could launch an attack on the twentieth day of mobilization, the Austro-Hungarian forces could not commence offensive operations for another three weeks.[26] Haymerle and Beck had recognized earlier that the slow mobilization and deployment of the Austro-Hungarian army made it, in effect, a reserve army for the Germans, who would have to win the initial battles alone.[27] By the forty-second day of the war, when Habsburg forces would finally become operational, a victorious German army might already be in Warsaw dictating terms of surrender that would neglect Austro-Hungarian interests. In a November 1882 memorandum on the current state of war planning, Beck charged that Austria-Hungary would have to shorten the time for mobilization if it was to remain a viable ally in German eyes.[28]

Beck and the Territorial Reorganization of the Army

In April 1881, Beck identified for Franz Joseph two fundamental reasons for the army's poor deployment capabilities.[29] First, he noted the inadequacy of the rail network, particularly those lines linking Galicia with the interior of the monarchy. Second, Beck contended that the existing organization of the common army--in the military parlance of the day its "extraterritorial dislocation" of forces--simply did not lead itself to speedy mobilization. The establishment of a territorial army organization, one in which units would be stationed in peacetime within their areas of recruitment, would simplify the task of mobilization more than any other single measure. Beck admitted that the diversity of the educational and cultural levels of the monarchy's various nationalities might create differences in troop quality from region to region. Still, these problems would be far outweighed by the advantages of garrisoning units within their replacement districts. In the event of war, troops in their home areas could be swiftly brought up to strength. Territorial organization would also ease the burden on the already overtaxed communications network, eliminating the shuttling of reserves to their units prior to deployment in the theater of operations.[30]

Beck's plans for the reorganization of the army were eminently reasonable. But the idea found little support among many of the leading military figures of the age, for it challenged existing notions of the army's primary role within the state. The war ministry, like the *Hofkriegsrat* before it, regularly rotated troops to garrisons outside their home areas to ensure their reliability in the event of civil disturbance.[31] Soldiers with no ties to the local population would have no qualms against firing into the midst of angry crowds. This gave the government the means to restore order without creating large police forces.[32]

Archduke Albrecht, Beck's ally on most issues, opposed him on the territorialization of the army. Having been the military governor of Vienna in 1848, Albrecht lived with the constant fear that revolutionary forces might some day threaten the monarchy's existence. The army had saved the dynasty then, and it might have to do so in the future. Albrecht saw the specter of revolution everywhere. In repeated letters to Beck, he harped upon the dangers to the established order posed by the "socialist-nationalist-liberal-democratic-anti-clerical internationale."[33] He particularly feared revolution in the imperial capital given its rapid growth after 1848, and called for the stationing there of "30,000 bayonets" to allow the government to react swiftly and decisively to the least sign of unrest.[34] Responding to Beck's memorandum, Albrecht voiced his apprehension that a territorial organization would ultimately lead to the "nationalization" of the army--the creation of what essentially would become provincial militias with no concern for defending the empire as a whole.[35] Albrecht also argued that the current extra-territorial dislocation allowed the army to exploit the strengths of each of the monarchy's nationalities. There was no better *Jäger* (light infantryman) than a Tyrolean or an Austrian, no better cavalryman than a Hungarian hussar, no better artillerist than a "cold-blooded" Bohemian, no better sailor than a Dalmatian. A territorial system, with its requirement that all combat arms be raised from within one general region, would negate these substantial advantages.

Many lacking Albrecht's conservative and stereotypical perspectives also opposed the reorganization of the armed forces on territorial lines. Franz Kuhn, whose liberal credentials were above reproach, lobbied the foreign office, war ministry, and general staff against the measure.[36] Unlike Albrecht, who feared territorialization would splinter the army, Kuhn merely dreaded its two-part division as a result of its territorialization. The Hungarian national army, against which he had struggled as minister, would become reality.[37]

Beck, however, felt that external threats posed a greater danger to the monarchy's security than domestic upheaval. Not even in Austria-Hungary's newest provinces, where serious internal unrest did indeed occur in 1881-82, did Beck believe revolution had the remotest chance of challenging the forces of order.[38] Within the monarchy proper, he believed that Austro-Hungarian troops would do their duty, even in the face of social unrest. In 1894 he opposed the construction of three army barracks in the Viennese working class districts of Donaustadt, Semmering, and Schmelz on the grounds that this might create a bad impression among the local inhabitants and was without regard to their possible need in suppressing a potential uprising.[39] Even in confronting the nationalist disturbances between Czechs and Germans in the Prague of the 1890s, Beck never wavered in his conviction that local forces could handle domestic unrest as well as those brought in from the outside.[40] While he made some allowances for the disobedience of Hungarian troops in his 1905 "Fall U" plan for a military coup in Budapest, Beck nevertheless remained convinced throughout his career that external, not internal, challenges posed a greater threat to the monarchy's existence.[41] To Beck, it made no sense to eschew the great mobilization benefits of a territorial organization of the armed forces for the negligible domestic ones offered by the current policy of stationing troops outside their home areas.

Among the monarchy's military leaders, only the outgoing chief of the general staff, Schönfeld, agreed with Beck's proposals concerning the reorganization of the army. Schönfeld had pressed repeatedly in early 1881 for the establishment of a territorial system for the army as a means of increasing mobilization speed. His last appeal arrived on the emperor's desk a scant month before Beck submitted his own memorandum on the subject.[42] Like Beck, Schönfeld wanted each military district to recruit, train, and mobilize locally raised troops. The district commanders would lead them in battle. Each district would provide for the material needs of its own units, eliminating the current burden of transporting horses to units during the first days of mobilization. With the exception of Tyrol and Dalmatia, all the military districts would form corps commands.[43] Unlike the various types of current military commands (*General-Kommanden, Militär-Kommanden, Truppen-Divisionen, und Militär-Kommanden*), all units stationed within a corps's command area in peacetime would remain attached to that corps in war.[44]

Ultimately, the reorganization of the army probably owed to Beck's combination of Schönfeld's ideas on army territorialization with the establishment of peacetime corps formations, for Archduke Albrecht had long cherished a corps organization for the army. The inspector general of the army had appealed in an 1875 memorandum for the establishment of peacetime corps to give general officers the opportunity to get to know the units that would be under their command in war.[45] Albrecht, seconded by then chief of the general staff Freiherr von John, repeated these calls for the reorganization of the army into corps commands in a military conference with the emperor.[46]   With the possible exception of his pet project concerning the creation of an inspector general of infantry, the establishment of a peacetime order of battle based upon the corps unit had topped Albrecht's list of priorities throughout the 1870s. He, therefore, made no attempt to veto any debate over Beck's proposals in the hopes that he might achieve a limited reorganization that would keep intact the traditional system of unit transfers.

The issue of army reorganization formed the basis for a series of discussions between the emperor and his top military advisers at the end of May 1881, before Beck had officially taken over as chief of the general staff.[47] Albrecht, Beck, Austrian Defense Minister Count Zeno von Welsersheimb, Josef Philippovich--now commander of the Vienna garrison--and Deputy War Minister Franz Vlasits attended the meetings, which became freewheeling debates over the future of the army.[48]   Franz Joseph merely stipulated that anything decided upon by the participants could not result in an increase in the military budget.

Beck outlined to those present the proposals contained in his April memorandum. The establishment of a territorially based corps organization would best provide for a rapid mobilization in wartime. He argued that all the other Great European Powers had adopted such systems, including Italy,[49] Russia and even the Ottoman empire. The current system of army organization was irrational. No uniformity existed in the current assignment of troops to the various military districts;   indeed, all those outside Hungary differed in size. Currently, only the units assigned to the Siebenbürgen military district formed a corps unit in war. Beck proposed the creation of sixteen corps of two line divisions each, with the commands at Innsbruck and Trieste receiving only one division in peacetime.

Beck's ideas met with mixed approval, with only Welsersheimb and Vlasits, two of the less influential members of the conference, announcing any support for organizational reform. Philippovich opposed all change, noting that the tense international situation would not allow the monarchy time to reorganize its armed forces. The best way to increase mobilization speed was to improve the rail network. Albrecht and Bylandt announced their readiness to consider renaming the existing military districts into corps commands but denied that reorganization on a territorial basis should necessarily follow. Naturally, the war minister's primary concern was that army reorganization not add to the military budget. Ongoing expenses in Bosnia-Herzegovina would account for cost overruns of 6,800,000 gulden for 1880-81 alone, and Bylandt was anxious to avoid further civilian wrath.[50] Albrecht liked the designation of peacetime corps, stating that these would give troops a "sense of belonging" to a larger, more important military unit. He also favored the creation of army commands composed of several corps areas. He rejected Beck's assertion that corps commands needed to be of the same size, citing examples of unequal corps in France and Prussia, and denied that faster mobilization necessarily meant greater efficiency. Troops had to arrive in the theater of operations in good order; otherwise the commander-in-chief would have to waste even greater amounts of time sorting things out.

A debate over the size of an army corps dominated the remaining discussions. All agreed with Albrecht that Beck's two division corps of approximately 25,000 men would be too weak and that three divisions made up a proper corps. Philippovich proposed the alternative of incorporating the militia forces by battalions into the organization of common army regiments, thereby increasing their battle strength. Austrian Defense Minister Welsersheimb noted that while he personally greeted such use of the Cisleithanian *Landwehr*, he doubted if the Hungarians would allow the splintering of *Honvéd* forces in such a manner. Welsersheimb added that he did not believe *Landwehr* forces were currently of first-line quality, but they could relieve common army units of rear area duties.

While the emperor correctly pointed out that such use of the militias would require legislative sanction in both halves of the monarchy, Beck nonetheless seized the opportunity to press for their inclusion in the common army organization. If the monarchy were forced to fight a two-front war, full combat use of the *Landwehren* would become a vital necessity. The incorporation of militia units by battalion as suggested by Welsersheimb was impractical. The Hungarians would never agree to such a submersion of the *Honvéd's* independent identity. The attachment, for example, of one militia division per corps would satisfy the Hungarian requirement for large-unit integrity while simultaneously providing a corps with a third division. This would require the reorganization and expansion of the militia forces.[51]

Bylandt and Vlasits liked Beck's plan for the incorporation of the militia forces into the common army organization. Bylandt, however, stuck to his view that the current military commands, with their unequal distribution of forces, should merely receive new designation as corps, with no attempt at reorganization. Albrecht interjected the somewhat mysterious viewpoint that different theaters would have different organizational requirements and that in the "narrow" deployment area of Galicia, militia forces would not be able to be deployed in division strength. Beck attacked these viewpoints, arguing that unequal corps sizes would seriously complicate troop deployments.[52] Bylandt shot back that Beck's equal corps would require the complete revamping of mobilization, supply, and other instructions and added the ultimate threat--the one guaranteed to carry the most weight with the emperor--that Beck's plans would cost more money. Initially, Bylandt's caveat impressed Franz Joseph, who vowed to reject any plan that would increase the military budget. By the third day of deliberations, however, perhaps after a little private lobbying by Beck, he changed his mind and instructed the war ministry to conduct a cost analysis of Beck's organizational plans.

By then, however, 1881 was already half over. Beck, establishing himself at the general staff, had little time to press the war ministry for immediate action on army reorganization. The matter instead was referred to a war ministry committee formed soon after the May 1881 meetings. On 3 June 1882, over a year after the first top-level discussions, Bylandt reported its findings to the emperor.[53] Beck, who sat on the committee, exploited these back-channel discussions to the fullest and succeeded in convincing the war minister to drop his earlier reservations.[54] The committee, instead of vetoing army reorganization, the inclination of both the war minister and his deputy in May 1881, came up with three alternative plans, each based roughly upon the territorial principle originally advocated by Beck and Schönfeld.

These plans, distinguishable from one another only in minor details, recognized--as Beck had in his original proposals--the impossibility of an absolute territorial system. Indeed, even Germany, again viewed as the model of army organization, had not adopted a rigid territorial system.[55] The alpine lands and Dalmatia did not have the population to support their defense needs and would still require the presence of troops recruited elsewhere. Bosnia-Herzegovina, given both their meager military resources and the volatile nature of the provinces themselves and the bordering Balkan states, also demanded further garrisoning by "non-local" troops.[56] The army would be divided into fifteen corps areas, plus one "military command" in Dalmatia, which would become a divisional headquarters in wartime.[57] The committee report warned that the work of reorganization would require a certain amount of time to accomplish, during which mobilization would be virtually impossible. If war threatened, reorganization of the army would have to be put off to a later date. Bylandt, now convinced of the need for reform, urged that the reorganization take place the coming fall, adding his personal conviction that a war with Russia would more likely come later, in 1884 or perhaps 1885.

Franz Joseph convened another military conference the week after Bylandt submitted the reorganization committee's report.[58] The war minister's change of heart on territorial reorganization lent a spirit of concord and cooperation lacking in the previous gathering of the emperor's top military advisers. Franz Joseph immediately announced his support for Bylandt's proposal to begin army reorganization in September. Both Beck and Deputy War Minister Vlasits stressed to those present that this would preclude the mobilization of the army before March 1883. Beck, however, supported Bylandt's wish to go ahead with the reorganization in the fall since no international disturbances appeared likely.[59] Even Albrecht, who had earlier so staunchly opposed the suggestion of a territorial military system, abandoned his earlier reservations (probably at Beck's urging) and announced his support for Bylandt's proposals.

It only remained for Bylandt to present the plan to the common ministerial council on 29 June 1882.[60]   Little resistance to the reform in principle was expected from either the Austrian or Hungarian government. Austrian Defense Minister Welsersheimb had been in on the early discussions and had supported the general staff's proposals on the grounds of efficiency. Military territorialization, something which they had insisted upon in regard to the *Honvéd*, had formed an underlying part of the moderate Hungarian nationalist program since the *Ausgleich*.   Only the price tag of 1.5 million gulden might arouse civilian resistance.

Bylandt explained to both minister-presidents that currently it took the common army longer to mobilize than its counterparts in neighboring states. To increase the war readiness of the monarchy, a reorganization of the army on a more or less territorial basis was unavoidable. The war minister remarked that the current international situation looked favorable for such a move in the coming winter.   Financially, the moment also seemed auspicious, for the withdrawal of 3,000 reservists from Bosnia-Herzegovina would save the war ministry 40,000 gulden. Bylandt added that, while the cost of shifting units to their new stations would cost 1.5 million gulden, a direct violation of the emperor's original instruction that the reorganization not increase expenditures, over half that amount could be saved elsewhere within the military budget. Total cost of the reform would be 650,000 gulden.

Bylandt explained that the new organization would divide the monarchy into fifteen corps areas.   Each area would contain all elements (troops, horses, supplies) that an army corps would need for its mobilization and deployment on the battlefield. There would be complete agreement between the peacetime and wartime orders of battle. Three senior corps commanders would command armies in wartime. Twenty-two new recruitment districts would be added to the eighty already in existence, for a total of one hundred two. Each recruitment district would provide the common army with one regiment of infantry.[61]   In general, all troops would be stationed within their recruitment areas, although some might still receive garrison assignments outside the home district. As a sweetener, Bylandt announced that the war ministry would allow the Hungarian ministry to communicate directly with the corps commands within the kingdom. Previously all contact with military agencies had to go through the war ministry in Vienna.

As expected, both governments announced their support for the proposed reorganization of the army.   Hungarian Premier Tisza seemed especially pleased at the decentralization of military functions that appeared would accompany the measure.[62]   While both governments naturally balked at any increases in the military budget, their respective parliaments approved the required appropriations the following November, allowing the operation to go forward as planned.[63]

Of the top military leaders involved, Beck must receive the most credit for the territorial reorganization of the common army. Walter Wagner has claimed a lion's share of the credit for Bylandt, since the committee that ultimately drafted the guidelines operated under war ministry auspices.[64] Franz Hlavac's more balanced assessment awards Bylandt and Beck an equal number of kudos, an assertion supported by the Pitreich family reminiscences.[65] Yet the early discussions reveal that Bylandt did not initially favor the reorganization of the army on a territorial basis and agreed to consider it only after repeated appeals by the general staff, first under Schönfeld, then Beck. True, his change of heart undoubtedly played a crucial role in enacting the reform, for Franz Joseph revealed no inclination to take sides in the early debate. Bylandt, however, did not provide the initial impetus for change. Beck's prestige, already great because of his close relationship with the emperor and enhanced by his success in the Bosnian operation, forced first the careful consideration and ultimately the adoption of a territorial system for the Habsburg common army.

As Bylandt informed the civilian ministers, the reorganization of the army did not achieve the ideal of absolute territorialization. Galician troops continued to make up for manpower deficiencies in the Dalmatian and Innsbruck commands. Cavalry forces recruited from all over the monarchy continued to be rotated to garrison duties in Galicia in order to cover the mobilization of the army against Russia.[66] The war ministry also continued to station troops from within the monarchy in Bosnia-Herzegovina.

Despite Beck's views that civil unrest could never seriously threaten state authority, the military leadership continued the policy of territorial dislocation in regard to the larger cities of the empire. Beck's own dispositions for the invasion of Hungary in 1905 reveal the presence of large numbers of Hungarian troops in Vienna.[67] After 1891, many of the Bosnian forces, considered unreliable in a war with the monarchy's Balkan neighbors,[68] received peacetime assignment to the Budapest and Vienna garrisons. There they aroused the ire of the local populations, which protested the government's use of these "Muslim mercenaries" to counter domestic unrest.[69] When local troops proved incapable of meeting domestic security requirements, the army high command did not hesitate to transfer them elsewhere. For example, in 1895 the war ministry abandoned the territorial principle when the Prager Hausregiment No. 28 proved unreliable in countering the burgeoning nationalist challenges to public order in the Bohemian capital.[70]

Railroads and Strategic Deployment to Galicia

With the conclusion of organizational reform in March 1883, Beck turned to surmounting the next, and probably greatest, impediment to the swift deployment of the army in war: the railroad network. Schooled by Heß in the importance of railroads, Beck had long been a strong advocate of the expansion of the Austro-Hungarian network. As head of the military chancellery, he had virtually dictated military priorities during the construction boom of the late 1860s and early 1870s.[71] On the other hand, the completion of the Carpathian railroads, the major achievement of this period of activity, had not produced a significant increase in the army's deployment speed versus Russia. In 1883 very few of the monarchy's railroads were double-tracked because of the expense involved, particularly in the case of the Carpathian lines, which required costly tunnels.[72] The *Kaiser Ferdinand Nordbahn*, and its eastern extension, the *Carl-Ludwig Bahn*, provided only single-tracked linkages between Galicia and the remainder of Cisleithania. The *Nordbahn* also passed within a few miles of the Russian frontier at several places, arousing grave concerns for its security in the event of war.

Beck had discovered many of these problems in an inspection tour of the Galician railroads immediately following his appointment as chief of the general staff. His early meetings with the Germans had served to heighten his uneasiness over the poor mobilization prospects in Galicia.[73] Moltke had made pointed appeals to Beck to improve mobilization conditions during their September 1882 conversations. Three months later, Beck had to ask Waldersee to suppress the appearance of an article critical of Austro-Hungarian mobilization conditions in the Prussian *Militärische Wochenblatt*.[74] At year's end Austria-Hungary could scarcely be expected to launch an offensive against Russia before the forty-fifth day of mobilization, over three weeks after Germany completed its deployment and a slender five days before Russian forces would reach full strength.[75] The monarchy needed to take swift and decisive action to improve the rail network if it were to retain its value to Germany as an ally.

The reorganization of the army had been, for the most part, an inner-military problem with an inner-military solution. The army leadership had only consulted the civilians only when it appeared that their reorganization proposals would lead to increases in the military budget. The 1867 Compromise, however, had left the responsibility for railroad construction in the hands of Vienna and Budapest, with no central agency to coordinate an empire wide policy. Kuhn had unsuccessfully attempted to usurp these functions for the war ministry in the early 1870s. As chief of the general staff, Beck took the lead in the formation of railroad policy for the entire monarchy. In February 1883,

Franz Joseph, at Beck's urging, convened a civil-military conference to discuss the future of Austro-Hungarian railroad development.[76]

Although the foreign minister and the two minister-presidents were in attendance, Beck clearly dominated the proceedings. He informed the conference of his grave concerns over the current state of the communications to Galicia. Only one single-tracked line connected the province with the western half of the monarchy. While the double-tracked portion of the *Nordbahn* to Oderberg (Stary Bohumín) could handle forty fifty-car trains per day, the single-tracked extension to Auschwitz (Oswiecim) could carry only twenty-six such trains. The single-tracked *Carl-Ludwig Bahn* between Cracow and Lemberg (Lvov) could take only twenty fifty-car trains per day. The two small mountain lines connecting Galicia and Hungary could bear only fifteen thirty-five-car trains. To transport an army corps required sixty trains of that size. Therefore, the shipment of the six Hungarian corps over the Carpathians would require thirty days; this on top of the two weeks needed to bring them up to war strength. The Austro-Hungarian army could, therefore, achieve complete war readiness in Galicia only forty-five days after the issuance of the mobilization order.

Beck proposed the construction of another "transversal" railroad in Galicia as protection against enemy interdiction of the exposed *Nordbahn*. The *Reichsrat* had authorized construction of such a line in 1881 but had done nothing since toward the realization of the project.[77] When built, this line should be double-tracked. Beck also challenged the Hungarian ministers to introduce legislation for the construction of two additional Carpathian lines, connecting Preßburg with the "tranversal" railroad and Hungary to eastern Galicia. These improvements, he argued, would improve mobilization speed by five or six days.

While the responsible ministers of both Austria and Hungary noted problems with Beck's proposals, particularly the double-tracking of the transversal railroad and the construction of the uneconomical "Munkacs-Stryj" line to eastern Galicia, the chief of staff ultimately succeeded in obtaining over the course of the next decade their compliance with his wishes.[78] Within a year, the "transversal" railroad reached completion, and the traffic capacity of the existing Carpathian routes increased through the construction of frequent sidings. Stretches of the *Nordbahn* and *Carl-Ludwig Bahn* were double-tracked, vastly improving their capacities. The important "Munkacs-Stryj" railroad, a project requiring the cooperation between Budapest and Vienna since it crossed the frontier between the two, was finished in 1887.[79] By 1892 there were five railroads leading to Galicia, two of them double-tracked.[80] The Austrian and Hungarian governments also proved cooperative in the acquisition of new rolling stock throughout the decade of the 1880s, including 1,678 locomotives and 22,310 cars of various descriptions, naturally of vital importance for the transport of troops and supplies in wartime.[81]

Beck's intervention in the expansion of the rail network in Galicia did not fundamentally alter the making of railroad policy in Austria-Hungary. In Hungary, the communications ministry retained control over the planning and concessioning of new lines and the submission of the appropriate legislation to parliament. The trade ministry continued to exercise a similar function in Cisleithania, although Vienna made some attempt at the coordination of civilian and military requirements by creating in February 1882 a general directorate for the Austrian state railroads. This body represented the Austrian state railroads as a whole in any negotiations with the military authorities and in case of war would merge with the army's "central directorate for military transport by rail," created by Bylandt in 1878.[82] In 1895, a separate railroad ministry was created and Beck's current deputy, Major General Emil von Guttenberg, placed at its head. These responsible ministries continued to dispatch biannual reports to the military chancellery concerning construction progress. Beck's successors at the head of this agency, however, possessed none of his earlier influence over railroad policy. Beck took this influence with him to the general staff, the military organ in Beck's opinion best equipped to determine army requirements.[83]

The continuous improvement of rail communications leading to Galicia led to repeated revisions in Austro-Hungarian war plans against Russia in the 1880s, a task against which Schönfeld had revolted but which Beck pursued with enthusiasm. Beck did not relish the idea of a war against Russia and had welcomed the conclusion of a written Three Emperors' League agreement in 1881.[84] Russia, however, was the only potential enemy of the monarchy able to destroy it without outside assistance. Within fifty days the Russians could raise a field army of over a million men, numbers which Austria-Hungary could never hope to match.[85]

His conversations with Waldersee and Moltke in 1882 provided Beck, as they had done in virtually all of his other endeavors of the early 1880s, with the basic premises for war plans versus Russia. In particular, the need to assist the Germans in the early offensives dominated his thinking. In a letter to Franz Joseph of 29 April 1883, Beck stressed the need to deploy eight operational corps by the eighteenth day of mobilization.[86] Austria-Hungary could not allow Germany to take on Russia alone in the early stages of a war. If Germany managed to emerge victorious from the early engagements without appreciable Austro-Hungarian support, the monarchy would have no claim to any of the fruits of victory.[87] "Our army," Beck wrote Franz Joseph in 1883, "needs victories too" in order to impart a long-lasting fear on the Russian neighbor.

Beck's first deployment plan against Russia, submitted to the emperor via the war ministry in September 1881, had not foreseen close cooperation with the Germans and had repeated Schönfeld's concern to get the most men to Galicia in the shortest span of time.[88]   Austro-Hungarian forces were divided into three groups: a western army positioned between Cracow and Tarnow to guard the exposed stretch of the *Nordbahn*, a center army deployed near the San River to operate on either bank of the Vistula, and a group stationed at Lemberg (Lvov) to protect the right flank of the main attack farther west.   Uncertain diplomatic relationships with Italy, Romania, and the Balkan states meant that initial Austro-Hungarian deployments in a Russian campaign would be limited to twenty-six common army infantry divisions, all seven divisions of the monarchy's cavalry, and six militia divisions, or a force totaling less than 500,000 men.[89]

The new understandings with the Germans, however, required a more refined approach.   In a November 1882 directive, Beck called for a concentration of the army farther east, to coordinate with the German drive from East Prussia and achieve the planned double envelopment of the Russian army in Congress Poland.[90]   The Austro-Hungarian right flank would brush the Dniestr, while the main attack would proceed northward or northeastward along both banks of the Vistula to link up with advancing German forces in central Poland.

The territorial reorganization of the army, coupled with steady improvements in railroad communications, enabled Beck to achieve his goal of sizable deployments in Galicia by the eighteenth day of mobilization.   On 6 November 1883, he reported to Archduke Albrecht that Austria-Hungary could commence offensive operations with eight corps, over half the army, on mobilization plus twenty.[91]   Given the low density of the rail network in eastern Galicia in the early 1880s, half of these forces would concentrate around Cracow, while the remaining four corps would cover the frontier to Lemberg.[92]   Certain corps, however, could not be made operational in Galicia until the thirty-fourth day of mobilization, and most not until a week later.[93]

Protection of the Galician railroads, therefore, remained a primary concern for Habsburg planners.   In September 1883, the Austro-Hungarian military attaché to St. Petersburg told Beck that the Russians, if so inclined, could move already on the second day of mobilization with forty-two line infantry, eleven reserve infantry, and eighteen cavalry divisions.[94]   While these units would be at their peacetime strengths, they nevertheless could pose a serious threat to meager Austro-Hungarian forces stationed in Galicia during peacetime.[95]   In particular, the 112,000 Russian cavalry troops in Poland caused Beck considerable consternation, for it was feared that these could strike quickly at exposed rail lines and disrupt the Austro-Hungarian deployment in Galicia and force the premature evacuation of the province.

Over the course of the 1880s, increasing numbers of Austro-Hungarian cavalry received peacetime assignments in Galicia to protect vital communications. In 1881 only eight of the monarchy's forty-two cavalry regiments were assigned to Galicia.[96] In 1883 their number was doubled to sixteen regiments and by 1895 doubled again.[97] Mobilization plans, of course, called for the deployment of all remaining cavalry divisions to Galicia as quickly as possible in the event of war.[98]

To safeguard the army's deployment against Russia, Beck also proposed the construction of new, and the drastic extension of existing, fortifications in Galicia. While 4.6 million gulden had been approved for new fortifications in the early 1870s, little construction had occurred, particularly at the important deployment points of Przemysl, Jaroslau, and Lemberg in central and eastern Galicia. Kuhn opposed large expenditures for fortifications as a waste of money, and his successor Koller cut the fortification budget to a bare minimum in the mid-1870s.[99] The occupation of Bosnia-Herzegovina forced the virtual elimination of the fortification budget during fiscal 1877 and 1878.[100]

Although by 1881 expenditure levels had again risen to their meager levels of the Koller years, Beck, confronted with the Russian steamroller in Poland, came to the general staff determined to force the pace of fortification development. He received the whole-hearted support of Bylandt and, perhaps more importantly, Foreign Minister Gustav Kálnoky, who pushed through drastic increases in the fortification budget over substantial resistance from the civilian governments.[101] Between 1882 and 1886 the monarchy spent per annum nearly as much on fortifications as it had for the entire decade of the 1870s.[102] By the mid-1880s, Beck had achieved the completion of central fortifications at Cracow and Przemysl and the buildup of Lemberg and its environs as well as of the San bridgeheads at Jaroslau and Sierdawa.[103] In so doing, he ensured that the army would possess protected staging bases to carry any future conflict into the heart of Russian Poland.

Planning for War in the South and Southwest

While the Galician theater received Beck's greatest attention throughout the 1880s, he remained ever mindful of security threats along the monarchy's other borders. Indeed, Beck had seemingly inherited the grim prospect of a three-front war from his predecessor Schönfeld. Italy had not made appreciable gains for its support of the Berlin settlement which had seen two other non-combatants, Austria-Hungary and Britain, pick up territory at the expense of the decrepit Ottoman empire. While the Italian government attempted to maintain good relations with the monarchy, irredentism remained an integral part of liberal Italy.

The Austrian empire had, of course, posed the greatest obstacle to Italian unification, and many Italians believed that the *Risorgimento* remained unfinished, despite the acquisition of Venetia in 1866. In particular, Italian nationalists coveted the port city of Trieste, the Istrian peninsula including the Habsburg fleet anchorage at Pola, and the Dalmatian coast. They also advanced more dubious claims to the Austrian Tyrol south of the alpine watershed (i.e., the top of Brenner Pass), inhabited largely by Germans. A number of irredentist societies were formed in the 1870s, committed to the completion of the reunification process.[104]

In the winter of 1877-78 Beck drafted his first plan for a war with Italy.[105] He adopted the commonly accepted premise within Habsburg military circles that Italy would never alone risk a conflict with the monarchy over the unredeemed lands but would instead seek its ends through alliance diplomacy. Austria's task would be to isolate Italy, particularly from such dangerous allies as Germany and Russia, and thus neutralize its pent-up aggression. But, even alone, Italy remained a foe worthy of a full mobilization of the Habsburg armed forces. Against an Italian army of twenty divisions (223,440 men), Beck proposed to deploy the entire common army of thirty divisions. The use of militia forces in an Italian campaign, however, was not anticipated. The common army would achieve war readiness along the Italian frontier within twenty-three days.[106] An Austro-Hungarian main body consisting of two armies would advance across the Isonzo on Venice, while a weaker flanking army of three corps would strike southward from the Tyrol. Beck did not anticipate much resistance until the Po River, where he expected the slower mobilizing Italian army to gather.[107]

The following year Schönfeld submitted the general staff's war plan against Italy, which varied significantly in timetable but little in overall strategic execution from Beck's earlier effort.[108] The chief of the general staff, with perhaps a better understanding of the monarchy's capabilities because of his institutional perspective, argued that the army could not cross the Isonzo before the thirtieth day of mobilization owing to deployment difficulties caused by the territorial dislocation of the army. Schönfeld also had a higher regard for Italian capabilities than Beck, believing the Italians capable of deploying along the Brenta in front of Venice by the twentieth day of mobilization. Also unlike Beck, Schönfeld did not rule out the possibility of an Italian offensive against the Isonzo around the twenty-fifth day of mobilization, when they would achieve a limited superiority in numbers over gathering Austro-Hungarian forces. Schönfeld regarded the chance that the Italians would not contest the early river crossings as slight and, unlike Beck, he certainly expected them to make a stand before Venice.

These differing estimations of Italian capabilities did not translate into their logical political conclusions. Beck, who deprecated Italian effectiveness, opposed the idea of a preventive war because of broader international complications. Schönfeld, who saw Italy as a more formidable opponent, argued for its elimination in a preventive strike.

Upon becoming chief of the general staff in 1881, Beck set to work immediately on improving the monarchy's position in the southwest, undertaking several inspection tours of the Italian theater during his first two years in office.[109] His original 1877-78 sketch guided his revision of Schönfeld's plans.[110] The army would need to push across the numerous water barriers in Venetia. To that end, Beck foresaw the deployment of units at their peacetime strength in the theater. Reservists would fill out active ranks only after seizure of the north Italian bridgeheads to the Tagliamento.[111] The central thrust, dictated by the existing railheads in the theater, remained across the Isonzo. Beck envisioned the deployment of twenty-six common army and six militia divisions from Monfalcone on the Adriatic to Tarvis in southern Carinthia.[112] An additional four divisions would guard Tyrol and move to flank the Italian army should it attempt to defend one of the forward river lines.

While initial plans foresaw the use of the entire army against Italy, Beck continued to doubt that international conditions would ever permit Austria-Hungary to wage war against Italy alone.[113] In 1884-85, a purely defensive plan was drawn up which envisioned the deployment of ten divisions against Italy and the remainder of the army in Galicia.[114] Despite the offensive nature of the initial planning, Beck believed that the political conditions would force the monarchy on the defensive and from the start urged the buildup of fortifications along the Italian frontier. In particular, he favored the fortification of the Tyrol and Carinthia against preemptive raids by Italian alpine troops, kept at near war readiness in border areas.[115] Fortifications in the north would also allow for greater troop commitments on the Isonzo front in an offensive war, something which Beck increasingly viewed as necessary in order to flank new Italian works put up over the course of the 1880s facing Tyrol.[116]

Despite Beck's great personal energy regarding an Italian threat, a variety of factors forced the military leadership ultimately to eschew preparations in this theater for greater war readiness in Galicia. The Triple Alliance, concluded in May 1882, ensured at minimum Italian neutrality in the event the monarchy became embroiled in a conflict with Russia.[117] As the latter seemed increasingly probable, preparations in the east led to stagnation in the Italian theater. The extremely friendly and forthcoming attitude of Italian governments under Francesco Crispi during the Bulgarian crisis, including an unsolicited offer of military assistance on the Galician front, did much to allay Habsburg suspicions of its ally. The diplomatic coup of the Italian alliance torpedoed the fortification programs advanced by the general staff and the war ministry, despite their modest and defensive character.[118] After 1887 the general staff abandoned its regular re-examinations of military plans regarding Italy and did not resume them for over a decade.

While the monarchy's security problems in the southwest eased after 1882, they remained ever constant in the south. The Congress of Berlin had given Austria-Hungary control over Bosnia-Herzegovina, the protective hinterland for the Dalmatian coast so fervently desired in the 1870s by the navy and certain sections of the army. The military occupation of these provinces, however, brought little improvement in the monarchy's strategic situation in the Balkans. Possession of Bosnia-Herzegovina meant long borders to defend against neighboring states who regarded the provinces as natural extensions of their own territories. Communications within the provinces were poor in the extreme. No railroads existed prior to the Austrian occupation, and the road network was in such miserable shape as to require extraordinary efforts from both the Habsburg treasury and the troops stationed in the provinces.[119] Hungarian fears of cheap Balkan foodstuffs flooding the Habsburg markets over the railroads ensured that only one narrow-gauge line would connect Sarajevo with the rest of the monarchy.[120] The lack of railroads, in turn, hampered the reinforcement of the meager forces stationed there in times of crisis.

As in the case of Italy, Habsburg planners did not expect that either Serbia or Montenegro could seriously threaten Austria-Hungary alone. A war with either one would occur only within the context of a larger conflict. In a March 1882 memorandum, however, Beck conceded that a Balkan war might, and probably would, precede military complications with Russia.[121]

Serbia, the larger of the monarchy's two southern neighbors, appeared, on paper at least, capable of causing Austria-Hungary greater difficulties in its political role as "the Piedmont of the Balkans." The Serbian "standing army" equaled about one infantry division, and the general staff assessed the capability of the so-called "national army" of eight reserve divisions to that of the monarchy's militia forces. The total strength of the mobilized Serbian field army amounted to 159,600 infantry, 5,050 cavalry, and 272 guns. Much of the infantry was equipped with Peabody & Green breechloaders; the artillery, however, remained mostly armed with older muzzleloading French La Hitte pieces.

Despite its impressive numbers, Beck observed significant weaknesses in both the Serbian army and its defense posture. The relatively small standing army and poor roads ensured an extremely slow mobilization. The Serbian field army would require forty days at minimum to become operational. Austria-Hungary could also cause serious delays in this already leisurely schedule. In the event of hostilities, the monarchy could cut off Serbian purchases of both horses and their harness in Hungary, forcing Belgrade to look for other suppliers. By virtue of its geographical position between Serbia and western Europe, Austria-Hungary could block the shipment of new weapons systems.[122]

The militia quality of the Serbian forces meant that Austro-Hungarian forces would face at most about 75,000 effectives. Habsburg troops would encounter the remaining 75,000 only in mop-up operations after the defeat of the main body. The key to success, as in Beck's other war plans, lay in the swift mobilization and defeat of the Serbian field army. To that end, the chief of staff proposed to wage war against Serbia with only common army forces that could be quickly mobilized and deployed. Three corps, deployed both along the Save-Danube frontier and Serbia's Drina River border with Bosnia-Herzegovina, would trap and destroy Serbian forces gathering in the northern half of the kingdom. If the campaign degenerated into guerilla warfare in southern Serbia, the *Ballhausplatz* should offer territorial inducements to local Albanian chiefs to counter irregular resistance.

Despite its diminutive size, Montenegro, led since 1848 by Prince Nikita Petrovich, worried Austro-Hungarian planners more than the larger Serbian kingdom. Montenegrin military prowess was so respected that the XV Corps at Sarajevo had the sole task of warding off a Montenegrin attack into southern Dalmatia and Herzegovina. Since deployment against Serbia could use the better lines of communication in southern Hungary, peacetime forces in Bosnia-Herzegovina would be needed to protect the remote southern frontier. Austro-Hungarian planners expected that the almost tribal Montenegrin mobilization system could produce an army of between thirty and forty thousand men within a matter of days, and repelling an attack from the south posed substantial problems for the twelve to fifteen thousand peacetime defenders of the provinces.[123] But since the Montenegrin army was almost completely lacking in artillery, the general staff found an effective counterweight to its numbers in the construction of fortifications along the frontier.[124]

The Habsburg diplomatic and military establishments appreciated the hostility within both Serbia and Montenegro caused by the monarchy's occupation of Bosnia-Herzegovina. Over the short term, Russia's inept handling of its Balkan allies during the 1877-78 war with Turkey eased an otherwise threatening political-military situation in the south. Serbia's King Milan, never an enthusiastic supporter of the aggressive policies of his country's radical nationalists, sought reconciliation with Austria-Hungary after Russia's abandonment of Serbian interests at the Congress of Berlin. In June 1881 he pledged to maintain friendly relations with Austria-Hungary in peacetime and neutrality if the monarchy should become involved in a war with another power.[125] Milan also agreed to suppress intrigues on Serbian territory directed against the monarchy and its occupation of Bosnia-Herzegovina. In return, the Habsburg government agreed to support Serbian territorial ambitions in the south and the assumption by Prince Milan of the title of king. Privately, the *Ballhausplatz*, at Franz Joseph's instruction, also gave Milan assurances that the

Habsburgs would ensure the financial security of his family should his dynasty be overthrown by its radical-nationalist opponents.[126]   When in the winter of 1883-84 this possibility loomed large, the foreign office, war ministry and general staff demonstrated their commitment to the Obrenovich dynasty by authorizing the intervention of Austro-Hungarian forces in Serbia should unrest threaten the ouster of the friendly Belgrade regime.[127]

Nikita of Montenegro played a more wily game with the Habsburg leadership. Like Milan, he issued continual and ardent declarations of loyalty to his Habsburg neighbor but openly coveted Austrian-occupied Herzegovina, allowing rumors to circulate in 1881 that he might seize the southern portions of the province.[128]   When confronting a revolt in Bosnia-Herzegovina the following year, a Habsburg ministerial council considered it prudent to pay Nikita personally 100,000 gulden to limit his covert involvement in the uprising.[129]   Three years later, Nikita dared to ask Beck himself to have Franz Joseph appoint him governor-general of Herzegovina, a request that elicited mildly sarcastic comparisons by the Austro-Hungarian chief of the general staff to the old German anecdote about the goat who wanted to be made a gardener.[130]

The Romanian Front

The monarchy's extensive frontier with Romania formed the fourth and final area of concern to Austro-Hungarian military planners. Romania had in the 1870s aligned itself with Russia as a means of obtaining its independence from the Ottoman Porte. Romanian assistance to Russia in the 1877-78 war with Turkey, however, had brought the country mixed gains. True, Russia had sponsored Romanian independence both in the Treaty of San Stefano and at the Congress of Berlin. But it had also forcibly seized the rich Romanian province of Bessarabia, giving Bucharest only the poorer and smaller Dobrudja in exchange. This ill treatment of a loyal ally had led to increasing doubts in Romania about the value of a Russian alliance and to personal inclinations of the Hohenzollern Romanian King Carol to arrive at an understanding with the Dual Alliance.[131]

From the start of his tenure as chief of the general staff, Beck had urged closer relations with Romania. In an 1881 memorandum to the emperor, he argued that an alliance with Bucharest would cut off Russia from Serbia, Montenegro, and Bulgaria.[132]   The 80,000-man Romanian army might also serve to tie down Russian forces in Bessarabia that would otherwise find their way into the Polish theater of operations. In a memorandum two years later, Beck argued that a Romanian alliance would also disarm the considerable domestic chauvinism for a greater Romanian empire, which naturally coveted those areas of eastern Hungary with Romanian populations.[133]

From a strategic standpoint, it was absolutely vital to secure Romania's friendship. The mountainous border with the neighboring kingdom, ordinarily considered a benefit to a defender, belied an essentially indefensible character. In a September 1883 report following an inspection trip, Beck noted that there were no fewer than thirteen mountain passes leading into Siebenbürgen from Romania plus an additional two into the Cisleithanian province of Bukovina.[134] That portions of the native population might offer aid and comfort to a Romanian invader made a peripheral defense a vital need.

Since it would not be possible for Austria-Hungary to commit sizable forces to the theater in the event of a general mobilization, permanent fortifications capable of withstanding several weeks of siege would have to be constructed to block a Romanian-Russian invasion of Siebenbürgen. Beck predicted that the Romanian army, while currently not a threat at five divisions, would increasingly become a potent force under a new military law passed the previous year.[135] The war ministry, however, resisted Beck's proposals, favoring instead the deployment of two common army divisions to secure the province. Bylandt left unstated his greater probable concern over the cost of such an ambitious fortification program.[136]

Fortunately for Beck, the importance of Romania was not lost on the Habsburg foreign office, which took general staff concerns seriously and recognized the opportunity offered by Russia's inept diplomacy of the late 1870s to conclude an alliance with Bucharest. Negotiations undertaken following Beck's inspection trip to Siebenbürgen in August 1883, which Glaise-Horstenau argues was made to scare the Romanians into an understanding, quickly produced their desired result. On 30 October of the same year, King Carol concluded a highly secret defensive alliance with Austria-Hungary against Russia with provisions for talks over eventual military cooperation.[137] One drawback of the agreement was Carol's insistence that the treaty not be ratified by parliament, leaving open to doubt the ability of the king and his ministers to enforce compliance with its provisions in a crisis situation.[138] The gradual evaporation of anti-Russian feeling in Romania over subsequent decades and the increasing irredentism against Austria-Hungary made the alliance a dead letter by 1914.[139]

While it had accommodated Beck's wishes in regard to Romania, the *Ballhausplatz* proved less enthusiastic about negotiating an alliance with Turkey, considered by the general staff an essential element of the monarchy's defensive posture in the Balkans. Beck had indicated to Waldersee at Strobl the desirability of Turkey as an ally, if only to hold the potentially hostile states of Serbia, Montenegro, and Bulgaria in check during a wider conflict involving Russia. The chief of the general staff reiterated these desires and concerns in a memorandum to the war ministry written sometime in late 1882 or early 1883.[140] Beck believed that the Ottoman empire could commit a quarter of a million men to the Balkan theater, more than enough to ensure the neutrality of the monarchy's potential enemies in the region. Turkish forces in Asia would also force Russia to deploy troops to defend the Caucasus that might otherwise be committed to the main theater in Poland. Foreign Minister Kálnoky, normally receptive to military viewpoints, did not see the value of an alliance with the Porte, believing that the liabilities entailed by any written obligation to that disintegrating state would far outweigh temporary military advantages.[141] Underlying foreign office reservations was the fear that the Turks might demand a return of Bosnia-Herzegovina.

Impact of the International Situation on the Army

Despite the success of Austro-Hungarian diplomacy in neutralizing many of the monarchy's potential foes, Beck's analysis of the strategic situation along the secondary fronts in Italy, the Balkans, and Siebenbürgen soon led him to realize the need for far-reaching reform of the entire Habsburg military system. Territorialization and improvements in railroad infrastructure had begun to improve the mobilization speed of the common army by the mid-1880s. The dangers confronting the monarchy from all sides threatened to stretch these first-line forces to the breaking point. The protective diplomatic masonry erected by the *Ballhausplatz* showed signs of instability from the moment the first bricks were laid in the early 1880s. Tiny fissures in the Italian, Serbian, and Romanian portions of the barrier could cause the diplomatic wall to come tumbling down at any moment under the weight of domestic, anti-Habsburg pressure groups. If this occurred, the monarchy would face disaster in a multifront war. A way had to be found to mobilize more of the monarchy's military manpower by expanding terms of service in the armed forces. The monarchy needed to harness the abilities of those men who completed their military service in the common army, *Landwehr*, or *Honvéd* through the creation of home defense forces, or *Landsturm*. The responsibility for guarding the secondary fronts would fall to these units, allowing the deployment of greater forces in threatened areas.[142]

The Austrian and Hungarian militias, currently filling the home defense role, would have to be transformed into organizations of first-line quality, capable of taking their place alongside the common army in the offensives against Russia. This would take considerable effort in overcoming both senior army prejudices against the state militias, particularly the *Honvéd*, and the disinclination of the civilians, especially in Austria, to agree to what amounted to back-door increases in military expenditures. The rise in tensions caused by renewed diplomatic conflict with Russia in the Balkans after 1885, however, would make this an absolute necessity if the monarchy were to survive the next European war.

Chapter 6

The Bulgarian Crisis:
Austria-Hungary Prepares for War

On 13 March 1884, Beck urged the war ministry to allow the general staff to make statistical studies of west Russia, including one of the quartering conditions there and in the Habsburg territories of Galicia and Bukovina.[1] The existing survey, undertaken by Schönfeld in 1877, provided general staff analysts mere administrative and population overviews of twenty-three Russian districts bordering the monarchy. Austro-Hungarian planners needed accurate information on the border areas to plan countermoves to an expected Russian offensive in the early stages of any future conflict. Any invasion would seriously disrupt the deployment of the army in Galicia. In September Beck submitted an additional request for statistical studies for Moravia, Silesia, and Hungary.[2] Within a month, the war ministry could announce their completion. By year's end, only those studies pertaining to the Volhynia, Podolia, and Kiev districts opposite the monarchy's eastern borders remained unfinished.[3] The *Ballhausplatz*, to whose consular officials the task of information gathering would fall, promised to pursue the matter with energy.

On the surface, Beck's fears concerning Russia appeared unfounded. Only three years before, the governments of Austria-Hungary, Germany, and Russia had renegotiated the Three Emperors' League. Indeed, the renewal, unlike the original agreement of the previous decade, had taken written form and appeared to usher in a new era of cooperation between St. Petersburg and Vienna. Russia had undertaken both to recognize a future Austro-Hungarian annexation of Bosnia-Herzegovina and restrain its puppet Bulgaria from a further destabilization of the Turkish Balkans.[4] Alexander III's new foreign minister, Nikolai Giers, appeared favorably disposed toward Austria-Hungary and less inclined to follow the rash councils of the PanSlavists.[5] In September 1884 the German, Austrian, and Russian sovereigns met at the tsar's retreat at Skiernewice, a meeting that highlighted the mood of rejuvenated amity among the three eastern courts of Europe.

For a time it appeared as if, with the Three Emperors' League, the foreign office had neutralized the primary threat to Habsburg security as effectively as it had dealt with the secondary ones by way of the Triple, Romanian, and Serbian alliance treaties. While the Three Emperors' League attempted to address the concerns of the signatories in the Balkans, it could not overcome a fundamental Austro-Russian distrust of each other's interests and activities in this area. In the early 1880s, St. Petersburg viewed Habsburg railroad enterprises in Serbia and Bulgaria with suspicion, while Vienna feared a renewed Russian drive on Constantinople and the Straits.

The Bulgarian Crisis

The monarchical solidarity and goodwill created by the Three Emperors' League might have continued to shield the monarchy from its greatest potential enemy for some time. But domestic and foreign political turmoil in Bulgaria soon transformed the underlying skepticism of the Austro-Russian relationship into open hostility.[6] Bulgaria, both under the Berlin Treaty and the Three Emperors' League renewal, fell within the Russian sphere of influence. Yet the Russian government appeared unable to control the country's German prince, Alexander von Battenberg. Battenberg showed an interest in the railroad projects of the Austrian Baron Hirsch, a disinclination toward similar Russian enterprises, and a dislike toward many of the military men sent by the tsar to rule Bulgaria in the prince's name. The ministries he appointed, both liberal and conservative, had also proven unwilling to consent to the railroad ventures put forward by St. Petersburg. In September 1883 Prince Alexander dismayed the Russians by removing Generals N.K. Kaulbars and L.N. Sobelev as ministers of war and interior respectively; both generals had disrupted Bulgarian parliamentary life over the Russian railroad issue without benefit to either Bulgaria or their overlord Tsar Alexander III. Then in 1884, Battenberg infuriated St. Petersburg still further by courting Princess Victoria of Prussia, dismissing Russian wishes that he marry an Orthodox Christian princess. Only the objections of Bismarck and Kaiser Wilhelm I to a Bulgarian-Prussian union forced Battenberg to abandon his marital ambitions in March 1885.

The break between Prince Alexander and his Russian overlords came six months later with the Bulgarian seizure of Eastern Rumelia, the southern portion of the original San Stefano Bulgaria which the Congress of Berlin had returned to Turkish control. St. Petersburg warned Alexander against the move; indeed the tsar had recalled all Russian officers serving in the Bulgarian army to punctuate his displeasure. While this deprived the Bulgarian armed forces of its officer corps above the rank of captain, the tsar's action did not deter Battenberg. Within a few days of the overthrow of the Turkish administration by a domestic insurgency, he arrived in Rumelia to declare its union with Bulgaria.

The lack of an immediate Turkish military response offered hope for a peaceful settlement of the Rumelian question and containment of the crisis, especially given Russia's new opposition--born of its troubles in controlling Battenberg--to any enlargement of the current Bulgarian state. Europe, however, had not reckoned with inner-Balkan rivalries. King Milan of Serbia, fearing the emergence of a powerful Slavic rival and responding to the popular outcry in Serbia against the Bulgarian action, declared war on 13 November 1885. Within a week, a surprise Bulgarian victory drew Austria-Hungary into the crisis, for Vienna could not allow the humiliation of its Serbian client. On 28 November the Austrian minister to Serbia demanded that Prince Alexander grant an immediate armistice or face Habsburg military action. Alexander, faced with the prospect of a widening war, agreed to peace.

This episode completely eroded the improved relations between Austria-Hungary and Russia since 1881. St. Petersburg suspected Habsburg machinations in Battenberg's behavior and recoiled at the prospect of an Austro-Hungarian military intervention in the Balkans, even if directed against Bulgaria. The Russian government now worked to settle accounts, first with Bulgaria, then with the Habsburg monarchy. It allowed the unification of Eastern Rumelia and Bulgaria to stand, albeit only under the rubric of a "personal union" under the Prince of Bulgaria--the reference to the title and not its current incumbent an intentional effort of Russian diplomacy. The Russian government then plotted and successfully executed the overthrow of Prince Alexander in August 1886. Battenberg's appearance in Habsburg Galicia following his ouster probably did nothing to allay Russian suspicions of Vienna's collaboration with the prince. After attempts by Stefan Stambulov, the head of the Bulgarian regency council, to orchestrate Alexander's return to the throne, Tsar Alexander III ordered a suspension of relations with Bulgaria and a withdrawal of all diplomatic and consular personnel on 17 November. A threat of armed intervention for the purpose of reorganizing Bulgarian affairs clearly accompanied this Russian *démarche*.

Austria-Hungary Prepares for Confrontation

Within the monarchy, the Hungarians loudly called for war if Russia invaded Bulgaria. Minister-President Kálmán Tisza denounced any Russian intervention as illegal, declaring that no power had the right to establish protectorates on Turkish territory. Kálnoky, lacking Tisza's personal animosity toward Russia, nonetheless echoed the Hungarian premier's sentiments in declarations before the Delegations in November 1886. The foreign minister even took Hungarian assertions a step further by stating the inadmissibility of any sort of Russian control in a reorganized Bulgaria that might infringe upon its autonomy.[7]

Working behind the scenes to give substance to these statements was Friedrich Beck. While he had been able to report to the emperor in April 1886 that an imposing force of seven cavalry and twenty-six infantry divisions could advance into Russian Poland on the twentieth day of mobilization, Beck realized that much work still needed to be done before the monarchy could wage war against Russia with any confidence.[8] He spent 1886 attempting to maximize existing military strength in Galicia. He shifted units slated for wartime deployment in the Bohemian fortresses to the field army in Galicia, arguing that existing works at Prague, Olmütz, Josefstadt, and Theresienstadt did not lie along the probable enemy lines of advance even in the unlikely event of an Austro-German war.[9]

Beck, however, realized that the foreign political situation placed new demands on war planning. Prior to 1886, deployment plans presupposed a full mobilization of the armed forces against one or more of the monarchy's enemies. At the end of 1886, he began to develop a series of measures preparatory to a full-scale mobilization, steps that would prepare the army for war without signaling its inevitability with a general call-up of forces.

Beck presented his proposals to a military conference on 21 December 1886.[10] The Galician corps commands had repeated the now familiar concern: that Russia might launch a preventive strike with troops immediately at hand in Congress Poland to disrupt a deployment of the Austro-Hungarian army.[11] Peacetime forces in Galicia would suffice to hold only a few key points. A Russian invasion, in addition to possibly cutting vital communication lines, would also disrupt the mobilization of reservists and *Landwehr* troops in the border areas. The advancing Russians would capture supplies and transport matériel intended for these forces. The army could not wait until a state of war existed before attending to these matters.

To facilitate the swift execution of a mobilization order, Beck prepared three lists of preparatory measures which the military council approved. The first list, the so-called "Group A" measures, contained steps such as the completion of several strategic railroads, including the vital Munkacs-Stryj line, the assembly at central points of locomotives and other rolling stock, an acceleration of their repair,[12] and the lighting of the larger stations. In short, the railroad authorities needed to start readying their lines for the demands of troop transport.

Since Montenegro was expected to side with Russia in the coming conflict, the completion of the landward fortifications of Cattaro and Castelnuovo in southern Dalmatia was absolutely necessary if the scanty forces there were to defend them successfully.[13]   All furloughed soldiers and untrained recruits of the current class needed to be called to the colors immediately.

Beck also wanted an increase in intelligence-gathering activity, particularly on the part of Austro-Hungarian consulates in the areas of the Russian empire bordering the monarchy. He expressed his great dissatisfaction with the current exchange of intelligence with the foreign office and that he was receiving two-month-old reports from the *Ballhausplatz*. To counter Russian information-gathering activities, Beck advocated an increase in gendarmerie forces in Galicia. The gendarmes, he noted, could also assist the military authorities in the requisitioning of vehicles for military transport.

The emperor, seconded by the remaining members of the military conference, approved all of Beck's "Group A" measures. Their cost, estimated at 27.5 million gulden, would be covered through borrowing from common funds (the so-called *Reichs-Activen*) in order to avoid a premature summoning of the Delegations which normally would have to approve such expenditures. Legislative action would significantly increase international tensions and the likelihood of war. All agreed that both civilian cabinets should be informed of these measures. The military conference also agreed that the measures of a more serious nature outlined in Beck's "Group B" and "Group C," including troop transfers to Galicia and call-ups in Bosnia-Herzegovina, would await a further deterioration of the diplomatic situation.

In the early months of 1887, the civilians, however, adopted a less than forthcoming attitude toward these military requirements. Austrian Finance Minister Julian Dunajewski torpedoed the military plan to use common funds for immediate preparations, despite the precedent of 1870 cited by Kállay.[14] While the Delegations approved the 28 million gulden credit, both cabinets resisted war ministry attempts to tap these financial resources.[15] Both Tisza and Dunajewski pressed for concrete reasons for the use of the money, rejecting the original excuse of uncertain international conditions offered the Delegations. Even Gustav Kálnoky, who as foreign minister had sponsored the credit bill along with the war minister, appeared no longer convinced that Russia meant to attack Austria-Hungary. In a letter to the Austro-Hungarian ambassador in Rome, he wrote that relations with Russia were good enough that Alexander III would inform Austria-Hungary if he were about to order military action against Bulgaria. For the moment, Kálnoky did not fear an imminent Russian attack.[16]

Militia (*Landwehr/Honvéd*) and Home Guard (*Landsturm*) Reform

While Beck's concrete preparations foundered on the rock of civilian resistance, the chief of the general staff achieved greater success in areas more fundamental in importance to long-term Habsburg security. In June 1886 both parliaments passed a *Landsturm* law with surprising speed and provided the monarchy with the legal basis for the organization of home defense forces. Beck had long favored the creation of *Landsturm* formations to take over the vital task of home defense. His investigations of the secondary fronts in Italy and Siebenbürgen early in his tenure as chief of the general staff had convinced him of their immediate necessity.

The military laws of 1868 had provided for the limited creation of home defense forces. Cisleithania possessed the so-called *Landesschützen* of Vorarlberg and the Tyrol, units with traditions dating back to the 1809 war of liberation against Napoleon. The organization and military obligation of these troops, however, remained informal and without legal foundation in the 1868 law. The Hungarian military law foresaw the creation of *Landsturm* units in wartime. Service in these formations, however, remained voluntary and with no provisions made in peacetime for their rapid mobilization in times of crisis.[17]

As in the case of army reorganization, Beck stood largely alone in his advocacy of the *Landsturm*. Albrecht was not enthusiastic about the prospect of handing out weapons to the government's social and nationalist enemies. At best, the Austrian government could introduce legislation formalizing a home defense obligation in the Alpine lands, areas unquestionably loyal to the Habsburg house.[18] The establishment of home defense forces in Hungary, however, was unacceptable to the archduke, who feared their use in renewed Hungarian attempts to split the empire.[19]

When the inner-military debate opened on the question in January 1884, still more opponents challenged Beck's calls for home defense forces.[20] Bylandt favored the organization of a small *Landsturm* which could be trained to a higher military standard than a *levée en masse*. Like Albrecht, the war minister distrusted certain national groups of the monarchy, citing a report by Schönfeld, now commander of the XII Corps in Siebenbürgen, which questioned the reliability of the Hungarian Székler population in defending the border with Romania. The creation of a Hungarian *Landsturm*, Bylandt argued, would also give renewed strength to Magyar efforts toward independence. If the government established large-scale home defense forces in peacetime, it risked arming elements hostile to the current constitution of the state.

Although Franz Joseph himself appeared initially convinced by these contrary arguments, Beck managed to win him over to a sweeping *Landsturm* reform. Beck's victory, like that in so many other military questions, owed much to his interpersonal skills and ability to convince skeptics of the correctness of his views. Beck was also indebted to a willingness on the part of the Austrian and Hungarian governments to introduce the necessary legislation to their respective parliaments. In a November 1884 crown council, Hungarian Defense Minister Baron Géza Féjerváry announced Hungary's agreement to an obligatory *Landsturm* for both halves of the monarchy that would create a force pool of between 400,000 and 450,000 men.[21] Shortly thereafter, Féjerváry's Austrian counterpart, Zeno von Welsershaimb, obtained an even more remarkable endorsement by a government never enthusiastic about even its *Landwehr* forces and even less so about the creation of new home defense formations.[22]

The *Landsturm* laws of 1886 laid the legislative groundwork for the mobilization of large segments of Habsburg society in the event of war.[23] All men between the ages of nineteen and forty-two not currently serving in the common army, the *Kriegsmarine*, or the two militias were subject to call-up during a general mobilization. A major portion of this manpower pool included those men who had completed military service in the army or militia; they would form between two and three hundred *Landsturm* battalions.[24] Among their tasks would be guarding important fortified works, including those protecting vital mobilization railroads in Galicia, and blocking invasion routes from Italy and Romania. They would free common army and militia forces from the performance of these duties, thus increasing the strength of the Habsburg field army.

A second group, made up of the younger recruits, would undergo intensive military training during the first weeks of war before being posted as replacements to common army and militia units.[25] The 1868 law had provided for an *Ersatzreserve* of 80,000 men, 10% of the statutory ceiling of common army and *Kriegsmarine* strength in wartime. Beck, however, realized that this would not begin to cover the expected losses during even the initial stages of a general European conflict.[26] The 1886 *Landsturm* law, therefore, also provided an essential and urgently necessary enhancement of the army's capability to replace the heavy casualties of modern warfare.

While both governments had acted quickly to pass the necessary *Landsturm* legislation, they proved less cooperative in appropriating money to equip the new units. Minister-President Kálman Tisza announced to a January 1887 ministerial council that no funds had been allocated in 1887 for the purchase of uniforms and equipment for the newly sanctioned *Landsturm* battalions.[27] Only 700,000 gulden out of a total requirement of 5.6 million to outfit the Hungarian *Landsturm* found a place in the 1888 budget. Both the Austrian and Hungarian finance ministers warned that an extraordinary funding request would have such an impact on money markets that the government might face resistance should it need to approach them later for war credits.

Civilian unwillingness to finance the creation of new *Landsturm* formations continued throughout 1887 and prevented their effective organization during the war scare with Russia. A shortage of retired officers fit for service in the *Landsturm* also hampered efforts to field these units.[28] Whereas *Landsturm* units had been formed in Galicia, neighboring Bukovina still lacked territorial forces by the spring of 1889.[29] Indifferently armed in the initial stages with a combination of the new Mannlicher repeaters and the older Werndl and Wänzl single-shot breechloaders, the home defense troops over the course of the 1890s gradually received the same armaments as their common army and militia counterparts. Material and organizational deficiencies were also soon corrected. By 1900, Austria-Hungary possessed both home defense forces to protect exposed frontiers and a replacement pool that at least approached the requirements of modern warfare.

Only with the 1890s would Beck's ambition that the *Landwehr/Honvéd* assume front-line duties alongside the common army be fulfilled. Both militias had suffered from neglect and underfunding in their first fifteen years of existence.[30] Since the army perceived them as home defense forces, it paid little attention to developing their full potential, including rapid mobilization in wartime. In the 1870s, budgetary disputes between the defense ministries and the war ministry over who would bear wartime armament and mobilization costs had marred relations and prevented serious cooperation.[31] Civilian desires to limit expenditures severely restricted the peacetime establishments of both militias. The peacetime strength of even the Hungarian *Honvéd*, which enjoyed much greater popular and governmental support than its Austrian counterpart, never exceeded 4500 infantry and 2,000 cavalry prior to 1890.[32] True, both militias inducted more than 10,000 men annually, but these recruits never remained with the colors longer than their eight-week training required.[33] Nor did the *Landwehr* and *Honvéd* possess nearly enough officers to staff their wartime formations.[34]

Consequently army leaders had written off the militias as effective fighting forces, particularly in the early stages of a conflict. In November 1875 Archduke Albrecht had declared that the militias would not be ready for action for three months after the initial mobilization order and, therefore, did not need to be incorporated in the common army order of battle then being drawn up.[35] Not that Albrecht and many like-minded officers initially lamented this lack of readiness. They still greatly disliked the idea of a *Honvéd* and feared both its further development into a true national army and its potential use against the common army in the kingdom's ongoing efforts to achieve greater independence from Vienna. The militias were excluded from common army maneuvers, their officers from officially attending the *Kriegsschule*.[36]

As chief of the general staff, Beck became a constant champion of the monarchy's militia forces. Immediate improvements in their war readiness, however, remained moderate. During the 1880s, he obtained permission for the militia to participate in army maneuvers from a skeptical emperor and dubious colleagues. While officer shortages, the subject of a frenzied military conference in early 1883, continued to plague both *Landwehr* and *Honvéd*, the situation improved gradually after 1885 through transfers from the common army.[37] By 1887, the Austrian defense ministry could assure the war ministry that the *Landwehr* could mobilize all of its infantry by the tenth day of mobilization and its cavalry within three and a half weeks.[38] The *Honvéd* ministry boasted an equal or greater readiness for the Hungarian militia. Both the Austrian and Hungarian militias, however, still suffered from inadequate training since both governments continued to furlough most recruits following the eight-week training period. This situation would improve only after 1890, when Beck and the war ministry took increased interest in militia development as a surrogate for common army improvements, made impossible by parliamentary turmoil in Austria and political sensitivities in Hungary.

Improvements in Overall Military Readiness

Beck did not ignore the common army in his drive to improve the monarchy's war readiness in the face of an impending war with Russia. To hasten its mobilization, Beck continued to press for the extension of the Austro-Hungarian rail network to Galicia. In 1887, the vital Munkacs-Stryj railroad, linking remote eastern regions of that province to the interior of the monarchy, reached completion.

In order to facilitate the deployment of the army still further, Beck began lobbying in February 1883 for the passage of a war requirements act (*Kriegsleistungsgesetz*) to allow the army to localize the collection of needed raw materials and the purchase of horses. During mobilization, the latter operation in particular absorbed vast amounts of time and energy during mobilization. The horse conscription law (*Pferdestellungsgesetz*), passed in 1876, forced stud farmers to sell their horses to the government on demand for fair compensation. In the past, the government obtained most of its horses from the great farms of the Pannonian Basin. A major stumbling block to the efficient procurement of their own horses by the individual corps remained the unequal distribution of animals throughout the monarchy. The mountainous regions of Cisleithania did not possess enough horses to meet the needs of troops stationed locally. Some 8,000 animals still had to be shipped from Hungary during mobilization.[39] This transport of animals from central Hungary to the various corps areas where they were needed continued to slow mobilization. As the abortive mobilization of 1870 proved, strict reliance on Hungarian suppliers also increased Budapest's leverage in a crisis situation. In 1883, Beck informed a military conference that current mobilization planning took into account the long-distance transport of 26,000 horses between adjacent corps areas and another 50,000 within the corps areas themselves.[40] At the same conference Deputy War Minister Franz Vlasits lamented the fact that horse procurement for the militias was not handled as a common matter, but rather independently by the two defense ministries.

The civilians, however, welcomed Beck's burden-sharing proposals. Budapest and Vienna reached an agreement in principle by the end of 1883 over the portion of the war requirements bill pertaining to horses. Each corps would make an effort to obtain its horses within its own area. If the number of local animals was insufficient, then purchasing agents could go to neighboring corps areas that had surpluses. Harder to achieve was an understanding over the army's appropriation of civilian conveyances during mobilization. The war ministry estimated that the military would need to requisition between ninety and one hundred thousand vehicles.[41]   In early 1887, with a war with Russia looming on the horizon, the Austrian and Hungarian Delegations approved a *Kriegsleistungsgesetz* that allowed for almost unrestricted acquisition by the government of vehicles and horses.[42]   The final version of the law even contained provision for the drafting of civilian personnel under the age of fifty as laborers and teamsters for the army.

The pressures of growing international crises in the late 1880s saw a civilian willingness to shoulder increasing military burdens.   Under joint pressure from the war ministry and general staff, the parliaments approved expenditures for the rearmament of the army with the newest piece of small arms technology, the repeating rifle. By the mid-1880s all the major armies of Europe had either tested or actually commenced use of repeaters in first-line units. The Austro-Hungarian war ministry itself had already begun conducting trials of Kropatchek repeaters in 1882 and extended testing to other models over the following three years.[43]   In March 1885, Franz Joseph ordered the purchase of 5,500 repeating rifles from the Werndl's Steyr works designed by the *Nordbahn* engineer Ferdinand Mannlicher.   Despite some early problems involving the bolt action of the piece, a military commission, made up of several corps and divisional commanders and presided over by Bylandt and Beck, approved the Mannlicher design for the entire common army in October 1886.[44] Werndl's large production capabilities undoubtedly weighed heavily in the decision to adopt the Mannlicher repeater. In order to use existing munitions stocks, the commission recommended the retention by the new pieces of the 11mm caliber of the Werndl single-shooter currently used by the army. On 27 January 1887 Franz Joseph ordered the common army to adopt the 11mm Mannlicher as the standard infantry weapon.[45]

With the imperial order the Steyr works went into full production. By the end of 1887, Werndl had delivered over 50,000 pieces and promised to manufacture an additional 100,000 by spring.[46]   Beck, however, almost immediately began to have second thoughts on the caliber issue. Already in 1886 he had alerted the war ministry to the desirability of shifting to a smaller caliber infantry weapon.[47]   Improvements in gunpowder had made smaller caliber weapons as accurate as their larger counterparts. Since smaller caliber munitions naturally weighed less, soldiers could carry more rounds.[48] On 10 March 1888, Franz Joseph ordered a change from the 11mm to the 8mm Mannlicher.[49] The 94,000 11mm pieces already manufactured were to be converted to the new standard caliber. By April 1890 all of the infantry and Jäger troops were equipped with the new repeaters, a remarkable achievement when compared with the production and procurement woes of the 1870s.[50]

Both the Austrian and Hungarian governments, while cautious on the issue of actual war credits in early 1887, demonstrated extreme forbearance on the rearmament issue and particularly toward the military's expensive switch to the 8mm. Between 1887 and 1890, they appropriated over 38 million gulden for the new repeating rifles.[51] At the same time they also financed a great expansion of the Austro-Hungarian railroad network and approved increased funding for the arming and extension of the monarchy's fortification system.[52]

The Unreliable German Ally

Fear of war with Russia relaxed the otherwise tight civilian purse strings. As the year 1887 opened, civilians and military men alike were truly alarmed by the magnitude of the international crisis confronting them. The major cause for concern centered on the uncertain attitude of the German ally. Would the Germans honor their alliance with the monarchy in the event of a war with Russia? In early 1887, indications were that they would not. In the summer of 1886, shortly before Alexander Battenberg's overthrow, Archduke Albrecht met with the Prussian *Generalquartiermeister* Alfred von Waldersee at Schloß Weissenstein in Bohemia.[53] The archduke's alarm at the situation in Bulgaria and his fears of a Russian intervention were shrugged off by the talkative Prussian. Russia, Waldersee explained, did not contemplate war in the near future, despite the Pan-Slavist leanings of the Russian general staff, troop increases in Congress Poland, and recent improvements in Russia's east-west rail network.[54] That the Russians had made relatively few improvements along the Bug and Narew rivers, the principal staging areas during mobilization, provided ample evidence of their basic passivity.

Waldersee's nervous verbosity, however, revealed to the Austrian political-military leadership the underlying reasons for German eagerness to discount the Russian danger. The Prussian *Generalquartiermeister* seemed to Albrecht preoccupied by a possible French war.[55] He dwelt on the construction of new fortifications along the border with Germany at Toul, Epinal, and Nancy. In a war with Germany, France would commit the vast majority of its army along this fortified frontier, since the rough terrain in the south would allow for the deployment of relatively few forces to guard against an Italian invasion.

French hatred for Germany, of course, had by 1887 long been an assumed element of European international politics. Although Waldersee would not directly admit it to Albrecht, what had suddenly reawakened German fears of French *revanche* was the appointment of General Georges Boulanger as French minister of war in early 1886. Boulanger had alarmed Berlin with a flurry of bellicose speechmaking and his forward defense policies in eastern France.[56] These actions, together with a sincere republicanism and a concern for the lot of the common soldier, had made him the darling of the nation by summer. A military figure much of the Gyulai stamp, Boulanger made an impressive parade-ground general and seemed to his peacetime audiences the embodiment of the Gallic martial spirit. His popularity in France reached cult proportions, with a variety of Boulanger souvenirs from ties to pipes selling in Parisian markets and songs extolling his virtue as "*Général Revanche*" on the lips of enthusiastic customers.[57]

The diversion of German attentions westward and the lackadaisical attitude of the Prussian general staff toward a war in the near future considerably worried the Habsburg civil-military leadership as 1886 drew to a close. In mid-December, Waldersee reiterated his convictions of Russia's fundamental passivity to the Austro-Hungarian Military Attaché Karl Steininger in mid-December.[58] More alarming to Austrian ears, however, were his hints that Germany would not honor the Strobl-Breslau understandings concerning its troop commitments in the east. Waldersee could offer only vague assurances that Germany would conduct "powerful offensives" on the Russian front but would not state the exact strength of the forces it planned to deploy there.

Several months of repeated badgering by Steininger finally produced a German answer to this vital question. Germany, Waldersee told the Austro-Hungarian military attaché, would deploy at least 200,000 men in the east in the event of war. While this still represented an impressive military effort, it was only half the level of the Strobl commitments and a quarter of the Austro-Hungarian common army.[59] This revelation altered the strategic balance of forces in the east, something which Archduke Albrecht was quick to point out in a situation report to the foreign office.[60] Russia could deploy sixty-two infantry divisions along its western frontier. To oppose them, the Dual Alliance could now muster only forty-eight infantry divisions, thirty-six of which were Austro-Hungarian. Albrecht lamented the one-sidedness of the Austro-German relationship and stridently argued that Germany was *obligated* to commit at least eighteen infantry divisions to offensive operations by the third week of mobilization. If allied, but untrustworthy, Italy used the opportunity of an Austro-Russian war to attack the monarchy, German liabilities on the eastern front would increase to thirty divisions to make up for reductions in Austro-

Hungarian forces. If Germany could not meet these responsibilities, Albrecht wrote Foreign Minister Gustav Kálnoky, Austria-Hungary should be released from all obligations of the alliance.

These haughty words, however, did not correspond to the political-military realities of early 1887. In October 1879, when Bismarck concluded the Dual Alliance with Andrássy, Germany had been the object of Russian wrath as a result of its thankless mediating role at the Congress of Berlin. In 1887, St. Petersburg glowered on the Habsburg empire, which had seemingly aided and abetted Battenberg's insubordination in Bulgaria. To weather this new international storm, Austria-Hungary now clearly needed Germany more than Germany needed Austria-Hungary. As Albrecht himself admitted in another memorandum of March 1887, the monarchy possessed few other friends in Europe capable of rendering meaningful assistance in a war against Russia.[61] Even nominal allies such as Italy, Romania, and Serbia were untrustworthy and ineffectual. Germany remained the monarchy's only hope in combating the Russian colossus.

These realities moderated the Austro-Hungarian response to steady Russian preparations in Congress Poland. Beck was particularly anxious to avoid anything that would offer Russia a pretext for war. He concentrated his efforts on non-provocative military preparations: the gradual purchase of munitions wagons, shoes, canned foods, coats, and cartridge boxes for the new repeating rifles.[62] Completion of the Galician fortresses and railroads and a ban on the sale of horses formed the most forward portions of the Austro-Hungarian readiness program in the spring and summer of 1887.[63] Beck, however, shied away from ordering increases in standing forces in Galicia. Indeed, Beck hastened to reassure the Russians that the general staff did not contemplate large troop transfers to the eastern frontiers.[64] In June a military commission approved the introduction of four-year active service for cavalry troops as an indirect means of increasing force levels in Galicia, where most of them were stationed. Arrangements for the execution of this policy decision, however, were left to the indefinite future.[65]

These limited measures, designed to please a peace-loving Berlin and placate a hostile Russia, failed to do either. Relations with St. Petersburg deteriorated rapidly after the crowning of Ferdinand of Saxe-Coburg as Prince of Bulgaria on 14 August 1887. From the Russian perspective, the election of another German prince to the Bulgarian throne was bad enough. What made it infinitely worse was Ferdinand's status as an active Habsburg army officer and the son of an Austrian general. Already suspicious of Austro-Hungarian motives in Bulgaria, the selection of Ferdinand by the Bulgarian diet appeared proof of Habsburg treachery to an enraged Russian government. Russia responded by ordering more troops to Congress Poland. In November an

agitated Tsar Alexander III threatened a frightened Prince Bismarck that the
deteriorating Austro-Russian relationship might yet lead to a disastrous war.[66]

These warnings, in turn, threw the Germans into a panic over Austro-
Hungarian preparations. On 30 November 1887, the Austro-Hungarian Military
Attaché Baron Karl Steininger reported the first of the many confused signals
that would emanate from Berlin over the next several months.[67] The Prussian
foreign office, for example, wanted the Habsburg government to raise troop
strengths in Galicia. *Generalquartiermeister* Waldersee, speaking for the
Prussian general staff, wanted the Austrians to wait. The tsar's visit, he told
Steininger, had offered hope that Russia would not opt for war. In any event,
Waldersee said, Russia would not dare start a campaign in the middle of winter.
On the other hand Waldersee's chief, Helmut von Moltke, favored an immediate
preemptive Austro-German strike before the Russians completed their
preparations.[68]

Steininger's report prompted a civil-military conference to consider
general staff proposals to increase military preparedness in Galicia.[69] Foreign
Minister Kálnoky utlined to those present Germany's obligations to Austria-
Hungary under the Dual Alliance and offered his conviction that Berlin would
honor the agreement if Russia suddenly attacked. Germany could not remain
idle while Russia crushed the monarchy. German participation in a war against
Russia under other circumstances, however, remained highly doubtful.

Kálnoky added that while relations with Russia could still be
considered "normal," events in Bulgaria had strengthened impressions in St.
Petersburg that Austria-Hungary presented the greatest hindrance to Russian
ambitions in the Balkans. While he did not feel that recent troop increases in
Poland reflected strains in the Austro-Russian relationship, Kálnoky agreed with
general staff fears that the increased troop levels gave Russia the ability to
invade Galicia without first mobilizing units to their full wartime strength. The
probability of such a direct offensive, however, was not great. More likely
would be some sort of Russian military action against Bulgaria. In that event,
Kálnoky reported, the monarchy could expect some assistance from Britain and
Italy under the Mediterranean agreement currently under negotiation.[70]

For Beck, this did not alter the current military relationships in the
probable theater of war. Austria-Hungary had some 33,000 men stationed in
Galicia opposite a Russian force over three times its size. The chief of the
general staff agreed with Kálnoky: the monarchy should do nothing that might
provoke the Russians and allow Bismarck to back out of the Dual Alliance. The
winter campaign advocated by Moltke was madness. Winters in Russia lasted
until May. The Bosnian campaign had illustrated that hostile climate and terrain
would decimate the fighting qualities of even well-trained units within a matter
of weeks.

Instead, Beck, in concert with War Minister Bylandt, again attempted to find a middle course that he hoped would both please the political and military leaderships in Berlin and deter the Russians from a rash offensive. The Second Infantry Division, currently stationed in Vienna, would be shifted to Galicia, and Beck proposed to raise forces already in Galicia to a near war footing. To increase cavalry readiness, each cavalry regiment would receive an additional twenty-five mounts.[71] The supply of preservative rations would be increased from the current low level of five to eighteen days.

Beck, meanwhile, got only a flood of confused signals from Berlin. Emmerich Count Széchenyi von Sávar und Felsö-Videk, the Austro-Hungarian ambassador to the German empire, wrote Kálnoky on 9 December that Waldersee still advised against troop increases in Galicia.[72] Two days later, he reiterated Moltke's pessimism in regard to St. Petersburg's intentions and his desire to go ahead with a winter offensive to forestall further Russian preparations.[73] The German military attaché to Russia, by odd circumstance on leave in Berlin during the height of the crisis, told Steininger that every day that Austria-Hungary and Germany waited to mobilize was a crime and that the sooner the allies launched their invasion, the better.[74] In Vienna, the German Military Attaché Major Adolf von Deines also pushed for preventive war and, on 20 December, warned his father to arrange his business affairs in anticipation of one by the end of January.[75]

What had prompted von Deines's timetable was a private assurance by Beck on 15 December that the Austro-Hungarian army could be ready by mid-January for an offensive into Russia if Berlin gave the word.[76] Neither Beck nor Albrecht wanted war, but both were anxious to play the good ally, particularly to the German military leadership, which, with the notable exception of Waldersee, appeared to desire a confrontation with Russia.

A ministerial council held on 18 December demonstrated that the civilians held cautious views.[77] Kálnoky, Taaffe, and Tisza all agreed: the monarchy should do nothing to provoke St. Petersburg. Offensive war was not an option. Public opinion, important to army morale in war given universal conscription, would not support a preventive strike into Russia. Moreover, while the Prussian general staff seemed to advocate war, Bismarck would never authorize offensive action against Russia. Nevertheless, Austria-Hungary needed to proceed with moderate preparations outlined by Beck in case the military-diplomatic situation worsened. The civilians also approved a war ministry proposal to return all Galician regiments currently stationed elsewhere to their areas of recruitment.[78] The foreign office could defend such a move as a continuation of the army territorialization begun in 1883. A crown council convened the following day to approve the 16 million gulden necessary to fund these operations.[79]

The ministerial council of 18 December recognized the essential paradox of the current Austro-German relationship. While the letter of the Dual Alliance was strictly defensive in nature, the practical military planning, undertaken with the knowledge and approval of both the German and Austro-Hungarian civilian governments, foresaw a defensive-offensive as the only way to victory over the ponderous Russian giant. When Kálnoky informed the conference of military discussions under way to clarify the *casus foederis* with Berlin, no voices were raised in objection.

Kálnoky had already given Beck advanced approval to open military talks with the Germans a week earlier.[80] Beck had informed Bylandt on 11 December of earlier discussions with the Germans over Austro-Hungarian use of German Silesian railroads.[81] Within a few days of the ministerial council, he forwarded to the foreign office a report from Karl Steininger containing Moltke's agreement to an unofficial exchange of views between the general staffs.[82] Indeed, Steininger's dispatch made military contacts seem all the more imperative, for it contained new warnings by Moltke against the troop increases in Galicia just approved by the ministerial council.

Shortly before Christmas, Beck sent Steininger a memorandum which both stated his position on the issue of military preparations and posed a series of questions which the attaché was to raise with von Moltke.[83] The Austro-Hungarian chief of the general staff stressed the need for the establishment of a simultaneous mobilization date in the event the political leaderships decided upon war. Austria-Hungary and Germany also needed to agree to issue their declarations of war on the same day. With the southwestern borders now secured by the Triple Alliance, Beck could promise that Austria-Hungary would commit its entire armed might against Russia with the exception of those forces necessary to secure Bosnia-Herzegovina. Austria-Hungary and Germany should reaffirm their earlier commitments to conduct the war in an offensive manner against the enemy's main forces in central Poland.

Beck's inquiries centered chiefly around the number of forces Germany planned to commit to a war against Russia and how soon these could be mobilized. To what extent was the Prussian general staff taking into account Italian assistance in the west? Should Germany and Austria-Hungary pressure Romania into active participation in a war with Russia? What would the allies do in the event of further threatening preparations by Russia? What consequences would the invasion of one of the empires have for the other?

Beck's missive, undertaken with the complete knowledge and approval of the *Ballhausplatz*, got a stormy reception in Berlin. Through diplomatic channels, Prince Bismarck abruptly dismissed the defensive-offensive premise of all Austro-German war planning against Russia since Strobl.[84] The chancellor declared his opposition to any arrangements that called for preemptive aggression against Germany's Russian ally. Bismarck expected

Vienna to walk a political-diplomatic tightrope. A Russian attack was certainly possible, and Germany did not want its ally to be surprised by it. But Austria-Hungary needed to take care not to antagonize Russia with military preparations. Germany would enter a conflict only after an unprovoked Russian attack. Bismarck charged that the Austro-Hungarian general staff wanted to change the defensive character of the alliance and warned Kálnoky not to let events slip from civilian control.[85]

Moltke, who earlier in December had so impetuously clamored for war, had now apparently been reined in by the chancellor. The Prussian chief of the general staff responded to Beck's memorandum with a stiff inquiry on the strength and location of Austro-Hungarian deployments against Russia, although he already possessed much of this information. Moltke claimed he would need to know Habsburg dispositions before he could draw up a scenario of what German forces could accomplish in the event of war. In an interview on 30 December, Moltke told Steininger what had long been appreciated by the civilian and military leaderships of the Habsburg empire: that Austria had nothing to gain from a war with Russia and that it should assiduously avoid such a conflict.[86]

Vienna recoiled under these blasts from its closest ally. On 5 January a hastily convened ministerial council concluded that--given the German response to Beck's memorandum--inaction was the best policy with the Delegations held in readiness for the moment war threatened.[87] A crown council four days later suspended all troop increases authorized the previous month except for the transfer of Galician regiments from peacetime stations in the southwest. These, Kálnoky assured the ministers, the *Ballhausplatz* could square diplomatically as a continuation of the territorial reorganization of the army.[88]

The Habsburg foreign office hastened to reassure Germany that Beck's attempt to coordinate an allied offensive applied only to the case when both governments determined that war with Russia was unavoidable.[89] A worried Kálnoky wrote Berlin twice on 12 January that Austria-Hungary in no way desired an offensive war against Russia. The foreign minister defended Beck, declaring that all earlier joint discussions between the Prussian and Austro-Hungarian general staffs had agreed upon an offensive-defensive strategy against Russia. To await a Russian attack might give up the important military advantage of the faster allied mobilization. Bismarck unfairly charged Vienna with warlike intentions: had not Moltke's memorandum of late November said that it was high time for Austria-Hungary to launch an offensive strike?

At the general staff, a young Major Franz Conrad von Hötzendorf revised the operation section's assessment of the strategic situation to accommodate the new, trickier relationship with the German ally.[90] While Russia had reinforced its peacetime garrisons in Congress Poland, Conrad now declared it was impossible to determine the extent of these troop transfers.

Conrad went still further to dismiss the threat, which had formed the basis of Beck's efforts throughout the 1880s, that Russian units would be capable of launching spoiling offensives at their peacetime strengths. Even the vaunted Russian cavalry, Conrad estimated, would first have to form up into brigades and divisions before attempting to disrupt the Austro-Hungarian mobilization. By then friendly forces would have gathered in sufficient numbers to repulse any impromptu Russian assault on the army's lines of communication.

Vienna's hasty retreat, unfortunately, did not halt the flow of contradictory signals from Berlin. On 14 January Waldersee informed Steininger that the Russians were moving four divisions to the western frontier, and that he now supported Beck's earlier wish for the coordination of countermeasures.[91] The Prussian *Generalquartiermeister* added that he thought the chancellor himself would soon agree to such action.

Bismarck, however, showed no signs of wanting to engage in joint crisis planning. Shortly after Steininger's interview with Waldersee, Herbert von Bismarck, the chancellor's son and German state secretary for foreign affairs, informed Vienna that Germany would permit Austria-Hungary to use the Silesian railroads only if it were subject to an unprovoked attack by Russia.[92] Since the Silesian lines were slated to perform vital mobilization functions, Herbert's declaration put to rest all thoughts of pre-war military measures by the allies.[93] A communication from father Otto on 24 January urging the virtual abandonment of Galicia in the event of war served notice that Germany expected Austria-Hungary to adopt an extremely conciliatory attitude toward Russia or risk losing the alliance.[94]

Both Beck and Kálnoky had to console themselves with offers of support from friendlier, but less important, allies. In early January, Italian Premier Francesco Crispi informed the Austro-Hungarian ambassador to Italy of his desire to dispatch an Italian expeditionary corps to Galicia in the event of a war with Russia.[95] A few days later, the idea received great attention in a series of joint Austro-German-Italian staff discussions in Berlin concerning the transport of Italian troops to the Rhine in the event of a Franco-German war.[96] The Prussian general staff eagerly endorsed the Italian proposal to send forces to Galicia, despite the fact that Chancellor Bismarck decried even Austro-Hungarian deployments there.[97]

Despite its obvious goodwill, Beck felt compelled to rebuff Crispi's cooperative gesture on practical grounds. Austro-Hungarian railroads could not transport an Italian expeditionary force to the lower Danube, at least in the early portions of a Russian campaign. By the time rolling stock became available for such a purpose, Italian troops would arrive too late to make decisive contributions to a campaign.[98] While he had initially supported Crispi's initiative, Kálnoky seconded Beck's negative assessment. The Italian army had too much to worry about already, both along the Rhine and its border with

France, without troubling itself with the dispatch of several army corps to the east.[99] While undoubtedly sincere in their concerns, both Beck and Kálnoky missed a golden opportunity, never again to reappear, to bind Italy tightly to the Triple Alliance with a special military convention.

The Romanian government also proved ready to support Austria-Hungary in a war against Russia. In late December 1887, Count Agenor Golouchowski, the monarchy's minister in Bucharest, informed the *Ballhausplatz* that Romania had begun quiet preparations for war. King Carol, the country's Hohenzollern monarch, was convinced that Russia intended to invade Romania without a declaration of war.[100] Like his Habsburg neighbor, Romanian Premier Ion Bratianu appeared anxious to avoid the appearance of open preparations, but had nonetheless procured new weapons, clothing, and munitions for his country's forces.[101] Golouchowski wrote that while the Romanian premier believed war with Russia inevitable, of the cabinet members only Bratianu and Foreign Minister Demeter Stourzda knew of the secret alliance with Austria-Hungary and Germany. Most of political Romania believed that the country would remain neutral in a war between Russia and the Dual Alliance.

Romania, however, appeared anxious in early 1888 to arrive at a definite understanding with it allies concerning the deployment of its troops in a war with Russia. Foreign Minister Stourzda was dispatched in early January to meet with Beck and Waldersee, and King Carol followed up these initial contacts with a royal visit to Berlin in March.[102] As with the Italian deployment proposals, Beck found little to rejoice in the Romanian military arrangements being formulated in Berlin. Despite recent improvements, Beck doubted the capabilities of the small Romanian army. He preferred Romanian neutrality over an eastward extension of the front which the Romanians would themselves be incapable of sustaining. The Siebenbürgen corps could not be spared from the initial battles in Galicia to assist the Romanians if they got into trouble. Carol complained, however, that the Romanian army was not strong enough to conduct offensive operations alone and would require the support of Austro-Hungarian forces to make an effective contribution to the campaign. To Beck's dismay, the Germans supported Carol's demands for the participation of Austro-Hungarian forces in a Romanian offensive.[103] Beck refused to alter his campaign dispositions, and the Romanian talks ended without conclusion.

Reflections on Modern Warfare

By March 1888, when Carol visited Berlin, the international crisis had begun to ease. Russia slowed its military preparations along the western frontiers and ended its anti-Habsburg rhetoric, developments assisted undoubtedly by the publication of the Dual Alliance in February 1888.[104] Germany became absorbed in the turmoil of transition government during the *Dreikaiserjahr*. In France, the Boulangist movement had become more an issue of domestic politics than an international problem. The general's reluctance to overthrow political opponents within the government and energetic action by the latter to suppress an army-led nationalist insurrection led to the rapid demise of the Boulangist movement. Boulanger's flight to Belgium in April 1889 finally ended the immediate danger of a Franco-German war.[105]

Beck used the opportunity afforded by the sudden easing of tensions to reflect upon the recent crisis and the nature of a future European war. In a March 1889 memorandum to the emperor, Beck blamed the armaments race, begun in France after its defeat in the 1870-71 war, for the current anxiety in Europe.[106] One hundred years before, European armies had averaged some 150,000 men. By the mid-nineteenth century, their size had more than doubled. In 1889, the Great Powers could field armies numbering in the millions.

To provide security from the huge military establishments of neighbors, European nations had begun to form peacetime alliances. While initially of defensive intent and purpose, these coalitions themselves contributed greatly to the probability of a general European war, for they could potentially transform local conflicts into continental conflagrations. Alliances also did not end the armaments race, as nations and their allies now had to measure themselves against rival blocs as well as individual potential enemies.

Combined, these factors made the next general European war a grim and terrible prospect. Aided by the modern technology of rail transportation, between seven and eight million men would clash almost immediately in the opening engagements. The development of repeating small arms and improvements in field artillery would ensure that many of the combatants, perhaps a third, would never return from the battlefield.[107]

The horrors of modern warfare, therefore, placed tremendous spiritual and moral obligations on the European political and military leaderships. No government should consider lightly the grave choice of war for, Beck warned, one that did so might end up buried in the rubble. On the other hand, while abhorrent, no government could ignore the necessity for war preparations. Beck's motto "*Si vis pacem, para bellum*"--he who desires peace must prepare for war--provided the only security in an international climate fraught with tension.

In proffering this nineteenth-century counterpart to the deterrence policies of the nuclear age, Beck appeared to knuckle under to the self-generating prerogatives of the arms race. But Beck largely conceived of preparedness in the limited, non-aggressive improvement of existing military organizations and structures. When he did advocate an expansion of the monarchy's military establishment, as he would almost continually until leaving office in 1906, his goal was always to catch up to, but never exceed, the military preparations of neighboring Great Powers. This, in part, owed to a realistic assessment of Austria-Hungary's political and financial limitations. But an examination of even his most forward expansion programs indicates that their adoption would still have left the monarchy militarily weaker than most of its potential enemies in both absolute and relative terms.[108]

Beck's moderation in the aftermath of the Bulgarian crisis, the greatest direct threat to the monarchy's security since 1866, illustrates this point. With crown council approval, he ordered in March 1888 the return of those Galician regiments with peacetime stations in the southwest to their home districts.[109] In response to reports in early 1888 of the transfer of two additional Russian corps to Congress Poland, Beck and the new War Minister Ferdinand Bauer obtained imperial sanction for the call-up of three *Ersatzreserve* classes during the summer and fall.[110] The following year, Beck proposed a more permanent countermeasure in the transfer of the Brünn military district to Galicia in order to strengthen the peacetime military establishment there.[111] In September 1889, Beck led both corps and cavalry maneuvers in Galicia involving the newly transferred X Corps, to sharpen the war readiness of those forces stationed along the Russian frontier.[112] To make sure these troops received timely reinforcement in war, he also continued to press for infrastructure improvements, achieving in 1889 a readiness gain of three days over the previous year.[113] Beck also persisted in his calls for improvements in the Galician fortification system, including the construction of new "*Gürtel*" (ring) works around the original central defenses in order to protect them from long-range, heavy artillery.[114]

Revision of the Military Law

The crisis of 1887-88 demonstrated the urgent need for a more fundamental increase in the monarchy's military capabilities. The German alliance, which had protected Austria-Hungary during the reform period of the 1880s, no longer appeared a solid guarantor of Austro-Hungarian security. In particular, the events of 1887-88 demonstrated that the monarchy needed the capability of protecting its own Balkan interests. They revealed a German civil-military leadership uncoordinated in its interpretations of and views toward the alliance with Austria-Hungary. A visit to Vienna by the bombastic new German emperor Wilhelm II in October 1888 did little to improve upon this negative impression of Germany.[115] Later in the fall, the Austro-Hungarian chargé d'affaires in Berlin repeatedly complained of German dissatisfaction with

Taaffe's reliance upon the Slavs in the Cisleithanian governmental coalition and fears that the monarchy would not "uphold its Great Power position" in Europe because of internal divisions.[116]

Beck believed Austria-Hungary needed a new military law that would increase army size and thus counter Russian preparations. Already at the height of the war scare with Russia, Beck had begun to press the war ministry for a revision of the existing 1868 law, due for renewal the following year as a part of the decennial renegotiation of the *Ausgleich*.[117] By the end of 1889, Beck estimated that the Russians would increase their forces along the Austro-Hungarian border by two divisions and complained that soon the armed forces of the monarchy, even with German assistance, would not be equal to the task of opposing Russia's military might.

From the military standpoint, the problems with the original 1868 legislation were legion.[118] By law, the Austro-Hungarian common army could not exceed 800,000 men in wartime, regardless of the military situation. No other European state possessed statutory limitations on the size of its armed forces during wartime. The 1868 military law also limited the number of men in the replacement pool (*Ersatzreserve*) to 10% of the army's wartime strength, or 80,000 men. Given the high casualty rates of modern warfare, this would hardly have met the army's replacement needs for the first weeks of a conflict alone, much less those of an extended campaign. The army granted exemptions to over 15,000 men annually, further reducing replacement numbers. Prior to 1882, these men received no military training and would have to undergo an eight-week training course during wartime to ready them for combat.[119] Moreover, the number of young men actually inducted into the army each year fell short of statutory limits because of an 8% attrition rate during training.[120]

Both the military leadership and the Vienna and Budapest governments had recognized these problems early in the Bulgarian crisis. A May 1885 military conference had obtained the emperor's approval for such measures as the elimination of legal limits on the size of the *Ersatzreserve*, the raising of the annual recruitment contingents for the common army, *Landwehr*, and *Honvéd*, and the elimination of service exemptions in wartime. In October 1887, the war ministry, after consultation with the general staff, officially proposed the lifting of restrictions on the wartime strength of the common army.[121]

The new military proposals quickly encountered trouble in the Hungarian diet, where more nationalist elements of the ruling liberal party pressed Minister-President Tisza to demand concessions to Magyar feeling. Hungarian Nationalist feelings against the army had been aroused when in 1886 Brigadier General Ludwig Janski, commander of the Budapest garrison, ceremoniously decorated the statue of the loyalist general who had held the city against Kossuth's revolutionaries in 1849.[122] By 1889, the Hungarians were ready for a showdown over the military law. Specifically, they demanded the introduction of the Magyar language of command for all regiments recruited under the Crown of St. Stephen. Beck led the military opposition to this drastic measure, citing the insurmountable communication problems two command languages would cause. The Hungarians, frightened by the recent crisis with their old enemy Russia, withdrew this most radical demand when such venerated conservative national figures as ex-foreign minister and *Ausgleich* negotiator Count Gyula Andrássy lent their support to the military viewpoint. Tisza, personally against the establishment of either a national Hungarian army or the Magyar language of command within a common military context, limited his requests to the insertion of the letter "u" (*und* = and) in the name of the common army and all common military agencies, including the war ministry and general staff. The implication of Hungarian separateness in the "imperial *and* royal" institutional label proved sufficient to obtain passage in April 1889 of a new army law incorporating much of the military's original proposals.[123]

The 1889 military law raised the annual recruitment contingent of the common army and *Kriegsmarine* from 95,500 to 103,100 men and fixed those of the *Landwehr* and *Honvéd* at 10,000 and 12,500 men respectively.[124] In addition, both militias received their own replacement pools.[125] Under the new law, exemptions from military service would be rescinded during wartime. The law also eliminated the ceiling on the wartime strength of the armed forces.

The increases, however, fell far short of force levels of the other major European land armies. In 1889, Germany and France each inducted over a quarter of a million men annually into their armed forces. Russia inducted a staggering 335,000. Austria-Hungary, by comparison, called less than half that number, a mere 125,600 men, to the colors each year. While the new military law abolished wartime limitations on army size, the common army would still number some 800,000 men during the initial stages of a conflict, since the modest recruitment increases were meant merely to compensate for training attrition. The lifting of the wartime ceiling meant only that the monarchy could eventually train and equip an army in excess of 800,000 men in the event of an extended conflict.

With the passage of the military law of 1889, the Austro-Hungarian armed forces were as strong as they would ever be for the next twenty-three years. Thanks to Beck's efforts throughout the decade of the 1880s, they had also reached the height of their effectiveness in terms of mobilization speed and overall war readiness. When Beck took over as chief of the general staff, the Austro-Hungarian army could scarcely hope to begin offensive operations in Galicia six weeks after receipt of a mobilization order. By 1889, improvements in the railroad network, undertaken at Beck's insistence and direction, ensured war readiness within twenty-three days. The effectiveness of the militia forces had increased steadily and they would in the 1890s be able to take their place alongside common army units in the front line. The 1886 *Landsturm* law, another Beck achievement, created units to guard the mobilization routes, provided the army with an adequate replacement pool in wartime and allowed for a greater exploitation of the monarchy's able-bodied manpower reserves. The lifting of limits on wartime army strength in 1889 allowed the army to take full advantage of the longer service obligations of the law.

Beck's Dominance in Military Affairs

The passage of the 1889 military law also marked the beginning of what would over the course of the following decade become Beck's complete dominance over the military affairs of the monarchy. In the 1880s, Beck had seized the initiative for military reform from the war ministry and had presided over the great improvements in the monarchy's military capabilities during the period. However, he had still to seek the cooperation of other actors within the military hierarchy, specifically the constitutional war minister and the inspector general of the army. Conciliatory by nature toward colleagues, Beck had not found this cooperation difficult, especially with a generally like-minded Archduke Albrecht. Bylandt, however, closely guarded the prerogatives of the war minister's office, including its oversight of the general staff, and sometimes opposed Beck on important issues such as army reorganization.

By 1889, however, the monarchy had a new war minister, capable but nonetheless impressed by Beck's successful reform of the Austro-Hungarian army and his influence with both the emperor and inspector general. Beck, for his part, still treated his nominal superior with the great respect which he personally felt he owed the man with the awesome responsibilities of war minister. Nonetheless, the relationship between the chief of the general staff and war minister assumed the character of one between equals. Beck remained the war minister's "*Hilfsorgan*" in name only. Albrecht, now almost seventy-five years old and nearly blind, trusted Beck completely and increasingly relied upon him to run the army. While Albrecht would remain the designated wartime commander-in-chief, all recognized by the end of the 1880s that Beck, not the archduke, would lead the monarchy's armed forces in the next war. When Albrecht died in February 1895, Beck stood directly beneath Franz Joseph at the pinnacle of the military power within the Austro-Hungarian monarchy.

Conclusion:
The Rebirth of an Army

The military reforms of the 1880s, originated to a large extent by Beck and realized with the cooperation of the war ministry and the Austrian and Hungarian governments, completed the transformation of the Habsburg army from the ineffective instrument of mid-century to a modern military machine, capable of the rapid mobilization and deployment heretofore associated only with the Prussian-German, and to a lesser extent, the French army. The buildup of the rail network permitted the quick assembly of the field army in Galicia. The *Landsturm* laws, passed in the middle of the decade, meant the military could call to the colors all able-bodied men to the age of forty-two in time of war. The 1889 military law, in addition to obtaining a slight increase in the annual recruitment contingent to offset training attrition, lifted statutory limitations on army size, allowing for the mobilization of Habsburg society in the event of a longer conflict. The monarchy would no longer, as it had at mid-century, have to surrender after the loss of a few initial battles. The empire now possessed the means to wage a longer, total war: the kind it would experience in 1914-18.

This amazing circumstance, Beck's personal achievement, was obscured by the subsequent deterioration of the monarchy's military position that occurred under his leadership after 1890. Beck, who would serve as chief of the general staff until November 1906, himself recognized early on that the empire would have to expand its military forces if it hoped to keep pace with the development of neighboring Great Power armies.[1] The 1889 law was merely designed to compensate for training attrition to allow Austria-Hungary to field a common army of 800,000 men during wartime. While the law had eliminated ceilings on army strength, it had not provided a corresponding expansion of the recruitment contingent that would provide additional trained manpower in war.

In the early 1890s Beck drew up a proposal for the expansion of the armed forces, which he presented personally to the common ministerial council in February 1893.[2] The grim situation, particularly versus Russia, had become even worse. Beck informed the council that Russia had increased its peacetime forces since 1886 by nearly 120,000 men and 526 guns. The German ally had strengthened its standing forces by 77,000 men since 1887. Beck conceded that the German army might be called upon to fight on two fronts against powerful adversaries, but cautioned that Austria-Hungary might also face a multifront war involving Russia, Italy and some Balkan states.[3] Russian peacetime forces in the Warsaw and Kiev districts alone totaled more than 288,000 men--more than seven Austro-Hungarian corps at full wartime strength! Beck realized that the Russians could overwhelm meagre Austro-Hungarian defenses during the first days of mobilization. Russia was also beginning to rearm with repeating rifles, which would mark a massive increase in Russian firepower on the battlefield.

       To counter these developments, Beck argued that Austria-Hungary had to increase dramatically both its active forces and reservoir of trained reserves. Approximately 217,000 men within the monarchy came of military age each year. Of these, about 188,000 men could actually be inducted into the various branches of the armed forces. Beck hoped to give the vast majority of this additional manpower to the common army and the *Kriegsmarine* and pushed for an annual recruitment contingent of 159,000 men for these services, more than a 50% increase over current recruitment levels.[4] Beck, however, did not abandon his idea of the 1880s that the militia forces needed to prepare themselves for front-line roles in a future war. He, therefore, argued for increases in the annual *Landwehr* contingent to 16,360 men. The current *Honvéd* recruitment level of 12,500 men satisfied its current wartime requirements.

       As in the push to expand Austro-Hungarian military capabilities in the 1880s, German attitudes toward the Dual Alliance proved decisive. In 1891, Wilhelm II removed the pro-Austrian Waldersee as chief of the Prussian general staff. His successor, Alfred von Schlieffen, quickly demonstrated a condescending attitude toward the Austro-Hungarian armed forces and an ambivalence toward close ties with the Habsburg military establishment. Contacts between the general staffs dwindled in the early 1890s. In 1893 the Prussian general staff, without prior consultation with Vienna, completely abandoned the double envelopment of the earlier Moltke-Waldersee dispositions in favor of a joint Austro-German offensive into Congress Poland from Silesia and Galicia. In late 1896, Schlieffen suddenly reverted to the original idea of a simultaneous advance from East Prussia and Galicia. Schlieffen, however, had no intention of increasing troop commitments to the east. While he ostensibly maintained the Moltke-Waldersee eighteen division East Army, Schlieffen increasingly shifted his first-line units to the west, replacing them with less effective reserve divisions.[5]

       Beck's proposals to expand army size encountered powerful and ultimately insurmountable civilian resistance. While the Vienna and Budapest governments did not deny the strategic imbalances portrayed by Beck, they nonetheless asserted (with some justification) that such a drastic military buildup was unnecessary given the gradual improvement in Austro-Russian relations throughout the early 1890s. Russia, after securing the French alliance in 1894, began to shift its interests to East Asia where it hoped to gain Mongolia and Korea. This shift became apparent after the reemergence of the Eastern Question in the Macedonian, Cretan, and Armenian revolts after 1895, when Russia sought cooperation with Austria-Hungary to maintain the Ottoman empire and the political status quo in the Balkans.[6] Russia's cooperative attitude in Balkan affairs effectively disarmed Beck's appeals for military expansion. After 1895 the probability of war seemed remote to most civilian ministers. Vast increases in the military establishment and the financial outlays required to support it appeared unnecessary from the civilian standpoint.[7]

From Beck's perspective, however, the strategic situation had greatly worsened by the mid-1890s, and he tried desperately to shake the civilian governments' complacency. In a situation report to the emperor in December 1896, he warned that latent political tensions might still give rise to a sudden European conflagration.[8] Despite its East Asian interests, Russia continued to enhance the military effectiveness of its European armies. All Russian forces in Europe had been completely rearmed with repeating rifles, and St. Petersburg had announced increases in the 1896 military budget of over 10% from that of the previous year.

While the Franco-Russian alliance perhaps posed a more immediate threat to Germany, it also gave rise to renewed Austro-Hungarian concerns about the security of the southwestern frontier. The substantial decline in Italian military might following the Ethiopian debacle at Adua in March 1896 meant fewer troops to defend both northern Italy and the Rhine against French assaults, which might force Germany to shift even greater portions of its army to the west in order to compensate for decreased Italian commitments.[9]

Moreover, Beck worried about the impact of the new naval balance of power in the Mediterranean created by the Franco-Russian understandings on Italy's value as an ally. If the Triple Alliance lost control of the Mediterranean, Italy would have to use its entire land power to defend against a possible amphibious invasion.[10] By the late 1890s the naval balance of power had shifted in favor of the Franco-Russian alliance. Only if Britain came to the assistance of Italy in the Mediterranean would the latter be able to meet its land commitments to the Triple Alliance. Whitehall, however, would presumably enter such a conflict only if Russia threatened to seize the Dardanelles. The Austro-Hungarian *Kriegsmarine*, the object of an almost studied neglect during the land buildup of the 1880s, would not have a decisive impact on the course of a naval war.[11] As Beck pointed out to the emperor in his 1896 memorandum, Austria-Hungary's greatest contribution in a European conflict would be its land war against Russia, for which it would increasingly have to bear the sole burden.[12] But it became apparent to Beck that the navy would soon need strengthening to fulfill even its limited mission of coastal defense within the narrow confines of the Adriatic.

Matériel shortcomings, particularly in the artillery arm, began to cast grave doubts on the monarchy's ability to wage a successful land war against Russia. By the turn of the century, the army's field artillery, most of which dated from the mid-1870s, had begun to wear out.[13] The 80mm and 90mm pieces, cast in steel-bronze using the Uchatius method, had deteriorated more rapidly than expected owing to the introduction of smokeless powder charges during the 1890s.[14] The monarchy's fortress artillery, much of it consisting of smoothbore pieces made in the 1860s, also needed replacing by 1900. This placed a tremendous additional burden on military finances and worked to postpone Beck's expansion program.[15]

Beck's last years in office were also troubled by new security threats in the southeast. In 1903, nationalist army officers overthrew the pro-Habsburg Obrenovich dynasty in Serbia. After the abdication of King Milan in 1889, Belgrade had slowly drifted away from its close alignment with Austria-Hungary of the early 1880s. Milan's son Alexander proved to be a weak ruler who exercised exceedingly poor judgment when he married his mistress, Draga Mashin, a woman of questionable repute, in August 1899. Serbian nationalists, never happy under Obrenovich rule after the late 1870s because of the dynasty's close identification with the Habsburg monarchy--a power which had thwarted their expansionist aspirations by occupying Bosnia-Herzegovina in 1878--plotted to remove the king who had so dishonored the nation. In June 1903, army officers forced entry into the royal palace, murdering Alexander, Draga, and several members of their court.[16]

Habsburg relations with the government of the new sovereign, the Karageorgevich King Peter I, never cordial because of the regicide which had brought the latter to power, deteriorated rapidly following a Habsburg ban on Serbian pork exports in 1905-6. The annexation of Bosnia-Herzegovina in 1908 created a mood of open hostility between Vienna and Belgrade that ultimately led to war in the summer of 1914. In the early 1880s the Habsburg civil-military leadership had favored armed intervention to maintain a friendly regime in Belgrade.[17] In 1903, however, the monarchy, paralyzed by the domestic crisis in Hungary surrounding the introduction of the new military law, did nothing.

The security of the southern frontier was even more severely undermined in 1905 by the Italian sale of artillery, including large caliber-siege pieces, to Montenegro.[18] General staff concerns over the military capabilities of the small Balkan principality had in the past been tempered by the Montenegrin army's lack of a significant artillery arm.[19] By 1906, general staff Captain Erik Edler von Merizzi estimated that all Montenegro would need to do to overwhelm the cordon defense of southern Dalmatia would be to build a paved road to the frontier for the transport of siege artillery.[20] Attaché reports from Rome warned of Italian cultural and political interests in Turkish Albania,[21] and other intelligence indicated certain covert Italian military preparations against the monarchy.[22] The general staff had also noticed a steady increase in Italian intelligence-gathering operations in the southwestern portions of the monarchy, including the dispatch of army officers to reconnoiter important railroads, causing Beck to bemoan the relative openness of the Austro-Italian border in Tyrol.[23]

These actions prompted a general discussion on Austro-Hungarian defenses in the southwest in 1904. Both Beck and War Minister Heinrich von Pitreich felt the situation of sufficient gravity to abandon at least partially the territorial system established during the 1880s. Specifically, they requested in December 1904 a reversal of the 1888 decision to transfer regiments from their original garrisons in the III and XIV Corps areas.[24] Old formulae of the 1870s were revived. The irredentist movement, Pitreich wrote the emperor, might force an otherwise friendly Italian government to acts of aggression against the monarchy. The reinforcement of local garrisons and fortified works was absolutely necessary to forestall successful surprise attacks across the Austro-Italian border.[25]

Within the general staff, the Italian sale of artillery to Montenegro gave rise to a new assumption that the two countries planned to make common cause in a future war against Austria-Hungary.[26] In particular, the operations section feared a combined land-sea offensive against Cattaro, the secondary fleet anchorage of the Austro-Hungarian *Kriegsmarine*. Oskar Potiorek, Beck's last deputy chief of the general staff, saw imminent war in the coincidence of renewed Italian activity with unrest in Hungary over the introduction of the military bill, citing 1848-49, when unrest in both places nearly toppled the Habsburg regime. Potiorek suggested a series of precautions against an Italo-Montenegrin preventive strike, including troop increases in Bosnia-Herzegovina. Lack of money brought on by the government's inability to collect taxes in rebellious Hungary, however, precluded such measures.[27]

Hungary's rejection of the military bill, Italy's apparent defection from the Triple Alliance, and the events in Serbia combined to sap the strength of an aging Friedrich Beck. After 1903, Beck gradually withdrew from active participation in political-military discussions, surrendering his former leadership role to the war minister, his friend and ex-deputy Heinrich von Pitreich. He reemerged briefly in 1905 to direct planning of the armed *coup d'état* against the Hungarian parliament, if only to temper the grandiose war of conquest planned by Major General Moritz von Auffenberg-Komarów, then commander of the 65th Infantry Brigade at Raab (Györ).[28] Beck had called for limited military intervention in Hungary as early as 1903 to accompany a suspension of the kingdom's constitution. But ever a committed proponent of the *Ausgleich*, he recoiled at Auffenberg's formula for civil war.[29]

Much to Beck's relief, a compromise resolved the Hungarian constitutional crisis the following year. The Hungarians agreed in principle to the raising of the recruitment contingent and the retention of the German language of command for the common army, while the military leadership permitted the *Honvéd* to organize its own artillery units. This made the *Honvéd* a fully equipped, independent fighting force. While this concession alarmed many within the military who saw in it the realization of their fears concerning the emergence of a national Hungarian army, it did not much trouble Beck, who had been urging the creation of a militia artillery arm for years.[30]

The year 1906 would also be Beck's last in office. In June, Franz Joseph made Beck a count on his twenty-fifth anniversary as chief of the general staff and bestowed upon him the Hungarian Order of St. Stephen. Honors and congratulations flooded into his office in the old war ministry building *Am Hof.* German Emperor Wilhelm II made Beck the colonel-proprietor of a Prussian infantry regiment, republican France inducted him into the Legion of Honor, and the Russian government sent him a diamond-studded portrait of Tsar Nicholas II. Numerous other decorations followed from the smaller German states.

These honors, as well as those received earlier in his career, reflected a life of service to the Austro-Hungarian monarchy. In 1906, Beck remained the only living and active *Ausgleich* negotiator. The political-military compromises of 1867, in no small measure Beck's achievement, secured the monarchy's Great Power status on the continent after the disaster at Königgrätz. Of greater importance to Beck's subsequent career, the *Ausgleich* gave the imperial army a respite for much needed reform. Specifically, the Compromise allowed the army time to work out administrative conflicts that would eventually lead to the introduction of a true general staff system on the Prussian model.

The establishment of a powerful general staff over the resistance of the imperial war ministry represented Beck's greatest achievement and one that provided a framework for his life's work of improving the war readiness of the Austro-Hungarian monarchy. Among those advising the emperor on military affairs in the late 1860s and early 1870s, only Beck remained steadfast in his advocacy of a Prussian-style general staff. His devotion to this cause, born of observations made in the early 1860s of Prussian institutions under the elder Moltke, was both heartfelt and selfless, for Beck could have had no idea that he would one day lead the general staff. Beck's crusade led him to challenge the most powerful military institutions of his day. The imperial war ministry, revived as a consequence of the 1859 defeat, reigned supreme over military affairs in the immediate post-*Ausgleich* era. Beck had also often taken up the cudgels against the army's dynastic overlord, Archduke Albrecht, a man who through both deed and lineage occupied an exalted position within the military hierarchy.

Beck won his battles through extraordinary interpersonal skill. Both his control over the flow of military paperwork and his presence among the emperor's immediate entourage as head of the military chancellery gave him an almost continuous opportunity to push his views with Franz Joseph. He bombarded the emperor with memoranda calling for the overthrow of both Albrecht's powerful *Armeeoberkommando* and Kuhn's war ministry. Beck also undoubtedly punctuated his arguments in personal meetings, of which no records were made. Ultimately, Franz Joseph sided with Beck simply because he liked him. The emperor admired Beck for his energy, pluck, tact, coolness and bravery on the battlefield, attributes that had proven of great assistance during the 1866 war and indispensable in the reorganization of the military that followed.

Beck's career mirrored the increasing bourgeois participation in the Habsburg officer corps. A military career, of course, had always offered the best path toward ennoblement within the monarchy, but in the mid-nineteenth century few commoners gained entrance into the highest echelons of the army.[31] When Beck enrolled in the Tullner *Pionierschule* in 1846, scarcely 8% of the monarchy's highest-ranking generals were of common origin. By the time of his retirement, two-thirds of the Habsburg senior generalcy shared Beck's bourgeois background.[32] Beck, however, was unique in that he became the publically acknowledged friend and colleague--eventually on terms approaching equality--of a major European sovereign.

Beck's close association with the emperor reveals something of Franz Joseph's character as it solidified into its well-known forms in the late 1860s and early 1870s. The emperor, to be sure, was no military expert and possessed no firm ideas on army administration other than that it should remain fundamentally responsible to the dynasty and not to any civilian agency or representative body. Perhaps cognizant of his meager abilities in the military sphere, Franz Joseph preferred to work through close, trusted associates. In the early days of his reign, this had led to reliance on the incompetent Grünne, a courtier driven solely by the exercise of power and without administrative or combat ability.

Beck, the emperor's second military favorite, represented a maturation of Franz Joseph's judgment. First, Beck, unlike Grünne, possessed both real ability and firm ideas as to what the army needed to do in order to recover from the Königgrätz disaster. Unlike Grünne, Beck was no "yes man," no courtier who always told the emperor what he wanted to hear. Beck's plans for the creation of a Prussian-style general staff system required the emperor to make drastic changes in army administration; indeed, in 1874 they forced him to reverse completely decisions reached just a few years before. Once Franz Joseph made the fundamental choice to follow Beck's advice, he sustained him against all opponents, even at times against members of his own family. The

1867 *Ausgleich* left matters of army administration solely in the emperor's hands. Without Franz Joseph's confidence and support, Beck would never have been able to reform the army.

The general staff created by Beck, with belated assistance from John and Albrecht, marked a radical departure from earlier concepts of military preparedness within the Habsburg monarchy. Unlike earlier elite organizations such as the adjutant general corps, membership in the general staff was determined solely on merit demonstrated in competitive examinations open to all members of the officer corps and administered on an armywide basis. As in Prussia, Beck designed the general staff to function as a sort of central nervous system for the monarchy's armed forces. The general staff bureaus, which formulated war plans, devised mobilization, transportation, and logistics schedules, and made fortification policy, formed the brain of the military organism. The dispersion of general staff officers trained in military science and well versed in the activities of the central bureaus throughout the army ensured the smooth execution of instructions from the brain during periods of crisis and war.

Before the reestablishment of the general staff corps in 1874, the Austro-Hungarian armed forces had never engaged in systematic peacetime military planning. The accomplishments in this vital area of military preparation by Beck's predecessor Schönfeld were marred by the latter's unwillingness to view such planning as a dynamic process. Beck systematized the planning and preparation for war within the general staff upon becoming chief in 1881. Planning against arch-enemy Russia underwent annual revision, while arrangements regarding potential enemies in the southwest and south received consideration as conditions warranted. Through extensive staff exercises and army maneuvers, Beck made sure that members of his general staff corps received some measure of experience in their execution. Gone were the days when divisional chiefs of staff would lead their troops in battle, such as Beck had done at Magenta. The new general staff officer assisted field commanders in the deployment of their forces according to the master designs of the staff bureaus in Vienna.

In the process of formulating deployment plans in the early 1880s, Beck came to recognize the acute weaknesses in the Austro-Hungarian military posture, the remedies for which would form the basis for all his subsequent career efforts. In the initial period of utter unpreparedness, Beck moved quickly to give military substance to the loose political alliance concluded by Bismarck and Andrássy in October 1879. The great disparity between German and Austro-Hungarian capabilities, particularly regarding mobilization and deployment speed, led Beck to push through a whole series of measures designed to improve Austro-Hungarian war readiness. These reforms included the total recasting of the army's principal societal role from domestic police force to protector against external aggression. Beck also obtained a drastic buildup of the monarchy's railroads leading to the main theater in Galicia.

The increasing size and effectiveness of neighboring Great Power armies forced a similar expansion of Austro-Hungarian military capabilities. Beck achieved as much in this regard as was possible under the constitutional arrangements of the *Ausgleich*. In the 1880s, this had meant shifting the two militias from home defense duties to active service with the Austro-Hungarian field army. The Hungarians welcomed the greater battlefield role for their *Honvéd* forces; the Cisleithanian defense ministry more grudgingly acquiesced to the wishes of the general staff. To protect the borders and garrison the empire's fortifications in the absence of the field army, Beck created new *Landsturm* formations.

Within the Habsburg context, the establishment of the *Landsturm* was a revolutionary political and military achievement. In 1867, Beck had gone against the majority of senior officer corps opinion in his advocacy of militia forces as a means of resolving the political-military impasse with the Hungarians. At that time, the notion of handing out weapons to civilians, some of whom had never had the "benefit" of the indoctrination provided by regular military service, would have been anathema to army reactionaries. These attitudes were reflected in the initial military laws of the dual monarchy, which limited *Landsturm* formations to the loyal alpine lands in Cisleithania and to volunteer participation in Hungary. In the mid-1880s, the *Landsturm* concept still had enemies in high places within the military, including Archduke Albrecht and Schönfeld. Beck overcame Albrecht's arch-conservatism by pointing to the military necessity of *Landsturm* forces, and the opposition of senior generals also quickly wilted under the stern imperatives of the grave political-military crisis at hand.

The procurement of arms and equipment for thousands of home defense soldiers meant a drastic increase in the direct military outlays of the Vienna and Budapest governments, for their defense ministries received administrative responsibility for the new *Landsturm*. That the Hungarians readily agreed is not surprising, for they welcomed every opportunity to expand the security role of the *Honvéd* ministry. The Austrian government, at the same time more sympathetic to army viewpoints but less enthusiastic about funding the military establishment throughout the 1867-1914 period, agreed to the increased *Landsturm* expenditures under the threat of war with Russia. That no foreign political crisis comparable to that over Bulgaria in the late 1880s existed in the 1890s goes a long way toward explaining Beck's inability to obtain passage of his program to expand the common army.

The lack of openly hostile external threats during his last fifteen years as chief of the general staff indeed made it impossible for Beck to continue the logical development of the common army into a true *Volksheer* (People's Army) that would exploit the monarchy's full manpower potential. Beck's efforts in this direction during the 1890s and early 1900s, seconded by Archduke Albrecht as well as successive ministers of war and foreign affairs, indicate that the civil-military leadership did not, as Norman Stone has asserted, shrink from enforcing the universal service obligation of the 1868 and 1889 military laws.[33]

In a certain sense, the expansion program of the 1890s fell victim to the pacific inclinations of its author, for Beck never dreamt of provoking an international crisis to boost army development. The experience of the late 1880s had proven that the German ally would not countenance Habsburg aggression in the Balkans. A balance of relations between Russia and Austria-Hungary, of course, had been a hallmark of Bismarckian foreign policy since the early 1870s. Despite the abandonment of the Russian connection by Bismarck's successors, the gradual erosion under Schlieffen of German strategic commitment to an allied defense against Russia remained a powerful restraint on Austro-Hungarian action in the southeast.

Beck, however, unlike his successor Conrad von Hötzendorf, did not need external checks of powerful allies to hinder aggressive impulses. While he had been instrumental in placing the acquisition of Bosnia-Herzegovina on the foreign political agenda, Beck wished above all to avoid a confrontation with Russia. A staunch conservative, Beck saw in the solidarity of the three continental empires the preservation of the social order. He viewed the Balkans as a legitimate area of operations for the Habsburg imperial mission after the monarchy's exclusion from German and Italian affairs and pushed hard throughout his career for Austro-Hungarian expansion to the Aegean. But Beck was not willing to risk war with Russia or any other Great Power to realize this goal.

Nor did Beck favor the use of war against the monarchy's lesser neighbors as a means of redressing strategic imbalances. In particular, he did not share the hatred for liberal Italy of a large segment of the senior officer corps and justly feared a preventive war would unleash a continental European struggle which the monarchy would not survive. Aggression against the Slavic states of Serbia and Montenegro, largely unnecessary before 1903 given preponderant Habsburg political influence, would very likely lead to an unacceptable confrontation with Russia.

Those who had to pay the price for the adventurism of General Conrad, that is, the monarchy's common soldiers, would later appreciate the services to the general European peace of his predecessor. The Social Democratic *Arbeiter Zeitung* wrote upon Beck's death in February 1920: "Undoubtedly it would have been much more useful for Europe had he remained the man at the top despite his advanced age."[34] Only when Conrad took over as chief of the general staff, the obituary continued, did aggressive, adventuristic elements gain the upper hand. Crown Prince Rudolf's sometime mouthpiece, the liberal *Neue*

Wiener Tagblatt, called Beck an embodiment of the Franz Joseph period, and described the general as a man of form who did not try to bluff or scare the emperor into taking action.

General Conrad, a man who urged war upon the monarchy's neighbors almost as a matter of routine, was, of course, the implied object of this comparison. While not Beck's personal choice as his successor, General Conrad could justifiably be considered a Beck legacy as a general staff product of the late 1870s and early 1880s.[35] At the time of his appointment, Conrad enjoyed a tremendous reputation within the officer corps. Unlike Beck, who never really held an independent command, Conrad was respected as a troop leader.[36] Between assignments with the line, Conrad taught tactics at the *Kriegsschule* and authored a two-volume book on the subject.

A captive of the cult of the offensive then sweeping European military circles, Conrad, despite the wall of fire which artillery shrapnel and repeating small arms could lay down by the late 1880s, believed the attack the essential element on the modern battlefield. He waxed eloquently on the magical qualities of the word *"Vorwärts"* (forward) and called for assaults by small columns of infantry to reduce casualties from artillery fire. On the strategic level, his concepts, while perhaps equally innovative, were also equally "offensive." His division of the army into A and B echelons (*Staffel*) was an attempt to make possible a preemptive strike against either Serbia or Italy. What Austria-Hungary would do with these territories once the *k.u.k. Armee* conquered them never received serious consideration.

The latter concept did indeed provide the first planning link between the war plans against Russia, Italy, and the Balkans states, which had remained highly compartmentalized during Beck's tenure in office. While they certainly represent a major innovation in the military sense, Conrad's war plans belie his poor political and Euro-strategic judgment. Gerhard Ritter's statement that Conrad certainly wanted war but just as certainly did not want a world war, reaffirmed by recent scholarship on general staff perceptions during the July crisis of 1914, was indicative of a bellicosity untempered by the military realities of the time: a bellicosity that would get the monarchy involved in a world war which Beck had correctly predicted it would not survive.[37] And since the origins of the Great War have since undergone an almost unprecedented historical scrutiny, Conrad's actions and attitudes, not Beck's, have dominated our subsequent perspective of the military role in the Austro-Hungarian monarchy.

Apart from an early extensive treatise to the emperor on battlefield tactics, Beck took little intellectual interest in the development of small-unit tactical doctrine apart from his insistence upon conducting realistic field exercises and maneuvers.[38] His best military understanding remained at the strategic and geopolitical levels. The military defeats early in Franz Joseph's reign dampened Beck's martial ardor every bit as much as they did the emperor's. The absolute necessity of peace, first to establish, then to solidify the empire's new constitutional dualism, remained an imperative in Beck's mind throughout his career. Conrad, by contrast, did not share the perspective of the defeated monarchy of mid-century and made assessments on the basis of the efficient military machine handed him by Beck.

Si vis pacem, para bellum--to preserve peace, one must prepare for war--defined Beck's career as it does that of many peacetime soldiers. Beck judged the immediate post-*Ausgleich* army as basically incapable of maintaining the empire's Great Power status and advocated a series of reforms to enable it to discharge its essentially defensive function. The greatest of these reforms, from which all Beck's other achievements flowed, was the establishment of a general staff charged with peacetime military planning and preparation for war. Staff planning during the early 1880s quickly uncovered weaknesses in the monarchy's strategic position. A coordinated political-diplomatic and military response in the improvement of the rail net, the conclusion of alliances, and the creation of new home defense forces combined to solve the most urgent of these security problems. These proved successful largely because they required relatively slight financial commitments from the civilian governments and occurred in the war-scare atmosphere of the late 1880s. This political-military consensus evaporated with the easing of Austro-Russian tensions in the early 1890s. Consequently, by 1893, Beck's proposals for the expansion of the standing army, which amounted to almost a doubling of the military budget over a ten-year period, had few chances of obtaining parliamentary approval in Austria or Hungary.

The Habsburg armed forces under Beck made their greatest war-readiness improvements against the potential Russian enemy, although deployments against Serbia and Italy received significant consideration. That all of the general staff's war plans presupposed the superiority of the offensive over the defensive in the limited strategic sense did not mean that Beck either desired war or believed it inevitable. In his 1882 conversations with Waldersee at Strobl, Beck steadfastly refused to consider the formation of unified war aims in regard to Russian Poland, fearing where such discussions might lead. Apart from some rather well-developed ideas on a post-Ottoman political order in the Balkans, Beck never made plans for the reconstruction of Europe following a general conflict. In this sense, he closely resembled his successor Conrad. But unlike Conrad, who actively sought to settle scores real or imagined with the monarchy's neighbors, Beck wanted to avoid war if at all possible.

Unfortunately these pacific attitudes did not remain a permanent part of the Beck legacy. Instead, the office of chief of the general staff, which Beck had spent a lifetime creating, was misused by an insecure and aggressive successor--to the monarchy's ultimate doom. While Beck's services to Europe as a military man of peace received recognition at the time of his death in 1920, they have since faded into the recesses of historical consciousness. In Austria today, Beck remains largely unknown, despite his long tenure in high military office during the commonly celebrated reign of Emperor Franz Joseph I. Conrad, the man probably most responsible for the defeat and dismemberment of Franz Joseph's empire, occupies a prominent, even honored, position within significant portions of the contemporary Austrian memory. During my visit to the Republic of Austria in 1988-89, I found no portrait of Beck hanging in either the Vienna Military History Museum or the old *Kriegsarchiv* in the *Stiftskaserne*, despite his paramount role in the shaping of the Austro-Hungarian army that fought the venerable empire's last war.[39] By constrast, a large picture of Conrad adorned the office wall of a principal military archivist. Similarly, the Austrian *Bundesheer* continued to lay wreaths to Conrad's memory at his final resting place in Hietzing cemetary, while Beck, who dedicated his life to the preservation of the Habsburg state and to the general European peace, lies in a shady corner of the Vienna *Zentralfriedhof*, the monarchy's forgotten general.

Notes

Introduction: The Forgotten *Feldzeugmeister*

1 . Beck received the rank of full general in 1916, eleven years after his retirement, when it was created in order to make Austro-Hungarian general officer ranks correspond to their counterparts in the allied Imperial German Army.

2 . High Court Chamberlain.

3 . Paul W. Schroeder, "The Status of Habsburg Studies in the United States," *Austrian History Yearbook* 3 (1967, pt. 3): 267-95.

4 . See Edmund von Glaise-Horstenau, *Franz Josephs Weggefährte* (Vienna: Amalthea Verlag, 1930).

5 . Originally a voluminous diary, numbering several thousand pages, was given to the *Kriegsarchiv* by Beck's family along with the remainder of his papers in the early 1920s. Alice von Beck, the general's granddaughter, apparently requested the return of the diaries shortly before the outbreak of World War II. For fifty years it was thought that they had been burnt during the war in the fire caused by Allied bombing which destroyed her apartment in the *Hohen Markt* in Vienna. In the early 1990s, Dr. Peter Broucek of the Vienna *Kriegsarchiv* located a copy of the diary in Switzerland which had survived in private hands. Glaise-Horstenau, however, so thoroughly and exclusively based his work on the diary that it offers little more than what has already been revealed. It also appears clear to Vienna archivists that while Beck called the huge manuscript his *Tagebuch*, or diary, the general dictated the contents to transcribers around 1900.

6 . The German general staff study during the interwar period edited by Kurt Wiedenauer reproduced much of the Beck diary pertaining to the latter's relations with the Prussian Chief of the General Staff Alfred von Schlieffen. This study is currently housed in the Potsdam Militärarchiv.

7 . See Gunther E. Rothenberg, *The Army of Francis Joseph* (West Lafayette, Ind.: Purdue University Press, 1976).

8 . Dieter Degreif, "Operative Plannung des k.u.k. Generalstabes für einen Krieg in der Zeit vor 1914 (1880-1914)" (Ph.D. dissertation, University of Mainz, 1983). Lothar Höbelt has clarified the nature of Austro-German alliance politics in the 1890s, in "Schlieffen, Beck, Potiorek und das Ende der gemeinsamen deutsch-österreichisch-ungarischen Aufmarschpläne im Osten," *Militärgeschichtliche Mitteilungen* 36 (1984/2): 7-30.

9 . István Deák, *Beyond Nationalism: A Social and Political History of the Habsburg Officer Corps, 1848-1918* (New York: Oxford University Press, 1990).

10 . Walter Wagner, *Geschichte des k.(u.)k. Kriegsministeriums, 1848-1888*, 2 vols. (Graz: Hermann Böhlaus Nachfolger, 1966 & 1971).

11 . KA Nachlaß Wolf-Schneider von Arno, B/197.

166   *Notes*

Chapter 1: Death and Rebirth

1 . Casualty figures are from Gordon A. Craig, *The Battle of Königgrätz: Prussia's Victory over Austria, 1866* (Philadelphia: J.B. Lippincott Company, 1964), p. 166.

2 . Arthur J. May, *The Hapsburg Monarchy 1867-1914* (Cambridge, Mass.: Harvard University Press, 1951), pp. 35-45; Carlisle A. Macartney, *The Habsburg Empire 1790-1918* (New York: Macmillan, 1969), pp. 349-52.

3 . Between 1867 and 1915, the term "Austria" was not used in the political parlance of the Habsburg empire. Habsburg lands outside Hungary became known officially as "the kingdoms and lands represented in the Reichsrat" and were unofficially referred to as "Cisleithania," meaning the lands on this (Cis-, or the western) side of the Leitha River which divided the Austrian crown lands from the Kingdom of Hungary. Conversely, Hungary became known as Transleithania (i.e., lands across the Leitha River). Austria-Hungary became the official name of the Habsburg state after 1867.

4 . Johann Christoph Allmayer-Beck, "Die bewaffnete Macht in Staat und Gesellschaft," in Adam Wandruska and Peter Urbanitsch, eds., *Die Habsburger Monarchie 1848-1918*, vol. V, *Die bewaffnete Macht* (Vienna: Verlag der österreichischen Akademie der Wissenschaften, 1987), p. 12.

5 . KA Nachlaß Wolf-Schneider von Arno, B/197, 6/VII, pp. 355-60; Antonio Schmidt-Brentano, *Die Armee in Österreich: Militär, Staat und Gesellschaft 1848-1867* (Boppard am Rhein: Harald Boldt Verlag, 1975), pp. 10-18; Walter Wagner, *Geschichte des k.k. Kriegsministeriums, 1848-1866*, vol. 5, *in Studien zur Geschichte der Österreichisch-Ungarischen Monarchie* (Graz: Verlag Hermann Böhlaus Nachfolger, 1966), pp. 55-65; Joachim Niemeyer, *Das österreichische Militärwesen im Umbruch: Untersuchungen zum Kriegsbild zwischen 1830 und 1866* (Osnabrück: Biblio Verlag, 1979), p. 154; Rothenberg, *The Army of Francis Joseph*, p. 40.

6 . KA Nachlaß Wolf-Schneider B/197, 6/VII, pp. 414-20; Rothenberg, *The Army of Francis Joseph*, p. 54. Anton Freiherr von Mollinary, *Sechsundvierzig Jahre im österreich-ungarischen Heere*, vol. 2 (Zurich: Verlag Art. Institut Orell Füssli, 1905), p. 60.

7 . For a complete treatment of Benedek's career, see Oskar Regele, *Feldzeugmeister Benedek: Der Weg nach Königgrätz* (Vienna: Herold, 1960). See also KA Nachlaß Wolf-Schneider, B/197, 6/VII, pp. 431-32.

8 . For the early history of the quartermaster general staff, see the unpublished manuscript by Wolf-Schneider von Arno in the Vienna *Kriegsarchiv*. For a published overview of the Habsburg general staff, see Oskar Regele, *Generalstabchefs aus Vier Jahrhunderten* (Vienna: Herold, 1966).

9 . Niemeyer, p. 149.

10 . For samples of student work at the *Kriegsschule*, see KA Nachlaß Beck, B/2, Fasz. III, No. 62. Beck graduated from the first *Kriegsschule* class. See also KA Nachlaß Wolf-Schneider, B/197, 6/VII, pp. 393-97; Wagner, "Die k.(u.)k. Armee: Gliederung und Aufgabenstellung," pp. 251-55; Niemeyer, p. 157.

11 . As quoted in Rothenberg, *The Army of Francis Joseph*, p. 60.

12 . Wagner, "Die k.(u.)k. Armee: Gliederung und Aufgabenstellung," pp. 158-67; Schmidt-Brentano, *Die Armee in Österreich*, pp. 41-43; Regele, *Feldzeugmeister Benedek*, p. 163; KA Nachlaß Wolf-Schneider, B/197, 6/VII, pp. 428-30.

13 . Friedrich's father, Josef Beck, was a professor of surgery at the University of Freiburg. See Edmund von Glaise-Horstenau, *Franz Josephs Weggefährte* (Vienna: Amalthea Verlag, 1930), pp. 11-12.

14 . Glaise-Horstenau, p. 17.

15 . Glaise-Horstenau, p. 18.

16 . For the Austrian army in Italy, see Alan Sked, *The Survival of the Habsburg Empire: Radetzky, the Imperial Army and the Class War, 1848* (London: Longman, 1979). See also Rothenberg, *The Army of Francis Joseph*, p. 17. For a biography of Radetzky, see Oskar Regele, *Feldmarschall Radetzky, Leben-Leistung-Erbe* (Vienna: Herold, 1957).

17 . Glaise-Horstenau, pp. 23-24.

18 . Glaise-Horstenau, pp. 30-31.

19 . For Austrian foreign policy during the Crimean War, see Paul Schroeder, *Austria, Great Britain and the Crimean War: the Destruction of the European Concert* (Ithaca, N.Y.: Cornell University Press, 1972); Norman Rich, *Why the Crimean War? A Cautionary Tale* (Hanover, N.H.: University of New England, 1985), p. 200.

20 . For a complete discussion of Heß's operative ideas, see Manfried Rauchensteiner, "Hess, Heinrich Freiherr von, Schriften aus dem Militärwissenschaftlichen Nachlaß mit einer Einführung in sein Leben und das operative Denken seiner Zeit," in *Bibliotheca Rerum Militärium, Quellen und Darstellungen zu Militärwissenschaft und Militärgeschichte* 41 (Osnabrück: Biblio- Verlag, 1975). For a contemporary observation of Heß's shortcomings, see Mollinary, vol. II, p. 47.

21 . Glaise-Horstenau, pp. 38-42.

22 . Glaise-Horstenau, pp. 44-45.

23 . Glaise-Horstenau, p. 53.

24. Wagner, "Die k.(u.)k. Armee: Gliederung und Aufgabenstellung," pp. 343-44.

25 . Glaise-Horstenau, pp. 67-72.

26 . For a good survey of the early development of the Prussian general staff, see Trevor N. Dupuy, *A Genius for War* (Englewood Cliffs, N.J.: Prentice Hall, 1977), pp. 24-47. See also Hajo Holborn, "The Prusso-German School: Moltke and the Rise of the General Staff," in Peter Paret, ed., *The Makers of Modern Strategy from Machiavelli to the Nuclear Age* (Princeton, N.J.: Princeton University Press, 1986), pp. 281-95.

27 . See the excerpt from Moltke's history of the 1859 war, in Daniel J. Hughes, ed., *Moltke on the Art of War: Selected Writings* (Novato, Calif.: Presidio Press, 1993), pp. 235-36. See also Dupuy, p. 66.

28 . On 1 May 1861, Beck would marry Rzikowsky's daughter, Anna.

29 . Glaise-Horstenau, pp. 73-4; KA Nachlaß Beck, B/2, Fasz. V, Nos. 105 and 106. Beck's ideas did not entirely lack appeal among his Prussian counterparts. Gerhard Ritter has noted that Moltke expressed in the early 1860s similar hopes of

Austro-Prussian cooperation against France. See Gerhard Ritter, *The Sword and the Scepter: The Problem of Militarism in Germany*, vol. 1, *The Prussian Tradition 1740-1890* (Coral Gables, Fla.: University of Miami Press, 1969), p. 217.

30 . Beck's report on the Prussian maneuvers garnered him high praise from the deputy chief of the general quartermaster staff, Major General Ladislaus Nagy von Alsó-Szopor. See KA Nachlaß Beck, B/2, Fasz. V, No. 117. See also KA Nachlaß Wolf-Schneider, B/197, 6/IX, pp. 686-87.

31 . KA Nachlaß Beck, B/2, Fasz. V, No. 125; Glaise-Horstenau, p. 80. See also KA Nachlaß Wolf-Schneider, B/197, 6/IX, p. 924.

32 . Glaise-Horstenau, pp. 81-82. After 1860, the parliament slashed military appropriations from 160 million gulden in 1861 to 96.5 million in 1865. For more complete discussion of military budget cutbacks during this period, see Wagner, "Die k.(u.)k. Armee: Gliederung und Aufgabenstellung," p. 300; Rothenberg, *The Army of Francis Joseph*, p. 58; Kurt Peball, "1866: Der Krieg und seine historische Symtomatik," in Dermot Bradley and Ulrich Marwedel, eds., *Militärgeschichte, Militärwissenschaft und Konfliktforschung: Eine Festschrift für Werner Hahlweg zur Vollendung seines 65. Lebensjahres am 29. April 1977* (Osnabrück: Biblio Verlag, 1977): 325-58.

33 . Glaise-Horstenau, pp. 85-87.

34 . KA Nachlaß Beck, B/2, Fasz. V, No. 135.

35 . KA Nachlaß Wolf-Schneider, B/197, 6/VII, p. 483; Glaise-Horstenau, p. 89.

36 . KA Nachlaß Beck, B/2, Nos. 108, 109, 120.

37 . As cited in Hughes, ed., *Moltke on the Art of War*, p. 96.

38 . In November 1874, Benedek privately told ex-war minister Franz Kuhn von Kuhnenfeld of his 1866 conversations with Archduke Albrecht. See Kuhn's diary entry for 3 November 1874 in KA Nachlaß Kuhn, B/670, No. 7, p. 284. Oskar Regele writes that there were widespread rumors at the time that Franz Joseph had furnished Benedek with a written assurance that he would not face a military court in the event of a Prussian victory. Regele adds, however, that there is no existing archival evidence to suggest such a deal. See Regele, *Feldzeugmeister Benedek*, p. 400.

39 . See the conference protocol of 14 March 1866, in MKSM 22-1 ex 1866, Sonderreihe, Sep. Karton 24, No. 5.

40 . Krismanich had headed the general staff's topographical bureau and was considered an expert on the Bohemian-Moravian theater of operations. He had also served as an instructor of strategy at the *Kriegsschule*. See KA Nachlaß Wolf-Schneider, B/197, 6/VII, p. 478; Craig, *The Battle of Königgrätz*, p. 15; Rothenberg, *The Army of Francis Joseph*, p. 67; Regele, *Feldzeugmeister Benedek*, p, 402; Schmidt-Brentano, *Die Armee in Österreich*, p. 261; Holborn, p. 293. For Krismanich's plans, see the documents assembled for his court-martial following the Austro-Prussian War, in MKSM 22-9 ex 1866, Sonderreihe, Sep. Karton 24, No. 5.

41 . For Beck's own report concerning his activities as imperial envoy to the North Army, see KA Nachlaß Beck, B/2, Fasz. V, No. 139. See also his telegrams to Vienna, in MKSM 69-4/3 ex 1866; Glaise-Horstenau, pp. 100-130.

42 . Lavender Cassels, *Clash of Generations: A Habsburg Family Drama in the Nineteenth Century* (London: John Murray, 1973), p. 16.

43 . May, pp. 35-45; Macartney, pp. 549-52.

44 . Gunther E. Rothenberg, "Toward a National Hungarian Army: The Military Compromise of 1868 and Its Consequences," *Slavic Review* 31 (1972): 805-16; Macartney, p. 19.

45 . Rothenberg, "Toward a National Hungarian Army," pp. 805-16.

46 . Walter Wagner, *Geschichte des k.u.k. Kriegsministeriums 1866-1888*, vol. 10, in *Studien zur Geschichte der Österreichisch-Ungarischen Monarchie* (Graz: Verlag Hermann Böhlaus Nachfolger, 1971), p. 11.

47 . See Albrecht's memorandum of 23 December 1867, in which he bemoaned Andrássy's lack of knowledge of army organization and despaired at what he considered the unreasonableness of his demands concerning the stationing of Magyar troops and officers outside the Kingdom of Hungary and the "Magyarization" of their service uniforms, in HHStA, Filmarchiv, Nachlaß Albrecht, roll 54; See also Albrecht's memorandum of February 1867 concerning the future powers of the war ministry, in HHStA, Filmarchiv, Nachlaß Albrecht, roll 53. See also Wagner, "Die k.(u.)k. Armee: Gliederung und Aufgabenstellung," p. 353; Rothenberg, "Toward a National Hungarian Army," pp. 805-16.

48 . The army initially opted to convert existing Lorenz muzzleloaders to breechloading through the construction of a trapdoor mechanism proposed by Franz Wänzel. This solution proved ultimately unworkable since most of the M1854 Lorenz rifles were already worn out and possessed poor ballistic qualities. The army ultimately adopted an 11mm breechloader designed by Steyr manufacturer Josef Werndl. Complete rearmament with the Werndl was not accomplished until the mid-1870s. See Wagner, "Die k.(u.)k. Armee: Gliederung und Aufgabenstellung," p. 604; Frederick Myatt, *The Illustrated Encyclopedia of 19th Century Firearms* (New York: Crescent Books, pp. 103-104.

49 . Rothenberg, "Toward a National Hungarian Army," pp. 805-16; Rothenberg, *The Army of Francis Joseph*, p. 75; Glaise-Horstenau, p. 144; Elfriede Jandesek, "Die Stellung des Abgeordnetenhauses der im Reichsrate vertretenen Königreiche und Länder zu Fragen des Militärs, 1867-1914" (Ph.D. dissertation: University of Vienna, 1964), pp. 6-9.

50 . See the minutes of the 14 February 1867 crown council, in HHStA, PA XL, Karton 283, KZ 322, MRZ 127.

51 . See the crown council protocol for 31 December 1867, in HHStA, PA XL, Karton 283.

52 . Glaise-Horstenau, p. 147; Wagner, *Kriegsministerium* II, p. 25; For Andrássy's post-*Ausgleich* political views, see Franz-Josef Kos, *Die Politik Österreich-Ungarns während der Orientkrise 1875-79: Zum Verhältnis von politischer und militärischer Führung* (Vienna: Böhlau Verlag, 1984); István Diószegi, *Die Außenpolitik der österreichisch-ungarischen Monarchie 1871-1877* (Vienna: Hermann Böhlaus Nachfolger, 1985).

53 .   See Beck's memorandum of 27 November 1867, "Gegen die Zweitheilung des Heeres," in both KA Nachlaß Beck, B/2, Fasz. V, No. 143, and MKSM 82-3/20 ex 1868. See also Beck's earlier memorandum on the future organization of the army written on the occasion of his preliminary discussions with Andrássy in March 1867, in KA Nachlaß Beck, B/2, Fasz. V, No. 141.

54 .   See Beck's recommendations to Franz Joseph at the close of his memorandum of 28 November 1867, in KA Nachlaß Beck, B/2, Fasz. V, No. 144.

55 .   See the protocol for the 31 December 1867 crown council, in HHStA, PA XL, Karton 283.

56 .   See the protocols for the ministerial council meetings held on 10 and 14 January 1868, in HHStA, PA XL, Karton 283. John remained chief of the general staff for another year, until removed from that post by his successor as war minister, Franz Freiherr Kuhn von Kuhnenfeld.

57 .   In his diary, Kuhn disparagingly compared the mental capacity of Hungarians to that of American Indians (whom he considered savages) and wrote that the Kingdom of Hungary "reeked of the steppes of Asia." Kuhn disliked the Compromise of 1867 since it removed Hungary from effective control of the Austro-Germans. The Danube, Kuhn wrote, would always remain a German river and warned political Hungary that it had a choice between an agreement with the "amicable" Austro-Germans now or domination by unyielding Prussians later. Events of the first half of the 20th century largely confirmed the farsightedness of Kuhn's predictions. See KA Nachlaß Kuhn, B/680, No. 7, pp. 11, 24-25, 55-56, 211-12.

58 .   Kuhn had been Gyulai's chief of staff in 1859 and had commanded the Austrian defense of the Tyrol in 1866.

59 .   Rothenberg, "Toward a National Hungarian Army," pp. 805-16. The defense ministries had, in theory, already been in existence after early 1867, when Franz Joseph entrusted Andrássy with the portfolio of Hungarian defense minister in addition to that of minister-president. See Tibor Papp, "Die königlich-ungarische Landwehr (Honvéd) 1868 bis 1914," in Adam Wandruska and Peter Urbanitsch, eds., *Die Habsburgermonarchie 1848-1918*, vol. V, *Die bewaffnete Macht* (Vienna: Verlag der österreichischen Akademie der Wissenschaften, 1987), p. 645.

60 .   See MKSM Sonderreihe, Karton 45, Wehrgesetz, for protocols of the steering committee proceedings; see also the crown council protocols of 5 and 8 March 1868 for the ministerial deliberations over the steering committee findings, in HHStA, PA XL, Karton 283. See also the 18 June 1868 crown council which debated the draft military bill, in HHStA, PA XL, Karton 283, KZ 2050, MRZ 72; see also Kuhn's version of the crown council, in KA Nachlaß B/670, No. 7, pp. 22-23. See also Walter Wagner's detailed description, in Wagner, *Kriegsministerium* II, pp. 43-47.

61 .   See the crown council protocol of 18 June 1868 cited above. See also Kuhn's version of his April 1868 exchanges with Andrássy on the subject of the military bill, in KA Nachlaß Kuhn, B/670, No. 7, pp. 17-19, 21.

62 .   See Kuhn's diary entries of 14-15 July 1868, describing an acrimonious train conversation with Andrássy, in KA Nachlaß Kuhn, B/670, No. 7, p. 26.

63 . Little written evidence exists detailing the exact nature of Beck's private negotiations with Andrássy in June-July 1868. On 10 August, Beck wrote the Hungarian minister-president that he was honored to have acted as the go-between in the negotiations with Budapest. Three days later, Andrássy thanked Beck for his services. See MKSM 82-3/12 ex 1868, Letter No. 2458, Beck to Andrássy, Vienna, 10 August 1868, and Letter No. 1020, Andrássy to Beck, Ofen, 13 August 1868.

64 . See Papp, "Die königlich ungarische Landwehr (Honvéd) 1868 bis 1914," p. 643.

65 . See MKSM 82-3/15 ex 1868, Telegram, Beck to Franz Joseph at Gödöllö, Vienna, 26 October 1868. The military law of 1868 ultimately signed by Franz Joseph did not include provision for the limitation of peacetime forces, although it did limit the common army's wartime strength to 800,000 men.

66 . For transcripts of the proceedings of 5-9 November 1868, see MKSM 82-3/20 ex 1868. See also Glaise-Horstenau, pp. 149-50; Wertheimer, pp. 364-65.

67 . Beck reportedly remarked that "a hussar is a hero in any uniform." Approval of the common army uniform for *Honvéd* cavalry quickly followed. See Glaise-Horstenau, p. 150.

68 . The idea for one-year volunteer reserve officers was borrowed from Prussia. See Rothenberg, *The Army of Francis Joseph*, p. 83; Allmayer-Beck, "Die bewaffnete Macht in Staat und Gesellschaft," pp. 75-79.

69 . The "language of command" consisted of approximately eighty German words regulating the disciplined movement of troops on the battlefield. The 1868 military law did recognize "regimental languages" governing routine administration and operations, including training. Regimental languages were those spoken by at least 20% of the recruits, and regimental officers had to learn them within three years of their posting and demonstrate competency in an oral examination. Failing the language examination placed the officer in question on the bottom of the regimental promotion list. See István Deák, *Beyond Nationalism: A Social and Political History of the Habsburg Officer Corps, 1848-1918* (New York: Oxford University Press, 1990), pp. 99-102; Rothenberg, *The Army of Francis Joseph*, p. 108; Antonio Schmidt-Brentano, "Die österreichische Armee von Erzherzog Karl bis Conrad von Hötzendorf," in Heinrich Lutz and Helmut Rumpler, eds., *Wiener Beiträge zur Geschichte der Neuzeit*, vol. 19, *Österreich und die deutsche Frage im 19. Jahrhundert* (Munich: Oldenburg, 1982): 231-55.

Chapter 2: The General Staff Question

1 . See the copy of the joint report by John and Albrecht concerning general staff performance during the 1866 war, in MKSM 50-4/1 ex 1866, Letter No. 4728, John and Albrecht to Franz Joseph, Vienna, 13 October 1866. See also Allmayer-Beck, "Die bewaffnete Macht in Staat und Gesellschaft," p. 71.

2 . See the Heß-Beck memorandum, "Gedanken über die gegenwärtige Organisation der Waffen und Branchen der Armee von FM Heß" of September 1863, in

KA Nachlaß Beck, B/2, Fasz. V, No. 130. See also Beck's later memorandum, "Die Organisation des Generalstabes," written sometime in 1865, in KA Nachlaß Beck, B/2, Fasz. V, No. 136.

3 . See Beck's "Promemoria über Armeeverhältnisse" of August 1867, in KA Nachlaß Beck, B/2, Fasz. V, No. 142.

4 . See Beck's memorandum, "Über die Stellung des Chefs des Generalstabes" of 23 December 1867, in KA Nachlaß, B/2, No. 153.

5 . In the pre-1866 Austrian army, the chief of the general staff did not exercise absolute control over the general staff corps. In the spring of 1866, chief of the general staff Major General Alfred von Henickstein had to obtain Lieutenant General Ludwig von Benedek's approval for all staff appointments within the Italian Army and then submit the coordinate list to the emperor via the war ministry for final sanction. See MKSM 69-1/7 ex 1866, Letter No. 1135, Franck to Franz Joseph, Vienna, 2 April 1866.

6 . See Josef Jakob Holzer, "Erzherzog Albrecht 1867-1895: Politisch-militärische Konzeptione und Tätigkeit als Generalinspektor des Heeres" (Ph.D. dissertation: University of Vienna, 1974), p. 1.

7 . See MKSM 9-4/5 ex 1866, Letter No. 5729, John to Franz Joseph, Vienna, 9 September 1866. See also Schmidt-Brentano, *Die Armee in Österreich*, p. 29; Wagner, *Kriegsministerium* II, pp. 11-14.

8 . MKSM 9-1/1 ex 1868, Letter No. 10, Albrecht to Franz Joseph, Vienna, 2 January 1868. See also Wagner, *Kriegsministerium* II, p. 32.

9 . See MKSM 9-1/3 ex 1868, Letter Präs. No. 181, John to Franz Joseph, Vienna, 15 January 1868. See also Wagner, *Kriegsministerium* II, p. 36.

10 . See MKSM 1-2/7 ex 1867, Letter Präs. No. 3377, John to Franz Joseph, Vienna, 11 November 1867. Essentially, John challenged the military chancellery's right to issue military instructions and resolutions independently from the war ministry or army high command. Beck viewed John's position as an infringement on the emperor's constitutional authority as supreme warlord.

11 . See Beck's note of 18 January 1868 appended to John's letter of 30 December 1867 offering reasons for his resignation as chief of the general staff, in MKSM 50-2.3 ex 1867, Letter Präs. No. 4396, John to the Military Chancellery, Vienna, 30 December 1867.

12 . MKSM 9-1/2 ex 1868, Letter, Military Chancellery to Kuhn, Vienna, 18 January 1868.

13 . One only has to read Kuhn's torrid diary entries. The war minister's almost insane rage against the army commander often robbed him of words to express his loathing, forcing him to insert long series of dots, dashes and exclamation points after a particularly scathing comment. See KA Nachlaß Kuhn, B/670, No. 7. See also Rothenberg, *The Army of Francis Joseph*, p. 79.

14 . See the entry for 8 October 1868, in KA Nachlaß Kuhn, B/670, No. 7, p. 34.

15 . See Wagner, *Kriegsministerium* II, pp. 37, 70-71; Wagner, "Die k.u.(k.) Armee: Gliederung und Aufgabenstellung," p. 354; Rothenberg, *The Army of Francis Joseph*, p. 79; KA Nachlaß Wolf-Schneider, B/197, 6/VII, p. 362.

16 . See Kuhn's notes on an audience with Franz Joseph in which the war minister received the emperor's permission to redefine Albrecht's role, in KA Nachlaß Kuhn, B/670, No. 7, pp. 47-48. For all the documents pertaining to the changes made in Albrecht's role in early 1869, see MKSM 9-1/1 ex 1869. See also Wagner, *Kriegsministerium* II, pp. 71-74 and KA Nachlaß Wolf-Schneider, B/197, 6/VIII, pp. 501-2.

17 . See Franz Joseph's reply to Kuhn of 4 March 1869 drafted by Beck, No. 704, in MKSM 9-1/1 ex 1869. Note Beck's elimination on point three of the draft letter which would have given Albrecht routine access to military chancellery records. See also Holzer, pp. 125-27; Wagner, "Die k.u.(k.) Armee: Gliederung und Aufgabenstellung," p. 357.

18 . See MKSM 9-1/14 ex 1868, Letter Präs. No. 3328, Kuhn to Franz Joseph, Vienna, 5 October 1868. See also KA Nachlaß Wolf-Schneider, B/197, 6/VIII, p. 503; Wagner, *Kriegsministerium* II, pp. 59-60.

19 . See the diary entries for 2 and 3 October 1868, in KA Nachlaß Kuhn, B/670, No. 7, p. 43.

20 . MKSM 70-2/5 ex 1869, Letter No. 1181, Kuhn to Franz Joseph, Vienna, 26 March 1869. See also Wagner, *Kriegsministerium* II, p. 74.

21 . KA Nachlaß Wolf-Schneider, B/197, 6/VIII, p. 506; Rothenberg, *The Army of Francis Joseph*, p. 80.

22 . Gunther Rothenberg writes that in 1870, 3.13% of general staff majors were over forty-three years of age, while 17% of their counterparts in the cavalry, 42% in the infantry, and 94% in the artillery had already reached this age. See Rothenberg, *The Army of Francis Joseph*, p. 81. István Deák notes that general staff officers were universally resented throughout the army for their distinctive bottle-green uniforms and plumed headgear similar to that of general officers. See Deák, p. 111. For an illustration of the uniform flourishes permitted to officers of the general staff, see the series of oil paintings by Lieutenant Oskar Brüch, in Günther Dirrheimer, *Das k.u.k. Heer 1895*, vol. 10, in *Schriften des Heeresgeschichtlichen Museums in Wien* (*Militärwissenschaftliches Institut*) (Vienna: Österreichischer Bundesverlag, 1983).

23 . See Beck's memorandum entitled "Bemerkungen zu den organischen Bestimmungen für den Generalstab," Vienna, 10 May 1870, in MKSM 71-9/1 ex 1870.

24 . See Albrecht's memorandum to Franz Joseph of 20 May 1870, in MKSM 71-9/1 ex 1870. See also Walter Wagner's discussion of Albrecht's objections to Kuhn's proposals, in Wagner, *Kriegsministerium* II, p. 95.

25 . Among the pro-Kuhn general officers on the committee were Major Generals Mollinary and Maroicic. Kuhn's director of the general staff, Brigadier General Josef Gallina, also received a seat on the committee. See Mollinary II, p. 188. Walter Wagner has quite correctly pointed out that most of the committee members did not belong to the ministry and that the committee, therefore, at least possessed the appearance of objectivity. See Wagner, *Kriegsministerium* II, p. 95.

26 . See Letter, Degenfeld to Franz Joseph, Vienna, 17 August 1870, in MKSM 71-9/1 ex 1870.

27 . See MKSM 64-1/2 ex 1869, Letter No. 334, Kuhn to Franz Joseph, Vienna, 24 January 1869.

28 . Kuhn's memorandum has been published by Glaise-Horstenau, pp. 457-60. See also Kuhn's diary entry of 14 July 1870, in KA Nachlaß Kuhn, B/670, No. 7, pp. 100-101.

29 . Key to understanding ministerial opinions during the July 1870 crisis are HHStA, PA XL, Karton 285, Ministerial Conference Protocol, KZ 3018, MRZ 66, 15 July 1870; HHStA, PA XL, Karton 285, Crown Council Protocol, 18 July 1870. Also important is Kuhn's contemporary version of the events of the 18 July council, as well as his later recollections thereof, in KA Nachlaß Kuhn, B/670, No. 7, pp. 101-2; Nachlaß Kuhn, B/670, No. 14, pp. 12-14.

30 . MKSM 69-2/1 ex 1870, Letter Präs. No. 2656, Kuhn to the Military Chancellery, Vienna, 26 July 1870.

31 . HHStA, PA XL, Karton 285, Ministerial Council Protocol, KZ 3113, MRZ 81, 30 August 1870.

32 . KA Nachlaß Kuhn, B/670, No. 7, p. 97.

33 . MKSM 64-1/3 ex 1870, Letter Präs. No. 3269, Kuhn to Franz Joseph, Vienna, 31 August 1870.

34 . See Kuhn's report to the emperor on the commission's findings, in MKSM 64-1/2 ex 1871, Letter Präs. No. 4268, Kuhn to Franz Joseph, Vienna, 6 January 1871.

35 . Andrew Wheatcroft, "Technology and the Military Mind: Austria 1866-1914," in Geoffrey Best and Andrew Wheatcroft, eds., *War, Economy and the Military Mind* (London: Croom Helm Rowman and Littlefield, 1976), pp. 50-56.

36 . According to an unsigned report to the emperor, probably by Beck, Werndl had set up his factory along "American" principles of mass production, which had required more time and experience to implement than Werndl had anticipated when he assumed the government contract. Machinery ordered from the United States had arrived late and delayed production, and Werndl's subcontracting of various portions of the manufacturing process had caused additional delays. See "Referat über die Werndl'sche Gewehrlieferungs-Angelegenheit," in MKSM 64-3/5 ex 1867.

37 . MKSM 64-1/11 ex 1871, Letter Abt. 7, No. 4693, Kuhn to Franz Joseph, Vienna, 18 November 1871.

38 . HHStA, PA XL, Karton 285, Crown Council Protocol, KZ 4344, MRZ 89, 5 November 1870.

39 . See Beck's memorandum entitled "Vorstudien für einen Verteidigungskrieg," probably written sometime after the start of the Franco-Prussian War, in KA Nachlaß Beck, B/2, Fasz. VI.

40 . See Beck's "Studie zu einer etwaigen Mobilisierung des k.k. Heeres," which he included in the file with Kuhn's analysis of the shortcomings of the Austro-Hungarian partial mobilization during the Franco-Prussian War. See MKSM 65-1/1 ex 1871, Memorandum, Beck to Franz Joseph, Vienna, 10 September 1870.

41 . In August 1870, Kuhn had become embroiled in a fierce struggle with Archduke Albrecht over the army wartime order of battle. Albrecht, supported by Franz

Freiherr von John, favored the organization of super-sized divisions of 20,000-25,000 men into corps numbering 70,000 men, which Kuhn felt were much too large. When Franz Joseph approved Albrecht's proposals, Kuhn threatened to resign. The emperor ultimately reversed himself, since he deemed it ill advised to change war ministers in the midst of a grave international crisis. See KA Nachlaß Kuhn, B/670, No. 7, p. 102; Holzer, p. 35.

42 . Kuhn instructed neither the war ministry nor the general staff to prepare concrete mobilization and deployment plans for wars against Prussia and/or Russia. The general staff, then under the direction of Brigadier General Josef Gallina, consequently did nothing to plan for Kuhn's offensive war in Poland or intervention in Germany. This suited Gallina's personal preferences, for he took little interest in war planning, concentrating his efforts as the "director" of the general staff on tactical problems. Gallina authored several textbooks on tactics and general staff fieldwork. See Allmeyer-Beck, "Die bewaffnete Macht in Staat und Gesellschaft," p. 129; KA Nachlaß Wolf-Schneider, B/197, 6/VIII, p. 510.

43 . See MKSM 69-1/1 ex 1872, Letter Präs. No. 1226, Kuhn to Franz Joseph, Vienna, 23 March 1872.

44 . See MKSM 69-2/1 ex 1874, Letter Präs. No. 861, Kuhn to Franz Joseph, Vienna, 9 March 1974.

45 . See Wagner, "Die k.(u.)k. Armee: Gliederung und Aufgabenstellung," pp. 573-74.

46 . The common army budget rose from 77.7 million gulden in 1871 to approximately 88.1 million in 1874-75. Funds allocated for extraordinary purchases, however, dropped off significantly in the years immediately following the Franco-Prussian War. See Rainer von Kesslitz, "Die Lasten der militärischen Rüstungen Österreich-Ungarns in neuster Zeit (1868-1912)," in KA, MS Allgemeine No. 54.

47 . See HHStA, PA XL, Karton 287, Crown Council Protocol KZ 593, MRZ 146, 23 February 1873.

48 . The Austrian and Hungarian ministries repeatedly slashed Kuhn's procurement budget throughout the early 1870s. Of the approximately 63.3 million gulden requested by the war minister for extraordinary purchases in 1872-73, only 21.4 million was ultimately approved. See HHStA, PA XL, Karton 286, Crown Council Protocol KZ 1057, RMRZ 108, 19 April 1871; MKSM 51-1/3 ex 1872, Letter Präs. No. 2193, Kuhn to Franz Joseph, Vienna, 21 May 1872; Kesslitz, p. 181.

49 . See Kuhn's diary entry for 19 February 1872, in KA Nachlaß Kuhn, B/670, No. 7, pp. 176-78. See also Wagner, "Die k.(u.)k. Armee: Gliederung und Aufgabenstellung," p. 450.

50 . See Beck's memorandum, "Stellung des Chefs des Generalstabes," in KA Nachlaß Beck, B/2, Fasz. VI, No. 164.

51 . See the following memoranda by Beck: "Studie in Bezug auf die für einen Krieg im Allgemein nöthigen Vorarbeiten," January 1872, in KA Nachlaß Beck, B/2, No. 159; "Studie über das Wesen der größeren Generalstabs-Übung," 8 January 1872, in KA Nachlaß Beck, B/2, No. 161. See also Wagner, *Kriegsministerium* II, pp. 118-19.

52 . See KA Nachlaß Beck, B/2, Fasz. VI, No. 167, Memorandum "Die wichtigsten militärischen Fragen," Beck to Franz Joseph, Vienna, 14 December 1873; Wagner, *Kriegsministerium* II, p. 120.

53 . For Beck's protests against war ministry slowness in updating the wartime order of battle, see his memorandum of 29 January 1873, in MKSM 65-2/4 ex 1873.

54 . See the diary entries for 13 and 22 February 1869, in KA Nachlaß Kuhn, B/670, No. 7, p. 47.

55 . See KA Nachlaß Kuhn, B/670, No. 7, pp. 56-57, 169; MKSM 29-1/21 ex 1873, Memorandum, Albrecht to Franz Joseph, Vienna, 20 December 1872.

56 . See MKSM 18-1/1 ex 1873, Memorandum ad KM Präs. No. 2215, "Entwurf des deutschen Reichs-Militär-Gesetzes," Albrecht to Franz Joseph, Vienna, 14 June 1873.

57 . See the entries in Kuhn's diary for 17 January and 5 February 1873, in KA Nachlaß Kuhn, B/670, No. 7, pp. 210, 215-16. See also Kuhn's comments on the artillery issue after leaving office, in KA Nachlaß Kuhn, B/670, No. 7, pp. 278-79.

58 . See MKSM 29-1/21 ex 1872, Memorandum, Albrecht to Franz Joseph, Vienna, 20 December 1872.

59 . See MKSM 29-1/8 ex 1872, Memorandum, "Bemerkungen über die Waffen Übungen des k.k. Heeres in den Monaten Juli, August und September," Albrecht to Franz Joseph, Vienna, 18 November 1872. Kuhn himself admitted in 1871 that the army maneuvers he had seen that year had not gone well, but blamed deficiencies on the generalcy and not on shortcomings in troop instruction or drill. See Kuhn's diary entries for 28-29 August, 6 September, and 13 September 1871, in KA Nachlaß Kuhn, B/670, No. 7, pp. 152-55.

60 . See MKSM 29-1/1 ex 1872, Letter Präs. No. 3817, Kuhn to Franz Joseph, Vienna, 2 February 1872.

61 . Albrecht had apparently passed along to the emperor complaints of several field commanders that the new Werndl rifles were too long and thus difficult for persons of small stature to fire. Kuhn countered with the observation that the French *chassepot* rifle, a weapon of recognized superior quality, was actually two inches longer than the Werndl. In a memorandum to the emperor, Kuhn also used Albrecht's observation that cavalry horses were being given too little fodder as another example of the overly critical nature of the inspector general's reports. See MKSM 29-1/33 ex 1871, Memorandum, Albrecht to Franz Joseph, Vienna, 9 September 1871.

62 . MKSM 64-1/6 ex 1873, Letter Präs. No. 1141, Kuhn to Franz Joseph, Vienna, 10 April 1873. Note especially the attached comments by Franz Joseph and Albrecht.

63 . See MKSM Sonderreihe, Karton 64, Memorandum, Albrecht to Franz Joseph, Vienna, no date, 1873. Albrecht did not mention himself as a member of the military conference, although it can be fairly assumed that, as the designated commander-in-chief of the monarchy's armed forces in wartime, he planned to preside over its deliberations in the absence of the emperor.

64 . See MKSM 69-2/10 ex 1870, Letter No. 849, Andrássy to the Military Chancellery, Budapest, 7 August 1870; MKSM 12-1/45 ex 1870, Letter Präs. No. 2820,

Kuhn to Franz Joseph, Vienna, 4 August 1870, Letter Präs. No. 3185, Kuhn to the Military Chancellery, Vienna, 31 August 1870, Letter, Andrássy to Franz Joseph, Vienna, 10 September 1870; KA Nachlaß Kuhn, B/ 670, No. 7, pp. 116-17. See also Wagner, *Kriegsministerium* II, p. 54.

65. HHStA, PA XL, Karton 284, Ministerial Council Protocol KZ 2581, RMRZ 58, 11 August 1869; HHStA, PA XL, Karton 284, Crown Council Protocol KA 2583, RMRZ 59, 13 August 1869; HHStA, PA XL, Karton 286, Ministerial Council Protocol, KZ 579, RMRZ 106, 14 March 1871. See also Gunther E. Rothenberg, *The Austrian Military Border in Croatia, 1740-1881: A Study of an Imperial Institution* (Chicago: University of Chicago Press, 1966), pp. 180-92; Rothenberg, *The Army of Francis Joseph*, p. 86. Walter Wagner gives the misleading impression that Kuhn cooperated in good faith with the Hungarians over the dissolution of the Military Border. In fact, Kuhn switched positions on the issue only when it became apparent that Croatian elements opposed to Budapest stood to gain the most from the dissolution of the Military Border. See Wagner, *Kriegsministerium* II, pp. 110-11; KA Nachlaß Kuhn B/670, No. 7, pp. 213-14.

66. See, for example, the debate over Kuhn's 1872 and 1873 budgets, in HHStA, PA XL, Karton 286, Ministerial Council Protocol KZ 2314, RMRZ 115, 10 July 1871. See also HHStA, PA XL, Karton 287, Ministerial Council Protocol KZ 2392, RMRZ 132, 4 July 1872. See also Kuhn's attempt to increase the size of the standing army by 28,000 men, also torpedoed by de Pretis, in HHStA, PA XL, Karton 287, Crown Council Protocol KZ 586, RMRZ 138, 8 October 1872.

67. See the diary entry for 1 January 1870 for Kuhn's denials of democratic-republican sympathies, in KA Nachlaß Kuhn, B/670, No. 7, pp. 78-79. See also the entry for 26 November 1874.

68. See, for example, Kuhn's diary entry of 5 May 1870, where the war minister complained of having received his war-readiness report back from the emperor without comment, save that it was "satisfactory." Kuhn blasted the page: "I have fully equipped 765,000 men--no other war minister had done that." See KA Nachlaß Kuhn, B/670, No. 7, p. 97.

69. See the diary entries for 29 May and 4 June 1872, in KA Nachlaß Kuhn, B/670, No. 7, p. 186. Kuhn wrote that the emperor's reaction belonged, at most, to the mentality of the 16th century!

70. See the diary entry for 6 December 1874, in KA Nachlaß Kuhn, B/670, No. 7, pp. 290-91.

71. See MKSM 8-(file number missing) ex 1872, Letter, Kuhn to Franz Joseph, Vienna, `13 May 1872.

72. See KA Nachlaß Wolf-Schneider, B/197, 6/VIII, pp. 577-79.

73. See KA Nachlaß Wolf-Schneider, B/197, 6/VIII, p. 570. Wolf-Schneider cites an example of an infantry major promoted to the rank of lieutenant colonel on 1 May 1872 and again to colonel six months later.

74. See MKSM 9-1/9 ex 1873, Letter Präs. No. 3548, Kuhn to Franz Joseph, Vienna, 10 October 1873.

75 . See MKSM 9-1/9 ex 1873, Memorandum No. 1854/MKSM, Beck to Franz Joseph, Ofen, 13 October 1873.

76 . See MKSM 9-1/9 ex 1873, Memorandum, Albrecht to Franz Joseph, Vienna, 21 January 1871.

77 . Koller would resign as war minister on 1 July 1876 for health reasons. Kuhn remarked in his diary on Koller's ill health and general lack of energy upon the latter's appointment as war minister in June 1874. See the diary entry for 15 June 1874, in KA Nachlaß Kuhn, B/670, No. 7, pp. 269-70.

78 . HHStA, Filmarchiv, Nachlaß Albrecht, roll 47, Letter, Albrecht to John, Vienna, 7 February 1874.

79 . See MKSM 50-2/1 ex 1874, Memorandum, John to Albrecht, Graz, February, 1874. See also Wagner, *Kriegsministerium* II, pp. 121-22.

80 . See Beck's 24 March 1874 memorandum, "Allerunterthänigster Referat betreffend den Wirkungskreis und die Stellung des künftigen Generalstab-Chefs," in MKSM 50-2/1 ex 1874. See also KA Nachlaß Wolf-Schneider, B/197, 6/VIII, p. 512; Wagner, *Kriegsministerium* II, pp. 121-22; Glaise-Horstenau, p. 241.

81 . See MKSM 50-2/1 ex 1874, Letter, John to Albrecht, Graz, 11 April 1874. See also Wagner, *Kriegsministerium* II, pp. 122-23; Glaise-Horstenau, pp. 240-41; KA Nachlaß Wolf-Schneider, B/197, 6/VIII, p. 513.

82 . See Franz Joseph's undated instructions to Koller and John, in MKSM 50-2/1 ex 1874. See also Wagner, *Kriegsministerium* II, p. 124.

83 . Foreign Minister Andrássy would remark in an 1875 ministerial conference that while he personally favored the reestablishment of the general staff corps, the approval of the Hungarian Delegation for such a measure would be difficult to achieve because Kuhn had just convinced its members of the opposite viewpoint. See HHStA, PA XL, Karton 288, Ministerial Council Protocol KZ 276, RMRZ 162, 26 June 1875. Koller, however, with Franz Joseph's backing, pushed through the general staff agreement of April 1874.

84 . HHStA, Filmarchiv, Nachlaß Albrecht, roll 40, Letter, Koller to Albrecht, Prague, 3 April 1874. Koller also solicited Beck's advice on personnel appointments within the war ministry. In April 1874, Koller wrote Beck asking for his opinions on who should head the various departments within the war ministry. Koller, however, ultimately did not accept all of Beck's recommendations. See MKSM 50-2/1 ex 1874, Letter, Koller to Beck, Prague, 17 April 1874; Letter, Beck to Koller, Vienna, 19 April 1874; Letter, Koller to Beck, Prague, 27 April 1874. See also Wagner, *Kriegsministerium* II, pp. 125, 261-67; KA Nachlaß Wolf-Schneider, B/197, 6/VIII, p. 513.

85 . Koller had been called to Vienna on the pretext of consultations on upcoming troop maneuvers. See KA Nachlaß Kuhn, B/670, No. 7, pp. 273-74.

86 . See Wagner, *Kriegsministerium* II, p. 126. Wagner writes that Franz Joseph felt somewhat intimidated by his temperamental minister and feared that Kuhn might become angry at his dismissal. The emperor was relieved when Kuhn did not react violently to notification of his ouster.

87 . This was no great feat of deductive reasoning, since Gallina had been relieved as "director" of the general staff on the same day Kuhn left the war ministry and since Kuhn would be replacing John at the Graz command.

Chapter 3: The Eastern Crisis and Beck's Rise to Power

1 . See KA Nachlaß Beck, B/2, Fasz. II, No. 44, Draft Memorandum, Beck (Heß) to Buol and Franz Joseph, Vienna, 1856. See also Beck's memorandum of the same year entitled "Nothwendigkeit von Kolonien," in KA Nachlaß Beck, B/2, Fasz. II, No. 46; Glaise-Horstenau, p. 38. Beck favored a large military role in an expansionist foreign policy à la the French example in Algeria.

2 . See Beck's memorandum of 1862-63 entitled "Zur politischen Frage des Adriatischen Meeres," in KA Nachlaß Beck, B/2, Fasz. V, No. 119. In particular, Beck worried that Italy or Montenegro might throttle Austrian access to the Mediterranean by seizing Turkish Albania and the Balkan side of the Straits of Otranto.

3 . See Beck's "Studie über die Okkupation von Bosnien," dated 1 August 1875, just weeks after the first uprisings in Bosnia and Herzegovina, in KA Nachlaß Beck, B/2, Fasz. VI, No. 171. Beck took great pains to demonstrate to Franz Joseph the value of Dalmatia to the empire, noting that it produced a 2 million gulden surplus annually. See the "Berichte über dalmatische Verhältnisse," in KA Nachlaß Beck, B/2, Fasz. VI, No. 180.

4 . See MKSM 82-1/1 ex 1870, Letter No. 283, Franz Joseph to Kuhn, Vienna, 15 February 1870; MKSM 82-1/1 ex 1870, Letter Präs. No. 600, Kuhn to the Military Chancellery, Vienna, 7 March 1870.

5 . See MKSM 39-1/9 ex 1872, Albrecht to Franz Joseph, Vienna, 13 October 1872. See also MKSM Sonderreihe 52/6, Military Conference Protocol, 17 February 1872; HHStA, PA XL, Karton 287, Crown Council Protocol KZ 73, RMRZ 140, 8 January 1873. See also Holzer, pp. 42-43.

6 . See Ernst Freiherr von Plener, *Errinnerungen*, vol. II (Stuttgart: Deutsche Verlags-Anstalt, 1921), p. 91;   Nicholas Der Bagdasarian, *The Austro-German Rapprochement 1870-1879: From the Battle of Sedan to the Dual Alliance* (London: Associated University Presses, 1976), p. 186. Franz-Josef Kos, *Die Politik Österreich-Ungarns während der Orientkrise 1874/75-1879: Zum Verhältnis von politischer und militärischer Führung* (Cologne: Böhlau, 1984), p. 53.

7 . Plener II, p. 91; Kos, p. 54.

8 . For Austro-Hungarian foreign policy aims in the early 1870s, see Bridge, p. 62; Diószegi, pp. 27-28. For military policy, see the protocol of the 17 February 1872 military conference, in MKSM Sonderreihe 52/6, Military Conference Protocol, 17 February 1872. Identification of Germany and Russia as the monarchy's principal threats was based more on the personal animosity toward these countries on the part of the war minister and inspector general of the army than on any real danger that they posed.

9. The Carpathian railroad debate of the late 1860s and early 1870s essentially centered around three basic routes: Hormona-Przemysl, Eperies-Dukla-Tarnów, and Munkacs-Stryj. Disagreements between the war ministry and various elements of both the Austrian and Hungarian parliaments blocked the necessary legislation prior to the Franco-Prussian War. The shift of strategic priorities to the east after 1871 eased the military task of convincing the civilians for the need of additional railroads connecting Galicia with the interior of the monarchy. The early 1870s saw the completion of lines connecting Przemysl and Tarnów with Hungary. For the fortification debate of the early 1870s, see MKSM 39-1/2 ex 1872, Memorandum No. 470/MKSM, Albrecht to Franz Joseph, Vienna, 28 March 1872; Letter No. 470/MKSM, Franz Joseph to Kuhn, Ofen, 11 April 1872. See also MKSM 39-1/4 ex 1872, Letter Präs. No. 2074, Kuhn to Franz Joseph, Vienna, 17 May 1872; HHStA, PA XL, Karton 287, Ministerial Council Protocol KZ 1862, RMRZ 122, 28 March 1872; HHStA, PA XL, Karton 287, Crown Council Protocol KZ 73, RMRZ 140, 8 January 1873; Wagner, *Kriegsministerium* II, pp. 400-402.

10. See MKSM 34-1/10 ex 1872, Letter No. 18247, Tisza to Franz Joseph, Budapest, 22 February 1872; Memorandum No. 280/MKSM, Beck to Franz Joseph, Ofen, 26 February 1872; MKSM 34-1/13 ex 1873, Memorandum, Beck to Franz Joseph, Vienna, 24 March 1873.

11. MKSM 34-1/23 ex 1872, Letter Abt. 5/No. 1876, Kuhn to Franz Joseph, Vienna, 14 June 1872.

12. See MKSM 78-1/1 ex 1872, Lónyai to Franz Joseph, Ofen, 14 April 1872.

13. Rodich, for example, favored the introduction of German language instruction in Dalmatian primary schools to combat Italian cultural dominance in the region evident since the time of Venetian hegemony. See MKSM Sonderreihe, Karton 61, Letter No. 799/pr., Rodich to the Interior Ministry, Zara, 25 October 1875.

14. For the Beck-Rodich correspondence, see KA Nachlaß Beck, B/2, Fasz. VI, No. 179. Beck ensured that Franz Joseph received Rodich's reports on conditions in Dalmatia and neighboring Montenegro and Turkey.

15. Mollinary II, pp. 309-10. While he knew of Mollinary's pronounced South Slav sympathies, Kuhn nonetheless had appointed him to the Agram command because of his supposed ability to get along with the Hungarians. This was seen as key, since the army commander in Croatia had the politically sensitive task of executing the transfer of the Military Border to Hungarian civil control.

16. For Andrássy's instruction, see MKSM 69-2/1 ex 1875, Abstract Telegram, Andrássy to Rodich, Vienna, 19 January 1875.

17. See MKSM 69-2/1 ex 1875, Letter No. 58/MKSM, Beck to Koller, Budapest, 19 January 1875.

18. See MKSM 69-2/1 ex 1875, Letter No. 58/MKSM, Beck to John, Budapest, 22 January 1875.

19. See MKSM 69-2/2 ex 1875, Civil-Military Conference Protocol, 29 January 1875. For other treatments of this important conference, see Kos, pp. 69-78; Diószegi, pp. 76-81.

20 . The general staff anticipated that the army would have to build its own road network to achieve the full occupation of Bosnia and Herzegovina.

21 . Diószegi, p. 76.

22 . See MKSM Sonderreihe, Karton 61, Telegram, Beck to Rodich, Vienna, 7 February 1875; KA Nachlaß Beck, B/2, Fasz. VI, No. 179.

23 . Beck prepared a detailed briefing on Dalmatia for the emperor, complete with a wealth of statistical information, including religious, educational, and agricultural data. Beck also included a wealth of information on the condition of the local road network, all fortifications since the period of Venetian rule, and the histories and geographical situation of about fifty Dalmatian towns. See KA Nachlaß Beck B/2, Fasz. VI, No. 170, Memorandum "Kaiserreise nach Venedig und Dalmatien," Beck to Franz Joseph, Vienna, April 1875.

24 . Mollinary II, pp. 281-82.

25 . See Beck's diary entry, reproduced in Glaise-Horstenau, p. 181.

26 . See Glaise-Horstenau, pp. 181-83.

27 . See William L. Langer, *European Alliances and Alignments, 1871-1890* (New York: Alfred A. Knopf, 1931), p. 71.

28 . See MKSM 69-2/14 ex 1875, Letter No. 1658/MKSM, Beck to Mollinary, Bruck an der Leitha, 23 August 1875.

29 . For the most detailed account of the diplomacy of the first year of the Eastern Crisis of 1875-78, see David Harris, *A Diplomatic History of the Balkan Crisis of 1875-78: The First Year* (Stanford, Calif.: Stanford University Press, 1936). For concise descriptions of Andrássy's diplomatic initiatives, see Kos, pp. 98-110; Diószegi, *Außenpolitik*, pp. 98-106. See also, Scott W. Lackey, "From Status Quo to Expansionism: Count Julius Andrássy and the Eastern Question, July 1875-April 1877" (M.A. thesis, University of North Carolina, 1986), pp. 12-14.

30 . This was the so-called Berlin Memorandum of May 1876. See Kos, pp. 110-15; Diószegi, *Außenpolitik*, pp. 106-9; Lackey, pp. 14-17.

31 . See KA Nachlaß Beck B/2, Fasz. VI, No. 179, Letter, Beck to Rodich, Bruck an der Leitha, 5 September 1875.

32 . Rothenberg, *The Army of Francis Joseph*, p. 93.

33 . See MKSM 69-1/2-1 ex 1876, Letter No. 199/MKSM, Beck to Rodich, Vienna, 31 January 1876; MKSM 69-1/4-2 ex 1876, Letter, Beck to Rodich, 21 February 1876. Beck wrote the latter at Andrássy's dictation. Beck issued similar instructions to Mollinary in Croatia. See MKSM 69-1/4-3 ex 1876, Abstract Letter, Beck to Mollinary, Vienna, 24 February 1876.

34 . Indeed, the general staff had accomplished little in the way of strategic planning during John's second tenure as chief, hindered mainly by the war ministry's failure to complete the mobilization instructions. See KA Nachlaß Wolf-Schneider B/197, 6/VIII, p. 525; Glaise-Horstenau, p. 243.

35 . See HHStA, PA XL, Karton 288, Ministerial Council Protocol KZ 2181, RMRZ 164, 8 July 1875; HHStA, PA XL, Karton 288, Crown Council Protocol KZ 4437, RMRZ 167, 8 October 1875. For figures on government income and expenditure, see Wysocki, *Die Wirtschaftliche Entwicklung*, pp. 93-100.

36 . See MKSM 69-1/4-5 ex 1876, Telegram, Beck to Rodich, Vienna, 10 July 1876. Beck did not, however, tell Rodich that Russia had agreed to let Austria-Hungary occupy the provinces only in the event that Serbia and Montenegro defeated the Ottoman empire.

37 . MKSM 69-1/4-5 ex 1876, Letter No. 1567/MKSM, Beck to Rodich, Vienna, 14 July 1876.

38 . See MKSM 69-1/8 ex 1876, Letter Präs. No. 3490, Bylandt-Rheidt to Franz Joseph, Vienna, 10 July 1876. The other three divisions were slated to be committed in the event Serbia or Montenegro moved to hinder the Austrian occupation of Bosnia and Herzegovina.

39 . See Degreif, p. 19; Wagner, "Die k.(u.)k. Armee: Gliederung und Aufgabenstellung," pp. 360-61; Wagner, *Kriegsministerium* II, pp. 152-56.

40 . See MKSM 69-1/8 ex 1876, Memorandum, Beck to Franz Joseph, Vienna, July 1876.

41 . That Serbia would not be an enemy in the upcoming operation was reflected in Franz Joseph's order to Bylandt-Rheidt, which directed the war ministry to draw up two deployment plans, one that dealt solely with the occupation of Bosnia and Herzegovina, another which added operations against Serbia with the three divisions of the Austro-Hungarian VII Corps. See MKSM 69-1/8 ex 1876, Letter No. 1603/MKSM, Franz Joseph to Bylandt-Rheidt, Vienna, July 1876.

42 . See Friedrich Haselmeyer, *Diplomatische Geschichte des Zweiten Reiches von 1871-1918* (Munich: Verlag Bruchmann, 1955), p. 105; Mihailo D. Stojanovic, *The Great Powers and the Balkans 1875-1878* (London: Cambridge University Press, 1939), p. 32; Wertheimer II, pp. 259-60; Bridge, p. 72. For the Turkish peace terms, see Letter No. 209, Stolberg to Bülow, Vienna, 16 September 1876, German Foreign Ministry Archives, T-139, roll 384, frames 0751-0756; Letter, Andrássy to Zichy, Vienna, 17 September 1876, HHStA, TF 74 039, Karton 116, folio 1-668; Theodore von Sosnosky, *Die Balkanpolitik Österreich-Ungarns seit 1866*, vol. I (Stuttgart: Deutsche Verlags-Anstalt, 1913), p. 154; George Hoover Rupp, *A Wavering Friendship: Russia and Austria, 1876-1878* (Cambridge: Mass.: Harvard University Press, 1941), pp. 172-74; Langer, p. 95; Haselmayer, p. 123; Lackey, pp. 64-65.

43 . KA Generalstab, OpB, Karton 668, Heft 1, "Memoire über den strategischen Aufmarsch der k.k. Armee in Galizien," 1876. See also Rosner, pp. 93-98; Rothenberg, *The Army of Francis Joseph*, pp. 94-95; Kos, pp. 179-82.

44 . For a transcript of the conference, see MKSM 69-1/25 ex 1876, Military Conference Protocol, Vienna, 13 November 1876.

45 . See Beck's "Denkschrift zur Lösung der Orient-Frage" of 1 December 1876, in MKSM Sonderreihe 28/2; see also Beck's "Studie über die Okkupation von Bosnien" of 1 August 1875, in KA Nachlaß Beck B/2, Fasz. VI, No. 171.

46 . For the text of the so-called Budapest conventions, see Pribram II, pp. 199-203.

47 . See KA Nachlaß Beck B/2, Fasz. VI, No. 179, Letter, Beck to Rodich, Vienna, 21 June 1877.

48 . MKSM 69-1/21 ex 1877, Letter No. 340 res., Schönfeld to Franz Joseph, 22 May 1877; Military Conference Protocol, Vienna, 23 June 1877.

49 . See KA Nachlaß Beck B/2, Fasz. VI, No. 179, Letter, Beck to Rodich, Hardensdorf, 21 July 1877.

50 . MKSM 69-1/2 ex 1877, Letter, Franz Joseph to Beck, Bad Ischl, no date. See also Glaise-Horstenau, p. 195.

51 . See MKSM 69-1/2 ex 1877, Telegram, Beck to Franz Joseph, Vienna, 11 August 1877.

52 . Langer, p. 129.

53 . Rothenberg, *The Army of Francis Joseph*, p. 97; Glaise-Horstenau, pp. 196-97.

54 . Holzer, pp. 84-86.

55 . See Schönfeld's "Memoire über die gegenwärtige Lage und die mögliche Verwicklungen; zugleich Besprechung der erforderlichen militärischen Maßnahmen," Vienna, 31 January 1878, in KA Generalstab, OpB, Karton 668, Heft 1. See also Rosner, pp. 123-26.

56 . See HHStA, PA XL, Karton 290, Crown Council Protocol KZ 50, RMRZ 191, 7 February 1878.

57 . Glaise-Horstenau, pp. 199-200.

58 . For the general staff's assessments of the military situation in February 1878, see MKSM 69-1/6 ex 1878, Letter No. 66 res., Schönfeld to Franz Joseph, Vienna, 12 February 1878; Generalstab, OpB, Karton 668, Heft 1, Memorandum, Schönfeld to Franz Joseph, Vienna, 14 February 1878; see also Schönfeld's memorandum to the emperor, "Wann erscheint eine Mobilisierung ohne sofortigen strategischen Aufmarsch nicht möglich oder wünschenswert," Vienna, 16 February 1878, in KA Generalstab, OpB, Karton 668, Heft 1.

59 . See HHStA, PA XL, Karton 290, Crown Council Protocol KZ 64, RMRZ 192, 24 February 1878.

60 . For Beck's fears concerning parliamentary approval of the 60 million credit, see KA Nachlaß Beck, B/2, Fasz. VI, No. 179, Letter, Beck to Rodich, Vienna, 7 March 1878; see also Glaise-Horstenau, pp. 172-73. The Treaty of San Stefano granted independence to Serbia, Montenegro, and Romania. Bulgaria, while remaining under Turkish suzerainity, was enlarged to include an Aegean coastline and, in direct violation of the Budapest Conventions, would be occupied by Russian troops for two years. Russia regained Bessarabia (lost in the 1856 Treaty of Paris) and acquired the Asia Minor towns of Kars, Ardahan, Batum, and Bayazid. See Langer, p. 138.

61 . Under Beck's compromise, three divisions would deploy to Bosnia-Herzegovina. One would invade Herzegovina from Dalmatia, while the other two would advance into Bosnia from Croatia and Slavonia. The army would mobilize two additional divisions but keep them in reserve. See Rosner, pp. 132-34.

62 . MKSM 69-1/23 ex 1878, Military Conference Protocol, Vienna, 16 April 1878.

63 . M.S. Anderson, *The Eastern Question 1774-1923* (London: Macmillan, 1966), p. 207.

184   *Notes*

64 . See MKSM 69-1/25 ex 1878, Military Conference Protocol, 6 June 1878.

65 . HHStA, PA XL, Karton 290, Crown Council Protocol KZ 62, RMRZ 205, 2 July 1878. See also MKSM 69-1/20-2 ex 1878, Letter, Andrássy to Franz Joseph, Berlin, 30 June 1878.

66 . See KA Nachlaß Beck B/2, No. 179, Letter, Beck to Rodich, Vienna, 23 May 1878.

67 . See KA Nachlaß Beck B/2, No. 179, Beck to Rodich, Vienna, 8 July 1878. For Andrássy's comment, see the memoirs of the Austro-Hungarian inspector general for engineers, Major General Daniel von Salis-Soglio, in Daniel von Salis-Soglio, *Mein Leben und was ich davon erzählen will, kann und darf* (Stuttgart: Deutsche-Verlags-Anstalt, 1908), vol. II, p. 76.

68 . For Beck's status within the army at the time of the occupation, see the unpublished family history "Geschichte der Familie Pitreich," written by August von Pitreich, the nephew of Heinrich von Pitreich, who would become one of Beck's deputy chiefs of the general staff and later imperial war minister, in KA Nachlaß Pitreich B/589, No. 3, pp. 120-31. Pitreich wrote that in 1878 Beck was already considered within the army as "the coming man" and the future chief of the general staff.

69 . See HHStA, PA XL, Karton 290, Crown Council Protocol KZ 70, RMRZ 207, 25 July 1878. For a copy of the instructions, see MKSM 69-1/27-1 ex 1878, Letter No. 1794/MKSM, Franz Joseph to Philippovich, Schönbrunn, 19 July 1878.

70 . See HHStA, PA XL, Karton 290, Crown Council Protocol KZ 79, RMRZ 210, 13 August 1878; HHStA, PA XL, Karton 290, Crown Council Protocol KZ 95, RMRZ 211, 18 August 1878.

71 . See the intelligence assessment delivered to the crown council by Schönfeld, who emerged briefly from sick leave in late August, in HHStA, PA XL, Karton 290, Crown Council Protocol, KZ 121, RMRZ 212, 19 August 1878. Bloody fighting continued throughout September and the first half of October around the town of Bihac in western Bosnia and to the east of Sarajevo along the Drina River. Major General Jovan Jovanovich's 18th Infantry Division did not clear Herzegovina of resistance until the end of September. See KA Nachlaß Beck, B/2, Fasz. VI, No. 179, Letter, Beck to Rodich, Vienna, 20 September 1878. See also Wagner, "Die k.(.u.)k. Armee: Gliederung und Aufgabenstellung," p. 311.

72 . See, for example, Philippovich's passionate letter to Beck of 28 August, in which he characterized the Muslim population as "wild people," who would require a long period of adjustment to law and order. He called the Begs marked by Andrássy's consular officials for Austro-Hungarian decorations as "moral zeros." Philippovich described the Ottoman officials he had met as "unreliable and inept," and complained of the neglected and unsanitary condition of Sarajevo and other cities. See MKSM 69-1/27-5 ex 1878, Letter, Philippovich to Beck, Sarajevo, 28 August 1878.

73 . See MKSM Sonderreihe, Karton 57, Letter, Beck to Philippovich, Vienna, 29 September 1878.

74 . See MKSM 69-20/3 ex 1878, Military Conference Protocol, 1 October 1878.

75 . For Beck's dispatches to the emperor during his inspection tour of Bosnia and Herzegovina, see MKSM 69-25/1 ex 1878. See also MKSM 69-25/7 ex 1878, Telegram, Beck to Franz Joseph, Sarajevo, 31 October 1878 for Beck's version of his meeting with Philippovich.

76 . In October 1878, a common ministry commission had assigned responsibility for Bosnia and Herzegovina to the common finance ministry and had devised a provincial administration headed by a military governor. See MKSM 69-16/3 ex 1878, Civil-Military Conference Protocol, 14 October 1878.

77 . See, for example, ex-minister Kuhn's critique in KA Nachlaß Kuhn, B/670, No. 11, p. 34. Kuhn wrote that Beck had mobilized more men for the Bosnian campaign than Radetzky had at his disposal in Italy in 1848-49.

78 . See, for example, the newspaper clippings on Beck's tour of Bosnia-Herzegovina, in KA Nachlaß Beck, B/2, Fasz. VI, No. 187.

79 . Kuhn made repeated references in his diary to Beck's leading role in the Bosnia-Herzegovina campaign. On 18 August 1878, he wrote "the leadership [for the campaign] resides with the military chancellery!--Beck--bird brain!" See KA Nachlaß Kuhn, B/670, No. 11, pp. 14-15. For a more positive assessment of Beck's increasing stature, see note 68.

Chapter 4: The Beck System

1 . See MKSM 20-1/1 ex 1880, Political-Military Conference Protocol, 7 January 1880.

2 . See MKSM Sonderreihe, Karton 57, Letter, Schönfeld to Beck, Vienna, 19 November 1878.

3 . Wagner, "Die k.(u.)k. Armee: Gliederung und Aufgabenstellung," pp. 361-62; Wagner, *Kriegsministerium* II, p. 187. Beck eventually compromised with Bylandt on this issue in 1888, when the railroad department of the general staff simultaneously became the 5th Department EB (*Eisenbahn*) of the war ministry.

4 . See MKSM 29-1/5-2 ex 1878, Letter No. 217, Schönfeld to Franz Joseph, Vienna, 11 May 1878; MKSM 29-1/2-1 ex 1879, Letter No. 52 res., Schönfeld to Franz Joseph, 4 February 1879. For the conflict between Bylandt and Schönfeld, see Rosner, pp. 137-38.

5 . See MKSM Sonderreihe Karton 57, Letter, Schönfeld to Beck, Vienna, 19 November 1878; KA Nachlaß Wolf-Schneider, B/197, 6/VIII, p. 527.

6 . For Conrad's views of Schönfeld, see KA Nachlaß Wolf-Schneider, B/197, 6/VIII, p. 531.

7 . See MKSM 1-2/2 ex 1878, Letter, Schönfeld to the Military Chancellery, Vienna, 23 September 1878.

8 . MKSM 1-2/2 ex 1878, Letter No. 2873/MKSM, Beck to the General Staff, 30 September 1878.

9 . Glaise-Horstenau, pp. 244-45.

10. See MKSM 68-1/1 ex 1874, Letter No. 173/MKSM, Franz Joseph to Kuhn, Vienna, 28 January 1874.

11. Glaise-Horstenau, pp. 248-49.

12. See KA Nachlaß Wolf-Schneider, B/197, 6/IX, p. 632; Glaise-Horstenau, pp. 250-52; Wagner, *Kriegsministerium* II, pp. 200-204; Rothenberg, *The Army of Francis Joseph*, p. 107.

13. In 1884, Beck told those officers honoring Bylandt's fifty years of military service that the war minister had the most difficult tasks to perform within the Austro-Hungarian military given his awesome responsibility for the material well-being of the common army and *Kriegsmarine*. See KA Nachlaß Beck, B/2, Fasz. VII, No. 228.

14. See MKSM Sonderreihe, Karton 57, folios 57-58, Letter, Albrecht to Beck, Vienna, 23 March 1881. See also Wagner, *Kriegsministerium* II, p. 201. Albrecht, however, did stress that the chief of the general staff needed to be "the master of his own house" with absolute authority over the direction of the general staff and its operations. Albrecht, however, knew he had little to fear from Beck's excluding him from operational questions. Beck had supported Albrecht's right to information in an 1879 dispute with the war ministry in which the latter had issued regulations and instructions to unit commands without first informing the inspector general. See the correspondence on this issue, in MKSM 9-3/1 ex 1879. See also Wagner, *Kriegsministerium* II, p. 146.

15. Glaise-Horstenau writes that Franz Joseph offered Beck the opportunity to move the general staff from its current quarters within the war ministry building Am Hof, thus accentuating the independent status of the corps. The ever diplomatic Beck, however, declined the emperor's kind offer, in which he saw the potential for increased tension and conflict between war ministry and general staff. He wanted close cooperation with the war minister and was willing to accept the cramped quarters on the fourth floor of the war ministry building to get it. Glaise-Horstenau, p. 261.

16. See KA Nachlaß Beck, B/2, Fasz. VII, No. 193, Memorandum "Notizen über Generalstabs-Offiziere," Schönfeld to Beck, Vienna, 13 May 1881. Among those singled out for high mention by Schönfeld were Arthur Freiherr von Bolfras, then a lieutenant colonel in the general staff and later head of the emperor's military chancellery from 1889 to 1916. Schönfeld also called Major Heinrich Ritter von Pitreich one of the most virtuous and loyal officers in the corps. Pitreich would later rise to become Beck's deputy chief of the general staff in the late 1890s and then war minister from 1902 to 1906. Franz Conrad von Hötzendorf also made Schönfeld's list, although the outgoing chief obviously did not know much about him except that he had successfully graduated (*mit gutem Erfolg*) from the *Kriegsschule* in 1878 and had recently been promoted to captain.

17. KA Nachlaß Wolf-Schneider, B/197, 6/IX, p. 776; Glaise-Horstenau, pp. 253-54. Franz Joseph agreed to retract the decoration. On 25 May, Franz Joseph had presented Beck with a portrait of himself, showing him in his daily work uniform in which he had received Beck's reports as head of the military chancellery. Glaise-Horstenau recounts the story that the artist, a Professor Angeli, apologized profusely to Beck for having had the emperor pose in his old tunic ("Bonjour!"). If he had known

that Franz Joseph intended to give the portrait to Beck, he would have had the emperor put on his new coat. Angeli had thought that the painting was only to go to Crown Prince Rudolf!

18 . See KM Präs. 45-8/2 ex 1881, Verordnungsblatt für das k.k. Heer, 20. Stück, 22 June, Circular Decree No. 71, Präs. No. 3265, 14 June 1881.

19 . Indeed, on the day Beck left the military chancellery for his new post, Franz Joseph instructed him to report to him each Wednesday at 11:00 a.m. on general staff affairs, a practice that would continue with precise regularity until Beck's retirement in November 1906.

20 . See KM Präs. 45-8/2 ex 1881, Letter, Franz Joseph to Bylandt, Vienna, 11 June 1881. Organizational studies conducted within the military chancellery during the 1880s continued to place the war minister at the top of the military structure. The chief of the general staff was listed just under the fifteen corps commanders but among the twelve lieutenant generals of the army, despite the fact that Beck would not attain this rank until late 1889. See MKSM Sonderreihe, Karton 64, "Studien über Höhere Commanden- und Beförderungs-Verhältnisse," 1882, 1886.

21 . See KA Nachlaß Beck, B/2, Fasz. VII, Nos. 194, 197.

22 . Glaise-Horstenau, pp. 255-56. Beck did not hesitate to make his admiration for the Prussian general staff public. On 29 October 1882, he wrote Helmut von Moltke on the latter's twenty-fifth anniversary as chief of the Prussian general staff, praising his achievement in creating a model institution for the rest of the world to emulate. In a gathering of his own staff officers at Christmas 1883, Beck proclaimed that his only goal was to achieve the position of trust and confidence for the Austro-Hungarian general staff already enjoyed by the Prussian general staff in Germany. See Glaise-Horstenau, pp. 263-64.

23 . Glaise-Horstenau, pp. 256-57.

24 . KA Nachlaß Beck, B/2, Fasz. VII, No. 195, "Antrittsrede Becks," Vienna, 2 July 1881. See also Glaise-Horstenau, pp. 262-63.

25 . Beck had already expressed most of the ideas concerning the duties of the general staff officer contained in his inaugural address in a March 1870 memorandum, "Studie über Manövrier und Gefechtstaktik," in KA Nachlaß Beck, B/2, Fasz. VI, No. 154.

26 . See MKSM 14-9/3 ex 1882, Letter, Bylandt to Franz Joseph, Vienna, 9 October 1882. Beck had set down his guidelines for the operation of the *Kriegsschule* in his 1873 memorandum, "Die wichtigsten militärischen Fragen," in KA Nachlaß Beck, B/2, Fasz. VI, No. 167.

27 . For Kuhn's views on military education, see the diary entry for 30 August 1874, in KA Nachlaß Kuhn, B/670, No. 7, pp. 275-77.

28 . See Beck's memorandum, "Die Kulturgeschichte im Rahmen der reorganisierten Kriegsschule," Vienna, 23 February 1882, in KA Nachlaß Beck, B/2, Fasz. VII, No. 203. However, after the late 1880s, treatment of the "liberal arts" at the *Kriegsschule* became increasingly limited to military applications. The cultural history course was later replaced by one entitled "The History of War and Its Methods." See

MKSM 14-7/3 ex 1887, Letter Präs. 5673, Bylandt to Franz Joseph, Vienna, 12 November 1887.

29 . KA Nachlaß Wolf-Schneider, B/197, 6/IX, pp. 904-905. Beck himself did not live up to his rigorous language requirements, unless one considers his rough knowledge of Italian. It must also be noted that the Wiener Neustadt Academy, from which most *Kriegsschule* students had graduated, already provided a liberal education comparable to the civilian gymnasia. Kuhn's curriculum reforms of the late 1860s and early 1870s, which introduced such subjects as economics, advanced mathematics and physics, astronomy, and Latin, were allowed to stand. See Wagner, "Die k.(u.)k. Armee: Gliederung und Aufgabenstellung," pp. 497-98.

30 . In 1905, Beck increased the prerequisite service with the troops to four years. See KA Nachlaß Wolf-Schneider, B/197, 6/IX, p. 748.

31 . See KA Nachlaß Wolf-Schneider, B/197, 6/VIII, pp. 594-604; Deák, p. 111. The preliminary examination, introduced by Kuhn, tested the aspirants' knowledge of French, field service, tactics, weapons, the pioneer service, the "art" of fortification, use of terrain, and situational drawing. The second exam tested these same areas in more depth. See Wagner, "Die k.(u.)k. Armee: Gliederung und Aufgabenstellung," p. 501. The military's desire to open career opportunities to as many nationalities as possible can be seen in an 1889 dispute over the abolition of German *Fraktur* script in both the civilian and military schools in Austria. The Austrian Ministry of Culture declared its opposition to such a reform, citing the fact that many books were still being published in *Fraktur*. Archduke Albrecht favored the introduction of Latin script in the military schools since it would help non-German nationalities. See KM Präs. 50-29/1 ex 1889, Memorandum of the 5th Department to Präs. No. 6623, Vienna, 21 December 1889.

32 . This included courses in strategy, tactics, military geography, general staff work, terrain studies, fortifications, engineering, and weapons.

33 . See, for example, Beck's personal notes concerning the tactical exercises of the first lieutenants assigned to duty with the general staff in Vienna, in Generalstab, Hauptreihe, Circular Letter No. 654 res., Beck to General Staff Officers, Vienna, 28 April 1882. See also Glaise-Horstenau, p. 361.

34 . While the general staff almost doubled in size during Beck's tenure as chief, it nevertheless only consisted of some 434 officers in 1911. See Deák, p. 112. Even line officers who had not undergone the rigorous *Kriegsschule* training resented their colleagues in the general staff. In 1900, Archduke Rainer, commander of the Austrian *Landwehr*, received an anonymous letter from an officer claiming to represent a large group of disgruntled active and retired line officers. They demanded an end to the promotion advantages of the general staff, calling its officers "*Kanzleihelden*" (desk heroes) with only theoretical knowledge. See MKSM 10-2/4 ex 1900, Letter, Anonymous to Archduke Rainer. The group threatened to distribute inflammatory brochures if their demands, which also included the sacking of the current war minister, Lieutenant General Edmund von Krieghammer, were not met by 1 November 1900. The army, of course, ignored these threats.

35 . Rothenberg, *The Army of Francis Joseph*, p. 107. This, however, was not out of step with the practice in other European armies. William Fuller, for example,

writes that general staff officers in the Russian army could expect, at the very minimum, to attain the rank of major general after thirty years of service, while line officers generally made it only as far as lieutenant colonel, and then only upon retirement. Martin Kitchen estimates that a posting to the Prussian general staff gave the officer in question the equivalent of approximately eight years of seniority over colleagues in the line. See William C. Fuller, *Civil-Military Conflict in Imperial Russia 1881-1914* (Princeton, N.J.: Princeton University Press, 1985), p. 21; Martin Kitchen, *The German Officer Corps 1890-1914* (Oxford: Clarendon Press, 1968), p. 7.

36. See Deák, pp. 111, 167-68. Deák puts the average age of captains as 34.8 in the general staff, 39.3 in the cavalry, 45.7 in the artillery, and a staggering 49.2 for officers in the supply troops. In 1890, Albrecht estimated that two-thirds of the army's divisional commanders and almost half of the brigadiers had, at one time or another, belonged to the general staff. KM Präs. 30-4/1 ex 1891, Memorandum, Albrecht to the War Ministry, Arco, 30 December 1890. Beck favored rapid promotion of staff officers for practical reasons. Since colonels and lieutenant colonels acted as corps chiefs of staff and as heads of the major general staff departments, Beck believed that they needed the vigor of youth to discharge these important offices effectively. Beck felt that ideally general staff colonels should be around forty years of age, a goal which he never attained. See KA Nachlaß Wolf-Schneider, B/197, 6/IX, pp. 778, 787.

37. See MKSM 14-7/3 ex 1887, Letter Präs. No. 5673, Bylandt to Franz Joseph, Vienna, 12 November 1887.

38. See Beck's undated memorandum on the organization of the *Kriegsschule*, in MKSM 20-1/12-2 ex 1887, in which he defended its main function as a general staff college. Beck had in 1884 allowed the officers of the railroad and telegraph regiment to attend the *Kriegsschule* instead of the higher engineering and artillery courses and gave in to Bylandt's request to allow engineering and artillery officers to take courses at the *Kriegsschule*. See KA Nachlaß Wolf-Schneider, B/197, 6/IX, p. 700. In 1888, Beck admitted far more engineering and artillery officers to the *Kriegsschule* in proportion to their overall numbers to make up for their under-representation in previous years. Of the forty-two officers admitted to the school that year, eight came from the artillery, twelve from the engineers, and only nineteen from the infantry and Jäger, although the latter two branches made up approximately 80% of the army. See MKSM 14-6/5 ex 1888, Letter Abt. 6 No. 3227, Bauer to Franz Joseph, Vienna, 17 October 1888.

39. See KM Präs. 31-15/1 ex 1886, Circular Letter Präs. No. 2672, War Ministry to the Commandant of the Kriegsschule, the Inspectors General of the Artillery, Engineers, the Heads of the Presidium, First and Fifth Departments of the War Ministry, Vienna, 20 July 1886.

40. See both KM Präs. 31-3/1 ex 1900, Letter, Pitreich to Krieghammer, Vienna, 5 January 1900; KM Präs. 31-3/3 ex 1900, Letter Präs. 392, Krieghammer to Franz Joseph, Vienna, 29 January 1900; KA Nachlaß Wolf-Schneider, B/197, 6/IX, pp. 732-38.

41. For Beck's assent, see KM Präs. 45-23/2 ex 1893, Memorandum No. 107 res., Beck to the War Ministry, Vienna, 29 January 1894. See also KA Nachlaß Wolf-

Schneider, B/197, 6/IX, p. 710. By the turn of the century, the files of the general staff *Hauptreihe* began to fill with personal letters by Beck to the disappointed families and mentors of general staff aspirants who had graduated from the *Kriegsschule* with excellent marks who nevertheless did not receive a general staff posting. For example, see Generalstab, Hauptreihe, 1-12 ex 1906, Letter, Beck to Heinrich Prade, Vienna, 2 August 1906; Generalstab, Hauptreihe, 1-13 ex 1905, Letter, Beck to Prince Philip von Sachsen-Coburg und Gotha, Vienna, 27 June 1905.

42 . "Schulden wie ein Stabsoffizier" (debts like a staff officer) became a common saying in the monarchy.

43 . Prussian chief of the general staff von Grolman began the practice of rotating staff officers to troop assignments in 1816. See Trevor N. Dupuy, *A Genius for War* (Englewood Cliffs, N.J.: Prentice Hall, 1977), pp. 34-35.

44 . The so-called "Enquête Commission," formed in 1880 to draw lessons from the occupation of Bosnia-Herzegovina, had recommended an end to the practice of attaching general staff officers to brigade commands. Line officers were to be specially trained to assist brigadiers in the administration and direction of their units. See MKSM Sonderreihe, Karton 64, "Generalstab-Reorganisation Enquête 1880: Auszug aus dem Sitzungs-Protokolle der mit allerhöchstem Befehlsschreiben vom 24 November 1878 einberufenen Enquête Kommission." See also KA Nachlaß Wolf-Schneider, B/197, 6/VIII, p. 622; Glaise-Horstenau, p. 269. Beck constantly reminded the members of his corps that the troops were their sole *raison d'être* and that their ultimate responsibility remained providing for their welfare. See, for example, Beck's speech to a gathering of general staff officers at the Hotel Metropol in Vienna on 24 April 1885, in KA Nachlaß Beck, B/2, Fasz. VII, No. 232.

45 . The examination for promotion to major consisted of both oral and written parts. The oral exam required the candidate to describe an historical military campaign in detail as well as to solve specific problems related to artillery, fortifications, army organization, and service with the general staff in general. The written test consisted of operative and tactical problems on the corps and divisional level. See KA Nachlaß Wolf-Schneider, B/197, 6/IX, pp. 899-900.

46 . General Karl Freiherr von Müffling, chief of the Prussian General Staff between 1821 and 1829, instituted the practice of annual general staff rides. See Dupuy, p. 48. In 1871, Brigadier General Josef Gallina led the first Austro-Hungarian *Generalstabsreise* in central Bohemia. See KA Nachlaß Wolf-Schneider, B/197, 6/VIII, p. 610; Wagner, "Die k.(u.)k. Armee: Gliederung und Aufgabenstellung," p. 377.

47 . Schönfeld generally attended, but did not personally lead, the *Generalstabsreisen* during his tenure as chief. See MKSM 29-1/3-1 ex 1877, Letter No. 51 res., Schönfeld to Franz Joseph, Vienna, 25 January 1877; MKSM 29-1/5 ex 1878, Letter No. 107, Schönfeld to Franz Joseph, Vienna, 5 March 1878. Beck continued his close personal direction of these rigorous exercises until his retirement in 1906, well past his seventieth year. See, for example, his report of the 1903 *Generalstabsreise*, in KM Präs. 30-2/4 ex 1903, Letter No. 2730, Beck to the War Ministry, Vienna, 13 November 1903.

48 . Beck formulated guidelines for the general staff exercises, like those regulating the many other aspects of his "system," years before he became chief of the general staff. See KA Nachlaß Beck, B/2, Fasz. VI, No. 160, "Studie über das Wesen der größeren Generalstabs-Übung," Vienna, 8 January 1872.

49 . See KA Nachlaß Wolf-Schneider, B/197, 6/IX, pp. 890-94; Wagner, "Die k.(u.)k. Armee: Gliederung und Aufgabenstellung," pp. 384-85; Glaise-Horstenau, pp. 267-68. For an evaluation of the participants of one of these general staff exercises, see Generalstab, Hauptreihe, "Relation über die Verwendung der Übungstheilnehmer--Generalstabsreise--Gruppe I 1885 - Ost Partei," No. 621 ex 1885. Wolf-Schneider writes that of the twenty-five *Generalstabsreisen* directed by Beck, nine were in Galicia, four along the Italian border, four along the Drina-Save-Danube frontier, two in Bosnia-Herzegovina, four in conjunction with the *Kriegsmarine* at Pola and two in Dalmatia.

50 . Beck would remain a *Feldmarschalleutnant* (major general) until 1889 when he was finally promoted to *Feldzeugmeister* (lieutenant general), the highest general officer grade in peacetime.

51 . See KA Nachlaß Wolf-Schneider, B/197, 6/IX, pp. 595-97, 612; Wagner, "Die k.(u.)k. Armee: Gliederung und Aufgabenstellung," pp. 384-85. Schönfeld had been even more extreme than Beck in his rejection of Philippovich's original suggestion, opposing both the participation of general officers in the *Generalstabsreisen* or the formation of an independent set of exercises. Before 1893 Albrecht limited the participation in the *Generalsreisen* to officers from one corps area. Thereafter, however, the approximately fifty participants were drawn from all commands and included more general staff officers than generals and colonels.

52 . See KA Nachlaß Wolf-Schneider, B/197, 6/IX, pp. 897-98; Wagner, "Die k.(u.)k. Armee: Gliederung und Aufgabenstellung," p. 385.

53 . See, for example, Beck's 1854 memorandum, "Über das Kriegsspiel," in KA Nachlaß Beck, B/2, Fasz. II, No. 32. Beck complained at that time that war games were too little used in the Austrian army.

54 . The club rules, drawn up by Beck on 10 November 1870, required only that members attend meetings on the nights the club was playing and that they be conversant with the rules. See KA Nachlaß Beck, B/2, Fasz. VI, No. 158.

55 . For a good discussion of the development of war gaming in Prussia, see Dupuy, pp. 51-52.

56 . See KA Nachlaß Wolf-Schneider, B/197, 6/VIII, pp. 607-08; Wagner, "Die k.(u.)k. Armee: Gliederung und Aufgabenstellung," p. 377.

57 . Wagner, "Die k.(u.)k. Armee: Gliederung und Aufgabenstellung," p. 385.

58 . See Beck's report, "Manöver des VII. und VIII. Armeekorps," in KA Nachlaß Beck, B/2, Fasz. V, No. 117.

59 . Most of the larger exercises took place in Italy, since Habsburg forces there were constantly kept on a war footing. Marshal Radetzky had long favored the institution of large-scale maneuvers and did hold one corps-level exercise in 1831 in which over 40,000 men participated. While the maneuvers were generally recognized as a success (Radetzky's instructions for maneuvers were published in 1833), corps exercises were not implemented because of the large costs involved. See Walter Wagner,

Von Austerlitz bis Königgrätz: Österreichische Kampftaktik im Spiegel der Reglements 1805-1864, in *Studien zur Militärgeschichte und Konfliktforschung*, vol. 17 (Osnabrück: Biblio Verlag, 1978), p. 45; Niemeyer, pp. 97-106.

60. John, for example, assisted Albrecht in the direction of the divisional exercises at Bruck an der Leitha in 1875. See MKSM 29-1/20 ex 1875, Letter No. 1591/MKSM, Franz Joseph to Albrecht and Koller, Laxenburg, 16 August 1875. For a description of army maneuvers at all levels undertaken that year, typical for those of the 1870s, see MKSM 29-1/34 ex 1874, Letter Abt. 5 No. 3931, Koller to Franz Joseph, Vienna, 14 December 1874.

61. See, for example, Koller's observations of the 1874 maneuvers, in MKSM 29-1 ex 1875, Memorandum, "Bemerkungen zu den Waffenübungen," Koller to Franz Joseph, Vienna, no date.

62. See Bylandt's complaints to Franz Joseph about the elimination of divisional exercises, in MKSM 29-1/2 ex 1880, Letter No. 450 Präs., Bylandt to Franz Joseph, Vienna, 21 February 1880.

63. See Generalstab, OpB, Karton 677, Letter, Beck to Albrecht, Vienna, 18 July 1881.

64. See Glaise-Horstenau, p. 274.

65. See KA Nachlaß, B/2, Fasz. VII, No. 214, "Voranschlag über die Kosten der preußischen Manöver."

66. See Glaise-Horstenau, p. 275.

67. Preparing four corps for these "super maneuvers" essentially meant the mobilization of about a quarter of the army. See KA Nachlaß Wolf-Schneider, B/197, 6/IX, pp. 915-19.

68. For example, officers of the *Kriegsmarine* cooperated with the general staff in periodic exercises at Pola. See, for example, Beck's speeches following such exercises in 1883 and 1900, in KA Nachlaß Beck, B/2, Fasz. VII, No. 223; KA Nachlaß Beck, B/2, Fasz. VIII, No. 294. Beck's supposedly mediocre performance at the 1906 "*Landungsmanöver*" (landing or amphibious maneuvers) in Dalmatia formed the basis for his ouster the following November.

69. See MKSM 20-1/1-2 ex 1886, Conference Protocol, "Programm über die unter A.h. Vorsitze Seiner k. und k. Apostolischen Majestät in der Conferenz am 26. Februar 1886 zur Berathung gelegenden Angelegenheiten." The participation of militia forces at the annual corps maneuvers did give rise to some thorny legal issues. Franz Joseph, for example, argued against the use of *Landwehr* units in the 1893 *Armeemanöver* in Hungary, since their deployment outside Austria would require *Reichsrat* sanction. See HHStA, Filmarchiv, Nachlaß Albrecht, roll 45, Letter, Schönaich to Albrecht, Vienna, 28 October 1892.

70. See, for example, MKSM 80-3/5 ex 1900, Letter No. 2280, Beck to the MKSM, Vienna, 25 September 1900, in which Beck informed the military chancellery of his departure the next day for southwest Hungary to reconnoiter the terrain for the 1901 fall maneuvers.

71. KA Nachlaß Wolf-Schneider, B/197, 6/IX, p. 915.

72 . A Daimler armored car was used for the first time in the 1906 maneuvers at Teschen, the last conducted by Beck. Motorcycles and private cars were used for carrying messages at Austro-Hungarian maneuvers after 1903. Balloons were first used in the 1895 maneuvers. See Wagner, "Die k.(u.)k. Armee: Gliederung und Aufgabenstellung," pp. 475-77. Wolf-Schneider, however, points out that the monarchy came relatively late to the art of aerial reconnaissance. Germany, France, Italy, Russia, and England all had begun to use balloons by 1885. See KA Nachlaß Wolf-Schneider, B/197, 6/IX, p. 106.

73 . The Habsburg military attaché reported in October 1901 that the *Berliner Tageblatt* had reported favorably on the Austro-Hungarian maneuvers of that year and had especially praised Beck's leadership. The attaché noted that the German maneuvers were no longer getting such good reviews in the press because of Kaiser Wilhelm II's interference in their conduct. See KA Nachlaß Beck, B/2, Fasz. VIII, No. 297. According to Glaise-Horstenau, the foreign military attachés in Vienna agreed that Austria-Hungary conducted the most realistic maneuvers of all the Great Powers. See Glaise-Horstenau, pp. 359-60. Fuller's negative assessment of Austro-Hungarian maneuvers is based upon Franz Ferdinand's later interference in their conduct. See Fuller, p. 43.

74 . MKSM Sonderreihe, Sep. Karton 24, No. 5, Letter, Beck to Franz Joseph, Vienna, 13 January 1902. See also Glaise-Horstenau, p. 410.

75 . Glaise-Horstenau, p. 410.

76 . See KA Nachlaß Wolf-Schneider, B/197, 6/IX, pp. 915-16. These generally took place in Galicia, where the bulk of the monarchy's cavalry was stationed.

77 . Beck, for example, complained in 1896 of the sloppy and hasty training of reserves in marksmanship. See MKSM 20-1/2 ex 1896, Military Conference Protocol, Vienna, 4 February 1896.

78 . See, for example, Beck's notification of the military chancellery of his intention to attend the artillery practice at Zircz. See MKSM 80-3/2 ex 1901, Letter No. 618, Beck to the MKSM, Vienna, 26 March 1901.

79 . For Beck's proposals see KM Präs. 45-13/2 ex 1883, Letter No. 977 res., Beck to the War Ministry, Vienna, 4 September 1882; KM Präs. 45-13/2 ex 1883, Letter No. 76 res., Beck to the War Ministry, Vienna, 15 January 1883. See also KM Präs. 45-13/2 ex 1883, Letter Präs. No. 350 res., Technical and Administrative Military Committee to the War Ministry, Vienna, 4 September 1882; KA Nachlaß Wolf-Schneider, B/197, 6/IX, p. 692; Wagner, *Kriegsministerium* II, p. 242; Wagner, *Die bewaffnete Macht*, pp. 469-71. These exercises generally consisted of the laying of telegraph lines and the construction of bridges, field railroad stations, and small stretches of track. For an idea of the conduct of the railroad and telegraph maneuvers, see Beck's descriptive report to the war ministry, in KM Präs. 15-12/2 ex 1900, Letter No. 2062, Beck to the War Ministry, Vienna, 31 August 1900.

80 . For Beck's proposals concerning the reorganization of the technical troops, see MKSM 38-1/7 ex 1890, Letter Präs. No. 4973, Bauer to Franz Joseph, Vienna, 26 September 1890; KM Präs. 45-2/4 ex 1891, Letter No. 1001 res., Beck to the War Ministry, Vienna, 21 November 1891; KA Nachlaß Wolf-Schneider, B/197, 6/IX,

194 *Notes*

p. 694; Wagner, "Die k.(u.)k. Armee: Gliederung und Aufgabenstellung," p. 372. Wilhelm von Pitreich charged in his family history that Beck harbored an intense hatred for the engineering corps and sought in the unification of the technical troops to impose the supremacy of the pioneers, Beck's original service branch. Pitreich noted that before the emergence of the Wiener Neustadt Academy and the *Kriegsschule*, the major educational institutions of the general staff, the engineering corps had formed the educated elite of the armed forces. See KA Nachlaß Wilhelm von Pitreich, B/589, No. 3, p. 147. Beck, however, did not wish to suppress a rival institution but rather favored the unification of the engineers and pioneers to simplify the work of the technical branches and to relieve himself of the unwanted burden of supervising the pioneer corps.

81 . For discussions of general staff organization, see KA Nachlaß Wolf-Schneider, B/197, 6/IX, pp. 886; Wagner, "Die k.(u.)k. Armee: Gliederung und Aufgabenstellung," pp. 376-77; Rosner, pp. 33-38.

82 . See KA Nachlaß Wolf-Schneider, B/197, 6/IX, pp. 767-68.

83 . See, for example, Beck's "Conduite-Liste" for 1854, which highlighted Beck's unsuitability for mapping duty, in KA, Qualifications-Liste Generaloberst Beck-Rzikowsky. See also Wagner, "Die k.(u.)k. Armee: Gliederung und Aufgabenstellung," p. 381. Kuhn lamented in 1887 that mapping no longer occupied a prominent place in a staff officer's duty. See the diary entry for 7-8 September 1887, in KA Nachlaß Kuhn, B/670, No. 13, p. 82.

84 . Wolf-Schneider, however, notes that most of the increases in the number of general staff officers during Beck's tenure as chief were absorbed by the growth in the number of staff positions with the corps commands and the creation of additional posts with various other military commands and installations (artillery brigades, fortresses, naval facilities, and so on). See KA Nachlaß Wolf-Schneider, B/197, 6/IX, p. 764.

85 . By 1905, Austria-Hungary had military attachés in the following capitals: Berlin, Rome, St. Petersburg, Paris, Brussels, London, Sofia, Constantinople, Athens, Bucharest, Belgrade, and Tokyo-Peking. See KA Nachlaß Wolf-Schneider, pp. 764, 778; Wagner, "Die k.(u.)k. Armee: Gliederung und Aufgabenstellung," p. 381. The military attachés could submit reports directly to the chief of the general staff via the intelligence section.

86 . Wagner, "Die k.(u.)k. Armee: Gliederung und Aufgabenstellung," p. 385. For the Austro-Hungarian response to the lessons of the Boer War, see Jay Stone and Erwin A. Schmidl, *The Boer War and Military Reforms*, vol. 28, *War and Society in East Central Europe* (New York: University Press of America, 1988), pp. 167-313.

87 . Wolf-Schneider writes that in 1883 only sixteen staff officers were attached to military schools as instructors. In 1908, over seventy served in this capacity. See KA Nachlaß Wolf-Schneider, B/197, 6/IX, p. 914.

88 . For a fuller treatment of Beck's deputy chiefs of the general staff, see KA Nachlaß Wolf-Schneider, B/197, 6/IX, pp. 880-84.

89 . August von Pitreich often described his uncle's duties as "thankless" and "unrecognized" by Beck, who stole the limelight from the deputy who actually "ran" the general staff bureaucracy. See KA Nachlaß August von Pitreich, B/589, No. 3, Geschichte der Familie Pitreich, p. 356. Beck, however, often recognized the work of

his top subordinates, including the deputy chiefs of staff, at the many of the "general staff evenings" (*Generalstabsabende*) which he periodically held at top Vienna hotels. See, for example, KA Nachlaß Beck, B/2, Fasz. VII, No. 237; KA Nachlaß Beck, B/2, Fasz. VIII, No. 278.

    90 . Glaise-Horstenau, pp. 414-15.

    91 . See, for example, Beck's letter to his wife in May 1899, reproduced in part by Glaise-Horstenau, pp. 414-15. August von Pitreich notes in his family history that Beck and his wife did not like to socialize informally with general staff officers at their homes or in the various garden restaurants of the capital city. Pitreich writes that the Hotel Victoria on the corner of Favoriten and Taubstummstraße was a favorite after-hours haunt for general staff officers posted to Vienna. See KA Nachlaß August von Pitreich, B/159, No. 3, p. 271.

    92 . See KM Präs. 30-4/1 ex 1891, Memorandum, Albrecht to the War Ministry, Arco, 30 December 1890.

    93 . For Hoen's criticisms, see Glaise-Horstenau, pp. 413-14.

Chapter 5: Defending the Dual Monarchy

    1 . Franz Hlavac, "Die Armeeorganisation der Jahre 1881-1883 in der Donaumonarchie" (Ph.D. dissertation: University of Vienna, 1973), p. 133.

    2 . For a text of the renewed Three Emperors' League, see Alfred Franzis Pribram, *The Secret Treaties of Austria-Hungary*, vol. I (Cambridge, Mass.: Harvard University Press, 1920), pp. 36-49.

    3 . See MKSM 20-1/1 ex 1880, Political-Military Conference Protocol, 7 January 1880.

    4 . See Beck's memorandum, "Die militärisch-politische Situation im Jahre 1880," in KA Nachlaß Beck, B/2, Fasz. VI, No. 185, Vienna, 31 March 1880.

    5 . See Beck's comparisons of the military might of the European Great Powers at the beginning of the 1880s, in KA Nachlaß Beck, B/2, Fasz. VII, No. 196. Beck estimated that Austria-Hungary could field an army of 405,000 first line troops versus an Italian force of 242,000 during the first six weeks of combat. He did, however, note that Italian second line and territorial forces outnumbered their Austro-Hungarian counterparts by a considerable margin, a factor of perhaps decisive importance if Italy were not defeated in the initial battles.

    6 . A Russian general, Alexander Kaulbars, dominated the Bulgarian army as minister of war and appointed other Russian army officers to staff the upper echelons of the Bulgarian army. See George F. Kennan, *The Decline of Bismarck's European Order: Franco-Russian Relations, 1875-1890* (Princeton, N.J.: Princeton University Press, 1979), p. 117.

    7 . See Beck's memorandum, "Österreich und Rußland" of 28 October 1854, in KA Nachlaß Beck, B/2, Fasz. III, No. 63, and his second "Memoire über russich-Pohlen," written sometime in 1856, in KA Nachlaß Beck, B/2, Fasz. II, No. 42.

8 . See Beck's 1860 "Entwurf eines Defensiv-Bündnisses" with Prussia against the possibility of a French attack, in KA Nachlaß Beck, B/2, Fasz. V, No. 105.

9 . For the text of this defensive alliance, see Pribram I, pp. 18-31.

10 . See the "Denkschrift eines Berichtes an die kaiserlich deutsche Botschaft in Wien," Berlin, 2 December 1879, in MKSM Sonderreihe, Karton 64, "Kundschaftsdienst im Auslande." The Dual Alliance of October 1879 stipulated only that the two powers would "come to the assistance of the other with the whole war strength of their empires." See Pribram I, pp. 26-27. Beck apparently prepared several memoranda for Bismarck on the subject which the latter passed on to the chief of the Prussian general staff, Helmut von Moltke, for his evaluation. Unfortunately, no copy of these notes exists in the Vienna *Kriegsarchiv*.

11 . For Bismarck's views on military cooperation with Austria-Hungary, see Gerhard Ritter, *The Sword and the Scepter: The Problem of Militarism in Germany*. vol. I: *The Prussian Tradition 1740-1890* (Coral Gables, Fla.: University of Miami Press), p. 231.

12 . Glaise-Horstenau, p. 248. According to Glaise-Horstenau, Moltke had apparently termed the Austro-Hungarian armed forces an *"Armee auf Kundigung"* (an army on short notice), a direct reference to the constitutional requirement of the 1867 *Ausgleich* which stipulated the renegotiation of the financial contributions to the common budget to be made by both halves of the monarchy.

13 . Albrecht was at this juncture more motivated by distrust of the Germans than by any desire for closer relations.

14 . The emperor may also have felt that the general staff had enough on its plate already with the formation of three new war plans -- one against Italy and two Russian scenarios--and perhaps wanted these preparations to go forward unimpeded and uninfluenced by promised German troop commitments in the east.

15 . Unlike the Prussian general staff, which tried to keep the substance of the military discussions from Bismarck and the Prussian foreign office, Beck kept the *Ballhausplatz* informed of every aspect of the negotiations. For example, see the memorandum concerning the contents of the Strobl meeting by the Austro-Hungarian chargé (later ambassador) in Berlin Count Ladislas Szögyény-Marich, "Auszug aus dem Berichte über die Besprechungen mit Glt. Grafen Waldersee," Berlin, August 1882, in HHStA, PA I, Karton 468, Liasse XXI.

16 . See Beck's memorandum, "Besprechung Beck-Waldersee in Strobl," 3 August 1882, in KA Nachlaß Beck, B/2, Fasz. VII, No. 207. Both the German emperor and chancellor knew and approved of Waldersee's trip to Strobl. Waldersee was appointed *Generalquartiermeister* in December 1881 to assist the aging Helmut von Moltke and performed much the same functions as the deputy chief of the general staff in the Austro-Hungarian army.

17 . Germany and Austria-Hungary agreed to assist Italy "with all their forces" in the event of an unprovoked attack by France. Italy entered into a reciprocal obligation to Germany in the event of French aggression but was only obligated to demonstrate benevolent neutrality toward Austria-Hungary if it were attacked by a single Great Power. Only if two or more Great Powers declared war on Austria-Hungary was Italy

bound to lend active military assistance under the terms of the Triple Alliance. See Articles II-IV of the Triple Alliance Treaty as reproduced in Pribrim I, pp. 66-67.

18 . See KA Generalstab, OpB, Karton 685, Letter, Albrecht to Franz Joseph, Vienna, 19 August 1882. Albrecht wrote the emperor that one could no longer doubt the goodwill of the German ally following Beck's discussions with Waldersee.

19 . For Beck's description of the meeting, see his memorandum "Unterredung mit Graf Moltke" Vienna, 22 September 1882, in KA Nachlaß Beck, B/2, No. 210. Moltke's attempt to keep the meeting secret did not succeed. Word leaked immediately that he had gone to see his Austro-Hungarian counterpart, and hundreds of people gathered outside Beck's hotel to see Moltke emerge from the meeting. However, little foreign political backlash resulted from the public disclosure of the talks between the two.

20 . Moltke had been surprised and dismayed by the popular resistance of the French people in the latter stages of the Franco-Prussian War, fearing the social consequences of "a people in arms." Since he was unwilling to have Prussia-Germany take such a decisive step toward full exploitation of universal service out of fear of the revolutionary dangers involved, Moltke recognized the difficulty of achieving rapid victory in a future war against a nation so mobilized. Prussian deployment plans of the 1870s versus France and Russia, which stressed an offensive-defensive strategy of spoiling attacks aimed only at a disruption of the enemy's mobilization, reflected Motlke's doubts about achieving victory through an all-out offensive. The encirclement plan agreed upon with Beck did not contravene this basic strategy. See Gunther E. Rothenberg, "Moltke and Schlieffen," in *Makers of Modern Strategy from Machiavelli to the Nuclear Age* (Princeton, N.J.: Princeton University Press, 1986), pp. 305-6.

21 . See KA Nachlaß Beck, B/2, Fasz. VII, No. 216, Telegram, Beck to Moltke, Vienna, 29 October 1882.

22 . See MKSM Sonderreihe, Karton 58, Letter, Moltke to Popp, Creison, 29 October 1882.

23 . See Generalstab, OpB, Karton 668, Heft 1, Letter, Steininger to Beck, Berlin, 17 February 1883.

24 . Steininger reported in July 1883 that the Prussian general staff viewed a war in the spring as inevitable and desirous, since delay would only benefit France and Russia. In October, Waldersee told Steininger that measures designed to strengthen the Russian army actually represented the beginning of a slow deployment against Austria-Hungary and argued that an early attack by the allies would be most advantageous. See Generalstab, OpB, Karton 666, Heft 1, Letter, Steininger to Beck, Berlin, 28 August 1883; Generalstab, OpB, Karton 668, Heft 1, Letter, Steininger to Beck, 14 October 1883.

25 . See "Abschrift eines Berichtes Seiner kaiserlichen Hoheit des Kronprinzen Rudolf über eine Unterredung mit Fürsten Bismarck," Berlin, 1 March 1883, in HHStA, PA I, Karton 468.

26 . See Beck's 7 December 1880 memorandum "Anträge zur Vorbereitung der Mobilisierung und des strategischen Aufmarsches der Armee," in Generalstab, OpB, Karton 668, Heft 1. At the time of the Strobl meeting, Austro-Hungarian forces would

have been hard-pressed to launch offensive operations against Russia before the forty-second day of mobilization. See Wagner, "Die k.(u.)k. Armee: Gliederung und Aufgabenstellung," p. 382.

27 . See Haymerle's undated memorandum of 1880, in Generalstab, OpB, Karton 668.

28 . See Beck's "Denkschrift über die militärischen Vorarbeiten für das Jahr 1883 als Grundlage für die Aufmarsch-Arbeiten," Vienna, 11 November 1882, in Generalstab, OpB, Karton 669.

29 . See Beck's "Studie über die Mittel zur Beseitigung jener Übelstände in der Dislokation und Ordre der Bataille der Armee, welche einer rashen Mobilisierung und einem beschleunigsten Aufmarsche hindernd im Wege stehen," in MKSM 65-2/7 ex 1881. See also Wagner, *Kriegsministerium* II, p. 213; KA Nachlaß Wolf-Schneider, B/197, 6/IX, pp. 665-66; Hlavac, pp. 44-46. Beck had advocated the reorganization of the Austro-Hungarian army on a territorial basis as far back as 1870. See KA Nachlaß Beck, B/2, Fasz. VI, No. 156, "Begründung für den Entwurf einer Stabs Ordre de Bataille," Vienna, 16 October 1870.

30 . In principle, the organization of the Austro-Hungarian army in 1881 closely resembled that of France in 1870. The impromptu organization of division and particularly corps-sized units, coupled with the separation of regiments and their reserve cadres in the home districts, had irreversibly crippled the French war effort against Prussia. While an 1873 military law upheld the principle of national recruitment in France, by the end of the decade most Frenchmen called to service were assigned to garrisons in their home districts. See Douglas Porch, *The March to the Marne: The French Army 1871-1914* (Cambridge: Cambridge University Press, 1981), pp. 29-32, 46.

31 . Units were also rotated regularly between the larger and smaller garrisons. See MKSM 65-2/1 ex 1873, Memorandum ad War Ministry No. 4960/Abt.5, Albrecht to the Military Chancellery, Vienna, 21 January 1873.

32 . A gendarmerie of thirteen regiments was formed only after the 1848 Revolution. While this force was later expanded to nineteen regiments, it nevertheless remained too small to meet the domestic security needs of the state without support from the regular military. See Rothenberg, *The Army of Francis Joseph*, pp. 19, 44-46. Radetzky's field instructions, however, said nothing about counterinsurgency fighting. See Niemeyer, pp. 62-63.

33 . See Holzer, pp. 66-71.

34 . See MKSM 65-2/27 ex 1873, Memorandum ad KM Präs. No. 1958, Albrecht to Franz Joseph, Vienna, 5 July 1873. The Vienna garrison numbered only some 7,840 men at the time Albrecht was writing, a scant two hundred more than in 1848, despite a doubling of the city's population to 900,000 over the same period.

35 . See Albrecht's April 1881 memorandum to the emperor, "Über Verbesserung unserer Heeres-Organisation," in MKSM Sonderreihe, Karton 1/16. See also the same memorandum in HHStA, Filmarchiv, Nachlaß Albrecht, roll 5. See also Wagner, *Kriegsministerium* II, pp. 212-13; Hlavac, pp. 37-40. The extent of Albrecht's fears in regard to the reliability of Austro-Hungarian troops stationed in their home areas can be seen in an 1873 memorandum in which he opposed the transfer of Infantry

Regiment No. 22 to Dalmatia on the grounds that it received over half of its replacements from there. See MKSM 65-2/1 ex 1873, Memorandum ad War Ministry No. 4960/Abt.5, Albrecht to the Military Chancellery, Vienna, 21 January 1873.

36 . See KA Nachlaß Kuhn, B/670, No. 12, pp. 23-70.

37 . In 1870 Andrássy had indeed called the reorganization of the army along territorial lines a "vital necessity." See MKSM 65-2/3 ex 1870, Letter, Andrássy to Franz Joseph, Ofen, 5 March 1870.

38 . Throughout the 1880s, Beck repeatedly opposed suggestions of the Sarajevo command to fortify key locations within the Bosnian capital against the possibility of domestic violence. Beck felt that money for fortifications in Bosnia could be better spent on building up border defenses along the Drina border with Serbia. See KM Präs. 33-5/52 ex 1882, Letter Präs. No. 3300, Sarajevo Command to the War Ministry, Sarajevo, 22 July 1882; KM Präs. 33-5/32 ex 1882, Letter Glstb. No. 962 res., Beck to the War Ministry, Vienna, 12 August 1882; KM Präs. 33-9/1 ex 1886, Letter No. 84 res., Beck to the War Ministry, Vienna, 22 January 1886.

39 . See KM Präs. 33-3/6 ex 1894, Military Conference Protocol, 7 March 1894; KM Präs. 33-3/11 ex 1894, Memorandum No. 1225 res., Beck to the War Ministry, Vienna, 4 November 1894. Beck favored the construction of any new barracks in the better sections of Vienna.

40 . While Beck, for example, in 1893 approved the transfer of two additional regiments to Prague to assist the local corps command in maintaining order in the city, these nevertheless came from Königgrätz, another Bohemian recruitment area. See KM Präs. 25-9/4 ex 1893, Letter Präs. No. 4494/II, War Ministry to Taaffe, Vienna, 14 September 1893; KM Präs. 33-1/1-1 ex 1898, Memorandum No. 48/MKSM, Bolfras to Franz Joseph, Vienna, 8 January 1898.

41 . For Beck's 1905 plans for a coup in Hungary, see KA Nachlaß Beck, B/2, Fasz. IX, No. 307; Kurt Peball and Gunther Rothenberg, "Der Fall U. Die geplannte Besetzung Ungarns durch die k.u.k. Armee im Herbst 1905," *Schriften des Heeresgeschichtlichen Museums in Wien* 4 (1969), pp. 85-126; Glaise-Horstenau, p. 406.

42 . See Wagner, *Kriegsministerium* II, pp. 210-11; Hlavac, pp. 30-47. Schönfeld, however, issued his greatest call for the establishment of a territorial system upon submitting his new war plan against Russia in January 1881. See Generalstab, OpB, Karton 669, Heft 4, Letter Glstb. Res. No. 98, Schönfeld to Franz Joseph, Vienna, 29 January 1881.

43 . Tyrolian and Dalmatian areas, with their lesser manpower resources, would form divisional commands.

44 . In 1881 the common army was organized into eight *General-Kommanden* (Vienna, Graz, Prague, Brünn, Budapest, Agram, and Sarajevo), six *Militär-Kommanden* (Cracow, Preßburg, Kaschau, Temesvár, Hermannstadt, and Zara), and two *Truppen-Divisions und Militär-Kommanden* at Trieste and Innsbruck. While the heads of the general and military commands would take charge of corps in wartime, according to the order of battle, they might end up losing some units to other corps while receiving some

from areas outside their peacetime control. See Beck's 1881 study as cited in note 29 above. See also Hlavac, pp. 12-15.

45. See HHStA, Filmarchiv, Nachlaß Albrecht, roll 4, Memorandum, Albrecht to Franz Joseph, "Studie über die Corps Einteilung der Armee im Kriegsfall," Vienna, end of November 1875.

46. See MKSM 64-1/2 ex 1876, Military Conference Protocol, 25 February 1876.

47. See MKSM 20-1/5-2 ex 1881, Military Conference Protocols, 26, 27 and 29 May 1882; Wagner, *Kriegsministerium* II, pp. 215-18; Hlavac, pp. 54-74.

48. The outgoing chief of the general staff Schönfeld did not attend.

49. This was incorrect. Italy retained territorial dislocation until World War I, fearing regionalism in the recently united Italian state. See Richard Bosworth, *Italy, the Least of the Great Powers: Italian Foreign Policy before the First World War* (London: Cambridge University Press, 1979), p. 22.

50. Bylandt had already begun to furlough troops before they completed their full three-year term of service in order to cut costs.

51. In his April memorandum, Beck had forwarded a somewhat different proposal for the use of the militia forces, assigning one militia brigade to each corps instead of a division. This proposal, however, considered for assignment only those portions of the militia slated under current plans for mobile operations (three *Landwehr* and seven *Honvéd* divisions), excluding from consideration those forces assigned to major garrisons. See MKSM 65-2/7 ex 1881.

52. Under Bylandt's scheme, the army would be composed of four corps of three divisions and nine corps of two divisions. Beck favored the organization of sixteen corps composed of two common army and one militia division.

53. See MKSM 38-3/2 ex 1882, Letter Präs. No. 2708, Bylandt to Franz Joseph, Vienna, 3 June 1882. See also Hlavac, pp. 104-17; Wagner, *Kriegsministerium* II, pp. 222-24.

54. Major General Vlasits chaired the committee made up of the heads of the second, third, fifth, and tenth war ministry departments, the chief of the general staff, three other staff officers, and an additional officer of the tenth department. See Wagner, *Kriegsministerium* II, p. 220.

55. The guard corps, for example, consisted of recruits from Prussia as a whole, not from any one district.

56. Beck's successor as head of the military chancellery, Major General Leonidas Popp, wrote shortly after Bylandt's submission to the emperor of the committee's report that even after the proposed reorganization, over one-fifth of the monarchy's regiments (22 out of 102) would still be stationed outside their recruitment districts. See MKSM 38-3/2 ex 1882, Memorandum No. 1311/MKSM, Popp to Franz Joseph, Vienna, 6 June 1882. Popp nevertheless urged Franz Joseph to order the immediate reorganization of the army along the lines of the war ministry proposals.

57. The Innsbruck command, which included only the recruitment districts of Tyrol and Vorarlberg, while it would receive the designation "XIV Corps," remained essentially a divisional command in peacetime.

58 . See 38-3/2 ex 1882, Military Conference Protocols, 10 and 11 June 1882. Albrecht, Bylandt, Beck, and Popp attended the meetings, as did the heads of the fifth and second war ministry departments, Colonels Alexander von Hold and Josef Stupka.

59 . Franz Hlavac incorrectly interpreted Beck's caveat concerning the impossibility of a mobilization before the completion of the reorganization of the army in March 1883 as a sudden lessening of his resolve in the matter. The conference protocol, however, clearly records Beck's endorsement of Bylandt's proposal to begin the reorganization in the coming fall. See Hlavac, p. 121.

60 . See HHStA, PA XL, Karton 293, Ministerial Council Protocol KZ 68, RMRZ 301, 29 June 1882.

61 . Each district was also responsible for the raising of one regiment of cavalry, field artillery, or fortress artillery. The technical troops were recruited from throughout the corps area, one battalion per corps. The railroad and telegraph regiment theoretically took recruits from all areas of the monarchy, although chiefly from the Austrian lands. For a good overview of the organization of the common army after 1881, see Günther Dirrheimer, *Das k.u.k. Heer 1895*, vol. 10, in *Schriften des Heeresgeschichtlichen Museums in Wien* (Vienna: Österreichischer Bundesverlag, 1986), pp. 12-99. The corps areas would also correspond to the divisional recruitment districts of the *Landwehr* and *Honvéd*, providing each common army corps with its third division. See Allmayer-Beck and Erich Lessing, *Die k.u.k. Armee 1848-1914* (Munich: Bertelsmann, 1974), p. 221.

62 . Beck was a major force behind the decentralization of military functions that pushed the war ministry to limit its role to the issuance of general mobilization guidelines, allowing individual corps commands latitude to draw up their own sets of detailed instructions. See Beck's memorandum, "Entwurf einer territorialen Organisation des k.k Heeres als Substrat für die kommisionellen Berathungen zur Beschleunigung und Vereinfachung der Mobilisierungs sowie zur Verbesserung der Aufmarschverhältnisse," in MKSM Sonderreihe, Karton 1/16. See also Beck's related request for the codification of army field regulations to assist commanders and general staff officers in completion of their duties in time of mobilization, in KM 47-7/1 ex 1883, Letter No. 163, Beck to the War Ministry, Vienna, 29 January 1883.

63 . Hlavac, pp. 190-91.

64 . Wagner, *Die bewaffnete Macht*, p. 364.

65 . August von Pitreich naturally credited his uncle Heinrich with having worked out many of the reorganization details but did mention that Beck had worked closely with Bylandt for organizational reform. See KA Nachlaß Pitreich, B/159, No. 3, pp. 142-43.

66 . Rothenberg, *The Army of Francis Joseph*, p. 111. The peacetime deployment of the large portions of the cavalry in Galicia for the purpose of protecting the army's deployment against Russia continued even after the organization of home defense forces toward the end of the 1880s.

67 . See KA Nachlaß Beck, B/2, Fasz. IX.

68 . The army high command harbored grave doubts about the loyalty of the Bosnian troops in a Balkan war and wanted them out of the provinces as quickly as

possible in the event of war. An 1887 war ministry directive stipulated the immediate transport of three battalions of Bosnian troops to Graz and a fourth battalion to Budapest on the third day of mobilization at their peacetime strength. Reservists would follow on the tenth day of mobilization. The territorial dislocation of some of these troops to Budapest and Vienna after 1891 in a sense fulfilled both internal and external security needs of the monarchy. See "Punktation für die Mobilisierung der bosnisch-herzegowinischen Truppen," in KM Präs. 86-2/9 ex 1887. Common Finance Minister Benjamin Kállay expressed similar doubts as to the reliability of Bosnian forces in the event of a Balkan war in an 1890 ministerial council. See HHStA, PA XL, Karton 295, Ministerial Council Protocol KZ 30, R.M.R.Z. 364, 28 April 1890.

69. See MKSM 65-1/5 ex 1891, Letter 2737/MKSM, Bolfras to the War Ministry, Vienna, 9 December 1891; Wagner, "Die k.(u.)k. Armee: Gliederung und Aufgabenstellung," p. 433. The Hungarian government lodged official protests against the deployment of Bosnian forces in Budapest, citing a 1640 law which prohibited the stationing of "foreign" troops within the kingdom. Common Finance Minister Benjamin Kállay, a Hungarian, silenced the objections of his countrymen by pointing out that Bosnian troops took the oath of allegiance to the same sovereign as did Hungarian forces and therefore could not be considered foreign within the context of Hungarian law. See HHStA, PA XL, Karton 295, Ministerial Council Protocol KZ 30, RMRZ 364, 28 April 1890.

70. See Allmayer-Beck, *Die k.u.k. Armee*, p. 149.

71. After 1873, the pace of new railroad construction dropped off radically for the remainder of the decade. For railroad development in the *Gründerzeit*, see David F. Good, *The Economic Rise of the Habsburg Empire, 1750-1914* (Berkeley, Calif.: University of California Press, 1984), pp. 100-103.

72. For the condition of the Austro-Hungarian rail network in the early 1880s from the military standpoint, see Beck's "Memoire betreffend den Ausbau der Eisenbahnnetzes zur Beschleunigung des Aufmarsches der Armee im Kriegsfall gegen Rußland," in MKSM Sonderreihe, Karton 64. See also Bylandt's resumé of the situation to the civilian ministers on the basis of general staff reports, in HHStA, PA XL, Karton 293, Ministerial Council Protocol KZ 24, RMRZ 292, 5 Febraury 1882.

73. For Beck's inspection report, "Verbindung zwischen der Donau und der Weichsel bei Oswiecim (durch das Waag- und Sola-Thal)," of August 1881, see KM Präs. 15-8/4 ex 1881. After his meeting with Waldersee, Beck became so concerned about the state of Austro-Hungarian railroads leading to Galicia that he dashed off a letter to Popp, his successor as head of the military chancellery, imploring him to raise with the emperor the matter of the concessioning of the so-called *"Tranversal-Bahn,"* an alternative east-west route to the *Nordbahn* less exposed to disruption by Russian forces during mobilization. See MKSM Sonderreihe, Karton 57, Letter, Beck to Popp, Vienna, 22 July 1882.

74. See Generalstab, OpB, Karton 668, Heft 1, Letter, Beck to Steininger, Vienna, 29 December 1882.

75. The fifty-day Russian mobilization speed noted for the early 1880s is based on an estimate made in 1890 by the head of the operations bureau of the Austro-

Hungarian general staff, Colonel Oskar Potiorek. See Generalstab, OpB, Karton 670, Heft 6, Memorandum, "Denkschrift über die Entwicklung des heutigen Aufmarsch-Elaborates für den Kriegsfall mit Rußland," Vienna, 11 October 1890.

76 . See MKSM 20-1/6-4 ex 1883, Civil-Military Council Protocol No. 310/MKSM, 4 February 1883.

77 . The "First Hungarian-Galician Railroad Company" had proposed to Beck the idea of a trans-Galician railroad already in 1880 while he was still at the military chancellery. See MKSM 34-1/1 ex 1880, Letter No. 463, "The First Hungarian-Galician Railroad Company," Vienna, 10 February 1880.

78 . For a good overview of the construction progress of the 1880s, see Generalstab, OpB, Karton 670, Heft 7, Memorandum, Potiorek to Beck, "Die Entwicklung des Eisenbahnwesens in Österreich-Ungarn und im Okkupations-Gebiethe vom 1881 bis Ende 1890," Vienna, 1891.

79 . See KM Präs. 15-8/3 ex 1887, Memorandum, Beck to the War Ministry, Neumarkt, 16 June 1887.

80 . See KA Nachlaß Wolf-Schneider, B/197, 6/IX, p. 823. See also the portion of Schönfeld's 1881 Russian war plan dealing with transportation to Galicia, in Generalstab, OpB, Karton 669, Heft 4, Letter Glstb. Res. No. 98, Schönfeld to Franz Joseph, Vienna, 29 January 1881. Wolf-Schneider notes that while in 1881 only thirty-three trains could depart daily for Galicia, a decade later this number had increased to ninety-six.

81 . These amounted to approximately a 50% increase in the total rolling stock between 1880 and 1890. See Generalstab, OpB, Karton 670, Heft 7, Memorandum, Potiorek to Beck, "Die Entwicklung des Eisenbahnwesens in Österreich-Ungarn und im Okkupations-Gebiete vom 1881 bis Ende 1890," Vienna, 1891.

82 . Hlavac, p. 220; Wagner, *Kriegsministerium* II, p. 174. In 1884, Beck obtained the creation of a Cisleithanian "railroad council" with military representation. The same year he secured from the Austrian trade ministry German as the language of operation for the general directorate of the Austrian state railroads, which greatly facilitated the mobilization and deployment of the army. Beck obtained Hungarian agreement to use German as the official language of railroad operation within the kingdom. Budapest, however, proved lax in its enforcement of language qualifications of railroad officials. See KM Präs. 55-3/5 ex 1884, Civil-Military Conference Protocol, 27 January 1884. See also KA Nachlaß August von Pitreich, B/589, No. 3, pp. 448-53.

83 . This was not the case throughout Europe. In Russia, for example, neither the war ministry nor the general staff exercised much control over railroad construction priorities. See Fuller, pp. 63-64.

84 . See Beck's memorandum of 20 January 1881, "Zu den Vereinbarung der Kabinette Wien, Berlin und Petersburg," in KA Nachlaß Beck, B/2, Fasz. VII, No. 189.

85 . Russian force totals based upon Austro-Hungarian general staff estimates contained in Beck's 1882 "Exposé: Militärische Situation in einem Kriege Österreich-Ungarn und Deutschland mit Rußland," in KA Nachlaß Beck, B/2, No. 205.

86 . See MKSM 69-2/1-3 ex 1883, Letter No. 682, Beck to Franz Joseph, Vienna, 29 April 1883.

87 . See the foreign ministry copy of Beck's 11 November 1882 "Denkschrift über die militärischen Vorarbeiten für das Jahr 1883 als Grundlage für die Aufmarsch-Arbeiten" to Franz Joseph, HHStA, PA I, Karton 466, Liasse XXb, folios 5-18. The general staff copy of this same memorandum survives, in Generalstab, OpB, Karton 669, Heft 4.

88 . Compare, for example, Schönfeld's 1881 war plan to Beck's calculations made the following year. See Generalstab, OpB, Karton 669, Heft 4, Letter Glstb. Res. 98, Schönfeld to Franz Joseph, Vienna, 29 January 1881; KA Nachlaß Beck, B/2, Fasz. VII, No. 205, Memorandum "Exposé: Militärische Situation in einem Kriege Österreich-Ungarn und Deutschland mit Rußland," Beck to Franz Joseph, no date, 1882.

89 . See the memorandum cited in note 85 above. See also Generalstab, OpB, Karton 669, Heft 4, Letter, Beck to Albrecht, Vienna, 23 February 1882.

90 . See note 85 above.

91 . See Generalstab, OpB, Karton 668, Heft 1, Letter, Beck to Albrecht, Vienna, 6 November 1883.

92 . When fully mobilized the centrally located third army would be the strongest of the three Austro-Hungarian armies at seven corps. See the May 1905 memorandum by Captain Lerch, "Geschichte des Aufmarsches gegen Rußland vom Jahre 1880 bis 1905," in Generalstab, OpB, Karton 670, Heft 7.

93 . For the most definitive work on Austro-Hungarian war planning in the Beck and Conrad eras, see Dieter Degreif, "Operative Plannungen des k.u.k. Generalstabes für einen Krieg in der Zeit vor 1914" (Ph.D. dissertation: University of Mainz, 1983). Hlavac's estimation that the army could mobilize against Russia within thirty-five days in 1883 appears to be overly optimistic. See Hlavac, p. 212.

94 . See Generalstab, OpB, Karton 668, Heft 1, "Resumé einer längeren Besprechung des Chef des Generalstabes FML Baron Beck mit dem Militär-Attaché in Petersburg Major Klepsch," Vienna, 4 September 1883.

95 . At the close of 1882, Beck estimated that, while Austria-Hungary could deploy a corp-strength force around Cracow in western Galicia by the sixth day of mobilization, early concentrations farther east, including around the major assembly point along the San River, remained weak. See MKSM 69-2/1-1 ex 1883, Letter Glstb. Res. No. 1466, Beck to Franz Joseph, Vienna, 21 December 1882.

96 . Eight cavalry regiments formed two cavalry divisions. See MKSM 20-1/1-2 ex 1881, Military Conference Protocol, 11 January 1881. Schönfeld told the conference that these forces could in no way protect the entire border from incursions by the fourteen regular Russian cavalry regiments stationed in Poland and would be merely capable of turning back the occasional cossack patrol.

97 . See Wagner, "Die k.(u.)k. Armee: Gliederung und Aufgabenstellung," pp. 437-38.

98 See, for example, the "Aufmarschskizze der Kavallerie Divisionen 1882," in KA Nachlaß Beck, B/2, Fasz. VII, No. 199.

99 . Less than 3 million gulden were expended for fortifications during the three fiscal years of Koller's tenure as war minister. See Kesslitz, p. 197. See also Wagner, "Die k.(u.)k. Armee: Gliederung und Aufgabenstellung," p. 403.

100 . Fortification expenditures fell to an abysmal 150,000-175,000 gulden per annum in 1877-78. See Kesslitz, p. 197.

101 . For Kálnoky's views, see HHStA, PA XL, Karton 141, Letter [excerpt], Kálnoky to Albrecht, Vienna, 12 December 1883. For the debates over the fortification budget, see HHStA, PA XL, Karton 294, Ministerial Council Protocol, KZ 55, RMRZ 318, 24 September 1884; HHStA, PA XL, Karton 294, Ministerial Council Protocol, KZ 56, RMRZ 319.

102 . Excluding the 1871 budget, which included the costs for the feverish preparations of the previous year along the Ens line and in Bohemia versus Prussia-Germany as well as in Galicia. See Kesslitz, p. 197.

103 . For Beck's original proposals regarding the construction of these fortifications, see MKSM 39-1/7 ex 1882, Letter Präs. No. 6447, Bylandt to Franz Joseph, Vienna, 10 December 1882; KM Präs. 33-9/1 ex 1883, Letter Glstb. No. 154 res., Beck to the War Ministry, Vienna, 27 January 1883; KM Präs. 33-17/2 ex 1883, Letter Glstb. Res. No. 505, Beck to the War Ministry, Vienna, 26 March 1883; KM Präs. 33-30/4 ex 1883, Letter Glstb. No. 1312 res., Beck to the War Ministry, Vienna, 8 November 1883. See also KA Nachlaß Wolf-Schneider, B/197, 6/IX, pp. 805-6; Wagner, "Die K.(u.)K. Armee: Gliederung und Aufgabenstellung," p. 405. Beck's efforts were supported by the inspector general of engineers, Daniel von Salis-Soglio. See Daniel von Salis-Soglio, *Mein Leben und was ich davon erzählen will, kann und darf* (Stuttgart: Deutsche Verlags-Anstalt, 1908), p. 161.

104 . See Richard Bosworth, *Italy and the Approach of the First World War* (New York: St. Martin's Press, 1983), pp. 55-56; John Whittam, *The Politics of the Italian Army 1861-1918* (London: Croom Helm, 1977), p. 119.

105 . See KA Nachlaß Beck, B/2, Fasz. VI, No. 176.

106 . Despite the fact that Beck at this point did not enjoy the institutional support of the general staff bureaus, his early war plan against Italy contains elaborate railroad timetables for each division and corps, stating when they would be transported and over what lines.

107 . Beck did not, therefore, foresee an Italian defense of the Isonzo, Tagliamento, Piave, Brenta or Adige, river lines. He did not mention in his war plan if he believed that the Italian army would attempt to defend Venice. It was estimated that the Italian army would require thirty days to mobilize and deploy. See Wagner, "Die k.(u.)k. Armee: Gliederung und Aufgabenstellung," p. 383.

108 . See the general staff's "Geschichte der Aufmärsche gegen Italien, I. Teil, 1880-1896," in Generalstab, OpB, Karton 691. See also KA Nachlaß Wolf-Schneider, B/197, 6/IX, pp. 855-57; Wagner, "Die k.(u.)k. Armee: Gliederung und Aufgabenstellung," p. 383.

109 . The first already in the fall of 1881. See Generalstab, Hauptreihe, Letter Generalstab No. 987 res., Beck to the War Ministry, Vienna, 27 October 1881.

110 . Given the more urgent task of preparing the Galician theater, only one Italian war plan was drawn up in full detail in the 1880s, although the general staff prepared several additional generalized alternatives. See KA Nachlaß Wolf-Schneider,

B/197, 6/IX, p. 851; Wagner, "Die k.(u.)k. Armee - Gliederung und Aufgabenstellung," p. 383.

111. See Beck's memorandum, Generalstab No. 378 res., 25 March 1882. For Beck's war plans versus Italy, see also KA Nachlaß Wolf-Schneider, B/197, 6/IX, pp. 857-58.

112. In 1883-84, two divisions were removed from the Italian theater for deployment with the XV Corps in Bosnia-Herzegovina. See the "Geschichte der Aufmarsch gegen Italien, II. Teil," in Generalstab, OpB, Karton 691.

113. Albrecht remained the big advocate of a preventive war against Italy, urging as late as 1885 its elimination to free the monarchy's hand against Russia. See Holzer, pp. 102-3.

114. See MKSM 69-2/4 ex 1884, Letter Generalstab No. 758, Beck to Franz Joseph, Vienna, 17 September 1884; Wagner, "Die k.(u.)k. Armee: Gliederung und Aufgabenstellung," p. 383.

115. See KM Präs. 72-21/1 ex 1882, Letter Präs. No. 1994, War Ministry to the Austrian Defense Ministry, Vienna, 30 March 1882; KM Präs. 15-8/4 ex 1882, Letter Präs. No. 3507/II, War Ministry to the Technical and Administrative Military Committee, Vienna, 10 July 1882; KM Präs. 33-7/4 ex 1882, Letter Präs. No. 660, Bylandt to Franz Joseph, Vienna, 23 March 1882. Walter Wagner writes that Austria-Hungary spent approximately 1.8 million gulden on fortifications in Carinthia and the Tyrol between 1883 and 1893, minor outlays compared to the amount of money spent for similar purposes in Galicia over the same period. See Wagner, "Die k.(u.)k. Armee: Gliederung und Aufgabenstellung," p. 405.

116. See MKSM 69-3/3 ex 1885, Letter Generalstab No. 514 res., Beck to Franz Joseph, Vienna, 11 July 1885.

117. For the provisions of the first Triple Alliance agreement, see Pribram I, pp. 64-73.

118. For example, the Delegations approved only one-tenth of the war ministry's total fortification budget for the Tyrol in 1883 of one million gulden. See KM Präs. 33-7/1 ex 1883, Letter Präs. No. 115, War Ministry to the XIV Corps Command in Innsbruck, Vienna, 15 January 1883. The war ministry instructed the XIV Corps Command not to use the money to begin construction of any of the planned walled fortifications, since it was highly doubtful that the army would ever receive the money to complete them. Beck would continue to complain of gaps in Austro-Hungarian fortifications versus Italy. See, for example, his complaints concerning the incomplete nature of the works around Trento, in KM Präs. 15-8/5 ex 1885, Memorandum, Beck to the War Ministry, Vienna, 21 August 1885.

119. In 1882, for example, Austria-Hungary expended 400,000 gulden on the construction of roads in Bosnia-Herzegovina. See KM Präs. 33-5/39 ex 1882, Letter Präs. No. 3385, War Ministry to the Sarajevo General Command, Vienna, 25 May 1882. This in a year in which Beck informed the war ministry of the great improvement of the road network since 1878. See Generalstab, Hauptreihe, Letter Generalstab No. 1208 res., Beck to the War Ministry, Vienna, 1 January 1882.

120 . See, for example, the Hungarian response to Common Finance Minister Kállay's proposed construction of a short Herzegovinian line between the provincial capital Mostar to Metkovich in 1883, in HHStA, PA XL, Karton 293, Ministerial Council Protocol KZ 61, RMRZ 314, 23 September 1883.

121 . See Beck's "Memoire betreffend das Verhalten der österreichisch-ungarischen Monarchie im Falle von Complicationen gegen Serbien," to the war ministry, Generalstab No. 388 res., Vienna, 28 March 1882. For Austro-Hungarian war planning versus Serbia, see also Degreif, pp. 42-46.

122 . In his 1882 memorandum, Beck mentioned the specific case of the Serbian order of 100,000 Mauser-Kosta rifles from Germany, only one-tenth of which had already been delivered.

123 . Schönfeld had already recognized the problem caused by the swift mobilization of Montenegrin forces. See Generalstab, OpB, Karton 668, Heft 1, Letter Generalstab No. 311, Schönfeld to Franz Joseph, 10 March 1881.

124 . Great efforts were made in the early 1880s to strengthen the landward defenses of the port city of Cattaro (Kotor), which anchored the cordon defense extending into Herzegovina. By 1886, much of the border with Montenegro had been fortified. A limited number of fortifications were also erected along the provinces' Drina frontier with Serbia to secure the border in the early stages of a Balkan conflict with a minimum number of troops. For the progress on works in southern Dalmatia and in Bosnia-Herzegovina, see Beck's inspection report of 25 May 1884, in KM Präs. 15-8/3 ex 1883. See also KM Präs. 15-8/5 ex 1886, Letter Generalstab No. 552 res., Beck to the War Ministry, Vienna, 3 June 1886. It must be noted, however, that the construction budget of the Sarajevo command remained extremely limited, with a large portion of monies allocated, at least in first years of the occupation, going toward the construction of adequate housing for Austro-Hungarian forces stationed there. See, for example, "Ausweis I der mit Reichs-Kriegs-Ministerial Erlaß vom 25. Mai 1882 Präs. No. 3385 bewilligten Bau-Herstellungen," in KM Präs. 33-5/58 ex 1882. In 1885, the war ministry had to caution the Sarajevo command not to exceed the 200,000 gulden construction budget approved for that year. See KM Präs. 33-4/1 ex 1885, Letter Präs. No. 56, War Ministry to the XV Corps Command, Vienna, 6 January 1885.

125 . For a complete text of the Austro-Serbian secret treaty of June 1881, see Pribram I, pp. 51-63.

126 . See HHStA, PA I, Karton 456, Liasse V, "Verhandlungen mit Serbien 1881-86," Letter, Haymerle to Franz Joseph, 28 June 1881.

127 . See the documents of KM Präs. 76-23/1 ex 1884 reprinted in Scott W. Lackey, "A Secret Austro-Hungarian Plan to Intervene in the 1884 Timok Uprising in Serbia; Unpublished Documents," *Austrian History Yearbook*, vol. 23 (1992), pp. 149-59.

128 . See the intelligence report of the General Command in Sarajevo to the war ministry of 7 January 1881, in KM Präs., 51-6/1 ex 1881.

129 . See HHStA, PA XL, Karton 293, Crown Council Protocol KZ 15, RMRZ 293, 12 February 1882. Major General Stephan Jovanovich, Rodich's replacement as Statthalter of Dalmatia, had noted already in 1881 that the people of

Herzegovina still looked upon Montenegro as their protector. See KM Präs. 33-4/1 ex 1882, Letter No. 95, Jovanovich to the War Ministry, Zara, 20 December 1881.

130 . See Glaise-Horstenau, p. 281. This episode, however, did not find its way into Beck's official report to the foreign office on his visit to Montenegro in 1884. See HHStA, PA XL, Karton 141, Letter Glstb. No. 634 res., Beck to Kálnoky, Vienna, 26 May 1884.

131 . Langer, pp. 331-34.

132 . See Beck's 1881 memorandum, "Diplomatisch-militärisches betreffend Rumänien," in KA Nachlaß Beck, B/2, Fasz. VII, No. 200.

133 . See Generalstab, OpB, Karton 669, Heft 5, Memorandum No. 519 res., "Exposé über die militärische Situation in Siebenbürgen während eines Krieges zwischen Österreich-Ungarn und Rußland," Vienna, spring 1883. Beck estimated at that time that 34% of the 8.5 million Romanians lived within the monarchy's borders.

134 . KM Präs. 15-8/11 ex 1883, Memorandum No. 1059 res., "Relation über die im August 1883 ausgeführte Informationsreise in Siebenbürgen und der Bukowina," Vienna, 6 September 1883.

135 . In his spring 1883 memorandum, Beck gave the current strength of the Romanian army at 76,800 infantry, 7,300 cavalry, and 264 guns plus an organized home defense levy of 40,000 men.

136 . Bylandt stymied Beck's proposals by referring them to a war ministry commission for consideration. See KM Präs. 76-3/10 ex 1883, Letter Präs. No. 6616, War Ministry to Beck, Vienna, 6 February 1884.

137 . For a text of the Austro-Romanian agreement, see Pribram I, pp. 79-85. The treaty also afforded Romania protection against Bulgaria, a hostile neighbor created by Russian diplomacy in 1878. Germany acceded to the treaty on the same day.

138 . At the time of its signing, only King Carol, Prime Minister Bratianu, and Foreign Minister Stourzda knew of its existence. See Elizabeth Heckl, "Erzherzog Franz Ferdinand und die Rumänienpolitik Österreich-Ungarns" (Ph.D. dissertation: University of Vienna, 1964), pp. 7-8.

139 . For an analysis of Romania's secretive relationship to the Triple Alliance powers, see Samuel R. Williamson, *Austria-Hungary and the Origins of the First World War* (New York: St. Martin's Press, 1991), pp. 94-97.

140 . See Beck's undated memorandum, "Direktion für die Mobilisierung und Versammlung der türkischen Streitkräfte im Falle eines russischen Conflictes mit Österreich-Ungarn und Deutschland und der damit verbundenen Verwicklungen auf der Balkan-Halbinsel," in Generalstab, OpB, Karton 668, Heft 1.

141 . See Kálnoky's reply to Turkish overtures for a written alliance, in HHStA, PA I, Karton 458, Telegram No. 17, Kálnoky to Calice, Vienna, 10 February 1882.

142 . Beck had been an advocate of *Landsturm* forces for the monarchy since 1868, including them in early drafts of the military law then under consideration. See KA Nachlaß Beck, B/2, Fasz. V, No. 148. Beck's inspection reports for the Italian and Siebenbürgen fronts in 1882 and 1883 contained calls for the permanent peacetime establishment of *Landsturm* forces. See KM Präs. 72-21/1 ex 1882, Letter Präs. No.

1994, War Ministry to the Austrian Defense Ministry, Vienna, 30 March 1882; KM Präs. 15-8/11 ex 1883, Memorandum, "Relation über die von August 1883 ausgeführte Informationsreise in Siebenbürgen und die Bukowina," Vienna, 9 September 1883.

Chapter 6: The Bulgarian Crisis

1 . See KM Präs. 27-7/1 ex 1884, Letter Generalstab No. 387 res., Beck to the War Ministry, Vienna, 13 March 1884.

2 . See KM Präs. 29-7/2 ex 1884, Letter Glstb. No. 927 res., Beck to the War Ministry, Vienna, 23 September 1884.

3 . See KM Präs. 29-7/5 ex 1884, Letter Präs. No. 4763, War Ministry to the Foreign Office, Vienna, 16 December 1884.

4 . See Langer, pp. 210-11.

5 . For a pen sketch of Giers, see George F. Kennan, *The Decline of Bismarck's European Order: Franco-Russian Relations, 1875-1890* (Princeton, N.J.: Princeton University Press, 1979), pp. 64-67.

6 . For the most detailed account of the Bulgarian crisis, see Part II ("The Bulgarian Gachis") of Kennan's work cited above. For a more traditional treatment stressing Great Power relationships and interactions, see Langer, chapters 10-11.

7 . See Langer, p. 368.

8 . See Generalstab, OpB, Karton 67, Heft 7, Letter Glstb. No. 379 res., Beck to Franz Joseph, Vienna, 22 April 1886. Beck noted that an additional cavalry division plus five infantry divisions would be ready by the twenty-third day of mobilization.

9 . See KM Präs. 33-12/1 ex 1885, Letter Präs. No. 5667, Bylandt to Franz Joseph, Vienna, 9 March 1886. See also Bylandt's order dissolving the fortress commands of Olmütz, Josefstadt, and Theresienstadt, in KM Präs. 33-12-/2 ex 1886, Circular Letter Präs. No. 1707, War Ministry to the IX, X, and II Corps Commands, Vienna, 4 April 1886. Under the current order of battle, Olmütz, for example, supposedly would have received a garrison of sixteen battalions (approximately 6,000 men) plus artillery without being a serious obstacle to either a German or a Russian advance on Vienna. See KM Präs. 39-1/2 ex 1886, Memorandum No. 23, Albrecht to the War Ministry, Vienna, 3 March 1886.

10 . MKSM 20-1/12-2 ex 1886, Military Conference Protocol No. 2796/MKSM, 21 December 1886.

11 . The Russian empire kept almost one million men under arms in peacetime to counteract the faster mobilization of neighboring armies. As the 1880s wore on, an increasing percentage of these peacetime forces were being stationed in Congress Poland near the German and Austro-Hungarian frontiers. See Fuller, p. 53.

12 . Beck estimated that 30% of the monarchy's locomotives were under repair at any one time.

13 . Beck wrote the governor-general of Bosnia-Herzegovina, General Johann Freiherr von Appel, in July 1886 that, while he expected that Serbia and Turkey would

remain neutral in an Austro-Russian war, Montenegro would use "insurrectionist elements" in southern Herzegovina to cause discomfort to the monarchy and might even side openly with Russia. Appel's primary task, therefore, would be to secure the borders of the provinces from outside agitators and repel any Montenegrin invasion. See Generalstab, OpB, Karton 671, Heft 8, Enclosure "Direktiven für das Verhalten des Commandanten der Armee-Gruppe im Occupations-Gebiete und Süd-Dalmatien in Kriegsfälle R und I," Letter Generalstab No. 524 res., Beck to Appel, Vienna, 26 July 1886.

14. See HHStA, PA XL, Karton 294, Ministerial Council Protocol KZ 1, RMRZ 335, 5 January 1887; HHStA, PA XL, Karton 294, Crown Council Protocol, KZ 14, RMRZ 336, 7 January 1887.

15. See the following ministerial and crown council protocols, in HHStA, PA XL, Karton 294, Ministerial Council Protocol RMRZ 340, 19 April 1887; HHStA, PA XL, Karton 294, Crown Council Protocol KZ 39, RMRZ 341, 20 April 1887.

16. See HHStA, PA I, Karton 471, Letter, Kálnoky to Bruck, Vienna, 27 February 1887.

17. See MKSM 20-1/1-3 ex 1884, Memorandum "Zur Landsturmfrage," Beck to Franz Joseph, Vienna, 20 January 1884.

18. See HHStA, Filmarchiv, Nachlaß Albrecht, roll 5, Memorandum "Über die Nothwendigkeit des Landsturms in den österreichischen Alpenländern," Albrecht to Franz Joseph, Vienna, 5 December 1877.

19. See HHStA, Filmarchiv, Nachlaß Albrecht, roll 6, Memorandum "Über die Verhältniß beider Landwehren, nämlich der k.u., in Beziehung auf Ergänzung von Mannschaft und Offiziere," Albrecht to Franz Joseph, Vienna, beginning of January 1883.

20. See MKSM 20-1/1-2 ex 1884, Military Conference Protocol MKSM No. 85, 8 January 1884.

21. There were some disagreements between the military leadership and the Hungarian government over *Landsturm* organization. The Hungarians hoped to further their aspirations for a national army by arguing for the use of the younger cadres in the new *Landsturm* formations rather than as replacements for the common army and the militias. Beck, supported by Bylandt, effectively opposed Hungarian proposals for *Landsturm* organization and obtained the commitment of the younger classes to the replacement pool in time of war. See KM Präs. 72-16/9 ex 1885, Letter Präs. No. 4905, War Ministry to Féjerváry, Vienna, 2 November 1885. See also in the same file, Memorandum to Präs. No. 4481, Glstb. No. 724 res., Beck to the War Ministry, Vienna, 19 October 1885. Somewhat surprisingly, Albrecht supported the Hungarian position, feeling that the less developed among the younger men would fall victim to disease under the rigors of field service. See MKSM 25-2/3 ex 1886, Memorandum "Studie über die Vermehrung der Wehrkraft der Monarchie," Albrecht to Franz Joseph, Vienna, end of December 1886.

22. For Welsersheimb's enthusiasm for Beck's initial proposals, see the military conference cited in note 20 above. For the views of both the Austrian and

Hungarian governments toward a *Landsturm* law, see MKSM 20-1/12-1 ex 1884, Civil-Military Conference Protocol MKSM No. 2804, 20 November 1884.

23 . For an outline of the eventual *Landsturm* law, see Beck's January 1884 memorandum cited in note 17 above. See also Wagner, "Die k.(u.)k. Armee: Gliederung und Aufgabenstellung," pp. 422-23; Rothenberg, *The Army of Francis Joseph*, p. 109.

24 . Retired common army and militia officers to the age of sixty were liable to call-up to command the *Landsturm* formations.

25 . A look at the 8 January 1884 military conference protocol cited in note 20 above reveals considerable disagreement as to which portion of the *Landsturm* to use to cover combat losses in the common army and the militias. Beck, with the support of Archduke Albrecht, won over Franz Joseph to their opinion that younger recruits, because of their greater physical stamina, should be used as replacements for linc units. Albrecht suspected a desire to further the cause of a national army in Féjerváry's advocacy of using the younger men to form the separate *Landsturm* units, for which the defense ministries were to assume administrative responsibility. For Féjerváry's early views on *Landsturm* organization, see also KM Präs 72-16/1 ex 1885, Letter No. 1038 szám/nöki, Féjerváry to Welsershaimb, Budapest, 14 March 1885; KM Präs. 72-16/2 ex 1885, Letter No. 1208 szám/lnöl, Féjerváry to Bylandt, Budapest, 14 April 1885. Féjerváry argued that it would take at least eight weeks before the younger *Landsturm* cadres would be sufficiently trained to serve in the line, while the older men with long service behind them could begin to replace losses from the very first battles.

26 . In the November 1884 civil-military conference, Beck noted that the Prussian Garde du Corps crossed the French frontier in 1870 with 30,000 men. Within seven weeks, only 9,000 remained. See note 22. For Beck's views on Landsturm organization, see KA Nachlaß Beck, B/2, Fasz. VII, No. 236, Memorandum, "Landsturmfrage," Beck to Franz Joseph, Vienna, 15 November 1885. Beck argued that the younger recruits, those nineteen- and twenty-year-olds of pre-military age, could only receive adequate training through the *Ersatzreserve* system.

27 . See HHStA, PA XL, Ministerial Council Protocol KZ 12, RMRZ 337, 29 January 1887.

28 . See Beck's laments over the officer shortage for the *Landsturm*, in KM Präs. 56-11/2 ex 1889, Letter Glstb. No. 253 res., Beck to Bauer, Vienna, 16 March 1889.

29 . See KM Präs. 56-9/1 ex 1889, Memorandum "Denkschrift über die Erweiterung der Landsturm-Organization in Galizien und der Bukovina," Beck to the War Ministry, Vienna, March-April 1889. The war ministry authorized the transfer of some 19,900 *Landsturm* men to the border guards (gendarmerie). See KM Präs. 56-9/7 ex 1889, Letter Präs. No. 5275, War Ministry to Beck, Vienna, 23 November 1889.

30 . The Hungarian defense ministry, for example, requested only 7.7 million gulden for 1876, despite the fact that in wartime it would be expected to have prepared a force numbering approximately 180,000 men, nearly a quarter of the size of the common army in war. See MKSM 12-3/3 ex 1875, Letter Präs. No. 2621, Hungarian Defense Ministry to the Military Chancellery, Budapest, 13 March 1875. In 1879 the Hungarian defense ministry noted in its operational readiness report for the *Honvéd* that it would

212

need over 2.5 million gulden in the event of mobilization to arm and equip wartime forces. See MKSM 12-1/44 ex 1879, Memorandum "Allerunterthänigster Referat zu dem a.u. Vortrage des ungarischen Landes-Vertheidigungs-Minister Szende vom 16. Mai 1879," Beck to Franz Joseph, Vienna, 6 June 1879.

31 . The problem first arose during the abortive mobilization of 1870 against Prussia and continued to poison army-militia relations throughout most of the following decade. Eventually a mixed commission of representatives from the war ministry and the two defense ministries concluded that the Vienna and Budapest governments would bear the costs of outfitting and arming their militias to their full wartime strengths while the war ministry would assume all costs involved in their mobilization. See HHStA, PA XL, Karton 288, Crown Council Protocol KZ 627, RMRZ 159; MKSM 69-1/1 ex 1875, Letter Präs. No. 4664, Kuhn to Franz Joseph, Vienna, 4 January 1874; MKSM 69-2/4 ex 1876, Letter, Bylandt to Franz Joseph, Vienna, 23 June 1876.

32 . For the most detailed examination of the *Honvéd*, see Tibor Papp, "Die königlich ungarische Landwehr (Honvéd) 1868 bis 1914," in Adam Wandruska and Peter Urbanitsch, eds., *Die Habsburgermonarchie 1848-1918*, vol. 5, *Die bewaffnete Macht* (Vienna: Verlag der österreichischen Akademie der Wissenschaften, 1987), pp. 634-86. Papp notes, for example, that the peacetime strengths of all the infantry battalions and cavalry squadrons scarcely exceeded the wartime strength of a single regiment. See, for example, KM Präs. 72-28/1 ex 1887, Memorandum "Schlagfertigkeitsbericht ad No. 2478/in 1887, über die königlich ungarischen Honvéd-Truppen für das Jahr 1887," Hungarian Defense Ministry to the War Ministry, Budapest, no date. Even a more optimistic (and erroneous) view expressed by Albrecht in 1885 placed the peacetime strength of both militias at a meager 16,000. See HHStA, PA I, Karton 466, Liasse XXb, Memorandum, Albrecht to the Foreign Office, Vienna, 13 April 1885.

33 . For manpower breakdowns in both militias, see MKSM 12-1/27 ex 1875, Memorandum Präs. No. 809, "Schlagfertigkeitsbericht der königlichen ungarischen Landwehr," Hungarian Defense Ministry to the Military Chancellery, Budapest, 16 March 1875; MKSM 12-1/45 ex 1878, Memorandum No. 986/MKSM, "Allerthänigster Referat zum Vortrage des königlichen ungarischen Landesvertheidigungs-Ministers Präs. No. 1764 vom 15. April 1878, womit die Relation über die Schlagfertigkeit der ungarischen Landwehr pro 1878 vorgelegt wird," Beck to Franz Joseph, Vienna, April 1878. See also Papp, "Die königlich ungarische Landwehr (Honvéd) 1868 bis 1914," p. 655.

34 . In a January 1883 military conference, Austrian Defense Minister Welsershaimb declared that only two of the five *Landwehr* divisions to be formed in the event of mobilization possessed the necessary staffs. The remaining three divisions had only designated commanders plus skeleton staffs of six officers and twelve men. See MKSM 20-1/3-2 ex 1883, Military Conference Protocol MKSM No. 295, 30 January 1883. The Hungarian defense ministry had reported a year earlier that it could currently meet only 50% of its wartime officer requirements. See MKSM 64-1/4 ex 1882, Letter Präs. No. 1861, Féjerváry to Franz Joseph, Budapest, 18 April 1882.

35 . See MKSM 65-1/5 ex 1876, Memorandum "Studie über die Corps-Eintheilung der Armee im Kriegsfalle," Albrecht to Franz Joseph, Vienna, end of November 1875. Albrecht repeated this assessment the following year. See HHStA, Filmarchiv, Nachlaß Albrecht, roll 5, Memorandum "Grundzüge zur Organisation der Artillerie," Albrecht to Franz Joseph, Vienna, August 1876. An 1884 readiness report of the Austrian *Landwehr* indicated that the force's relatively weak cavalry arm would not achieve war readiness until the twelfth week of mobilization, noting anticipated problems in procuring horses prior to that date. See KM Präs. 72-39-1 ex 1884, Enclosure "Schlagfertigkeitsbericht der k.k. Landwehr," Letter Präs. No. 770 res., Welsershaimb to Bylandt, Vienna, 6 May 1884.

36 . Still as head of the military chancellery, Beck argued in February 1881 in favor of the participation of *Landwehr* and *Honvéd* forces in annual maneuvers so that the army leadership could observe their capabilities. See MKSM 20-1/4-2 ex 1881, Military Conference Protocol, 15 February 1881.

37 . For the debate over the militia officer question, see MKSM 20-1/6-3 ex 1883, Military Conference Protocol No. 311/MKSM, 3 February 1883. For an early report on improvements, see KM Präs. 72-8/2 ex 1885, Memorandum "Schlagfertigkeitsbericht über die königlichen ungarischen Honvéd Truppen für das Jahr 1885," Hungarian Defense Ministry to the War Ministry, Budapest, no date.

38 . KM Präs. 72-29/1 ex 1887, Memorandum "Bericht im Bezug auf die Vorbereitungen für eine Mobilisierung der k.k. Landwehr und des Landsturmes im Jahre 1887," Austrian Defense Ministry to the War Ministry, Vienna, no date. Hungarian Defense Minister Géza Féjerváry, however, noted in a letter to the war ministry in the fall of 1887 that the movement of *Honvéd* forces should not occur before the twentieth day of mobilization at the earliest to allow officers to mold them into units. Féjerváry's estimate of the readiness of the *Honvéd's* hussar formations was even more pessimistic: six weeks would be needed before they could take the field. See KM Präs. 25-5/4 ex 1887, Letter No. 6883 eln., Féjerváry to Bylandt, Budapest, 1 September 1887.

39 . See Bylandt's figures, in MKSM 20-1/6-6 ex 1883, Military Conference Protocol, 4 March 1883.

40 . See MKSM 20-1/6-2 ex 1883, Military Conference Protocol No. 312/MKSM, 2 February 1883. After the operation in Bosnia-Herzegovina, the war ministry took great pains to increase the number of horses maintained by the army in peacetime. In 1879, the common army possessed in peacetime only 48,030 horses out of a total wartime requirement of 166,333. In 1883, Beck placed mobilization needs at 76,000 animals. See MKSM 64-1/1-2 ex 1879, Letter Präs. No. 2210, Bylandt to Franz Joseph, Vienna, 12 June 1879.

41 . See Bylandt's report on the matter, in KM Präs. 62-1/6 ex 1888, Letter Präs. No. 6670, Bylandt to Franz Joseph, Vienna, 27 December 1887.

42 . See KM Präs. 62-1/4 ex 1887, Memorandum Glstb. No. 199 res., Beck to the War Ministry, Vienna, 18 February 1887; KM Präs. 62-1/7 ex 1887, Letter No. 392 Präs./Ia, Welsershaimb to Bylandt, Vienna, 7 March 1887; KM Präs. 62-1/1 ex 1887, Draft of Kriegsleistungsgesetz.

43 . See MKSM 64-2/1 ex 1882, Letter Präs. No. 2677, Bylandt to Franz Joseph, Vienna, 30 April 1882; MKSM 64-4/1 ex 1883, Letter Präs. No. 3623, Bylandt to Franz Joseph, Vienna, 1 August 1883. The war ministry tested repeaters by Schulhof, Kropatchek, and Murata but oddly enough seemingly did not consider any of the various Mauser models, then beginning production in Germany.

44 . KM Präs. 32-15/1 ex 1886, Military Commission Protocols, 18 and 19 October 1886. The bolt action of the Mannlicher did not have the well-known rolling motion of the more famous Mauser rifle. Instead, the firer pulled straight back on the bolt to eject the spent cartridge and reload the rifle from the magazine. This allowed for much less leverage in operating the bolt, a problem that became especially acute after repeated firing of the piece, since the heat generated made the bolt expand, which significantly impaired reloading. According to the report of the Austro-Hungarian military attaché in Paris, the Mannlicher acquitted itself well in 1889 tests in Belgium against the Mauser. See KM Präs. 47-3/5 ex 1889, Letter No. 10/res., the Military Attaché in Paris to the War Ministry, Paris, 23 January 1889.

45 . See MKSM 4-1/1 ex 1887, Letter Abt.7/No. 254, Bylandt to Franz Joseph, Vienna, 25 January 1887. Mannlicher received 130,000 gulden in royalties on his patent.

46 . MKSM 4-1/3 ex 1887, Letter Abt.7/No. 2779, Bylandt to Franz Joseph, Vienna, 25 August 1887; MKSM 4-1/4 ex 1887, Letter Abt.7/No. 3680, Bylandt to Franz Joseph, Vienna, 12 October 1887.

47 . See KM Präs. 32-6/1 ex 1886, Internal Memorandum, "Referat über die Construction und Einführung eines neuen Infantrie-Munitions-Fuhrwerks," Seventh Department to the War Ministry Presidium, 6 March 1886.

48 . Beck's study (cited above) indicated that a soldier could carry four 8mm rounds for every three 11mm rounds. The shift to 8mm munitions, therefore, would reduce the burden of the foot soldier by 25% or allow him to carry that much more ammunition, an important consideration with repeating small arms. An 1887 war ministry study indicated that a foot soldier could carry 110 rounds of 8mm as opposed to the 80 rounds of 11mm ammunition which formed the current standard issue. See MKSM 4-1/4 ex 1887, Letter Abt.7/No. 3680, Bylandt to Franz Joseph, Vienna, 12 October 1887.

49 . See MKSM 4-2/2 ex 1900, Memorandum, "Darstellung des Verlaufes der Neubewaffnung des k.u.k. Heeres mit 8 mm Repetier-Handfeuerwaffen," War Ministry to Military Chancellery, Vienna, no date.

50 . Nonetheless, this switch in calibers meant that during the 1887-88 war scare with Russia, the Austro-Hungarian armed forces were equipped with rifles of differing calibers. See MKSM 20-1/5 ex 1889, Military Conference Protocol, 3 September 1889. Russia, it must be noted, did not begin to rearm its army with its Mosin repeaters until 1892 and did not obtain all the three million necessary pieces until ten years later. See Fuller, p. 54.

51 . See Kesslitz, p. 197.

52 . Kesslitz estimates that over the same period the monarchy spent more than 14 million gulden on fortified works, mostly in Galicia. See Kesslitz, p. 197.

53. See Albrecht's report of the meeting, in MKSM Sonderreihe, Karton 69, Memorandum No. 40, "Gespräch des Erzherzogs Albrecht mit Graf [sic] Waldersee am 22. Juli 1886 zu Windisch-Mattai." See the copy of the same memorandum in Generalstab, OpB, Karton 685. For Waldersee's less detailed version of the meeting and his praise for Albrecht's moderate attitude toward Russia, see Alfred Graf von Waldersee, *Denkwürdigkeiten des General-Feldmarschalls Alfred Grafen von Waldersee*, vol. I (Berlin: Deutsche Verlags-Anstalt, 1922), p. 295.

54. Fuller has argued that Russian achievements in the construction of strategic railroads remained extremely slender before the great infusion of French money at the turn of the century. Neither the Russian war ministry nor general staff possessed the slightest influence over the construction agenda, controlled by the finance ministry, and the vast majority of the lines constructed cannot be considered as having been strategic in nature. See Fuller, pp. 63-64.

55. See also Martin Kitchen's pen sketch of Waldersee's ideas on preventive war and his fears concerning France in 1886, in Kitchen, pp. 66-67. While Kitchen shows that Waldersee's attentions wavered between France and Russia, Vienna believed him to be preoccupied with the French threat throughout the 1887-88 crisis.

56. See Kennan, p. 246.

57. See Langer, pp. 374-75.

58. HHStA, PA I, Karton 466, Liasse XXb, Letter, Karl Steininger to Beck, Berlin, 14 December 1886.

59. See HHStA, PA I, Karton 466, Liasse XXb, folio 124-30, Letter No. 361 res., Steininger to Beck, Berlin, 9 March 1887. Karl Steininger added that the figure of four corps (twelve divisions) was the one most often mentioned in high German military circles. The Prussian general staff had agreed at the Strobl-Breslau meetings to deploy a force of at least twenty line and six reserve divisions in the east. See the previous chapter for the Strobl-Breslau conversations.

60. See HHStA, P.A. I, Karton 466, Liasse XXb, Memorandum, "Zur Situation," Albrecht to Kálnoky, Vienna, 7 March 1887.

61. See Holzer, pp. 106-107.

62. See the list of required preparations submitted for crown approval on 30 January 1887, in HHStA, PA XL, Karton 294, Crown Council Protocol KZ 22, RMRZ 338, 30 January 1887.

63. For preparation of the fortresses, see KM Präs. 33-6/5 ex 1887, Letter Glstb. No. 113 res., Beck to the War Ministry, Vienna, 30 January 1887; KM Präs. 33-6/16 ex 1887, Letter Präs. No. 2642, War Ministry to I Corps Command, Vienna, 19 May 1887. The Munkacs-Stryj railroad reached completion in the late winter of 1887, allowing for operational readiness in Galicia of twenty-four infantry divisions and seven cavalry divisions by the twentieth day of mobilization. See MKSM 69-2/1 ex 1887, Letter Glstb. No. 391 res., Beck to Franz Joseph, Vienna, 31 March 1887. Beck also pursued better coordination and planning concerning the transition between peace and wartime operations with the various railroad directorates. See KM Präs. 5-48/1 ex 1887, Letter Glstb. No. 673 res., Beck to Bylandt, Vienna, 30 June 1887. See also Degreif, pp. 33-34.

64 . The Russians apparently feared the transfer of the XV Corps in Bosnia to Galicia. See MKSM Sonderreihe, Karton 57, Letter, Beck to Popp, Vienna, 1 March 1887. While he was not planning the immanent transfer of the XV Corps to Galicia, Beck did advocate putting it on a war footing later the same month. See KM Präs. 77-5/1 ex 1887, Letter Präs. No. 1497, Bylandt to Kálnoky, Vienna, 16 March 1887.

65 . KM Präs. 26-2/3 ex 1887, Military Commission Protocol, 3 May 1887.

66 . See Kennan, p. 334; Langer, pp. 426-27, 443. In October 1887, Beck reported to a crown council that the Russians had a total of twelve infantry and seven and a half cavalry, divisions stationed opposite the Austro-Hungarian frontier alone. The military districts of Moscow and Kiev possessed a peacetime strength of 102,000 infantry, 27 cavalry and 616 artillery pieces. See MKSM 20-1/9-2 ex 1887, Crown Council Protocol No. 2428/MKSM, 30 October 1887.

67 . HHStA, PA I, Karton 464, Liasse XIX, folios 380-86, Letter No. 416 res., Steininger to Beck, Berlin, 30 November 1887.

68 .   Perhaps underlying Waldersee's passivity was his deep personal conviction, revealed in his memoirs, of the decreasing effectiveness of the Austro-Hungarian army brought on by what he inexplicably perceived as its increasing nationalist character. See Waldersee, p. 294. Adolf von Deines, the German military attaché in Vienna, viewed the creation of the *Honvéd* with Magyar language of command as the major weakening factor in the Habsburg military structure. See his letter of 17 June 1887 to his father, in Militärarchiv Freiburg, Nachlaß Deines, "Briefe an Seinen Vater 1887-89."

69 .   MKSM 20-1/10-2 ex 1887, Civil-Military Conference Protocol No. 2650/MKSM, 8 December 1887.

70 . The 1887 Mediterranean Agreements between Austria-Hungary, Great Britain, and Italy, with limited participation by Germany and Spain, called for the maintenance of the Balkan status quo. The Second Mediterranean Agreement, signed by Austria-Hungary, Britain, and Italy just four days after the 8 December civil-military conference, stressed the importance of keeping Bulgaria free of foreign troops and authorized either joint or unilateral action by the signatories in the event Turkey did or could not prevent an invasion of its Bulgarian territories. The treaty also stipulated that Turkey must not give up its rights to the Straits or territories in Asia Minor to foreign powers.

71 . Beck wanted to raise the number of horses per cavalry regiment by fifty but was overruled by Bylandt and the emperor.

72 .   See HHStA, PA I, Karton 464, Liasse XIX, folios 274-77, Letter, Széchenyi to Kálnoky, Berlin, 9 December 1887.

73 .   See HHStA, PA I, Karton 464, Liasse XIX, folio 282-83, Letter, Széchenyi to Kálnoky, Berlin, 11 December 1887. Széchenyi wrote another extensive letter the following day outlining Moltke's views. See HHStA, PA I, Karton 464, Liasse XIX, folios 307-15. The German ambassador to Vienna, Prince Heinrich von Reuß, transmitted a memorandum by Moltke on the subject of Russian armaments on the same day as Széchenyi's second letter. See HHStA, PA I, Karton 464, Liasse XIX, folios 284-300, Memorandum, "Die Entwicklung der Wehrkraft Rußlands seit 1878 unter

besonderer Berücksichtigung seiner Rüstungen im laufenden Jahr 1887," Moltke to Bismarck, Berlin, end of November 1887.

74. See HHStA, PA I, Liasse XIX, folios 305-6, Letter No. 424, Steininger to Beck, Berlin, 12 December 1887.

75. See Deines's letter to his father of 20 December, in Militärarchiv Freiburg, Nachlaß Deines, "Briefe an Seinen Vater 1887-89." See also HHStA, PA I, Karton 534, folios 227-33, Letter, Kálnoky to Széchenyi, Vienna, 17 December 1887.

76. See HHStA, PA I, Karton 464, Liasse XIX, folio 331, Telegram No. 3807, Széchenyi to Kálnoky, Berlin, 15 December 1887. Beck later clarified his statement to mean that 15 January was the earliest possible date that he could *order* an Austro-Hungarian mobilization. See HHStA, PA I, Karton 464, Liasse XIX, folios 343-46, Letter, Kálnoky to Széchenyi, Vienna, 17 December 1887.

77. See HHStA, PA I, Karton 294, Ministerial Council Protocol KZ 85, RMRZ 346., 18 December 1887.

78. This involved four cavalry and five infantry regiments (approximately 12,000 men) stationed in Dalmatia and the Tyrol to compensate for local recruitment deficiencies in these areas. See Chapter 5.

79. See HHSTA, PA XL, Karton 294, Crown Council Protocol KZ 86, RMRZ 347, 19 December 1887.

80. See HHStA, PA I, Karton 464, Liasse XIX, folio 392, Letter Präs. No. 6415, Bylandt to Kálnoky, Vienna, 11 December 1887.

81. See HHStA, PA I, Karton 464, Liasse XIX, folio 393, Letter Glstb. No. 1166 res., Beck to Bylandt, Vienna, 11 December 1887. Beck wrote Kálnoky a similar letter ten days later. See HHStA, PA I, Karton 534, Abstract, Letter, Beck to Kálnoky, Vienna, 21 December 1887. These dispatches indicate that Beck had kept certain aspects of the Austro-German military relationship secret from both the foreign office and his technical superior, War Minister Bylandt.

82. HHStA, PA I, Karton 464, folios 396-99, Letter No. 928 res., Steininger to Beck, Berlin, 19 December 1887.

83. See the publication of this document, in Glaise-Horstenau, pp. 461-62. Beck's note was based closely upon one drawn up earlier in the month by Archduke Albrecht. See the latter's "Punktation für eine Militär-Convention mit Berlin" of 10 December 1887, in Generalstab, OpB, Karton 677. Beck sent a copy of his memorandum to the foreign office on 21 December. See HHStA, PA I, Karton 464, Liasse XIX, folios 401-2, Enclosure to Letter No. 63/geh., Beck to Kálnoky, Vienna, 21 December 1887. Kálnoky thereupon communicated the context of Beck's memorandum to Ambassador Széchenyi in Berlin. See HHStA, PA I, Karton 534, Letter No. 1, Kálnoky to Széchenyi, Vienna, 22 December 1887.

84. See HHStA, PA I, Karton 534, folios 263-64, Note, Reuß to Kálnoky, Vienna, 30 December 1887. See also Kálnoky's memorandum on Reuß's dispatch, in HHStA, PA I, Karton 464, Liasse XIX, folios 693-96.

85. Bismarck repeated this charge in an interview with Austro-Hungarian Ambassador Széchenyi on 31 December. See HHStA, PA I, Liasse XXa, Letter No. 118, Széchenyi to Kálnoky, Berlin, 31 December 1887.

86. See HHStA, PA I, Karton 465, Liasse XXa, Letter No. 436 res., Steininger to Széchenyi, Berlin, 30 December 1887. See also Steininger's similar communication to Beck of following day, reprinted in Glaise-Horstenau, pp. 462-63.

87. See HHStA, PA XL, Karton 295, Ministerial Council Protocol KZ 3, RMRZ 348, 5 January 1888.

88. See HHStA, PA XL, Karton 295, Crown Council Protocol KZ 6, RMRZ 349, 11 January 1888.

89. See HHStA, PA I, Karton 464, Liasse XIX, folios 726-29, Letter No. 1, Kálnoky to Széchenyi, Vienna, 12 January 1888; HHStA, PA I, Karton 534, folios 268-72, Letter No. 2, Kálnoky to Széchenyi, Vienna, 12 January 1888.

90. Generalstab, OpB, Karton 791, Memorandum, "Studien über die Alarmierungs-Gruppierung in Galizien," Conrad to Beck, Vienna, winter 1887-88.

91. See HHStA, PA I, Karton 484, Liasse XIX, folios 470-76, Letter, Steininger to Beck, Berlin, 14 January 1888.

92. See HHStA, PA I, Karton 484, Liasse XIX, Letter, Kálnoky to Bylandt, Vienna, 17 January 1888.

93. The Austro-Hungarian 1888 deployment plan versus Russia called for the transport of the two common army divisions of the X Corps plus the 21st and 26th *Landwehr* divisions over the German Silesian railroads. Units of the X Corps, stationed in the Brünn military district in peacetime, were to have been among the first units to arrive in Galicia upon mobilization. See Generalstab, OpB, Karton 671, Heft 8, Letter Glstb. No. 360 res., Beck to Franz Joseph, Vienna, 7 April 1888.

94. See HHStA, PA I, Karton 464, Liasse XIX, Memorandum, Bismarck to Reuß, Berlin, 24 January 1888. See another copy of the same communication, in HHStA, PA I, Karton 534.

95. See HHStA, PA I, Karton 464, Liasse XIX, Letter No. 3, Bruck to Kálnoky, Rome, 9 January 1888. A report by the Austro-Hungarian military attaché the following month indicates that Crispi's proposal enjoyed widespread support within the Italian officer corps. See HHStA, PA I, Karton 464, Liasse XIX, Letter No. 392, Forstner to Beck, Rome, 22 February 1888.

96. Karl Steininger indicated in these discussions Beck's willingness to honor the prior understanding that Austria-Hungary would place certain Tyrolian railroads at Italy's disposal for the transport of forces to the Rhine to assist Germany in the defense of its western frontier. See HHStA, PA I, Liasse XIX, folios 480-81, Letter, Kálnoky to Széchenyi, Vienna, 15 January 1888. Kálnoky, on the other hand, used the opportunity presented by the staff talks on the matter to punish Bismarck for his contrariness regarding the Silesian railroads to inform the *Wilhelmstraße* that Austria-Hungary would be unable to honor earlier arrangements concerning the Tyrolian railroads in the event of a Franco-German conflict. See HHStA, PA I, Karton 534, folios 274-78, Kálnoky to Széchenyi, Vienna, 12 January 1888.

97. See HHStA, PA I, Karton 464, Liasse XIX, folios 615-17, Moltke to the Foreign Office, Berlin, 14 January 1888; HHStA, PA I, Karton 464, Liasse XIX, folios 360-361, Telegram No. 5080, Széchenyi to Kálnoky, Berlin, 17 January 1888.

98 . See HHStA, PA I, Liasse XIX, Telegram No. 8, Kálnoky to Széchenyi, Vienna, 19 January 1888.

99 . HHStA, PA I, Karton 471, Letter No. 2, Kálnoky to Bruck, Vienna, 7 February 1888; HHStA, PA I, Karton 471, Letter, Kálnoky to Golouchowski, Vienna, 17 February 1888.

100 . See HHStA, PA I, Karton 460, Letter, Golouchowski to Kálnoky, Bucharest, 21 December 1887.

101 . In December 1888, Bratianu also held the war ministry portfolio.

102 . See HHStA, PA I, Karton 466, Liasse XIX, folio 446, Telegram No. 1, Golouchowski to Kálnoky, Bucharest, 2 January 1888; HHStA, PA I, Karton 464, Liasse XIX, folio 562, Telegram No. 48, Széchenyi to Kálnoky, Berlin, 19 March 1888.

103 . See HHStA, PA I, Karton 484, Liasse XIX, folios 537-38, Letter No. 462 res., Steininger to Beck, Berlin, 23 February 1888.

104 . See the sarcastic reference to the Austro-German friendship in the 4 February 1888 entry in Kuhn's diary, in KA Nachlaß Kuhn, B/670, No. 3, p. 97. Although Kuhn could not know of all the details of the political-military exchanges of the previous months, his disdain for the German relationship had some basis in fact.

105 . See Langer, pp. 462-63. Boulanger remained in Brussels until committing suicide in 1891.

106 . See KA Nachlaß Beck, B/2, Fasz. VII, No. 244, Memorandum, "Über Zukunftskriege," Beck to Franz Joseph, Vienna, March 1889.

107 . Beck cited the casualty figure of 36% of the attacking Russian forces at Plevna in 1877.

108 . See, for example, the comparisons made to the other Great European Powers in the addendum to Beck's military expansion program of 1893, in KA Nachlaß Beck, B/2, Fasz. VIII, No. 266, "Studie über den Ausbau der Wehrmacht."

109 . See MKSM 65-1/2 ex 1888, Letter No. 797, Bylandt to Franz Joseph, Vienna, 5 March 1888.

110 . See HHStA, PA XL, Karton 295, Ministerial Council Protocol KZ 28, RMRZ 352, 29 April 1888; MKSM 72-9/3 ex 1888, Letter Präs. No. 3159, Bauer to Franz Joseph, Vienna, 7 July 1888.

111 . The matter was raised by War Minister Bauer in an April 1889 ministerial council and undertaken later the same year. See HHStA, PA XL, Karton 295, Ministerial Council Protocol KZ 29, RMRZ 356; KM Präs. 45-3/12 ex 1888, Letter Glstb. No. 1100 res., Beck to Bauer, Vienna, 21 November 1888. See also Wagner, "Die k.(u.)k. Armee: Gliederung und Aufgabenstellung," p. 397.

112 . See MKSM 29-1/12 ex 1889, Letter No. 962, Beck to the Military Chancellery, Vienna, 1 September 1889.

113 . See Beck's 1889 revision of the "Kriegsfall R," in Generalstab, OpB, Karton 671, Heft 9, Letter Glstb. No. 402 res., Beck to Franz Joseph, Vienna, 6 May 1889. Beck announced that general staff planning indicated that eight cavalry, twenty-eight infantry, and nine *Landwehr* would be operational in Galicia by the twenty-third day of mobilization, an improvement over 1888 projections by three days.

114. See KM Präs. 33-17/4 ex 1889, Memorandum Glstb. No. 550 res., "Bemerkung zu Präs. No. 3372 ex 1889 des Reichskriegsministeriums," Beck to Bauer, Vienna, 1 July 1889. After falling from record levels in fiscal years 1887-88 of 8.6 million gulden to slightly over 1 million gulden per annum in 1889 and 1890, fortification expenditures leveled off in the 1890s to roughly 1.5 to 2 million gulden annually. See Kesslitz, pp. 197-98. Much of the money spent during this period went toward the construction of smaller works designed largely to protect vital railroad bridges of the exposed *Nordbahn* and *Carl-Ludwig Bahn*. These fortifications were to be manned by local *Landsturm* forces during mobilization. See KM Präs. 33-15-1 ex 1888, Circular Letter Präs. No. 1933, War Ministry to the Inspectors General of Engineers, Artillery, the Chief of the General Staff, and the Technical-Administrative Military Committee, Vienna, 19 May 1888. Not everyone within the military hierarchy felt that such large fortification outlays were such a good idea. Archduke Wilhelm, the inspector general of artillery, for example, bemoaned the vast sums spent on fortifications during the late 1880s and early 1890s. See HHStA, Filmarchiv, Nachlaß Albrecht, roll 47, Letter, Wilhelm to Albrecht, Vienna, 21 April 1889.

115. For a good description of Wilhelm II's first foreign tour as emperor, see Frederic Morton, *A Nervous Splendor: Vienna 1888/89* (Boston: Little Brown, 1979), pp. 103-10. Wilhelm openly insulted Austrian Minister-President Eduard Taaffe by not including him in a decoration ceremony. The German emperor also criticized the Austro-Hungarian army's decision to adopt the 8mm Mannlicher repeater, declaring the caliber too large to allow foot soldiers to carry adequate ammunition. This despite the fact that the standard German infantry weapon, the Mauser repeater, was of only minimally smaller caliber at 7.92 mm.

116. See HHStA, PA I, Karton 468, Letter, Eisenstein to Kálnoky, Berlin, 14 November 1888; HHStA, PA I, Karton 468, Letter, Eisenstein to Kálnoky, Vienna, Berlin, 30 November 1888.

117. See KM Präs. 45-3/1 ad 2 ex 1888, Letter Glstb. No. 142 res., Beck to Bylandt, Vienna, 26 January 1888. The first renewal of the compromise in 1878 was postponed a year owing to initial resistance of the Austro-German progressive liberals to another decennial settlement of the military's size. See William A. Jenks, *Austria under the Iron Ring 1879-1893* (Charlottesville, Va.: University of Virginia Press, 1965), pp. 41-50; Elfriede Jandesek, "Die Stellung des Abgeordnetenhauses der im Reichsrate vertretenen Königreiche und Länder zu Fragen des Militärs, 1867-1914" (Ph.D. dissertation, University of Vienna, 1964), pp. 54-60.

118. See, for example, Albrecht's 1885 memorandum on the subject, in KM Präs. 26-10/1 ex 1885, Memorandum, "Memoire über die ungünstigen Verhältnisse der Ergänzung der bei der mobilen Armee entstehenden Abgänge--dann über die zu diesem Zwecke höchst wünschenswerten Verbesserungen des Wehrgesetzes und der Durchführungsbestimmungen zu demselben," Vienna, 17 March 1885. See the same memorandum, in HHStA, Filmarchiv, Nachlaß Albrecht, roll 7. The Austrian and Hungarian diets had undertaken no revisions in the original law when renewing it in 1879.

119 . The call-up of the *Ersatzreserve* to an eight-week training course formed an 1882 novelle to military law renewal of 1879. See Wagner, "Die k.(u.)k. Armee: Gliederung und Aufgabenstellung," p. 492. Since they did not receive regular training, it was assumed that the men assigned to the replacement pool would have to undergo refresher courses even after 1882.

120 . See KM Präs. 45-3/2 ex 1888, Letter Präs. No. 841, War Ministry to the Austrian and Hungarian Defense Ministries, Vienna, 17 February 1888.

121 . See MKSM 22-1/4 ex 1887, Letter Präs. No. 4806, Bylandt to Franz Joseph, Vienna, 3 October 1887.

122 . See Rothenberg, *The Army of Francis Joseph*, p. 119.

123 . See Rothenberg, *The Army of Francis Joseph*, pp. 119-20.

124 . See KM Präs. 26-2/13 ex 1888, Letter No. 3667 szám/eln, Féjerváry to Bauer, Budapest, 6 July 1888: See also the draft of the military law, in KM Präs. 26-2/17 ex 1888; Wagner, "Die k.(u.)k. Armee: Gliederung und Aufgabenstellung," pp. 492-93.

125 . Manpower shortages in the common army's *Ersatzreserve* had been somewhat compensated for within the provisions of the *Landsturmgesetz* of 1886. See Chapter 5.

Conclusion: The Rebirth of an Army

1 . In 1894, Beck noted the following annual recruitment for the remaining European continental powers: France 240,000 men; Germany 250,000 men; Italy 100,000 men; Russia 295,400 men. He also gave the following peacetime military establishments: France 510,887 men; Germany 557,112 men; Italy 252,117 men; Russia 1,017,000 men. Austria-Hungary inducted a total of 126,013 men into all services including the militias, making a total peacetime establishment of 325,946 men.

2 . See the following ministerial council protocols: HHStA, PA XL, Karton 296, Ministerial Council Protocol KZ 11, RMRZ 377, 2 February 1893; HHStA, PA XL, Karton 296, Ministerial Council Protocol KZ 20, RMRZ 378, 19 February 1893. See also HHStA, PA XL, Karton 296, Crown Council Protocol KZ 28, RMRZ 379, 28 March 1893. For a copy of Beck's expansion program, see KA Nachlaß Beck, B/2, Fasz. VIII, No. 266.

3 . Beck also pointed out that the Galician front was actually more like two fronts, an eastern and a northern, given Russian deployments in the Polish salient.

4 . These recruitment figures were ultimately obtained in the military law of 1912, albeit with a reduction of the active service requirement to two years. See Wagner, "Die k.(u.)k. Armee: Gliederung und Aufgabenstellung," p. 494.

5 . See the Riegenauer documents, in Militärarchiv Potsdam, W-10/50222. See also Gerhard Ritter, *Der Schlieffenplan: Kritik eines Mythos* (Munich: Oldenbourg Verlag, 1956), pp. 13-35; Lothar Höbelt, "Schlieffen, Beck, Potiorek und das Ende der gemeinsamen deutsch-österreichisch-ungarischen Aufmarschpläne im Osten,"

Militärgeschichtliche Mitteilungen, 36 (1984), pp. 7-30. In 1914 the German VIII Army in East Prussia numbered only thirteen divisions, of which only half were first line. See Stone, *Eastern Front*, p. 55.

6 . See Bridge, pp. 211-88; Berthold Sutter, "Um Österreich-Ungarns Großmachtstellung am Balkan: Sicherung des europäischen Friedens durch Teilung der Balkanhalbinsel zwischen Russland und Österreich-Ungarn - Eine militärische Denkschrift anläßlich der Kaiserentrevue 1897," in Walter Höflechner, et. al., eds., *Domus Austriae: Eine Festgabe Hermann Wiesflecker zum 70. Geburtstag* (Graz: Akademische Druck- und Verlagsanstalt, 1983), pp. 391-406.

7 . Beck tried to head off civilian resistance in this regard by advocating only gradual increases in military outlays over a ten-year period. The raising of the recruitment contingents would ultimately result in a total annual increase of more than 75 million gulden in ongoing expenditures for the common army, the *Kriegsmarine*, and the militias at the end of ten years. The 105 million gulden in one-time expenditures would similarly be divided over the span of a decade. See, for example, the financial schedule for Beck's expansion project, in KM Präs. 26-1/10 ex 1896, "Jahrgangsweise Darstellung des Mehrerfordernisses aus Anlaß des Ausbaus unserer Wehrmacht auf Grund eines erhöhten Rekruten-Contingentes."

8 . See MKSM 25-1/1 ex 1897, Memorandum "Denkschrift über die allgemeinen militärischen Verhältnisse Ende 1896," Beck to Franz Joseph, Vienna, 30 December 1896.

9 . Beck estimated an almost 20% decline in Italy's peacetime standing army from 194,000 men to between 160,000 and 170,000 men following the Adua disaster. The Italian war ministry furloughed substantial numbers of troops to compensate for expenses incurred during the campaign. See MKSM 25-1/1 ex 1897, Memorandum No. 729/geh., "Denkschrift über die allgeimeinen militärischen Verhältnisse Ende 1895," Beck to Franz Joseph, Vienna, 30 December 1896.

10 . At the end of 1896, Beck estimated that the Franco-Russian alliance could muster a force of twelve battleships and nine cruisers in the western Mediterranean and another twelve battleships and four cruisers in the Black and eastern Mediterranean seas. The French could mobilize their naval units in Mediterranean waters within forty-eight hours, while the Italian navy could muster only three battleships and ten cruisers to meet this immediate threat. Beck feared that the Russians could mobilize a landing force of twenty-four infantry battalions within two days for a surprise seizure of the Dardanelles. Without the support of the British Mediterranean fleet of seventeen battleships and twenty-one cruisers, Triple Alliance forces would be at a distinct disadvantage in a naval war. See MKSM 25-1/1 ex 1897, Memorandum No. 729/geh., "Denkschrift über die allgeimeinen militärischen Verhältnisse Ende 1895," Beck to Franz Joseph, Vienna, 30 December 1896.

11 . Austria-Hungary built only three armored cruisers in the 1870s and no capital ships in the 1880s. Only after 1891 did the *Kriegsmarine* leadership, which had flirted during the previous decade with small ship concepts of the French *jeune école*, embark on a program of capital ship development. Most of this naval building, however, occurred after 1900. For the newest treatments of the Austro-Hungarian *Kriegsmarine*

after 1848, see Lothar Höbelt, "Die Marine," in Adam Wandruska and Peter Urbanitsch, eds., *Die Habsburgermonarchie 1848-1918*, vol. V, *Die bewaffnete Macht* (Vienna: Verlag der österreichischen Akademie der Wissenschaften), pp. 687-763. See also Lawrence Sondhaus, *The Naval Policy of Austria-Hungary, 1867-1918: Navalism, Industrial Development and the Politics of Dualism* (West Lafeyette, Ind.: Purdue University Press, 1994).

12 . This is not to say that Beck did not think highly of the *Kriegsmarine* or purposely neglect its interests. As discussed in an earlier chapter, he placed the greatest emphasis on cooperation between the general staff and the navy and conducted several joint exercises as well as full-scale *Landungsmanöver* in cooperation with the *Kriegsmarine*. Naval priorities, however, were not nearly as pressing during the 1880s, particularly following the conclusion of the Triple Alliance with Italy, as the deficiencies in the monarchy's defense posture in Galicia which demanded the decade-long attention of the general staff to overcome. In the early 1880s, Beck advocated a drastic increase in the defensive capabilities of the main fleet anchorage at Pola, including the deployment of an extensive system of water mines and the construction of sea fortifications. See KM Präs. 30-33/2 ex 1883, Letter Generalstab No. 902 res., Beck to the War Ministry, Vienna, 6 July 1883.

13 . In certain remote areas, such as Bosnia-Herzegovina, the old M1863 muzzleloading cannon were still in use as late as 1889. See KM Präs. 33-17/4 ex 1889.

14 . Beck discussed the impact of smokeless powder charges on steel-bronze barrels in an 1899 report to the war ministry. See KM Präs. 32-8/1 ex 1899, Letter Generalstab No. 574, Beck to Krieghammer, Vienna, 15 March 1899.

15 . One of the greatest weaknesses of the M1875 field artillery piece was its lack of a recoil mechanism for the barrel which made it necessary to re-aim the piece each time it was fired. The problem was ineffectively addressed in the 1890s with the attachment of a tail spur in an attempt to anchor the gun when firing. Austro-Hungarian field artillery also lacked protective gun shields, making crews vulnerable to infantry fire. The M1905 pieces, introduced gradually over a five-year period, possessed recoil mechanisms but still lacked protective shields. The army spent nearly 80 million gulden between 1906 and 1910 in the rearmament of the field artillery. See Rothenberg, *The Army of Francis Joseph*, pp. 126-27; Wagner, "Die k.(u.)k. Armee: Gliederung und Aufgabenstellung," pp. 449-50; Kesslitz, p. 198.

16 . One of the major conspirators against Alexander was the young army officer Dragutin Dimitrievich (Apis), who later as chief of Serbian army intelligence organized the assassination of Archduke Franz Ferdinand at Sarajevo in June 1914. See the biography of Dimitrievich by David Mackenzie, *Apis: The Congenial Conspirator; The Life of Colonel Dragutin T. Dimitrievich*, in vol. 255, *East European Monographs* (New York: Columbia University Press, 1989).

17 . See Lackey, "A Secret Austro-Hungarian Plan to Intervene in the 1884 Timok Uprising in Serbia: Unpublished Documents."

18 . The general staff dispatched Lieutenant Rudolf Kutschera to spy on the delivery of the artillery at Antivari on 26 September 1905. Kutschera observed the unloading of forty-eight artillery pieces, including ten 120mm bronze siege cannon and

four 210mm cast iron howitzers, five hundred 70kg barrels of powder from the Tossano factory south of Turin, and large amounts of munitions. While most of the artillery consisted of old bronze pieces, it nevertheless would have been effective against the Austro-Hungarian cordon defenses of southern Dalmatia and Herzegovina. Kutschera estimated the total value of the shipment at 500,000 gulden. See MKSM 50-3/1 ex 1905, Memorandum, "Italienische Geschütz- und Munitionssendung nach Montenegro," Beck to Franz Joseph, Vienna, 28 October 1905. Italy had supplied Montenegro with approximately 15,000 infantry rifles in the mid-1890s, but this had been of much less concern to the general staff because the sale mostly involved older single-shot models and did not increase Montenegrin effectiveness against fortified defenses. See HHStA, PA XL, Karton 152, Abstract Letter No. 31 res., Gendarmerie Post Lastva to the District Office, Lastva, 25 July 1896.

19 . See, for example, the undated memorandum by Potiorek of the early to mid-1890s concerning Montenegrin military capabilities, particularly those of the extremely scanty and ill-equipped artillery arm, in Generalstab, OpB, Karton 796, Fasz. 172, Memorandum, Potiorek to Beck, no date. Potiorek estimated that the Montenegrins possessed only about twenty operational cannon but lacked the trained personnel to operate even these. He wrote that they would have a difficult time in overcoming the fortifications of the Austro-Hungarian cordon defense.

20 . See Generalstab, OpB, Karton 729, Memorandum, "Bericht über die im Sommer 1906 in Süddalmatien und Tyrol vorgenommenen Rekognoszierungen," Merizzi to the Operations Bureau, Vienna, no date.

21 . See, for example, the excerpt from the military attaché report No. 1192/geh. of 12 January 1903, in KA Nachlaß Beck, B/2, Fasz. IX, No. 304.

22 . A loyalist Italian peasant inhabitant of Habsburg Tyrol, for example, reported to the provincial Statthalter that he had observed preparations in a recent trip to Italian Vicenza for a call-up of all local men between eighteen and sixty for a guerilla strike into the Tyrol in the event of Franz Joseph's death. See KM Präs. 51-44/9 ex 1903, Abstract Letter No. 3899/pr., Statthalter of Tyrol and Vorarlberg to the Cisleithanian Minister-President, 7 August 1903. In a more detailed intelligence report to the war ministry, Beck wrote that the irredentist "Società Trento e Trieste" planned a putsch against Habsburg rule in the Trentino and had shipped some 500 rifles to Udine near the Austro-Hungarian frontier for that purpose the previous month. See KM Präs. 51-44/1 ex 1903, Letter Generalstab No. 1528 res., Beck to the War Ministry, Vienna, 25 June 1903.

23 . See KM Präs. 51-44/14 ex 1903, Letter No. 1263, Beck to the War Ministry, Vienna, 13 November 1903; KM Präs. 48-21/1 ex 1906, Memorandum No. 1041, "Bemerkung zum Geschäftsstücke Präs. No. 4785 ex 1906," Beck to the War Ministry, Vienna, no date.

24 . See KM Präs. 25-9/6 ex 1904, Letter Präs. No. 8893, Pitreich to Franz Joseph, Vienna, 18 December 1904. See also KM Präs. 25-9/3 ex 1904, Circular Letter Präs. No. 7541, the War Minister to the Austrian Minister-President, the Foreign Minister, the Austrian Defense Minister, and the Hungarian Defense Minister, Vienna, 21 November 1904.

25 . In the circular letter cited above, Pitreich noted, for example, that the Pola and Cattaro garrisons did not possess the manpower to man all the fortress artillery stationed there. Michael Behnen sees the increasingly strained Austro-Italian relationship as a consequence of Habsburg provocations and ignores the initial Italian act of selling siege artillery to the Montenegrins. The Austro-Hungarian measures cited by Behnen, such as the return of the Galician regiments to their original garrisons in the southwest, were undertaken as a result of general staff assumptions that the Italian sale of artillery to Montenegro indicated a possibility that the two countries were planning military cooperation against the monarchy. See Michael Behnen, *Rüstung--Bündnis-- Sicherheit: Dreibund und informeller Imperialismus 1900-1908* (Tübingen: Max Niemeyer Verlag, 1985), pp. 100-118, 124-82.

26 . See Generalstab, OpB, Karton 694, Memorandum, "Zusammenstellung der behufs Besserung der militärischen Lage in der Boche di Cattaro und in der Herzegowina nöthigen Maßnahmen," Potiorek to Beck, Vienna, 14 November 1905.

27 . For the most recent work on Potiorek's career, see Rudolf Jerábeck, *Potiorek: General im Schatten von Sarajevo* (Graz: Styria Verlag, 1991).

28 . Auffenberg's plan called for a full-scale concentric invasion of Hungary by troops stationed in the Cisleithanian corps areas. Auffenberg hoped this would provoke a national insurrection, which the common army would easily crush, as he calculated that the Hungarians could rely only on the support of the *Honvéd*, the hussar regiments, 20% of the regular infantry, and almost none of the artillery. Beck envisioned a much more limited military response, consisting primarily of securing land and water communications between Vienna and Budapest and the occupation of the latter by two infantry divisions and one regiment of dragoons. The X and XI Corps in central and eastern Galicia would merely increase their readiness by retaining with the colors those soldiers in their third year of active service scheduled to be furloughed in the fall. See KA Nachlaß Beck, B/2, Fasz. IX, "Maßnahmen zur Besetzung von Ungarn." See also Rothenberg, *The Army of Francis Joseph*, pp. 134-35; Kurt Peball and Gunther E. Rothenberg, "Der Fall U," in *Aus drei Jahrhunderten: Beiträge zur österreichischen Heeres- und Kriegsgeschichte von 1645 bis 1938*, in *Schriften des Heeresgeschichtlichen Museums/Militärwissenschaftlichen Instituts*, vol. 4 (Vienna: Österreichischer Bundesverlag, 1969), pp. 85-126.

29 . See Glaise-Horstenau, pp. 403-4.

30 . The Austrian government, not the Austro-Hungary military leadership, offered the greatest resistance to the creation of *Honvéd* artillery, largely because it would then have to make similar appropriations for the *Landwehr*. See, for example, HHStA, PA XL, Karton 303, Crown Council Protocol KZ 24, GMCPZ 4456, 5 May 1904.

31 . Arno Mayer estimates that between 1700 and 1914, army officers received 50% of all patents of nobility issued. See Arno J. Mayer, *The Persistence of the Old Regime: Europe to the Great War* (New York: Pantheon Books, 1981), p. 111.

32 . See the figures of Nikolaus von Preradovich as cited in Deák, *Beyond Nationalism*, pp. 160-61.

33 . See Stone, *The Eastern Front*, p. 71.

34 . KA Nachlaß Beck, B/2, Fasz. IX, No. 357. *Arbeiter Zeitung* No. 40, 10 February 1920.

35 . Beck wanted his last deputy, Major General Oskar Potiorek, to succeed him as chief of the general staff in 1906. Franz Ferdinand, however, pushed through Conrad's appointment.

36 . Conrad had held battalion (1892-94), regimental (1895-99), brigade (1899-1903), and divisional (1903-6) commands before becoming chief of the general staff. See Peter Broucek, "Taktische Erkenntnisse aus dem Russisch-Japanischen Krieg und deren Beachtung in Österreich-Ungarn," *Mitteilungen des Österreichischen Staatsarchivs* 30 (1977): pp. 191-220.

37 . See Ritter, *The Sword and the Scepter*, vol. II, pp. 227-28; Samuel R. Williamson, *Austria-Hungary and the Origins of the First World War* (New York: St. Martin's Press, 1991), pp. 47-51.

38 . See Beck's 171-page "Studie über Manövrier und Gefechtstaktik," written in March 1870, in KA Nachlaß Beck, B/2, Fasz. VI, No. 154.

39 . The *Kriegsarchiv* has moved to the new Austrian State Archives Building in the Nottendorfergasse since the author's research in Austria. Perhaps Conrad's portrait did not accompany the transfer of documents to the new location.

Bibliography

Archives

Austria-Hungary

1.   Kriegsarchiv, Vienna

      a.   Private Paper Collections
          1.   Nachlaß Beck
          2.   Nachlaß Bolfras
          3.   Nachlaß Kuhn
          4.   Nachlaß Pitreich
          5.   Nachlaß Wolf-Schneider von Arno

      b.   Official Documents
          1.   Generalstab, Operationsbüro, 1876-1906
          2.   Generalstab, Hauptreihe 1881-1906
          3.   Militärkanzlei Seiner Majestät des Kaisers Franz Joseph), 1867-1906
          4.   Militärkanzlei Seiner Majestät des Kaisers, Sonderreihe
          5.   Kriegsministerium, Präsidium, 1881-1906

2.   Haus-, Hof- und Staatsarchiv, Vienna

      a.   Private Paper Collections
          1.   Nachlaß Erzherzog Franz Ferdinand
          2.   Hausarchiv Kronprinz Rudolf

      b.   Filmarchiv
          1.   Nachlaß Erzherzog Albrecht

c.   Official Documents

Politisches Archiv, Austro-Hungarian
Foreign Ministry

1.   Interna,Gemeinsame Ministerratsprotokolle,
      PA XL/283-305
2.   Korrespondenz mit inneren und
      Militärbehörden 1883-84, PA XL/141
3.   Korrespondenz mit inneren und
      Militärbehörden, PA XL/149
4.   Kabinette des Ministers, PA I/656
5.   Verhandlungen mit Serbien 1881-92, PA
      I/456, Liassen V and VI
6.   Plan eines Bündnisses zwischen Türkei,
      Österreich-Ungarn und Deutschland 1882;
      Annäherung der Türkei an Österreich-
      Ungarn und England und Italien, 1887-
      88, PA I/458, Liasse VIIIa
7.   Veröffentlichung geheimer Verhandlungen
      1882-87, Eventualität eines Krieges mit
      Rußland 1887-88, PA I/464, Liassen XVII,
      XVIII and XIX
8.   Varia Generalia, PA I/465
9.   Varia Militaria 1882-95, PAI/466, Liasse
      XXb
10.   Varia betreffend Deutschland 1881-95, PA
      I/468, Liasse XXI
11.   Kronprinz Rudolf, Korrespondenz nach
      Seinem Tode 1889-1910, PA I/470, Liasse
      XXVII
12.   Verhandlungen mit Italien betreffend Tunis
      1890, PA I/471, Liasse XXIX
13.   Verhandlungen mit Rumänien 1886-92, PA
      I/471, Liasse XXX

Germany

1.   Militärarchiv Freiburg, Freiburg, Germany

      a.   Nachlaß Adolf von Deines

2.   Militärarchiv der Deutschen Demokratischen Republik, Potsdam, formerly East Germany

a.   W-10/150222, Materialsammlung zur Darstellung der operativen Verhandlungen des Grafen Schlieffen mit Österreich-Ungarn, ed. Kurt Wiedenauer

Published Primary Sources

Auffenberg-Komarów, Moritz Freiherr von. *Aus Österreichs Höhe und Niedergang*. Munich: Drei Masken Verlag, 1921.

Bardolff, Carl Freiherr von. *Soldat im alten Österreich*. Jena: E. Diederichs, 1938.

Eisenmenger, Victor. *Erzherzog Franz Ferdinand: Seinem Andenken gewidmet von seinem Leibarzt*. Vienna: Amalthea Verlag, 1930.

Geramvögli, Judit, ed. *Quellen zur Genesis des ungarischen Ausgleichgesetzes von 1867*. Munich: Ungarisches Institut, 1979.

Heß, Heinrich von. *Schriften aus dem militärwissenschaftlichen Nachlaß mit einer Einführung in sein Leben und das operative Denken seiner Zeit*. Manfred Rauchensteiner, ed., in *Bibliotheca Rerum Militarium, Quellen und Darstellung zu Militärwissenschaft und Militärgeschichte* 41. Osnabrück, 1975.

Hötzendorf, Franz Conrad von. *Aus meiner Dienstzeit*. 5 vols. Vienna: Rikola Verlag, 1921-25.

Hötzendorf, Franz Conrad von. *Mein Anfang: Kriegserinnerungen aus der Jugendzeit 1878-1882*. Berlin: Verlag für Kulturpolitik, 1925.

Margutti, Albert Alexander Freiherr von. *Kaiser Franz Joseph: Persönliche Erinnerungen*. Mainz: Mainz'sche Verlags- und Universitätsbuchhandlung, 1924.

Mitis, Oskar Freiherr von. *Das Leben des Kronprinzen Rudolf: Mit Briefen und Schriften aus dessen Nachlaß*. Leipzig: Im Insel Verlag, 1928.

Mollinary, Anton Freiherr von. *Sechsundvierzig Jahre im österreich-ungarischen Heere*, vol. 2. Zurich: Verlag Art. Institut Orell Füssli, 1905.

Moltke, Helmuth von (the Elder). *Ausgewählte Werke*. Ferdinand Schmerfeld, ed. Berlin: E.S. Mittler & Sohn, 1929.

Moltke, Helmuth von. *Die deutschen Aufmarschpläne, 1871-1890*. Eberhard Kessel, ed. Potsdam: A. Protte, 1936.

Nostitz-Reineck, Georg, ed. *Briefe Kaiser Franz Josephs an Kaiserin Elizabeth 1859-1898*. 2 vols. Vienna: Herold, 1966.

Plener, Ernst Freiherr von. *Erinnerungen von Ernst Freiherrn von Plener.* vol.
    2. Stuttgart: Deutsche Verlags-Anstalt, 1921.
Pribram, Alfred Franzis. *The Secret Treaties of Austria-Hungary.* 2 vols.
    Cambridge, Mass.: Harvard University Press, 1920-21.
Ronge, Max. *Kriegs- und Industrie-Spionage: Zwölf Jahre Kundschaftsdienst.*
    Vienna: Amalthea Verlag, 1930.
Roskiewicz, Johann. *Studien über Bosnien und die Herzegovina.* Leipzig: F.A.
    Brockhaus, 1868.
Rudolf, Crown Prince of Austria. *Majestät ich warne Sie: geheime und private
    Schriften.* Brigitte Hamann, ed. Munich: Amalthea Verlag, 1979.
Salis-Soglio, Daniel von. *Mein Leben und was ich davon erzählen will, kann
    und darf.* Stuttgart: Deutsche Verlags-Anstalt, 1908.
Schlieffen, Alfred von. *Dienstschriften.* Generalstab des Heeres, ed. 2 vols.
    Berlin: E.S. Mittler & Sohn, 1937-38.
Schweinitz, Hans Lothar von. *Briefwechsel des Botschafters General von
    Schweinitz.* Berlin: R. Hobbing,   1928.
Schweinitz, Hans Lothar von. *Denkwürdigkeiten des Botschafters General von
    Schweinitz.* 2 vols. Berlin: R. Hobbing, 1927.
*Stenographische Sitzungsprotokolle der Delegation des Reichsrathes: Neunte
    Session.* Vienna: Aus der kaiserlich-königlichen Hof-, und
    Staatsdruckerei, 1876.
*Stenographische Sitzungsprotokolle der Delegation des Reichsrathes: Elfte
    Session.* 2 vols. Vienna: Aus der kaiserlich-königlichen Hof-, und
    Staatsdruckerei, 1878.
Waldersee, Alfred von. *Aus dem Briefwechsel des Generalfeldmarschalls
    Alfred von Waldersee.* Heinrich Otto Meisner, ed. 2 vols. Stuttgart:
    Deutsche Verlags-Anstalt, 1928.
Waldersee, Alfred von. *Denkwürdigkeiten des General-Feldmarschalls Alfred
    Grafen von Waldersee.* 2 vols. Berlin: Deutsche Verlags-Anstalt,
    1922.
Waldersee, Alfred von. *Generalfeldmarschall Alfred Graf Waldersee in seinem
    militärischen Wirken.* Hans Mohs, ed. 2 vols. Berlin: Verlag R.
    Eisenschmidt, 1929.
Zebegeny, Wilhelm Ritter Gründorf von. *Memoiren eines österreichischen
    Generalstäblers 1832-1866.* Stuttgart: R. Lutz, 1913.

Secondary Sources: Books

Alfoldi, Laszlo, ed. *The Armies of Austria-Hungary and Germany 1740-1914,*
    in *U.S. Army Military History Research Collection, Special*

Bibliography Series, No. 12, vol. 1. Carlisle Barracks, Pa.: U.S. Army History Research Center, 1975.

Allmayer-Beck, Johann Christoph, and Lessing, Erich. *Die k.u.k. Armee 1848-1914*. Munich: Bertelsmann, 1974.

Anderson, M.S. *The Eastern Question 1774-1923*. London: Macmillan, 1966.

Bagdasarian, Nicholas Der. *The Austro-German Rapprochement 1870-1879: From the Battle of Sedan to the Dual Alliance*. London: Associated University Presses, 1976.

Behnen, Michael. *Rüstung-Bündnis-Sicherheit: Dreibund und informeller Imperialismus 1900-1908*. Tübingen: Max Niemeyer Verlag, 1985.

Bosworth, Richard. *Italy and the Approach of the First World War*. New York: St. Martin's Press, 1983.

Bosworth, Richard. *Italy, the Least of the Great Powers: Italian Foreign Policy before the First World War*. London: Cambridge University Press, 1979.

Bradley, Dermot, and Marwedel, Ulrich, eds. *Militärgeschichte, Militärwissenschaft und Konfliktforschung: Eine Festschrift für Werner Hahlweg zur Vollendung seines 65. Lebensjahres am 29. April 1977*. Osnabrück: Biblio Verlag, 1977.

Bridge, Francis Roy. *From Sadowa to Sarajevo: The Foreign Policy of Austria- Hungary 1866-1914*. London: Routledge & Kegan Paul, 1972.

Brusatti, Alois, ed. *Die wirtschaftliche Entwicklung*, vol. 1, in Wandruska, Adam, and Urbanitsch, Peter, eds., *Die Habsburgermonarchie 1848-1918*. Vienna: Verlag der österreichischen Akademie der Wissenschaften, 1973.

Calvocoressi, Peter and Wint, Guy. *Total War*, vol. 1. New York: Ballantine Books, 1972.

Cassels, Lavender. *Clash of Generations: A Habsburg Family Drama in the Nineteenth Century*. London: John Murray, 1973.

Corti, Egon, and Sokol, Hans. *Der alte Kaiser Franz Joseph I*. Vienna: Verlag Anton Pustet, 1955.

Craig, Gordon. *The Politics of the Prussian Army 1640-1945*. London: Oxford University Press, 1955.

Craig, Gordon. *The Battle of Königgrätz*. Philadelphia, Pa.: Lippincott Co., 1964.

Crankshaw, Edward. *The Fall of the House of Habsburg*. New York: Viking Press, 1963.

Crankshaw, Edward. *The Habsburgs: A Portrait of a Dynasty*. New York: Viking Press, 1971.

Deák, István. *Beyond Nationalism: A Social and Political History of the Habsburg Officer Corps, 1848-1918*. New York: Oxford University Press, 1990.

Diószegi, István. *Die Außenpolitik der österreichisch-ungarischen Monarchie 1871-1877*. Vienna: Hermann Böhlaus Nachfolger, 1985.

Dirrheimer, Günther, ed. *Das k.u.k. Heer 1895*, vol. 10. *Schriften des Heeresgeschichtlichen Museums in Wien (Militärwissenschaftliches Institut)*. Vienna: Österreichischer Bundesverlag, 1983.

Donia, Robert J. *Islam under the Double Eagle: The Muslims of Bosnia and Herzegovina, 1878-1914*. East European Monographs No. 78. Boulder, Colo.: East European Quarterly, 1981.

Dupuy, Trevor N. *A Genius for War*. Englewood Cliffs, N.J.: Prentice Hall, 1977.

Engel-Janosi, Friedrich. *Geschichte auf dem Ballhausplatz: Essays zur österreichischen Außenpolitik 1830-1945*. Graz: Verlag Styria, 1958-60.

Engel-Janosi, Friedrich, ed. *Probleme der franzisko-josephinischen Zeit 1848-1916*. Munich: Verlag Oldenburg, 1967.

Eyck, Erich. *Bismarck and the German Empire*. London: George Allen & Unwin, 1958.

Fritsch, Gerhard. *Feldherr wider Willen: Das Leben des FML Ludwig von Benedek*. Vienna: Österreichischer Bundesverlag, 1966.

Führ, Christoph. *Das k.u.k. Armeeoberkommando und die Innenpolitik in Österreich, 1914-1917*. Graz: Böhlau, 1968.

Gall, Lothar. *Bismarck: The White Revolutionary*, vol. 1. Trans. J.A. Underwood. London: Allen & Unwin, 1986.

Glaise-Horstenau, Edmund von. *Franz Josephs Weggefährte*. Vienna: Amalthea Verlag, 1930.

Good, David F. *The Economic Rise of the Habsburg Empire, 1750-1914*. Berkeley, Calif.: University of California Press, 1984.

Gottas, Friedrich. *Ungarn im Zeitalter des Hochliberalismus: Studien zur Tisza-Ära 1875-1890*. Studien zur Geschichte der österreichisch-ungarischen Monarchie No. 16. Vienna: Verlag der Akademie der Wissenschaften, 1976.

Hamann, Brigitte. *Rudolf: Kronprinz und Rebell*. Vienna: Amalthea Verlag, 1978.

Harris, David. *A Diplomatic History of the Balkan Crisis of 1875-78; The First Year*. Stanford, CA: Stanford University Press, 1936.

Haselmayer, Friedrich. *Diplomatische Geschichte des Zweiten Reiches von 1871-1918*. Munich: Verlag Bruchmann, 1955.

Höhne, Heinz. *Der Krieg im Dunkeln: Macht und Einfluß des deutschen und russischen Geheimdienstes*. Munich: Bertelsmann, 1985.

Howard, Michael. *The Franco-Prussian War: The German Invasion of France, 1870-1871*. London: Rupert Hart-Davis, 1961.

Jaszi, Oscar. *The Dissolution of the Habsburg Monarchy*. Chicago: University of Chicago Press, 1929.

Jelavich, Charles. *The Habsburg Monarchy: Toward a Multinational Empire or National States?* New York: Rinehart, 1959.

Jenks, William A. *Austria under the Iron Ring 1879-1893*. Charlottesville, Va.: University of Virginia Press, 1965.

Jerábeck, Rudolf. *Potiorek: General im Schatten von Sarajevo*. Graz: Styria Verlag, 1991.

Johnson, William M. *The Austrian Mind: An Intellectual and Social History 1848-1938*. Berkeley, Calif.: University of California Press, 1976.

Kann, Robert A. *The Multinational Empire: Nationalism and National Reform in the Habsburg Monarchy 1848-1918*. 2 vols. New York: Columbia University Press, 1950.

Kann, Robert A. *The Habsburg Empire: A Study in Integration and Disintegration*. New York: Praeger, 1957.

Kann, Robert A. *A History of the Habsburg Empire, 1526-1918*. Berkeley, Calif.: University of California Press, 1974.

Kann, Robert A. *Erzherzog Franz Ferdinand Studien*. Vienna: Verlag für Geschichte und Politik, 1976.

Kann, Robert A., Kiraly, Béla K., and Fichtner, Paula S., eds. *The Habsburg Empire in World War I: Essays on the Intellectual, Military, Political and Economic Aspects of the Habsburg War Effort*. Studies on Society in Change No. 2. Boulder, Colo.: East European Quarterly, 1977.

Kennan, George F. *The Decline of Bismarck's European Order: Franco-Russian Relations, 1875-1890*. Princeton, N.J.: Princeton University Press, 1979.

Kennedy, Paul, ed. *The War Plans of the Great Powers 1880-1914*. Boston: Allen & Unwin, 1984.

Kiraly, Béla, and Rothenberg, Gunther, eds. *War and Society in East Central Europe*, vol. 1. *Special Topics and Generalizations on the 18th and 19th Centuries*. Brooklyn College Special Studies on Society in Change No. 11. New York: Brooklyn College Press, 1979.

Kiszling, Rudolf. *Die Revolution im Kaisertum Österreich 1848-49*. 2 vols. Vienna: Universum Verlagsgesellschaft, 1948.

Kiszling, Rudolf. *Erzherzog Franz Ferdinand von Österreich-Este: Leben, Pläne und Wirken am Schicksalsweg der Donaumonarchie*. Graz: Hermann Böhlaus Nachfolger, 1953.

Kos, Franz-Josef. *Die Politik Österreich-Ungarns während der Orientkrise 1874/75-1879: Zum Verhältnis von politischer und militärischer Führung.* Cologne: Böhlau, 1984.

Langer, William L. *European Alliances and Alignments, 1871-1890.* New York: Alfred A. Knopf, 1931.

Listowel, Judith. *A Habsburg Tragedy: Crown Prince Rudolf.* New York: Ascent Books, 1978.

Lutz, Heinrich, and Rumpler, Helmut, eds. *Wiener Beiträge zur Geschichte der Neuzeit,* in vol. 9, *Österreich und die deutsche Frage im 19. Jahrhundert.* Munich: Oldenburg, 1982.

Lutz, Heinrich. *Österreich-Ungarn und die Gründung des Deutschen Reiches: Europäische Entscheidungen 1867-1871.* Frankfurt: Propyläen Verlag, 1979.

Luvaas, Jay. *The Military Legacy of the Civil War: The European Inheritance.* Chicago: University of Chicago Press, 1959.

Macartney, Carlisle A. *The Habsburg Empire 1790-1918.* New York: Macmillan, 1969.

Mackenzie, David. *Apis: The Congenial Conspirator: The Life of Colonel Dragutin T. Dimitrievich.* East European Monographs No. 255. New York: Columbia University Press, 1989.

Marek, George R. *The Eagles Die: Franz Joseph, Elizabeth and Their Austria.* New York: Harper and Row, 1974.

Markus, Georg. *Der Fall Redl: Mit unveröffentlichen Geheimdokumenten zur folgenschwersten Spionage-Affaire des Jahrhunderts.* Vienna: Amalthea Verlag, 1984.

Markus, Georg. *Der Kaiser Franz Joseph I: Bilder und Dokumente.* Vienna: Amalthea Verlag, 1985.

May, Arthur J. *The Habsburg Monarchy 1867-1914.* Cambridge, Mass.: Harvard University Press, 1951.

Mayer, Arno. *The Persistence of the Old Regime: Europe to the Great War.* New York: Pantheon Books, 1981.

Mitchell, Alan. *Victors and Vanquished: The German Influence on Army and Church in France after 1870.* Chapel Hill, N.C.: University of North Carolina Press, 1984.

Morton, Frederic. *A Nervous Splendor: Vienna 1888/89.* Boston: Little Brown, 1979.

Niemayer, Joachim. *Das österreichische Militärwesen im Umbruch: Untersuchungen zum Kriegsbild zwischen 1830 und 1866.* Osnabrück: Biblio Verlag, 1979.

Paret, Peter, ed. *The Makers of Modern Strategy from Machiavelli to the Nuclear Age.* Princeton, N.J.: Princeton University Press, 1986.

Pflanze, Otto. *Bismarck and the Development of Germany*. Princeton, N.J.: Princeton University Press, 1963.

Porch, Douglas. *The March to the Marne: The French Army 1871-1914*. Cambridge: Cambridge University Press, 1981.

Rath, R. John. *The Viennese Revolution of 1848*. Austin, Tex.: University of Texas Press, 1957.

Regele, Oskar. *Feldmarschall Conrad: Auftrag und Erfüllung 1906-1918*. Vienna: Herold, 1955.

Regele, Oskar. *Feldmarschall Radetzky: Leben-Leistung-Erbe*. Vienna: Herold, 1957.

Regele, Oskar. *Feldzeugmeister Benedek: Der Weg nach Königgrätz*. Vienna: Herold, 1960.

Regele, Oskar. *Generalstabchefs aus Vier Jahrhunderten*. Vienna: Herold, 1966.

Rich, Norman. *Why the Crimean War? A Cautionary Tale*. Hanover, N.H.: University Press of New England, 1985.

Ritter, Gerhard. *Der Schlieffenplan: Kritik eines Mythos*. Munich: Oldenburg Verlag, 1956.

Ritter, Gerhard. *The Sword and the Scepter: The Problem of Militarism in Germany*, vol. 1. *The Prussian Tradition 1740-1890*. Coral Gables, Fla.: University of Miami Press, 1969.

Roberts, Walter. *Tito, Mihailovich and the Allies, 1941-1945*. New Brunswick, N.J.: Rutgers University Press, 1973.

Ropp, Theodore. *War in the Modern World*. Durham, N.C.: Duke University Press, 1959.

Rothenberg, Gunther E. *The Austrian Military Border in Croatia 1740-1881: A Study of an Imperial Institution*. Chicago: University of Chicago Press, 1966.

Rothenberg, Gunther E. *The Army of Francis Joseph*. West Lafayette, IN: Purdue University Press, 1976.

Rothenberg, Gunther E. *The Austrian Military Border in Croatia 1522-1747*. Illinois Studies in the Social Sciences No. 48. Urbana, Ill: University of Illinois Press, 1980.

Rupp, George Hoover. *A Wavering Friendship: Russia and Austria, 1876-1878*. Cambridge, Mass.: Harvard University Press, 1941.

Schmidt-Brentano, Antonio. *Die Armee in Österreich: Militär, Staat und Gesellschaft 1848-1867*. Boppard am Rhein: Harald Boldt Verlag, 1975.

Schroeder, Paul. *Austria, Great Britain and the Crimean War: The Destruction of the European Concert*. Ithaca, N.Y.: Cornell University Press, 1972.

Shanahan, William O. *Prussian Military Reforms 1786-1813*. New York: Columbia University Press, 1945.

Showalter, Dennis E. *Railroads and Rifles: Soldiers, Technology, and the Unification of Germany*. Hamden, Conn.: Archon Books, 1976.

Sked, Alan. *The Decline and Fall of the Habsburg Empire 1815-1918*. London: Longman, 1989.

Sked, Alan. *The Survival of the Habsburg Empire: Radetzky, the Imperial Army and the Class War, 1848*. London: Longman, 1979.

Sokol, Hans Hugo. *Des Kaisers Seemacht: Die k.k. österreichische Kriegsmarine 1848-1914*. Vienna: Amalthea Verlag, 1980.

Sondhaus, Lawrence. *The Habsburg Empire and the Sea: Austrian Naval Policy, 1797-1866*. West Lafayette, Ind.: Purdue University Press, 1989.

Sondhaus, Lawrence. *The Naval Policy of Austria-Hungary 1867-1918: Navalism, Industrial Development and the Politics of Dualism*. West Lafayette, Ind.: Purdue University Press, 1994

Stadelmann, Rudolf. *Moltke und der Staat*. Krefeld: Scherpe-Verlag, 1950.

Stavrianos, Leften S. *The Balkans Since 1453*. New York: Rinehart & Company, Inc., 1958.

Stojanovich, Mihailo D. *The Great Powers and the Balkans 1875-1878*. London: Cambridge University Press, 1939.

Stone, Jay, and Schmiedl, Erwin A. *The Boer War and Military Reforms*. War and Society in East Central Europe No. 28. New York: University Press of America, 1988.

Stone, Norman. *The Eastern Front, 1914-1917*. New York: Charles Scribner's Sons, 1975.

Tapié, Victor Lucien. *The Rise and Fall of the Habsburg Monarchy*. New York: Praeger, 1971.

Taylor, Alan J.P. *The Habsburg Monarchy 1809-1918: A History of the Austrian Empire and Austria-Hungary*. London: H. Hamilton, 1948.

Turnbull, Patrick. *Solferino: The Birth of a Nation*. New York: St. Martin's Press, 1985.

Urbanski, August von. *Conrad von Hötzendorf*. Vienna: 1938.

Wagner, Walter. *Geschichte des k.u.k. Kriegsministeriums 1848-1888*. 2 vols. Vienna: Verlag Hermann Böhlaus Nachfolger, 1966 and 1971.

Wagner, Walter. *Von Austerlitz bis Königgrätz: Österreichische Kampftaktik im Spiegel der Reglements 1805-1864*. Studien zur Militärgeschichte und Konfliktforschung, No. 17. Osnabrück: Biblio-Verlag, 1978.

Wandruska, Adam, and Urbanitsch, Peter, eds. *Die Habsburgermonarchie 1848-1918*, vol. 5, *Die bewaffnete Macht*. Vienna: Verlag der österreichischen Akademie der Wissenschaften, 1987.

Wertheimer, Eduard von. *Graf Julius Andrássy: Sein Leben und Seine Zeit.* 3 vols. Stuttgart: Deutsche Verlags-Anstalt, 1910-13.

Whittam, John. *The Politics of the Italian Army 1861-1918.* London: Croom Helm, 1977.

Williamson, Samuel R. *Austria-Hungary and the Origins of the First World War.* New York: St. Martin's Press, 1991.

Wrede, Alphons von. *Geschichte der k.u.k. Wehrmacht.* 5 vols. Vienna: 1898-1905.

Secondary Sources: Articles & Dissertations

Allmayer-Beck, Johann Christoph. "Das Heerwesen in Österreich und in Deutschland." In Kann, Robert A., and Prinz, Friedrich, eds., *Deutschland und Österreich: Ein bilaterales Geschichtsbuch* (Vienna: Jugend und Volk, 1980): 490-517.

Allmayer-Beck, Johann Christoph. "Das Heerwesen." In Engel-Janosi, Friedrich, and Rumpler, Helmut, eds., *Probleme der franzisko-josephinischen Zeit* (Vienna: Verlag für Geschichte und Politik, 1967): 67-78.

Allmayer-Beck, Johann Christoph. "Das Schicksaljahr 1866." *Geschichte in Wissenschaft und Unterricht* 18 (1967): 321-32.

Allmayer-Beck, Johann Christoph. "Der Ausgleich des Jahres 1867." *Österreichische Militärische Zeitschrift* 5 (1967): 495-501.

Allmayer-Beck, Johann Christoph. "Der Ausgleich von 1867 und die k.u.k. bewaffnete Macht." In *Der österreich-ungarische Ausgleich von 1867: Vorgeschichte und Wirkungen* (Vienna: Herold, 1967): 113-26.

Allmayer-Beck, Johann Christoph. "Die bewaffnete Macht in Staat und Gesellschaft." In Wandruska, Adam, and Urbanitsch, Peter, eds., *Die Habsburgermonarchie 1848-1918*, vol. 5. *Die Bewaffnete Macht* (Vienna: Verlag der österreichischen Akademie der Wissenschaften, 1987): 1-141.

Askew, William C. "The Austro-Italian Antagonism, 1896-1914." In Wallace, Lillian Parker, and Askew, William C., eds., *Power, Public Opinion and Diplomacy: Essays in Honor of Eber Malcolm Carroll by His Former Students* (Durham, N.C.: Duke University Press, 1959): 172-221.

Binion, Rudolf. "From Mayerling to Sarajevo." *The Journal of Modern History* 47, No. 2 (June, 1975): 280-316.

Brettner-Messler, Horst. "Die Balkanpolitik Conrads von Hötzendorf." Ph.D. dissertation, University of Vienna, 1966.

Broucek, Peter. "Die Handschriftensammlung des Kriegsarchivs." *Scrivium* 11 (1974): 22-35.

Broucek, Peter. "Taktische Erkenntnisse aus dem russisch-japanischen Krieg und deren Beachtung in Österreich-Ungarn." *Mitteilungen des österreichischen Staatsarchivs* 30 (1977): 191-220.

Crowl, Philip A. "Alfred Thayer Mahan: The Naval Historian." In Paret, Peter, ed., *The Makers of Modern Strategy from Machiavelli to the Nuclear Age* (Princeton, N.J.: Princeton University Press, 1986): 444-77.

Degreif, Dieter. "Operative Plannung des k.u.k. Generalstabes für einen Krieg in der Zeit vor 1914 (1880-1914)." Ph.D. dissertation, University of Mainz, 1983.

Diószegi, István. "L'Autriche-Hongrie et les perspectives d'un guerre russo-turque, à la automne 1876." *Revue d'histoire moderne et contemporaine* 27 (January-March 1980): 85-93.

Egger, Rainer. "Der Militärkanzlei des Erzherzog Thronfolgers Franz Ferdinand und ihr Archiv im Kriegsarchiv Wien." *Mitteilungen des österreichischen Staatsarchivs* 28 (1975): 141-63.

Egger, Rainer. "The Kriegsarchiv." *Austrian History Yearbook* 6-7 (1970-71): 39-66.

Engel-Janosi, Friedrich. "Austria in the Summer of 1870." *Journal of Central European Affairs* 5, no. 4 (January 1946): 335-53.

Engel-Janosi, Friedrich. "The Resignation of Count Kálnoky as Foreign Minister of Austria-Hungary in May 1895." *Journal of Central European Affairs* 9, no. 3 (October 1951): 259-78.

Engel-Janosi, Friedrich. "Der Monarch und seine Ratgeber." In Engel-Janosi, Friedrich, and Rumpler, Helmut, eds., *Probleme der franzisko-josephinischen Zeit* (Vienna: Verlag für Geschichte und Politik, 1967): 9-24.

Fellner, Fritz. "Kaiser Franz Joseph, Kronprinz Rudolf und Kronprinzessin Stephanie: Drei Biographen." *Österreichische Osthefte* 21 (1979): 47-51.

Haag, John, and Houston, Robert W. "Materials for Austrian History in the National Archives Microfilm Series." *Austrian History Yearbook* 4-5 (1968-69): 335-43.

Hanak, Peter. "Hungary in the Austro-Hungarian Monarchy." *Austrian History Yearbook* 3, pt. 1 (1967): 294-302.

Hantsch, Hugo. "1866 und die Folgen." In *Der österreich-ungarische Ausgleich von 1867: Vorgeschichte und Wirkungen* (Vienna: Herold, 1967): 51-63.

Hantsch, Hugo. "Kaiser Franz Joseph und die Außenpolitik." In Engel-Janosi, Friedrich, and Rumpler, Helmut, eds., *Probleme der franzisko-*

josephinischen Zeit (Vienna: Verlag für Geschichte und Politik, 1967): 25-40.

Hellbrand, Erich. "Die Kartensammlung des Kriegsarchivs Wien." *Mitteilungen des österreichischen Staatsarchivs* 28 (1975): 183-96.

Hickl, Elizabeth. "Erzherzog Franz Ferdinand und die Rumänienpolitik Österreich-Ungarns." Ph.D. dissertation, University of Vienna, 1964.

Hlavac, Franz. "Die Armeeorganisation der Jahre 1881-1883 in der Donaumonarchie." Ph.D. dissertation, University of Vienna, 1973.

Höbelt, Lothar. "Die Marine." In Wandruska, Adam, and Urbanitsch, Peter, eds., *Die Habsburgermonarchie 1848-1918*, vol. 5. *Die bewaffnete Macht* (Vienna: Verlag der österreichischen Akademie der Wissenschaften, 1987): 687-763.

Höbelt, Lothar. "Schlieffen, Beck, Potiorek und das Ende der gemeinsamen deutsch-österreichisch-ungarischen Aufmarschpläne im Osten." *Militärgeschichtliche Mitteilungen* 36, pt. 2 (1984): 7-30.

Holborn, Hajo. "The Prusso-German School: Moltke and the Rise of the General Staff." In Paret, Peter, ed., *The Makers of Modern Strategy from Machiavelli to the Nuclear Age* (Princeton, N.J.: Princeton University Press, 1986): 281-95.

Holzer, Josef Jakob. "Erzherzog Albrecht 1867-1895: Politisch-militärische Konzeptionen und Tätigkeit als Generalinspektor des Heeres." Ph.D. dissertation, University of Vienna, 1974.

Jandesek, Elfriede. "Die Stellung des Abgeordnetenhauses der im Reichsrate vertretenen Königreiche und Länder zu Fragen des Militärs, 1867-1914." Ph.D. dissertation, University of Vienna, 1964.

Kann, Robert A. "Die Italienpolitik des Thronfolgers Erzherzog Franz Ferdinand." *Mitteilungen des österreichischen Staatsarchivs* 31 (1978): 363-71.

Kann, Robert A. "The Social Prestige of the Officer Corps in the Habsburg Empire from the Eighteenth Century to 1918." In Kiraly, Béla and Rothenberg, Gunther E., eds., *War and Society in East Central Europe*, vol. 1 (New York: Brooklyn College Press, 1979): 143-60.

Kesslitz, Rainer von. "Die Lasten der militärischen Rüstungen Österreich-Ungarns in neuster Zeit (1868-1912)." Kriegsarchiv Wien, MS Allgemeine No. 54.

Kiszling, Rudolf. "Die militärischen Vereinbarungen Österreich-Ungarns 1867-1914." *Österreich in Geschichte und Literatur* 10 (1966): 427-35.

Kiszling, Rudolf. "Erzherzog Franz Ferdinand und seine Pläne für den Umbau der Donaumonarchie." *Der Donauraum* 8, no. 5 (1963): 261-66.

Kriegl, Gertrud. "Die deutsch-österreichisch-ungarischen Beziehungen während des Rückversicherungsvertrages von Juni 1887-Juni 1890." Ph.D. dissertation, University of Vienna, 1942.

Lackey, Scott W. "From Status Quo to Expansionism: Count Julius Andrassy and the Eastern Question, July 1875-April 1877." M.A. thesis, University of North Carolina, 1986.

Lackey, Scott W. "A Secret Austro-Hungarian Plan to Intervene in the 1884 Timok Uprising in Serbia: Unpublished Documents." *Austrian History Yearbook* 23 (1992): 149-59.

Papp, Tibor. "Die königlich ungarische Landwehr (Honvéd) 1868 bis 1914." In Wandruska, Adam, and Urbanitsch, Peter, eds., *Die Habsburgermonarchie 1848-1918*, vol 5. *Die Bewaffnete Macht* (Vienna: Verlag der österreichischen Akademie der Wissenschaften, 1987): 635-86.

Peball, Kurt. "1866: Der Krieg und seine historische Symptomatik." In Bradley, Dermot, and Marwedel, Ulrich, eds., *Militärgeschichte, Militärwissenschaft und Konfliktforschung: Eine Festschrift für Werner Hahlweg zur Vollendung seines 65. Lebensjahres am 29. April 1977* (Osnabrück: Biblio Verlag, 1977): 325-58.

Peball, Kurt, and Rothenberg, Gunther E. "Der Fall U: Die geplannte Besetzung Ungarns durch die k.u.k. Armee im Herbst 1905." *Schriften des Heeresgeschichtlichen Museums in Wien* 4 (1969): 85-106.

Pribram, Alfred Franzis. "Zwei Gespräche des Fürsten Bismarck mit dem Kronprinzen Rudolf von Österreich." *Österreichische Rundschau* 17 (January 1921): 57-68.

Rosner, Willibald Richard. "Feldmarschalleutnant Anton Freiherr von Schönfeld als Chef des Generalstabes: Eine Studie zur Geschichte des österreichisch-ungarischen Generalstabes." Staatsprüfungsarbeit, University of Vienna, 1986.

Rothenberg, Gunther E. "The Habsburg Army and the Nationality Problem in the Nineteenth Century, 1815-1914." *Austrian History Yearbook* 3 (1967): 70-87.

Rothenberg, Gunther E. "Toward a National Hungarian Army: The Military Compromise of 1868 and Its Consequences." *Slavic Review* 31 (1972): 805-16.

Rothenberg, Gunther E. "Problems of a Multi-Ethnic and Multi-National Force: The Habsburg Army 1868-1918." In Colling, B. Franklin, ed., *Essays in Some Dimensions of Military History*. 3 vols. Carlisle Barracks, Pa.: U.S. Army Military History Research Collection, 1974, vol. II, pp. 52-61; and vol. III, pp. 38-46.

Rothenberg, Gunther E. "The Army of Austria-Hungary, 1868-1918: A Case Study of a Multi-Ethnic Force." In Weigley, Russel F., ed., *New Dimensions in Military History: An Anthology* (San Rafael, Calif.: Presidio Press, 1975): 242-56.

Rothenberg, Gunther E. "The Habsburg Army in the First World War: 1914-
1918." In Kann, Robert A., Kiraly, Béla, and Fichtner, Paula, eds., *The
Habsburg Empire in World War I: Essays on the Intellectual, Military,
Political and Economic Aspects of the Habsburg War Effort* (Boulder,
Colo.: East European Quarterly, 1977): 73-86.

Rothenberg, Gunther E. "Moltke and Schlieffen." In Paret, Peter, ed., *The
Makers of Modern Strategy from Machiavelli to the Nuclear Age*
(Princeton, N.J.: Princeton University Press, 1986): 296-325.

Rupp, George Hoover. "The Reichstadt Agreement." *American Historical
Review* 30 (April 1925): 503-10.

Schmidt-Brentano, Antonio. "Die österreichische beziehungsweise
österreichisch-ungarische Armee von Erzherzog Carl bis Conrad
von Hötzendorf." In Lutz, Heinrich, and Rumpler, Helmut, eds.,
Wiener Beiträge zur Geschichte der Neuzeit, vol. 19 *Österreich und die
deutsche Frage im 19. Jahrhundert* (Munich: Oldenburg, 1982): 231-
55.

Schroeder, Paul W. "Austro-German Relations: Divergent Views of the
Disjoined Partnership." *Central   European History* 11, No. 3
(September 1978): 302-12.

Stone, Norman. "Constitutional Crisis in Hungary, 1903-9." *Slavonic and East
European Review* 46 (1967): 163-82.

Sugar, Peter. "An Underrated Event: The Hungarian Constitutional Crisis of
1905-6." *East European   Quarterly* 15, no. 3 (Fall 1981): 281-306.

Sutter, Berthold. "Um Österreich-Ungarns Großmachtstellung am Balkan:
Sicherung des europäischen Friedens durch Teilung der
Balkanhalbinsel   zwischen Rußland und Österreich-Ungarn--Eine
militärische Denkschrift anläßlich der Kaiserentrevue 1897." In
Höflechner, Walter, et al., eds., *Domus Austriae: Eine Festgabe für
Hermann Wiesflecker zum 70. Geburtstag* (Graz: Akademische
Druck- und Verlagsanstalt, 1983).

Wagner, Walter. "Die k.(u.)k. Armee: Gliederung und Aufgabenstellung." In
Wandruska, Adam and Urbanitsch, Peter, eds., *Die
Habsburgermonarchie 1848-1918*, vol. 5. *Die bewaffnete Macht*
(Vienna: Verlag der österreichischen Akademie der Wissenschaften,
1987): 142-634.

Wheatcroft, Andrew. "Technology and the Military Mind: Austria 1866-1914."
In Best, Geoffrey, and Wheatcroft, Andrew, eds., *War, Economy and
the Military Mind* (London: Croom Helm Rowman   and Littlefield,
1976): 45-75.

Wischall, Susanne. "Das Ministerium Haymerle." Ph.D. dissertation,
University of Vienna, 1964.

Wysocki, Josef. "Die österreichische Finanzpolitik." In Brusatti, Alois, ed., *Die wirtschaftliche Entwicklung*, vol. 1, in Wandruska, Adam, and Urbanitsch, Peter, eds., *Die Habsburgermonarchie   1848-1918* (Vienna: Verlag der österreichischen Akademie der Wissenschaften, 1973): 68-104.

Index

Abdul Aziz 65
Adjutant General Corps 20, 158
Adriatic Sea 119, 153
Adua, Battle of 153
Aegean Sea 60, 75, 160
Agram. *See* Zagreb
Albania 154
Albrecht, Archduke 4, 32, 34, 67, 80, 103, 116, 158, 159; appointment as commander-in-chief of the Habsburg armed forces 24; appointment as inspector general of the army 34; attitude toward Hungarian nationalism 24, 25; attitude toward Prussia-Germany 100, 101, 138; attitude toward war with Italy 84; attitude toward war with Russia 73, 141; Beck-Andrássy military compromise, opposition to the 26; Bosnia-Herzegovina, criticism of Schönfeld's plans for the occupation of 72; Bosnia-Herzegovina, views on the occupation of 60, 63; dismissal of Schönfeld as chief of the general staff 86; general officer staff rides 92; general staff officers, assignment as adjutants to 95; general staff question, opinion on the 54; general staff, views on the role of the chief of the 32, 86; "Kuhn System," opposition to the 47, 48, 49, 50, 51; order to Benedek to accept command of the North Army in 1866 21; praise for Beck's leadership of the general staff 96; recommendation of Kuhn as minister of war 33; relationship with Franz Joseph 38; relationship with John 52, 53; relationship with Koller 52; relationship with Schönfeld 84, 85; reorganization of the army, opinion on the 42, 106, 109, 110; role in army maneuvers 93, 94; role of *Landwehr/Honvéd/Landsturm* forces 132, 134; support for Carpathian railroad construction 61; support for peacetime corps formations 107; Weisenstein meeting with Waldersee 137
Alcksinach, Battle of 69
Alexander III 60, 99, 128, 129, 131, 139
Andrássy, Count Gyula von 77, 99, 157; appointment as Minister-President of Hungary 22; attitude toward the military 23; Bosnia-Herzegovina, attitude toward the occupation of 6; Bosnia-Herzegovina, indifference to the administration of 76, 80; Compromise of 1867, military negotiations with Beck 25, 26, 27; Compromise of 1867, rejection of Kuhn's military compromise 27; Compromise of 1867, role in negotiating the 11; Congress of Berlin, role at the 75, 77; foreign policy during the Eastern Crisis of 1875-78 6, 63, 64, 65, 71, 72, 73, 74, 75; Gatling gun controversy 49; Military Law of 1889, support for 149
Armeemanöver 15, 93
Armeeoberkommando. See Army High Command

About the Author

SCOTT W. LACKEY has a Ph.D. from the University of North Carolina. He is Chief of the Combat Training Center Warrior Information Network Division of the U.S. Army Combined Arts Center History Office/Army Knowledge Network, Ft. Leavenworth, Kansas.

ISBN 0-313-29361-9

9 780313 293610

90000>

HARDCOVER BAR CODE

EAN